LET THE KICKING MULE KICK

KICK

Keith A. Horn

Formal picture of my dad, 1ˢᵗ Lieutenant, Ladd L. Horn, taken while in flight training at Goodfellow Field, San Angelo, TX between March and May 1943.

LET THE KICKING MULE KICK

Personal Stories From a WWII B-26 Bomber Pilot to His Family

1st Lieutenant Ladd L. Horn

and

Keith A. Horn

Cover design by the BookBaby design team.

Cover image: USAAF official picture of Crew 12A in front of a B-26 at Lake Charles Army Air Base, Lake Charles, LA, February 19, 1944. From left to right: Pilot, Ladd L. Horn; Co-Pilot, Paul M. Roseman; Bombardier, William C. Webb; Radioman, Warren E. Tupper; Armorer, Harmon R. Summers; Engineer, Bernard Fineman.

Inside cover image: Formal studio picture of Dad, 1st Lieutenant Ladd L. Horn, taken at Goodfellow Field, San Angelo, TX sometime between March and May of 1943.

Scripture quotations taken from The Holy Bible, New International Version® NIV® Copyright © 1973 1978 1984 2011 by Biblica, Inc.™ Used by permission. All rights reserved worldwide.

The author has made every effort to provide accurate Internet addresses as of the time of publication. The author does not assume any responsibility for errors or changes that occur after publication.

ISBN 978-1-66788-907-8

Printed in the United States of America by BookBaby 7905 N. Crescent Blvd. Pennsauken, NJ 08110

This book is dedicated to:

Alyson, Erin, Gabriel, Rosalina, Alma, Elijah, Abigail and Naomi (Gracie). It is my hope that you will know something of the man my father was and the sacrifice he made for our freedom.

'

And to Judy. I hope that these stories and pictures help you remember.

Dad, you gave three years of your life for our freedom. Thank you for trusting me with your story.

Dad, age ninety-four, on his front porch in front of the fireplace on his 70th wedding anniversary.

Dad's photo of an embroidered insignia of the 17th Bombardment Group of the 42nd Wing of the US Army Air Force.

Always in *(into)* Danger—Official Insignia of the Seventeenth Bomb Group. That is what the sign outside the headquarters in Sardinia (and the other locations we were headquartered) was like.

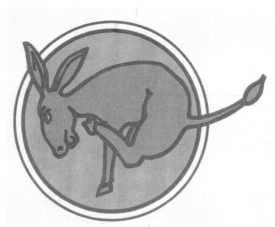

The "Kicking Mule" insignia of the 95th Bombardment Squadron of the 17th Bombardment Group, the squadron my dad, 1st Lieutenant Ladd L. Horn, was assigned to. This insignia is the origin of the title of this book.

All textual notes and comments that are not my father's original words are marked by italics and any substantial spelling, punctuation and grammatical errors that are in the original documents and letters are marked with the classical [*sic*].

All pictures included in this book are either from original prints made by Ladd L. Horn or from negatives or prints that were given to him by S2 or were obtained for services rendered.

The appearance of US Department of Defense (DoD) visual information does not imply or constitute DoD endorsement.

CONTENTS

Acknowledgments

Dad, thank you for your love and care, for all you taught me and for your love for Christ. Thank you too for this "grand story" of your experience during the war. I wish you had lived to see this book.

I am grateful to Bernard Fineman for providing my father with copies of his engineer's flight log which assisted in establishing accurate dates for both Crew 12A's trip from the USA to Telergma, Algeria and for those missions he flew as engineer or bombardier with my father. I am also thankful to his children, Steven and Amy, for providing permission for the use of his detailed flight information in this book.

I must also thank Robert Ringo, my father's tentmate, whom I interviewed in 2015 and for his letter about my dad that is included in this volume.

And lastly, thank you members of Crew 12A for your part in the fight for our freedom! You were an integral part of my father's war experience. He never forgot you.

LET THE KICKING MULE KICK

"The righteous perish, and no one takes it to heart; the devout are taken away, and no one understands that the righteous are taken away to be spared from evil."

—Isaiah 57:1

PREFACE: The Origin of Let the Kicking Mule Kick

My father, 1st Lieutenant Ladd L. Horn, B-26 pilot, experienced things I only glimpsed through his stories. He was a good storyteller, but the activities of life, my mom's reticence to have him talk about WWII (she would say something like, Ladd, don't talk about the war. Nobody wants to hear that old stuff.) and perhaps the magnitude and gravity of what he did, and saw, kept him from telling us more for many years. When I was young and still at home, he would sometimes tell bits and pieces of funny stories, or crazy "shenanigans," as he would say, from his time as a B-26 pilot. He would tell about guys putting .45 caliber rounds in the holes in their tent posts and hitting them until they went off and shot through the tent, or about the time he chased a farmer on his tractor across his newly-plowed field as he brought his plane in for an emergency landing during a cross-country training exercise. But the difficult things he saw and the really tough stories were held back for nearly seventy-five years except for three short pieces he wrote; "Condensed Record of Military Service," "Let the Kicking Mule Kick," which is the origin of the title of this book, and another written sometime between 1988 and 1995 entitled, "Recollections of 95th Squadron Activities: Sardinia, Corsica and Dijon; 50 Years After the Fact."

When my father and mother were in their nineties (for a brief life history see Appendix 1), and they needed more help around the house and with medical appointments, I began spending a few days a week with them. Perhaps the sense my dad had that he would only live a few more years coupled with my more extended times with him (something that had not been possible for over forty years since my family and I had lived out of state for most of that time) changed the picture. He seemed to feel that he needed to tell the stories— even the sad and difficult ones. I sensed that in a way he felt it was his "duty" to tell the next generation what he had done and to give them a sense of the lives of the flight crews who had fought in WWII. Dad knew that most of the

WWII veterans were gone and only a few remained to actively transmit a picture of that great global war. So many pilots and flight crew members had died during the war, and now, most of the remaining ones were approaching one hundred years old. In 2014, only one of his many crew members and tentmates was still alive, Robert Ringo, a bombardier. So, at some point, never really planned, and without too much of a decision, we both agreed that he would tell stories and I would type.

Whenever our day's work was at a lull or we were between appointments and errands, we would sit on the couch in the living room and he would start a story and I would type on my laptop. He always complained that I was not going fast enough (I am a reasonably fast typist but a stenographer would have been better because it is just about impossible to keep up with oral storytelling!). We would never spend a long time at one sitting, but we did sit down quite often. When I would go back to my home in Rochester, NY, I would often "Google" something from the story or stories we had just recorded—a plane, a pilot, an engineer or bombardier, a location in Africa or Europe—and the story would continue to take shape and color. I would either mail that information or take it to him on my next visit and he would pick up on it and tell me more of the last story or start a new one.

Most of the stories were told in 2015 and 2016. His memory was great even at age 95, and he had always had an intense interest in how things work. He could remember details about flight speeds, fuel consumption rates, how air bases were laid out, which men were tentmates, which crew members were flying with him on specific missions (even though flight crews were often changed on a mission by mission basis) where planes were damaged, which ones went down, what happened to men who were captured, and events, locations and even some of the people from villages around their bases. His stories are filled with detail. However, as for anyone trying to remember events from seventy-plus years earlier, some details are lost. That is part of oral storytelling.

As time went on, we started through his picture album from the war. During high school, he had learned to develop film and when he entered the military, he would buy or bargain for cameras and film, take pictures of the war—people and planes and places—and then develop them. He was able to make prints of the negatives in his improvised darkrooms built on the side of his tents in Sardinia and Corsica. The negatives or prints were then sent home to his parents or my mom (his girlfriend at the time). Once other soldiers discovered that he could develop film, they would request that he develop their film as well. He would then trade development of their film for prints of their pictures. Thus, his album is rich with pictures from the 95th Bombardment Squadron of the 17th Bombardment Group. As we began to record each picture with the details of personnel and locations in them, Dad would tell new stories and I would capture those as well.

The number of stories grew and I began to think that I should pull together all of the isolated stories and the history of his military service for his grandchildren and great-grandchildren so they would know something of the man he was and his experiences. But the more stories I recorded, the more I realized that these stories were different than many other military stories I had heard and that they might be of interest to other people. Most military books fall into a small number of categories: (1) global or regional conflict mostly consisting of information about countries, alliances, strategies, generals, and groups of soldiers; (2) equipment—planes, tanks, artillery and etc.; and, (3) stories of heroic events of capture and survival. I realized that the stories Dad was telling didn't fit any of these categories. His stories were about people, events, places, friends and animals caught up in the middle of war. They were alive and interesting—not a set of facts that some poor high school kid would have to write an essay about or memorize to pass the next exam. I also realized that what he had experienced was as intense and riveting as the action in some of the recent books and war films I had read or seen. And yet, they were told in a low-key way. I would often "miss" the intensity and emotion while I was typing but they would hit me later as I drove home or when I read the story to someone else. Once in the middle of a story I stopped typing and told him, "If I had read these stories in my high school history class, WWII would have come alive to me." More than once since I have "choked up" reading them to others. And so, I began thinking about putting his stories in a book.

This storytelling process went on for about a year and a half or perhaps a little longer (2015–2016). Dad always complained that we weren't moving fast enough. I know he felt he was steadily getting weaker and that at the pace we were going we would not get through all he wanted to tell. He was right. On October 16, 2016, he died and we had not finished.

The storytelling came to an end.

However, Dad was also something of a family record-keeper or "historian," and he kept pictures, antiques and keepsakes from multiple generations. Over the years, I learned that in the same fashion, he had kept many military records and mementos. When I bought my first car, a 1965 Ford Custom 500 in 1972, he gave me one of his Army blankets (see the story, "Stolen Army Blankets") to keep in the car in case I was ever stranded on a cold winter day in Buffalo. I still have that blanket in my 2019 Ford F150 in 2022. Before we started working on his stories he had also already passed his military awards on to my sister and me, each with exactly half of his insignia and medals. But, as he told me stories, I continued to get a better picture of which records and things he had saved. Some he gave to me while we were recording the stories. He had the common things people keep, such as medals, pictures and uniforms. Then there was his mess kit and his flying boots (purchased for a dollar in Natal, Brazil). There was his flight bag which contained orders (you weren't really supposed to keep orders, but my dad had a penchant for keeping things pertaining to him) and training manuals, exams and notebooks, lists of men in his squadron, his engineer's (Bernard Fineman's) flight log and so much more. After his death, I put all of his military records together and soon began to search for more information about him through Army records, museum archives and the Internet. The idea of a book of his stories with his pictures kept growing.

This book is the realization of that idea.

The stories have been left for the most part as they were captured, much as if you were sitting on the couch with us, hearing the story together with all of its interruptions, natural glitches, uncorrected phrasing, grammar and flow. While I have edited them to remove typographic errors, I have not edited them to remove all mistakes, or even to make them read smoothly. I felt that editing them would potentially take away my dad's character or insert my own personality and thus would put you one step farther away from the personal feeling in the stories. In a few places, I have added a few words or a phrase where it was necessary for a reader's understanding and I have added a few notes (always italicized; often captured at the beginning or end of the story). I have also tried to put at least one or more pictures that my dad took with every story to make it real. Most of the story titles are mine, a few are Dad's. My titles often come from his words.

Since the stories were spontaneous and were often based on things my dad and I were talking about that day, they are only approximately assembled in sequential time order. You can mentally create a general timeline given that his enlistment and training were in the US in 1942 and 1943, he was transferred to North Africa (Telergma, Algeria) via the South Atlantic Air Ferry Route in March of 1944, and then was moved to Sardinia in April of 1944, followed by Corsica (October 1944) and finally Dijon, France (November 1944). He returned home to the US in April of 1945. The stories therefore cover a little less than two years of training and a single year of overseas service.

There are several exceptions to the format of orally transmitted stories. The exceptions include some stories that came from the three summaries written by Dad somewhere between 1988 and 1995. The first he titled, "Condensed Record of Military Service." The second Dad titled, "Let the Kicking Mule Kick: Recollections of a Marauder Pilot (WWII)." The "kicking mule" is a reference to the insignia of his squadron, the 95th in the 17th Bombardment Group. This latter piece, a *Readers Digest*-like, condensed story, was Dad's attempt to give you an overall feeling for the life of the pilots and the flight crews of the 95th Bombardment Squadron. It was written years before we began our storytelling/"recording" sessions and uses general information from multiple missions and events to put together a "composite" story. This second "exception piece" is included as the first story in this book. The full stories and detail for each of the events described in "Let the Kicking Mule Kick: Recollections of a Marauder Pilot (WWII)" can be found in other stories within this volume. The third summary he wrote was his, "Recollections of 95th Squadron Activities: Sardinia, Corsica and Dijon; 50 Years After the Fact." It was written sometime between 1988 and 1995. (Dad titled the account as "50 Years After the Fact." This would place the latest possible timing of the writing of this piece in 1995. However, in the piece, he wrote, "I also kept the nameplate from a B-26. The nameplate was sliced off by a piece of propeller blade that came through the cockpit. After forty-four years, I can't find that either." Using 1944 as the year of the crash associated with that nameplate, and adding forty-four years would place the time of the writing as 1988 instead of 1995. The discrepancy remains unresolved.) I have divided this third written summary into several stories and included some of the information as additional detail in identical stories he told me orally in 2015–2016. The stories that come from divisions of this written summary include, "Toulon: A Right-Wing Plane is Lost," "The Second Right-Wing Plane Lost," "The Third Right-Wing Plane Lost," "The Zundapp," "Flying Co-Pilot for Paul Roseman,"

"Flying with Schoeps—Told Twice," "Mademoiselle," "Long Mission to Central Germany," "The Courier Trip," "The Most Fun I Ever Had with a B-26" and "Dad's Crew."

The other "non-oral" stories are the stories that came from the letters he wrote to my mother, Ethel J. Horn (O'Neil), who was his girlfriend at that time. From July 11, 1942 when he left for Fort Niagara as a draftee, to the day he was discharged, July 11, 1945, he wrote faithfully and often. She kept 339 of those letters in two boxes in their attic. After Dad died, I opened those boxes and after seventy-eight-plus years, was able to read his "real-time" thoughts and stories. He, of course, always told her how much he loved her, how lovely she was (and how he was nothing much to look at), how lonely he was and his desire to get married after the war. He mixed in stories about daily living in training and in war, with stories of flying and accidents that had happened. He held little back. He told the good with the bad, the funny with the sorrowful. He would as easily tell her of some "close call" or of men dying as about what they had for dinner (or didn't have as was often the case). Having read all 339 letters, I now say that I have a far better understanding of why my mom was "afraid" of flying for all of her life! The letters are a rich treasure trove of stories. I have selected a few letters to include in their entirety and many excerpts which are short stories in their own right. They are placed in, "PART II The War Through the Lens of Love," immediately after the stories Dad narrated to me. The letters are in chronological order.

Other information that may be of interest or that may clarify the overall picture of my dad's experiences is collected in a set of appendices.

Any uncertainties, inaccuracies and errors are most likely mine, though there are details of which Dad was uncertain and which we could not verify by other means. I left out just one of Dad's oral stories. It was one about Uden Uden's Oil Burner. I left it out because after quite some time reviewing the information it appeared to be a mixture of the story of Uden Uden's Oil Burner bombing Roccasecca Bridge from Villacidro, Sardinia and Capt. William R. Pritchard's flight with Coughin' Coffin during the bombing of Trapani Milo, Italy with a return landing at Djedeida in Tunisia.

While I have tried to verify all information in the stories I have included, I apologize ahead of time for any mistakes and would love to hear from you, the reader, if you have more accurate information. I would also love to hear from any families whose family members served with my father. They are an incredible group of men and women who deserve to be recognized. In some stories, or pictures, my dad would remember their names and faces in an instant—just as if he were still there. Others escaped his memory. He would, and I do, apologize for missing both individual and group names.

I want to especially acknowledge Jesus, my dad's and my Savior, for giving us the many days and hours we had together before he died. It was an incredible gift to me. While my dad will only specifically reference his relationship with Christ in three of the stories in this book, he would want you to know that the Lord was with him, personally, and held his life in his hands during those days of training and active duty. He would also want you to know that He loved Jesus to his last day on Earth. And he would want you to know Christ as well.

Keith A. Horn
Son of the late Ladd L. Horn (7/28/1921–10/16/2016)

INTRODUCTION: *What You Should Know as You Read*

War leaves an indelible mark on the men and women who serve. It shapes them in ways that even they do not fully understand or recognize consciously. Their experiences are a powerful reality that is rarely ever surpassed even when one lives for over seventy years beyond them. And the experiences come at a young age. Those of us who have never served cannot fully understand the impact, for "the shaping" is not just one of locations, equipment, technology and logistics mixed with people, rather it goes to the root of who people are and to what they believe about humanity. It has far too often left our veterans broken and isolated and, unfortunately, PTSD is too frequently a life-long reality.

Thankfully my dad was not broken by the events of his combat service even though he survived crash landings, flew and landed planes that had been terribly damaged by flak, saw uncounted numbers of his crew and squadron members killed in action (KIA) and came home with injuries (knee), neurological conditions (neuropathy) and perhaps facial cancer (from sun exposure in North Africa and flying at high altitude without UV screens in cockpit canopies) that affected him until he died on October 16, 2016. Dad was a very thoughtful and generally quiet man. He was slow to anger. He was caring. In emergencies he was strong, thoughtful and a man of action. He didn't react much to pain (though you could always recognize he was hurting by his quiet grunts and moans). And, Dad was a good storyteller. Oh, not in the way extroverts might be the life of a party through telling stories, but if he were with a bunch of his friends or with our family or our friends, he could tell stories of his childhood or the war for hours. And people loved to listen.

Dad was born on July 28, 1921 and was just twenty years old when he enlisted in the USAAF (United States Army Air Force; Serial # 0-687596) in 1942 (He turned twenty-one just seventeen days after he entered the Army. For additional details of his life history, see Appendix 1.) Interestingly, he was also drafted that same year (Army; Serial # 32380034. See records at https://aad.archives.gov/aad/record-detail.jsp?dt=893&mtch=1&cat=all&tf=F&q=Ladd+L.+Horn&bc=&rpp=10&pg=1&rid=3001647). Appendix 2 provides historical background on the USAAF relative to the US Air Corps and the US Air Force for your understanding as you will hear him refer to each throughout his stories. You will hear my father tell the story of how he enlisted, yet was also drafted, as you read the rest of this book. He was a 1st Lieutenant and B-26 "Marauder" pilot in the 17th Bombardment Group, 95th Bombardment Squadron of the USAAF and saw active duty in North Africa, Sardinia, Corsica and France, flying sixty-four bombing missions over Italy, Germany and France before he returned home in 1945. Sixty of his missions are recorded on his discharge papers. His last four missions, which he flew from Dijon, France, had not yet been reported back to the USA at the time of his discharge. He, of course, flew many more times, but no crew received credit for unsuccessful missions (e.g. when the weather was bad and you couldn't drop your bomb load, you missed the target, etc.). His stories in "PART I" of this book are the recollections of a 94- to 95-year-old who was making sure that our family and the next generation knew something of what he saw, felt and did while in active combat as a 21- to 23-year-old. And, his letters to Mom in "PART II" are the thoughts, emotions and storytelling of a 21- to 23-year-old written while engaged in war.

In order to understand his stories, you also need to know that my dad loved mechanical things. At nine or ten years old, he and his friends rebuilt a Ford Model T engine and they would drive that car around the neighborhood. At the same age, he would refinish floors, paint, and change out electrical outlets in his father's apartments. On his own, when he was in high school, he learned how to develop photographic film. Then, shortly before the war, he got a job at a local auto shop and in his short time there learned many skills that would be useful as he was around equipment during his combat years. After the war

Dad graduated from the University of Buffalo with a degree in electrical engineering. Later he migrated to mechanical and design engineering as his career developed through Fedders Air Conditioning, Dustex and American Precision Industries. His mechanical "bent" gave him a mind to analyze and remember details about the planes, guns, bombs, bombsights, jeeps and motorcycles of WWII. While his stories and this book are not about those details, in a few cases, the details did help us clarify parts of the story.

His knowledge of film developing served him well during his time on active duty. Initially he had no darkroom and few or none of the correct chemicals for the developing and stop baths. However, he was great at improvising and used his helmet and mess kit under a blanket in his tent in Telergma, Algeria as a makeshift "darkroom" to develop rolls of negatives. Later in Sardinia as his "film-developing fame" grew, many others asked him to develop their film. Eventually he and his crew built a darkroom on the side of their tent. Developing chemicals were in short supply and so he improvised, using a local alkaline laundry soap in the developing bath and various acids (e.g. citrus fruit juices) for the stop baths. As they relocated to Corsica, the new tent was modified to have a darkroom. In Dijon, France he had to once again resort to using his helmet and mess kit under a blanket for developing as he had no darkroom there. Often he traded his developing skills for copies of prints from the film he developed for others. His albums of black and white pictures from the war are a rich compilation, mostly of his pictures, but with select pictures of key planes or events that were taken by other crew members or official war photographers. (In several cases the 95th Squadron's S2 intelligence officers shared negatives or prints with him.) The pictures that were sent home were kept by his mother and father and Ethel J. O'Neil. As I assembled this book, there were approximately 700 pictures in his binders. Those pictures were the catalysts for a number of the stories in this book. As Dad and I sat together in 2015 and 2016, we spent some time going through the pictures in his binders. Many pictures reminded him of people and places and stories and so we captured those as well. Handwritten notes on the backs often filled in a few relevant details. Dad's memory did the rest, though there were gaps. Several pictures in his collection are "famous" in other historical works about the 17th Bombardment Group and the 95th Bombardment Squadron. Dad had often taken the picture or had the original or a quality copy and had shared them with those authors.

The stories you will read are not about generals and troops and numbers and campaigns. Rather, they are about people and places. They are about what it felt like and how men reacted. They are what he wanted our family to know about him and the experiences that shaped him. What the stories might lack from not being told as soon as he returned from combat is more than made up for by the perspective and wisdom gained through reflecting on those events for more than seventy years after they were experienced.

As you read these stories, try to imagine yourself, or maybe better yet, your children being where my dad was, doing what he and his crew did and surviving (or not!). Remember that some of these "men" celebrated their eighteenth (some had lied about their ages in order to join the USAAF) and nineteenth birthdays in Africa, Sardinia, Corsica and France. My dad was actually one of the older men having joined at the age of 20. By age 23 my dad had already flown a crew across the Atlantic Ocean, led them on bombing missions and watched crew members die.

While anyone can read these stories, and enjoy them without any background or WWII history, reading other sources about some of the events that my dad talks about may make the experience richer. There are a great many resources (and even films) out there giving details of the events and places my dad tells about—the North Africa Campaign, the Bolzano Bridge, Villacidro, Monte Cassino, the Rome-Arnot Campaign, Toulon, the invasion of southern France (Operation Dragoon), etc.

The planes my dad flew were Martin B-26 Marauders. If you have no knowledge of B-26 bombers, there are many great published and online resources that tell the entire story of these bombers. The remastered training film, "How to Fly the Martin B-26 Marauder (1944)," at https://www.youtube.com/watch?v=tuTOFcqGPys, is a great original training film (Love the "retro-style" acting!) that can give you some real "feel" for the plane. The plane was a twin-engine plane (two Pratt and Whitney engines, one mounted on each wing; 2,000 hp each) that served as a medium-range bomber. It had the highest loading per wing area of any plane made at that time. The B-26 was touted as having the lowest combat loss rate during the war. However, it was also known to be a very difficult plane to fly with significant issues during takeoff and landing (the stall speed for B-26s was around 140 mph, considerably higher than all trainers and most other aircraft of that time). Runaway props were also problematical. Thus, the B-26 Marauder received many nicknames: "The Widowmaker," "The Flying Prostitute," "The Baltimore Whore," "The Flying Vagrant," "The Wingless Wonder," "One-Way Ticket," "Martin Murderer," "The Flying Coffin," "The Coffin Without Handles," and the "B-Dash Crash." (see the URL below) During 1942, there were so many B-26 training crashes at MacDill field in Tampa, FL that the phrase, "One a day in Tampa Bay" was coined. Keep these B-26 "idiosyncrasies" in mind as you read my dad's stories about the crash at Telergma and about takeoffs, "Takeoffs are a Dangerous Thing." You can read a summary of the specific issues with B-26 bombers at http://www.joebaugher.com/usaf_bombers/b26_5.html .

As you read about the missions Dad flew, let your imagination take you into an approximately 34,000 lb aluminum and steel fuselage with several tons of bombs, no insulation, no heaters, no oxygen and six to eight crew members packed into tight spaces. Then fill it with the throbbing roar of two, 2,000-hp Pratt and Whitney engines just outside your window. You are dressed in your heaviest clothes (possibly a flight jacket, but likely not), a flak jacket and Mae West. Your communication is through headsets with microphones placed on your voice box because of the interior noise. Now fly at between 10,000 and 18,000 ft for three or four hours to your destination and back in numbing cold, short on oxygen, filled with anticipation and the fear of flak and German fighters and the constant consuming thoughts of, "Will I have enough fuel to make it back to base?" and, "Will my crew and I return at all?". Then, perhaps, his words will really come alive and you will get an even greater sense of what these flight crews went through.

My dad was a pilot. However, you will hear him talk of flying as a co-pilot in a number of his stories. There are three scenarios where this occurred. First, Dad had a B-26 training certificate, and he sometimes acted as the co-pilot for a pilot who was transitioning from other aircraft to the B-26s. Second, when a co-pilot was deemed ready to transition to pilot, an experienced pilot like my dad would take the co-pilot's seat on the first mission the new pilot flew. An example of this occurs in his story, "Flying as Co-Pilot for Paul Roseman." The third situation in which he would fly as co-pilot would be when he would be called up to fly with the flight leader of a mission. The flight leader led the mission and had to fly with extreme precision and immaculate timing. They were top pilots and needed experienced men as their co-pilots. This is the situation in Dad's story about Joseph Schoeps.

My father's official service records were burned in the National Personnel Records fire of 1973 in Overland Missouri. The records he saved, the pictures he took, the things he kept and the stories he told are the only records we have. It is likely that families of his flight crew and tentmates have additional information about him. I would love to hear from them.

How does a man or woman live through war in such constant contact with death? Part of my dad's strength lay in the fact that he had given his life to the Lord Jesus Christ at a young age. He loved Jesus. He trusted Jesus. He trusted

Jesus with his life—not just in general terms, but literally. You will hear a story of his training when he heard the "quiet voice of the Lord behind him" telling him to only partially complete a maneuver and how that decision to actively follow the Lord's command saved his life and that of his instructor. You will also hear him talk with Jesus Christ in the face of "certain" death as 20 or 30 mm tracer bullets came directly in at his cockpit windshield. My dad's (and my) real hope would be that you could know Christ as he did.

So, sit back and enjoy the ride with your guide, 1st Lieutenant Ladd L. Horn, B-26 Marauder pilot.

Keith A. Horn
Son of the late Ladd L. Horn (7/28/1921–10/16/2016)

PART I

The War As I Heard It

Let the Kicking Mule Kick
Recollections of a Marauder Pilot (WWII)
95ᵗʰ "Kicking Mule" Squadron

This first "story" is a composite of events from various missions on which my dad was pilot or co-pilot. It is not one of his oral stories, but, rather, a written account in which he attempted to capture an overall feeling for what pilots and their crews went through on a regular basis. Details of each of the events in this account will be found in the full oral stories that follow it.

Six B-26 Marauders in formation—unknown location.

Day after day we coaxed the roaring planes into the air, flak-battered, weary and worn, we never felt quite sure the planes would make it. Often overloaded we lifted them off the pockmarked dirt and gravel runway more by sheer will power than by any special skill we might have. Once airborne they staggered under the load of fuel, bombs, ammunition and essential crew and equipment, often flying through Marauder cumulus, the billowing black column of smoke from a burning Marauder that didn't make it. Blown tires were numerous as sharp stones and shrapnel pieces took their toll. Now and then there would be a runaway propeller and the screaming, tearing, snarling sound of it sent chills down the spine of every man on the base. Still we survived and went on flying

Paul Roseman *(Dad's co-pilot from Crew 12A)* sitting in the pilot's seat of one of our B-26s. The picture was taken mainly to show the cockpit and the range of dials and levers. *Note on back of the picture:* Lt. Roseman at Pilot's seat in ship, Aug. 1944 Sardinia.

One day our right propeller ran away just as we became airborne. We flew around the field in a wide arc and sat back down on the start of the runway never having attained more than about 50' to 75' of altitude and never having picked up our gear or flaps. The mission ended before it started.

Another time we raised the gear and the cockpit filled with billowing, choking, lavender-colored smoke. We couldn't see, we couldn't breathe. Scared? Yes! We snatched open the windshield vents and tried to hold the plane level with a slight climb. The flight engineer opened the cockpit entrance door (located in the floor) and even denser smoke billowed into the cockpit. He closed it quickly and we all got the same idea at the same instant. Three hands grabbed for the gear handle, down went the gear and in seconds we got fresh air in the cockpit. The smoke subsided rapidly. We could see and breathe. We were still airborne. Once again, we flew a wide, low-level arc around the field and sat back down on the runway glad to be alive. We were still choking and wheezing and our eyes running, but we were alive.

During takeoff on the rough runway we had ruptured the nose wheel cylinder and the hydraulic fluid leaking under high pressure (1,200 psi) had atomized to a high degree and also sprayed onto the hot nose wheel bearing. The coloring in the hydraulic fluid had caused the lavender smoke color. I had never realized that the wheel bearing got hot on takeoff although I had seen a main wheel bearing that had literally melted down. I assumed that was because of wear, maladjustment or faulty lubrication. But apparently, they got hot even under normal conditions.

Following normal takeoffs, we climbed out slowly making a gradual turn on the heading for the target, the idea being to conserve as much fuel as possible. Climbing rate and speed were a compromise; we climbed at 182 to 185 *(mph)* most times and gradually closed formation on course for the target. As we went through 10,000 feet we would open out, throttle back and shift the superchargers to "High Blower." During this time, the gunners would take position and test fire their guns.

View out of the pilot's window at low altitude.

As we penetrated enemy air space we tightened formation, six ships per group in a close, tight box. The first burst of flak always brought a "There she blows," a cheer and a squabble of chatter on the intercom. Enemy fighters evoked a similar reaction.

We were always most vulnerable as we approached the target area. At a flare pistol signal from the group leader, all flights went into a train and then fanned out and each approached the target from a slightly different angle and heading. We used glide-bombing techniques almost exclusively. The pilot nosed down slightly and maintained a specified rate of descent. The Norden bombsight had a preset error cranked in to compensate for the rate of descent and the bombardier could sight normally. The bomb would be right on. This procedure reduced the accuracy of the flak quite effectively as long as the gunners had to do manual tracking. They expected the bombers to be in level flight on the bomb run and the small change of altitude was not easily noted or corrected for. With the development of radar-controlled guns no evasive tactics did any good. We fought back by dumping tons of "window" to deflect the radar. "Window" was the name for thin strips of aluminum foil, paper backed on one side only. It fluttered down slowly through the air, reflecting radar and radio waves that confused radar sighting.

Flying formation.

The pilots were too busy on the bomb run to get to see much of what went on. Holding the bombers in tight formation to achieve an accurate, concentrated bomb drop took intense concentration. We did not have the luxury of formation sticks and were already weary from the long flight in to the target, always in tight formation for least vulnerability to fighter attacks.

As we approached the bomb run we increased engine RPM [*sic*] and put the fuel mixture controls into "auto rich." This gave quicker power response and better overall control of the aircraft.

The flak could be murderous. The pilot, without watching, sensed the close bursts by a flash of orange-red light followed by a concussion wave that made the plane buck and rock. You knew that was close enough to be lethal and never ceased to marvel that the engines were still running and the plane answering to controls. You scanned all instrument readings anxiously and waited for the next jolt. Small pieces of spent shrapnel rattled off the plane like hail, black smoke from other bursts drifted through the formation. The chatter on the intercom gave you a rough idea of the overall picture but you couldn't really look. Check the instruments, keep in tight, no sudden moves or accelerating that might throw the bombs and spoil the pattern. The bomb bay doors are open. It's only a few seconds more 'til "bombs away." The intercom squabbles away almost dense static on the earphones, "Number two flight is really getting it. They have one plane on single engine. Just lost his number two man. He's going down trailing black smoke (from the waist). He just "salvo'd [*sic*] his bombs, no chutes yet (from the tail)." In the midst of it all the bombardier comes through clear with "bombs away" and the plane bucks from the sudden decrease in load. "All bombs released. Bomb bay doors closing." follows a second later. All right! Break for it! The intercom is screaming, "Let's get out of here!"

Picture of Lindsey, a first pilot that went over about the same time I did and he was with me all the time I was there. He is sitting in the cockpit of a B-26 with the insulated headphones on and a throat mike. That is what we wore for all of our intercom communications. They were strapped up against your Adam's apple so they picked up your voice without all the noise going on in the plane. They were uncomfortable, but did the job pretty well. *Dad wrote a note on the back of this picture which had partially peeled off in glue. The following is my best re-creation of the full note:* One of the fellows of *(the)* 95th in a B-26. Can't remember his name *(arrow added later pointing to "Lindsay" sp?)*. Saw him last in field hospital in a wheel chair both legs broken and full of flak. Shell exploded just forward of *(the instrument?)* panel. His co-pilot made an emergency landing in Italy.

Paul Martinson in the cockpit of a B-26. You can see the intercom
microphone close to his neck.

I firewall everything; 2,700 RPM, [*sic*] full-rich mixture, full throttle, nose
down, break left, a diving gradual turn generally in the direction of home base.
The flight is opening out, speed is building up, the roar of the two Pratt &
Whitneys is deafening to my already aching ears. The air speed climbs to
275 … 300 … 350. Ooops. There's a redline at 353. Who cares? We're not
keeping up with the rest of the flight. The needle moves well beyond the
redline but we're leveling out now and it starts to recede. The open formation
at high speed and changing altitude was less vulnerable to the heavy flak. Now
we are clear of the worst. Got [*sic*] to tighten up now for fighter protection.
Got [*sic*] to slow down to conserve fuel. We cut the RPM [*sic*] all the way

back to 1,800, pull the mixture into manual lean and maintain just enough throttle to pull up to the rest of the flight and snuggle in tight. As soon as we're in position we shift to lower blower as an additional conservation measure.

Planes of the 95th Bomb Squadron just after bombing *(a)* huge ammunition dump in Germany. May have been the Laudersbach ammunition dump. That explosion was felt 200 miles away. It broke windows 80 miles away. One plane lost its engine from the concussion of the explosion. I took this picture. *Note: this was Siegelsbach, Germany not Laudersbach and was a February 25, 1945 mission from Longvic Field, Dijon, France.*

We've been out nearly 4 hours. The rarified air and bone-chilling cold along with the tension and stress has taken its toll. We are bone-weary, but it's not over yet. The turret gunner comes on the intercom; "There are fighters at 3 o'clock, very high." A few minutes later he comes on again, "They're closing, look like 109s." A few moments of silence and then, "ME-109 *(Messerschmitt Bf 109)* at 1:00 high." I can see him now, he is dropping fast, going to attack our flight head on. There is nothing to do but hold in there. It's all up to the gunners now. His 20 mm cannon shells start popping around us, red tracers arc out to meet him. He starts a "split S" and slides under through us belly up. The last glimpse I get of him tracers are bouncing off his armor-plated belly.

Postcard cropped from Dad's picture.

We had penetrated German territory nearly as far as the "heavies" with just as large a bomb load. The only reasons we could do it were our extra speed and no time wasted joining up a large formation. But we didn't have the fuel supply, only about 1,000 gallons for two big engines, the rest of this mission would be sweating out fuel. The auxiliary tanks were already empty and the main tanks dangerously low. As we approach base the flight engineer comes forward and taps my elbow. "I've checked over the plane," he says. "We've got damage, nothing serious that I can find. No fuel leaks, no hydraulic leaks and the electrical systems are functional." I acknowledge and he kneels down in front of the control pedestal perusing the engine instruments dutifully. He flips the selector switch back and forth on the fuel gauge, and then repeats the procedure. He taps me on the throttle elbow to get my attention. "Lt.," he says, "All fuel gauges are reading empty." I nod and he remains silent. I am no longer reading gauges; I am counting minutes on my stopwatch.

1944. Narrow neck of land with water above and below. Bombing mission over Italy. [*sic*] We were bombing a bridge. It looks like a good bombing pattern, but it missed the bridge. It was taken by one of the Air Force photographers. This shows an excellent bomb pattern.

The airwaves are alive with frantic calls from pilots in the same situation seeking permission to land first. I've flown long enough. I know their requests will not be honored. It is against the rules and for good reason. You flew and you take your chances the same as the next guy.

1944. Note on back of picture: Two of the oldest planes in the 95th at the time. Note the number of missions painted on, particularly on the far plane. Also still in camouflage paint. Flying over Italy near Naples headed home to Sardinia. *Note: this picture was taken out of the co-pilot's window.*

I hated the fly-over requirement. Returning from a mission, all flights flew the length of the runway in train before making their landing approach. This gave the "powers that be" a quick check on how many planes were missing and which ones. It wasted some time and fuel, but I guess it made somebody happy. Our flight was intact; we were third place to land. That wasn't too bad. One plane ground-looped and cracked up at the edge of the runway. Our landing was OK and both engines were still running even as we pulled onto the hard stand and parked.

The ground crew cheered and threw their hats in the air. I wasn't used to this grand a welcome home. The cheering and commotion continued. I tried to fill out the flight form and then gave up. I handed it to the co-pilot and told the flight engineer, "Get out and see what the commotion is about." He climbed through the nose wheel door and went over to the group and looked where they were pointing. He cheered and threw his hat in the air. He came back and stuck his head up through the door. "Lt.," he says, "An 88 mm shell went through our right wing without exploding, left a hole big enough to throw your hat through. Missed both fuel tanks, the hydraulic lines, the gas lines and the electrical conduit, but it cut the main wing spar clean off." I broke into a cold sweat. Talk about surviving by the skin of your teeth! But tomorrow will be another day, there will be another plane, another mission. Maybe some of us will survive the war.

Sardinia 1944. Truck dragging in one of our planes that was shot up and had to crash land on the auxiliary field. If you knew you were coming in for a crash landing you had to land on the auxiliary field (if you could make it there). They would bring these planes back to the main field to see if they could be repaired. This was a very early model because you can barely see the air scoops. They built them for air speed but they were inadequate for the conditions (they needed large air scoops and large filters). The next models coming over had larger air scoops. The following models had even larger ones. Look at the nose swivel gun. It is still hooked to its swivel and is pointing up in the air. The transmitter antenna is in an odd location. *The plane is most likely Li'l Angel's Big Sis, Taffy.*

Frontline picture. Observation picture after we bombed. It was taken from a little higher altitude—around 15,000 ft. Location Central Italy. [*sic*] I don't know the name of the town.

Frontline picture. This is an observation photograph taken from 25,000 ft. The white specs are bomb craters. This is the actual battle front in Central Italy. Based on the type of farmland, it was up beyond Rome or Naples toward Europe. *Picture labeled,* Occ Buildings Mil Activity Rebel *(?)* Pesns *(?)* Comm Diggings and Communications center diggings M453153.

Some Funny Things Happened on My Way to the USAAF

In 1942 a friend of mine, Chuck Goodier, from Blasdell, NY (B-17 bomber crew member) had just transferred from the US Army to the US Army Air Force and was home on leave until the paperwork was completed. During that leave, he talked with me and told me he was sure I had been drafted or would soon be drafted. Based on what he had seen in the army he advised me that it would be better to enlist instead of waiting to be drafted.

At that time, I had not received a draft notice. However, draft decisions were made and notices went out in order to provide draftees with two weeks of time between when they received the draft notice and when they would have to show up. Therefore, the draft notice I received the evening of June 20, 1942 might have been made as many as twenty-four days before the following story and June 20th 1942 when I was inducted into the USAAF.

The following is the sequence of events that resulted in my being a pilot in the USAAF.

I went in to Buffalo about the 6th of June to order a leather-bound Schofield Bible (at Monroe's) for my girlfriend of about four years, Ethel Jane O'Neil (my wife of seventy years as of the telling of this story). They didn't have a leather-bound version in stock that day. However, they told me that if ordered that day it could be delivered in time for Ethel's birthday on June 20th. So, I put a down payment on it and completed the order.

On June 20th, 1942, I had to get in to Monroe's to pick up the Bible. I learned that the USAAF enlistment team would be in Buffalo on that same day. So, I decided that I would enlist in the morning and then pick up the Bible in the afternoon so I could give it to Ethel that evening. I mistakenly assumed that I would fill out some small amount of paperwork for the enlistment team and my enlistment would be done pretty quickly. It didn't turn out that way.

Ethel J. O'Neil 1942

When I contacted the enlistment team, they told me that I had to be in by 9:00 a.m. So, I borrowed my dad's car, drove in, parked and went to the building where the enlistment team was. When I arrived, there was a very long line of men waiting to enlist. The enlistment team quickly split us up into groups of 25 and a USAAF leader was put in charge of each group. Initially I filled out forms, most of which, requested general information. Next, they gave me a complete physical—and it was complete! Anyone who didn't pass the physical was eliminated and could not enlist. Next, they gave exams: IQ, aptitude, logic, reasoning capabilities, etc. all of which were graded on the spot. The USAAF personnel in charge would show you your score as soon as you completed the exam and it had been graded and they also showed you your ranking on their charts. This series of exams continued right on through noon, through lunch and into the afternoon. At 3:00 p.m. I was still taking tests. Finally, after the end of one of the last tests, the USAAF leader showed me that I had scored at a high level compared to the others. He told me that I was "acceptable" for the USAAF, but that I still had to go through an interview. They sent me to another part of the building where four or five officers were lined up along the wall. Each had charts and files on specific candidates. When one was free he called my name. He showed me my test scores and then said that I had done pretty well. He told me that I was accepted into the Air Force but that I had to go upstairs and go through a "swearing-in" ceremony. Unfortunately, time was running out and I had to get to Monroe's to pick up the Bible, drive home, change and meet Ethel for her birthday.

I went upstairs as they instructed me and I went through the "swearing in" ceremony. It was very formal much like the formal process of selecting a jury. They then told all of us that they had so many people enlisting that day that they couldn't keep up with the paperwork. So, we should go home and wait for the paperwork and indicated that it would take perhaps ten days to a couple of weeks. I quickly left, and made it to Monroe's before they closed. I picked up the Bible and went home. I wrapped the Bible, changed clothes and went up to Ethel's house on Big Tree Road in Hamburg and presented the Bible to her and told her I was now in the USAAF.

Ethel didn't want to accept the Bible when she opened it. She said it was too expensive a gift even though we had been going together pretty steady for about four years. She just thought that paying $17 for a Bible (nearly a week's salary) was too much. However, on the basis that it was both for her birthday and I was going into the USAAF she accepted it as sort of a "memory gift." Ethel was really pleased with the Bible even though she didn't want to accept it. How did Ethel respond to my enlistment? It actually wasn't very strong— partly because it was her personality not to react too strongly and I hadn't told her that I was going to enlist. In the end, it was kind of "Oh."

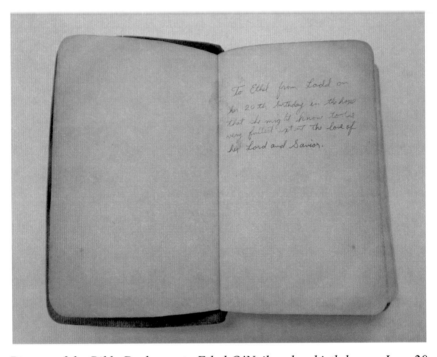

Picture of the Bible Dad gave to Ethel O'Neil on her birthday on June 20, 1942, the day he enlisted in the Air Force. This picture was taken in 2022. The note reads, "To Ethel from Ladd on her 20th birthday in the hope that she might know to the very fullest extent the love of her Lord and Savior."

When I got home from Ethel's house, my draft notice for the Army was there. It had arrived that day. The notice said to report to Hamburg the 11th of July for transportation to Fort Niagara.

A few days later I went to Hamburg, NY to the Army induction board. I told them that I had received an Army draft notice but that I was already an enlisted member of the USAAF. They asked me for the paperwork. When I told them that I had enlisted on June 20th and didn't have the paperwork yet but had been told to wait for it, they responded suspiciously and told me I still had to show up on July 11th. I tried a second time, but they again simply were skeptical and told me that they had "heard that story before." So, on the 11th of July I showed up.

The Army had olive-drab vans that they used to transport us to Fort Niagara. One of the other draftees in that group was Phil Wagner's brother-in-law. Phil Wagner lived four blocks from my house but I didn't know him until after the war. After the war, I became friends with Phil and worked with him at Fedders, Air Conditioning, Andco and Dustex where he was one of my draftsmen. Phil Wagner and I remained friends until Phil died at ninety-eight in 2015.

At Fort Niagara, the Army ran us through a series of tests again and I again did well. They told me that I had done well enough that I could qualify for the U.S. Army Air Force so I would have to take the Air Force exams. Once again, I told them that I had already enlisted in the Air Force. The officer in charge said, "No way! That is not possible." I told them the story of how I had gone in to the enlistment team in Buffalo on June 20th and had taken all of the exams, had taken the oath and was waiting for the official papers.

The officer told me that I still had to go to another building to take the exams, so I went. They passed out the exam and at the top it had an affidavit that I had to sign that certified that I had never seen or taken this exam before. When I read it, I told the officer in charge that I had taken this exam on June 20th in Buffalo and that all the questions were the same. The officer argued with me that it couldn't be true, but I still told him that I couldn't sign it or I would be lying. At that point, four other guys raised their hands and said that they had also taken the exam and were already enlisted in the US Army Air Force. They took all five of us away and told us to wait for further orders. They had no idea what to do with us and eventually we were sent to the barracks and signed up for some basic jobs while they (and we) waited.

We were at the Niagara base for a total of about two weeks *(actually closer to four weeks—his draft service date was July 11 and his last letter from Fort Niagara is dated August 5th)*. At the end of the second [sic] week, there was a notice posted on the bulletin board that had all five of our names on it. The orders were for us to pack our bags and be ready early the next morning to leave for Mitchell Field, Long Island.

Ladd L. Horn and Ethel J. O'Neil at Niagara Falls, August 2, 1942.

The next morning we left for Mitchell Field. *(Dad and I were interrupted at this point so I don't know whether they took the train or used vans).* When we arrived, they dropped us off at the edge of the base where there were enlisted men and barracks. The area was pretty much like a swamp. *(The conditions were terrible. See Dad's description in his letter from Camp Mills, Mitchell Field dated August 12, 1942 in "Part II The War Through the Lens of Love.")* They had no orders for us at Mitchell Field and no one knew what to do with us. Eventually a young 2nd Lieutenant came and helped arrange a tent for us. We were given tasks (I had latrine duty) but we were not allowed into the mess hall or onto the main base. We all were really hungry, but had no status, couldn't get money, and weren't allowed off the base. We had no salary or other source of income so we pooled our remaining money to buy things from the vending machines. We basically lived on coke and candy from the machines. We were told that we were in the US Army, not the US Army Air Force.

Ladd L. Horn, his parents and girlfriend (future wife) at Fort Niagara, Lewiston, NY on Sunday August 2, 1942. From left to right: Leonard August Horn, Freida May (Wenz) Horn, Ladd Leonard Horn and Ethel J. O'Neil.

After about a week or eight days, they posted a notice with our names. Once again, we were to pack our bags for transportation the next day. We were being moved to Blytheville, Arkansas. So, the following day we were taken by ten-wheeler trucks to Grand Central Station, given tickets and from there we went on the train to Buffalo where we were given new papers and train tickets for Blytheville and transferred to a different train. That first day leaving Buffalo for Blytheville we were in sleeper cars and we sat overnight on the bridge over the Niagara River. The train was loaded with many soldiers heading for Blytheville, but was not equipped with dining cars or food.

We arrived in Blytheville around the beginning of August. *(approximately the 17th of August based on the dates on letters he wrote from Mitchell Field— last date 14th—and from Blytheville—first date 18th—see "PART II The War Through the Lens of Love")* In Blytheville, a truck picked us up from the train station. At Blytheville, Arkansas there was a combined Army and Air Force base and there were many other draftees and recruits there. At that time, Blytheville served basically as a "holding base" for many recruits until they could be reassigned, though there was one group of US Army Air Force cadets being trained there. For me Blytheville turned out to be a holding location until the USAAF located me.

The four others I had traveled with and I went into basic training with the other recruits at Blytheville, most of whom were US Army recruits. Eventually I was separated from the other four I had been with up to that point. Interestingly, I did see Phil Wagner's brother-in-law once on some other part of the base.

We all marched and drilled and then were assigned to specific jobs on the base. I was assigned to permanent KP and assigned to a new barracks (the barracks were brand new, raw wood barracks) close to the mess hall. That job was tough! I got up at 4:00 a.m. to get to the mess hall to have everything ready for breakfast for all the men. After everyone else finished breakfast I could eat. Then immediately I had to start getting ready for lunch. Once again, I ate after the others had finished and then repeated the same sequence in the afternoon to get ready for supper. After supper, I cleaned up and went back to my barracks anywhere between 7 and 10 p.m. Then I'd repeat the same thing the next day.

I remained at Blytheville for most or all of August.

It was now about the end of August or the beginning of September. *(September 7ᵗʰ)* I came back from the mess hall one night and there was a nice guy in the barracks that told me that I should go down and check the bulletin board. He thought he had seen an order with my name on it. So, I went down and sure enough, there was an order and my name was the only one on it. It said that I should report for transportation early in the morning and that I was in the US Army Air Force and was headed for the classification center in Nashville Tennessee.

At Last! Out of the Army and into the USAAF Pre-flight Training in San Antonio, TX

When I arrived in Nashville there was no question that I was in the USAAF and I immediately started training. I was only in Nashville for five days but while in Nashville I was classified for pilot training. Based on your test results they decided what you would be trained for—pilot, bombardier, navigator, engineer... After five days, they shipped me from Nashville to San Antonio, TX that at the time was the largest USAAF aviation cadet-training center.

The trip to San Antonio was quite an ordeal. We were loaded on a train for San Antonio, but the train couldn't stay on schedule because of the large trainloads of soldiers moving from base to base had to be integrated with the civil passenger and freight trains that received scheduling priority. In order to accommodate the standard train traffic, we would be put on a siding and sit there for as much as half a day while the civil trains would pass through. Then we would get back on the tracks for a few hours and be routed onto another siding. The trains we rode on had no dining cars/mess halls and no food. We were able to get a little food from the Salvation Army or from kids at the station who could take our orders/money, run for the food and get back before the train left the station. Once in a while the Salvation Army would bring food and would be ready when we arrived in a station/location. They would "swarm" the train when we stopped and give out sandwiches for free.

Kids would all gather around our train at stations. We would send them for food, but often they wouldn't get back before the train left the station and once again we would be left without food.

We eventually made it to the Mississippi River. At the river, they had to transport the trains across on barges because there were not enough bridges for all of the civilian trains plus all of the troop-carrying trains. They would decouple the cars and load up to six cars on a barge, ferry them across the river, dock, unload and get them on the next track and then return for the next load. It took a long time and all the while we still didn't have any government-provided food. After we crossed the Mississippi River, there were sugarcane fields where we waited for the rest of the train to be brought across the river. We were so hungry that some of the guys got off the train and cut sugarcane for all of us. I'm sure the farmers weren't happy, but what are you going to do when you are that hungry? The sugarcane tasted pretty good.

Following the crossing of the Mississippi River we went south to San Antonio. We made good time relative to the earlier part of the trip because there was much less rail traffic on the north-south lines. It seemed that the east-west lines had the most train traffic at the time. In total, we were on the train for about five days.

When we arrived in San Antonio, the base had large groups of ten-wheelers there to greet the train. They loaded as many of us as possible on each one, drove us to the base and dropped us off at the entrance. Each person took his own luggage. Many lay [sic] down on their luggage right there at the entrance to the camp. It was really hot. Most of the men (boys really—ranging from a few as young as sixteen who had illegally entered the armed forces to about twenty-one years old) weren't used to the heat. In addition, no one had eaten much in five days and there was nothing to drink there at the base without getting into the mess hall. Many passed out and were picked up by first aid trucks and taken to the sick bay. Somehow, I survived ok—maybe it was the sugarcane.

I immediately started ground school training in San Antonio. The base was run well and set up well for a country that really was not prepared for war. They didn't even have current USAAF uniforms.

They checked us over and then took our army uniforms and exchanged them for coveralls since at that time they didn't have any (or enough?) USAAF uniforms. At the time the USAAF was in the process of changing from the older blue Army Air Force Uniforms (blue for the sky? USAAF song first line: "Off we go into the wild blue yonder"). However, they had decided that they needed something different for USAAF troops in combat and so they were migrating from blue uniforms to olive drab. Eventually we were given official USAAF uniforms. There were three kinds: (1) straight olive drab. It was ok to wear olive drab pants like the olive drab army uniforms with the olive drab "blouse" (sport jacket) and suntan shirt; (2) olive drab with pink pants (subdued pink pants that "matched" the olive drab "blouse") and a suntan shirt; and, (3) in the summer you could go with all "sun tan."

San Antonio, TX was ground school. The barracks were brand new and made with logs. The first three weeks consisted of routine things like physicals, tests for mental fitness, other aptitude tests, etc. and then came "pre-flight" training.

The man in front is wearing a monkey suit

Barracks for the cadets at SAACC, San Antonio, TX. Each dorm held forty-six men.

Cadets "Falling In" for Chow formation in front of the barracks at SAACC, San Antonio, TX.

This is My Outfit

My Flight

Hand-placed stone signs outside the barracks for Group 1, Squadron 2, Flight A, Dad's squadron placement at SAACC, San Antonio, TX, 1942.

Pre-flight training consisted of courses—college-like classes only condensed. Each course was about a month long and then you would start another class. The courses covered everything from physics to shortwave radio to internal combustion engines, extra math, trigonometry for navigation (a lot of this),

Morse code to communicate on the radio or by signal lights, etc. A lot of the courses were related to ground stuff, but then some for air communication.

Rear view of cadet "Drum Corps." Picture taken at SAACC, San Antonio, TX. The buildings in the back are classrooms (the second from the left is the "code" classroom) and the building to the right is the newly finished gym.

No 15 "Officers Club"   (over)

No. 15 "Officers Club." This is what you see when you reach the top of the hill in No. 14 *(picture #14 of a series taken along the cross country route)*. If you look very closely you will find two large buildings at the extreme left edge of the picture. They appear as two gray spots on the horizon and are two of the hangers on Kelly Field. *(Dad put an arrow in pen on the frame of the picture pointing to the two hangers.)*

The very heart of San Antonio - Note River Light

Picture of the river in downtown San Antonio, TX, Fall/Winter 1942.

The Alamo

Rear View of Alamo

The front and rear of the Alamo, Fall 1942.

Roosevelt and the Bugle Corps

President Roosevelt came to inspect the San Antonio training base while I was there in training. At that time, the population of the base was about 20,000. The parade grounds was something the size of a football field, and each wing would line up and march together into the parade area led by a drum and bugle corps. We didn't have much time to prepare for the review and so most of the preparation was done the day before or the morning of the review.

Our squadron was known for our good bugler. He was not only a great bugle player and musician but he also composed original pieces for drum and bugle corps. Our bugler was picked to lead the drum and bugle corps for our wing for the Roosevelt review. Our bugler and the drum and bugle corps practiced separate [*sic*] from the rest of the squadron and wing and our bugler composed an original piece of music for the occasion.

On the morning of the review, we practiced on the parade grounds with our wing. We marched and were shown where to enter the field and where the drum and bugle corps leading our wing would start playing. It was about a third of the way down the edge of the field and a relatively short distance from the reviewing stand where Roosevelt would be located. As each wing would approach that spot, their drum and bugle team would start playing and continue past the reviewing stand and beyond for a short distance. However, during the practice our drum and bugle team were [*sic*] not there, but were, [*sic*] instead, practicing on their own.

When it was time for the review, we lined up with our wing in the proper order with the rest of the wings and waited for our turn. We marched out into the stadium and as we got to the spot where the drum and bugle corps was to start playing, they broke into the song, "Der Fuhrer's Face" with its loud "raspberry" or "Bronx Cheer" and each shouted "Heil!" *Note: "Der Führer's Face" was a popular song of 1942 written by Oliver Wallace and popularized by Spike Jones and His City Slickers. It was a mockery of the Nazi Party's national anthem, "Horst Wessel Lied."* Everyone in our wing and in the whole stadium was in shock. No one knew the intent of our bugler and the drum and bugle corps. Did they intend the song for Roosevelt or were they simply playing a popular song against Hitler? The entire parade field grew tense and quiet. Almost 20,000 people were suddenly on edge. It was almost an eerie feeling. You could see some of the higher-ranking officers stand up and leave the parade grounds. Other ranking officers stood and looked nervous. Roosevelt stood there looking the same as he always did while reviewing troops. He seemed not to be phased and certainly didn't show any significant emotion to the crowd.

We continued to march past and beyond the reviewing stands. As we got beyond President Roosevelt, the drum and bugle corps switched to playing the original bugle piece that our bugler had composed. That piece was beautiful. The crowd visibly relaxed.

Our bugler received a lot of compliments on the bugle piece he had written. We never found out what he and the drum and bugle corps meant by playing that popular song about the Führer.

Visit of President Here Revealed as Trip Ended

White House Permits Press to Tell of Inspection By Chief Executive in San Antonio Last Sunday

Only in wartime could the President of the United States come into San Antonio, spend most of the day inspecting Army posts and camp and depart without newspaper readers having the full story of his visit immediately.

But it is wartime and President Roosevelt did just that last Sunday, the White House revealing Thursday that he had returned to Washington from an 8,754-mile trip which carried him over the Nation and included a lengthy stop in San Antonio.

Many San Antonians had seen him here and the fact that he was here was well known to the press but at the White House no mention was made of the visit until it was officially announced Thursday.

An Associated Press account of his visit in San Antonio reveals that he spent the morning at Uvalde, leaving there shortly after noon. The Associated Press tells of his visit here:

"Two hours later he reached Kelly Field at San Antonio, where several thousand aviation cadets are completing their advanced courses with twin-engined training planes. When they get through, they will be bomber pilots.

Cadets Lined Up

"The cadets and some of their ships were lined up along a mile-long runway, while four flights of 18 ships each dipped low over the flying field and came by the Chief Executive in echelon formations.

"Kelly Field, which was established some 25 years ago, now turns out a class of pilots every five weeks.

"On a nearby hill, once a bombing range, the President visited the San Antonio Aviation Cadet Center, where approximately 12,000 sun-bronzed young men are being classified to become pilots,

bombardiers or navigators or are getting the calisthenics, close order drills and other activities constituting pre-flight training.

"The center took in its first class last November. Before its spick and span buildings could be erected, hundreds of dud bombs had to be extracted from the site.

Tours Duncan Field

"The cadets at the center were assembled on the drill field, some in uniform, some in jumpers and some in shorts and jerseys. Fifteen were Latin Americans. A band saluted the Commander-in-Chief with ruffles and flourishes and then played the National Anthem.

"Mr. Roosevelt also toured Duncan Field, an Air Corps supply depot which provides parts, engines and supplies for approximately a fifth of the country and for the Panama Canal Zone. Some of the parts are manufactured at the field, which adjoins Kelly Field.

"In hangars and machine shops and on runways outside, the chief executive saw how aircraft are repaired or even rebuilt, chiefly by civilian workers. A number of B-18 and B-24 bombers were being put back into shape under the open sky.

Goes to Fort Sam Houston.

Moving over to Fort Sam Houston, an infantry post, the President saw a division and its equipment which almost covered a parade ground three miles in circumference. It was the Second Infantry, commanded by Maj.Gen. Walter M. Robertson, and it had just

Continued on Page 2, Column 4

Visit of President Here Revealed

Continued From Page 1

returned from three months of maneuvering in Louisiana.

Its seasoned regulars were drawn up in companies and massed in mobile equipment. Stretching far up the field were lines of jeeps, some trailing 37 millimeter and anti-tank guns, squad cars with men holding fingers on triggers of machine guns, trucks trailing field pieces up to the size of 155 millimeter Howitzers, field kitchens, water haulers, hoists and ambulances.

At Randolph Fied.

Moving over to Randolph Field late in the afternoon, the President passed between lines of cadets standing at present arms and circled among the buildings and across to flying fields.

Randolph Field, beautifully landscaped and laid out like a model town, gives cadets 10 weeks' basic training course, in which they are instructed in formatio flying, acrobatics and use of instruments. Most of the personnel was lined up along the roadway for inspection, but a score of single-motored trainers were in the air, their motors whining.

The inspections at San Antonio were the first Mr. Roosevelt had made since leaving San Diego two days ago and turning eastward through a bit of Mexico, Arizona and New Mexico. From San Antonio, he headed toward Fort Worth, to have a look at a bomber assembly plant.

Governor Greets Him.

Coke Stephenson, Democratic governor of Texas, and Lt.Gen. Walter Krueger, commanding officer of the 3d Army with headquarters at Fort Sam Houston, greeted the President at San Antonio.

He also met Maj.Gen. Hubert R. Harmon, commanding the Gulf Coast Air Force training center, with headquarters at Randolph Field; Maj.Gen. Richard Donovan, commanding the 8th Service Command of the service of supply, Fort Sam Houston; Maj.Gen. Geo. E. Stratemeyer, chief of the air staff, who was representing Lt.Gen. H. H. Arnold, chief of the Army air forces; Lt.Col. S. D. Grubbs, commanding officer at Kelly Rield; Col. M. H. Davis, commanding the Aviation Cadet Center, and Col. Walter C. White, commanding Randolph Field.

——Remember Pearl Harbor——

San Antonio Express October 2, 1942 article about President Roosevelt's visit to SAACC. Dad wrote in a letter dated October 2, 1942 that, "…the highway into camp was guarded by a man every 40 inches for as far as you could see. I was one of the men in that guard." See the description of the visit to Randolph Field in the article above.

Secretly Taking Pictures on Training Bases

I had a Brownie Number 8 camera that I had brought from home. But you couldn't get film for it. But, in 1942, Kodak was selling a little, molded-plastic, hand-size camera with size 127 film for around $2–$2.50. *(I believe this was Kodak's Baby Brownie based on Dad's letter dated February 15, 1943.)* You could readily get the film and it had a reasonable number of negatives per roll. When I was at *? (Most likely Bruce Field, Ballinger, TX)* training base, I went into town to the camera shop and looked at cameras. I decided that small plastic Kodak camera would do what I wanted. I could get more pictures per roll and I decided it would let me get the camera onto the base. Cameras weren't allowed on the base as it was illegal to take pictures. The base security guards would check all of your possessions whenever you entered the base. So, the first thing I did after I purchased that plastic camera was to smash it into about six pieces. When I got back to the base, the security guards saw the broken pieces of the camera. I told them that it was just a bunch of broken pieces of plastic from one of those plastic Kodak cameras and that I just wanted to use the lens from the camera. They let me through.

On base, we had some type of putty or material that was sticky but didn't get hard. Once I was on base, I carefully put the camera back together temporarily using this sticky stuff. I then was able to take pictures with it. After I exposed my roll of film, I pulled the camera apart, took the film out, cleaned the sticky stuff off and saved the pieces. I then sent the film home to be developed. The Army security never stopped me with that "broken camera" at any of the various bases I trained at. Of course, I couldn't ever let anyone see me taking pictures with that little camera.

Rowena, Texas. One mile down and five miles away as seen from ship #20 on my graduation day at Bruce Field. The Colorado River is in the Foreground. The Ballinger Field to San Angelo, TX highway runs diagonally across the picture. This picture was taken with the little broken plastic camera.

Flight Training, Ballinger, TX
Chinese Instructors and Chasing A Farmer Through
His Field

Following pre-flight training I entered twenty-seven weeks of flight training. It was divided into three nine-week sessions. After each session, you were moved. So, I went from San Antonio to Ballinger, TX for primary training.

At Ballinger, I had a Chinese instructor from the Chinese Air Force.

Primary flight training. Young G. Wong, Chinese flight instructor standing on the small walkway. You weren't supposed to walk on any other part of the wing. PT-19s were made of plywood and fabric. Wong was my flight instructor from the Chinese Air Force who was getting extra training so they could go back to China to teach the Chinese Air Force. They never got them back to China because of the aggression of the Japanese. He is wearing a nice leather flying jacket. We as pilots only got them long enough to take pictures. We were never issued them contrary to what the movies show today. Wong is the one who asked me to do a three-turn spin while at too low an altitude.

Each instructor had three students to train. The other two students Young G. Wong had were James M. Cain from Mississippi (he was kind of a real "louse up") and Bennett *(Chester B. Bennett; Vestal, NY)* from Endicott, NY. Bennett was very nice. He was also very short. He is on the wing and still shorter than the others." *(Left to right: James M. Cain, Chester B. Bennett, Young G. Wong and Ladd L. Horn. The plane was #13. Dad refers to this plane multiple times in his letters.)*

He had been sent to the USA to be taught to be an instructor for the Chinese Air Force. The Chinese conflict was going so badly that they didn't know how to get them back to their Chinese base so they were here in the US working with the US Air Cadets in training. Not everyone got a Chinese instructor, but I was assigned one. One of the Chinese instructors was very funny. When he got excited about something that didn't go right, he could no longer speak English. Once he got lost with a student on a flight and it was getting dark so everyone was worried. The student on that flight said that the instructor got so excited he couldn't find his way back. Finally, he found a railroad and followed it until he saw a train station with a name and then got out his highway map and tried to get back. They eventually got back to Ballinger TX about 2 hours late. He was upset because they didn't have night clearance or anything. It took about two days to calm him down. The student just took it as "I was along for the ride."

I was about three-fourths of the way through primary flight training. The training planes were PT-19s. They were two-seat open-cockpit, low-wing planes. They had in-line, six-cylinder, air-cooled, Franklin automobile engines. They had the reputation of being the toughest engines ever built. They would take mileage, speed, they didn't use any coolant and as an emergency practice they built them into the PT-19s.

The Chinese instructor took me up for a routine training flight. He had me take off from Ballinger and move out to a training quadrant. He was doing clipboard work on the way. At some point, he told me to do a three-turn spin. We weren't supposed to do a three-turn spin unless we were over 3,000 ft. I don't think we were above 2,000 ft. I gave the plane throttle to gain altitude. After a little bit, he hollered at me to "do a three-turn spin." We would say "willco"—will comply. I put it back to full throttle to gain altitude. He yelled at me again. I thought he is trying to find a way to "wash me out." I decided to do a two and a half turn, thinking maybe I could pull through ok. But, something in the back of my head said only do a two-turn spin. I thought, if I do that, he will think I didn't count right or I lost my bearings and wasn't doing it right. But he yelled at me again to do a three-turn spin. So finally, I gave it full throttle, pulled up as hard as I could and kept it there until the plane was about to stall and then did a very precise two-turn spin and pulled back on the stick as hard as I dared to avoid a high-speed stall. We leveled out at about ten feet altitude and he yanked the throttle off to zero and held it there and yelled "emergency landing." (This was the first time since I joined the Air Force that I positively felt that there was some spiritual power controlling my actions and the results.) There was a farmer driving a tractor ahead of me full throttle standing up in his seat, shaking his fist at me—probably thinking I was a crazy pilot trying to scare him to death on purpose. All I could do was touch down because the instructor was holding the throttle off. So, I put it down on the fresh worked dirt without hitting the farmer. (By holding the throttle down, he was forcing me to break the rules because even when an instructor said "emergency landing" you were to come close to the ground, but not make an actual landing.) We no more than stopped than he was out of the cockpit out on the wing up the walkway screaming unintelligibly at me—half in Chinese—half English and half mixed swear words. Even in Chinese you could tell it was swearing. So, once he began to talk more normally, I realized he was yelling at me to get out of the cockpit. I climbed out onto the wing walk, and he said, "Go to the rear cockpit. Look in. What do you see?" I didn't know what to say or what I was supposed to see. I looked in and the altimeter read 3,000 feet. So, I said, "Your altimeter is reading 3,000 feet." He said, "What should it be reading?" I said, "Zero." Then he said again, "What is it reading?" I said, "3,000 feet." "Are you sure?" I said, "Yes!" "What should it be reading?" I said, "Zero." He said, "I broke every rule in the book that I taught you young guys not to do. I was doing paperwork and didn't do what I was supposed to." He then said, "Get back in the cockpit, buckle yourself in, we're going back to the main field." He took off, flew the plane back to the main field with me as a passenger in the rear cockpit. I didn't know what was coming. He had made me break enough rules that I could be washed out. He climbed out of the cockpit at the home field, came back to the rear cockpit and said, "Get out!" Now, having the instructor fly you back to the home field in the rear cockpit meant that you had graduated, but I figured I had washed out. He told me to go into the field room and, "I'll see you there." because the instructor would review the training session with you and review how it went. So, when he came in, he came over to the table where I had set [*sic*] down. He sat down but said nothing to me and got out his papers and clipboard and stuff like that. He said something about next training session, then left. Everybody that saw this assumed that I had made an early graduation. I didn't know what to think or what it meant. I went back to my barracks and my bunk and normal operations.

Next time I went back for training, he came in and tried to explain to me that he was a "stupid jerk," that I had behaved properly under the circumstances, and if the others wanted to think I had graduated, let them think that. He explained that he had been so far behind in paperwork that he had behaved improperly in doing paperwork while flying and he was in the wrong. That is the last I ever heard of it. I graduated with the class and moved on to San Angelo, TX.

The following is what Dad wrote about this event in his description of his spiritual journey:

I saiah says:
> Whether you turn to the right or to the left, your ears will hear a voice behind you, saying, "This is the way; walk in it."
>
> —Isaiah 30:21

Elijah says (on Mount Horeb):
> Then a great and powerful wind tore the mountains apart and shattered the rocks before the LORD, but the LORD was not in the wind. After the wind there was an earthquake, but the LORD was not in the earthquake. After the earthquake came a fire, but the LORD was not in the fire. And after the fire came a gentle whisper.
>
> —I Kings 19:11,12

…Only a few seconds later he cut the throttle and started swearing at me followed by, "I told you to do a three-turn spin. Now do it!" I looked at the altitude and my brain said, "Do a two and one half and say you misjudged on your recovery start." A little voice right behind me said, "Two turns." My brain argued, "He'll never accept that. I'll be washed out." I pulled the nose of the plane up to a stall and let it fall off into a spin. My brain said, "Do two and one half turns and make the quickest recovery you can." Right behind me the little voice said, "Two turns."…

> …anyone who comes to him must believe that he exists and that he rewards those who earnestly seek him.
>
> —Hebrews 11:6

Rewards?

1. I was still alive—otherwise none of this "epistle" could be written.
2. Being moved to the rear cockpit was an advancement indicating I was qualified for graduation from primary training without regard to further instruction.

An Engagement Ring and the "Check" Ride Goodfellow Field, San Angelo, TX

In San Angelo, we were given Vultee B-13 basic trainers. They were quite a step up from the PT-19s. They were heavy, clunky, single radial-engine planes with open cockpits—front and rear. Some had sliding canopies. We had a few Curtis BT-9s but I never had a chance to fly one of them. I had an instructor from Brooklyn, NY. No one liked his personality, but he did stick up for me. There were no major incidents in training there. It was a nine-week session.

Postcard Dad sent home: "On the Line"—San Angelo, TX—Goodfellow Field. The planes are Vultee BT-13 Valiants.

Me [*sic*] in front of a Vultee B-13 Valiant commonly known as the Vultee Vibrator. It vibrated like no other plane you ever flew. But it was very rugged compared to the Curtis Wright planes we had. The propellers were 9' long and weighed about 900 lb. This was large and heavy for the size and horsepower of the engine and the plane was so rigidly built that if one thing shook, then everything shook with it. *March 21–May 24, 1943*

Me [*sic*] in a Vultee BT-13 Valiant at Goodfellow Field, San Angelo, TX.

In San Angelo I purchased Mom's *(Dad is referring to Ethel J. (O'Neil) Horn his wife; my mother.)* engagement ring. I bought it on time since I didn't have cash. It was the only thing like that I bought on time. The jewelry store owner said that he had had good luck with time payments from cadets. So, I made sure he got all of his payments. My plans were to ask Mom to marry me when I graduated from flight training.

Dad carried Mom's picture and engagement ring on all sixty-four missions he flew. When we contacted Robert Ringo (tentmate; bombardier for other pilots) in 2015, one of the first things Dad wanted to make sure Bob Ringo knew was that he (Dad) had married the girl in the picture he carried with him on every mission and that he had been married to her for seventy years.

Ethel J. Horn in Dad's military uniform.

I was about three-quarters of the way through and did well in my courses. They then put me up for a check ride. A higher-level officer would fly with you and give you commands that you had to follow and he would judge whether you were trained well enough for the stage you were in. In the check ride, I passed all but one thing. The check-ride officer flunked me on the check because he said I couldn't do a decent slow roll (he had me do three or four slow rolls). The plane wasn't a good plane to do slow rolls in. The check ride officer told the instructor he had flunked me. You'd better take him out and do slow rolls. The instructor said, "He does the nicest slow rolls I ever had a student do." The instructor was really "hot"—totally mad at the check-ride officer. He took me out and we got to altitude and he told me to do a slow roll. I did a perfect slow roll. He said, that's enough, we're going in. So, we went back into the building and into the room for pilots to wait in. My instructor went over to the check-ride officer. He didn't even salute him and he lit into him. He said, "I took him out and he did the most perfect slow roll I've seen. You probably don't know how to do a slow roll yourself." He was fuming. He really told the guy off and kept going at him even though he was about three ranks higher than him. I thought, oh, no, here is where we both get sent to the infantry. Everyone was looking and watching. I just stood there and didn't know what to do. But, the higher officer eventually backed down and the guy said, "OK, he passes." The instructor motioned for me to come and he strutted off like a fighting rooster.

Picture copied from the "Goodfellow Field, Army Air Force's Basic Flying School, A Pictorial Review," San Angelo, TX. Dad wrote on the page, I have flown each of the three planes in the picture both day and night.

"French Leave" (AWOL)

At Druce *(Dad misspoke here. It was Goodfellow Field)* Airfield in San Angelo, TX, there was a short and stocky guy in our training group. Unfortunately (or maybe for him, fortunately) I can't remember his name. This guy, we'll just call him "Bob" for the sake of this story, and the military just didn't mix. He was always in trouble and always looking for a way to get out of the Army. He talked about how he had a car and how he knew how to get across the border into Canada. He said that one day he would leave, go to Canada and disappear into the far north. He told everyone that he would survive on the supplies he had and, he said he would wait until the war was over and then come back. No one ever took him too seriously because no one who was going to actually go AWOL would ever speak openly about it. He did have a car on base and the car was filled with supplies.

Well Bob couldn't stay out of trouble. He was constantly being caught breaking some rule. As punishment, he would be given "gigs." "Gigs" were demerits *(general inspection grade)* that were handed out for minor infractions. The magnitude of the demerit was determined based on the severity of the infraction. Records were kept and the gigs were added up. Gigs had to be "worked off," usually by marching on the walkways and ramps during a soldier's free time. There would be groups of guys marching for hours— maybe an hour for each gig. And so, Bob always found himself "walking off gigs." Bob would start to march, but after a little while he would disappear.

The first few times Bob disappeared, the officers in charge couldn't find him. The rest of the men kept marching and Bob was nowhere to be found. It turns out that there was a small ravine adjacent to the ramp they used for marching off the demerits. Bob would simply wait for a time when officers weren't looking, slip out of line and disappear down the ravine. He would then spend the rest of the time in the ravine. One day when Bob disappeared, a wisp of smoke started coming up out of the ravine. As the officers explored, they found Bob with a small fire going cooking coffee—which I am sure resulted in another round of gigs being added to his tally.

One day Bob came up missing from the base. His car was gone. He was never found and there was a lot of speculation. I believe I know where he went. I think he did exactly what he said he was going to do—take off for Canada and the far north to survive until the war was over.

Walking off gigs on Sunday afternoon at San Angelo, TX. Everything you got reprimanded for as a cadet you had to walk one hour on the ramp on Sunday afternoon. The ramp got very crowded after a while. Everyone had so many gigs (some were up in the hundreds) and there wasn't enough time to walk them all off. These uniforms were all olive drab enlisted men's uniforms that they issued to us just to make us look alike.

"Helicopter" Flying AT10's, Hurricanes and Graduation But No Engagement!

After graduation, I moved up to Advanced training and moved to Houston TX. The field was Ellington Field. There I flew all AT-10s. They were also called the "Bobcat." (*They were*) dual-control, twin-engine, bombing trainers. Because at some place along the line when I had filled out some questionnaire I had said that I would like to be a multi-engine pilot and they honored that at that time.

Two interesting things happened at that training field. The first one was that the AT-10 had the capability of "slow flying." Basically, you could make the twin engine plane fly like a helicopter. What you did to "slow fly" one would be to get the plane cruising at normal cruising speed and then cut back on throttle and pull up on the nose so that you could keep the plane flying. You would continue to slow the plane until you could no longer maintain altitude. You then had to add throttle back in and continue feeding more throttle in and hold the plane at altitude using nose attitude. You would do this until you got the plane up to full throttle and the plane was essentially hanging in the air by the propellers like a helicopter. You then practiced holding the plane in that position as long as you could. You would see how many minutes you could hold it there. The position was very sensitive to any movement on the controls. Each pilot was required to be capable to hold the plane that way for a sustained length of time. They had a total time set that you had to fulfill during that part of your training that consisted of "slow flying." So, I was sent out one day and told I had to get in so many more minutes of "slow flying" (around 50 minutes). I went out and had the plane hanging on its props and a student fighter pilot came by with a single-engine advanced trainer and as he caught up to me he kept slowing down and decided he was going to "fly formation" with me. As he got slowed down to some place near my speed, his plane stalled and fell.

He recovered from his stall, got his plane up to flying speed, flew a wide circle around me and very carefully pulled back on my right wing to fly formation with me and when he was close enough he smiled and waved at me and his plane stalled and fell out from under him again. He recovered, climbed back up to my altitude, cruised past me slowly with the funniest look on his face, waved to me and I waved back. I don't think he understood why he couldn't fly in formation with me.

The second thing that happened in Houston *(Ellington Field)* was that my mom and dad and Ethel decided to come for my graduation on my birthday. The day after they arrived, the worst hurricane to hit that area in years struck the base. That was on July 25th, three days before graduation. It destroyed the theater building we were going to graduate in, and blew about 30% of the buildings on the base to bits. One of the barracks behind the one I stayed in actually rolled over in the wind and landed on one slope of its roof before eventually blowing apart. For some reason the double barn doors on one side of it were the only things left of the building after the storm. One of the things we watched from our barracks during the storm was the storm clearing the adjacent parking lot of cars. The wind took the cars down the street sideways— hopping up and down due to the friction of the tires. There were none left in the parking lot after the storm. There were very few planes left in good condition after the storm. They had some of the guys hang onto the planes and a few broke the guy-wires and flipped with guys in them. Some held and were ok afterwards.

One of the hangers withstood the storm so it was decided to hold the graduation ceremony on time, as best as they could [*sic*] in the hanger. I've never understood why that building held together—it was steel beams and sheet metal construction. So, Ethel and my mom and dad came for the graduation, saw me get my certificate, greeted me on the hanger floor and we had a great time there. I was technically out of the Air Force for one day then.

They had rented a solid brick motel that held together during the storm. The weather was pleasant after the storm. So, I proposed to Ethel that day and she turned me down flat! She was not going to have anything to do with me and marriage until I came home from the war. But she did help me shop for my uniforms at the huge store there.

CADETS' ALL-NIGHT VIGIL SAVES ELLINGTON PLANES

Cadets at Ellington were out on the field all Tuesday night holding down planes to keep them from "taking off" in the high wind. Several hundred cadets were called on duty to keep watch in shifts. Only six planes were badly damaged, according to Maj. C. L. Jordan, Ellington public relations officer. Thirteen cadets and nine soldiers were injured at the field. (Other storm pictures on Pages 2, 3 and 4.)

Picture from The Houston Press Wednesday July 28, 1943. The headline was, "Five Known Dead in Hurricane." One article was entitled, "Worst Storm Since 1915 in Galveston," and another "Winds Reach Top Velocity of 132 Miles."

Graduation day, July 29, 1943, Ellington Field, Houston, TX. Dad's girlfriend (and future wife) and his parents drove to Houston for his graduation and birthday: Left to right, Ethel J. O'Neil, Freida M. (Wenz) Horn and Leonard A. Horn. Three days earlier, July 25th, was the major hurricane that hit Houston, but they were ok in the brick hotel.

Summer uniform worn at graduation from Ellington Field July 29, 1943.

Crush cap and side or garrison cap worn with the graduation summer uniform pictured on the previous page. This picture was taken in 2022.

B-26 Training Dodge City, KS

The next day I received orders to go to Dodge City, Kansas for B-26 bomber transition training. A number of us were chosen for the training and the rest were sent to combat crew training. I arrived in Dodge City in the middle of the night via train along with one other guy. The train was nearly empty, scheduled for midnight but was a few hours late. We went to the largest hotel in town and they didn't have any space. They told us ungraciously that there was no room in the other hotels around town. We begged the desk clerk to sleep in the easy chairs in the lobby and they eventually agreed.

The B-26s were a huge difference from the trainers we had flown in. Learning to fly them was a real workout. We went from low-speed, light-weight training planes to a plane with the highest wing loading of any military or civilian aircraft of that time. The official wing loading was 51 lb/sq ft. They used to kid that it was the only plane the Air Force had that couldn't fly. We made the jump from 200 hp engines to over 2,000 hp engines. We went from a takeoff speed of 45–50 mph, to a takeoff speed of 125-150 mph. I did above-average in the ground school and flight training—enough so that I received a letter of commendation from the base commander who happened to be "Barney" Oldfield (Charles Bernard Oldfield). As far as I know I was the only person to receive a commendation like that—and to get one from him was special.

"Barney" Oldfield was the top-level auto racing man and top-level airplane racing man in the country just prior to WWII, period. He arranged the first aircraft—auto race to prove that airplanes could accomplish anything an auto could. The auto won, but barely and only because the plane couldn't turn short enough. He was a competitor, developer, experimenter and a general rabble-rouser in the Air Force. He was a very nice person. A few of the fellows that got to fly with him were a little upset when he changed glasses two or three times on the final approach with a high-speed bomber (he would let go of the controls and change glasses). He was later noted for encouraging the Air Force to use the B-24 to fly the Hump because they needed the air transport so badly.

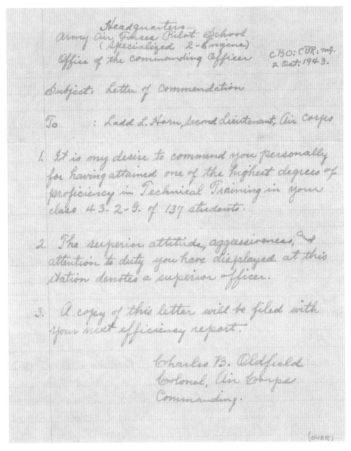

Handwritten commendation letter from Charles B. Oldfield, October 2, 1943.

Very few of the Air Force planes could make it. The Air Force told him that if he thought the B-24 could fly the hump, you prove it by flying one over. As far as I know, he did and they used them because it was a four-engine "boxcar"-like plane.

I completed training there in October 1943. I was then ordered to Lake Charles, LA for combat crew training.

One of the B-26 training planes. This was an official Air Force picture.
Those pointed tails were the early models of the B-26s. We called them
Straight As. They had a single 50-caliber swivel gun in it. They quickly
decided this was not enough rear protection and changed them.

B-26 MARAUDER
DODGE CITY ARMY AIR FIELD
DODGE CITY, KANSAS

Official Air Force picture of a B-26. This is a very early model because of the all plexiglass nose. Later these were reinforced because when you started firing machine guns through there and they were mounted to the plexiglass you started breaking things apart. The B-26 plane was designed by an aeronautical engineer who had just graduated from school. The Martin aircraft corporation didn't think they would get the contract, so they gave the job to him with the military specs. He did such a good job of designing it that they got the contract. It had the highest wing loading of any plane ever built up to that time. It was 51 lb/ sq ft. His name was Payton McGruder. *(Peyton M. Magruder)*

Combat Training, Lake Charles, LA

With the letter of commendation, I left Dodge field and went into combat crew training at Lake Charles LA. That was where I trained until February 1943. We learned to skip bomb, bomb tanks, strafe and all types of mission work including some long-distance flights to simulate bomber combat flights overseas.

Multiple times as I was growing up, Dad told me about their flight training preparation for high-altitude flying. Since it was expected that on missions in Europe they would be flying without oxygen at altitudes of from 10,000 to approximately 18,000 feet, they were taught to recognize the symptoms of altitude sickness and to be able to effectively operate aircraft under low oxygen conditions. Dad told how pilots would be placed in a large, controlled-atmosphere chamber with a notebook. They were instructed to continuously and carefully write the children's poem, "Mary Had a Little Lamb" in their notebooks during the entire session. The chamber was then sealed and the partial pressure of oxygen in the chamber was slowly lowered to match the atmospheric conditions at high altitude. Dad said that as the oxygen content went down you still felt great and you focused on writing the poem carefully in your notebook. He said he would feel that he was doing a great job of writing the poem and staying focused. However, as they raised the oxygen partial pressure at the end of the session, he would look at his notebook and would be shocked that when the oxygen content was low, his poems had drifted down and off the page with very poor handwriting. After multiple sessions in the chamber, he said that he could recognize the symptoms and he was able to correct his actions and improve his performance.

On one of the bomb-mission training flights I did out of Lake Charles I let one gunner ride along. We'd occasionally let other flight crew members ride along—e.g. gunners or others. He wanted to ride up in the cockpit where he could see well because we were going near his family's farm in Texas. He was disappointed when we weren't going quite as far as his family's farm. We located it on the map and I decided it wasn't too far outside my range and so I decided to fly a bit faster and that we could make it without being in trouble. So, he told me he'd continue to ride in the nose and he would pick out the farm and guide me to it. He wanted me to buzz the farm. It was outside regulations. So, we buzzed the farm at low level at about 300 mph and went right down through the farm. You could see chickens and animals and people running and yelling. We just made one pass. He thought that was great. I never heard what his parents said about it.

A New B-26C for the Free French Air Force
Hunter Field, GA to Homestead, FL

While in Lake Charles LA where I received combat training, I received orders to take my crew and go to Hunter Field, GA (Savannah, GA). We went by train with my crew (Crew 12A). When I arrived at Hunter Field I accepted delivery of a brand new, off-the-line B-26 (definitely a B—maybe a B1 or 2; *records show it was a B-26C*). I signed a receipt for $356,000 and I received a lend-lease agreement to deliver to the French Free Air force. I was supposed to get a counter receipt from the French Free Air Force when I turned it over that would absolve me from the $356,000 cost. It was a hard decision to make because there was a guy at the base who was working off one of these debts because he had signed for a locomotive that had never arrived. He would have to be in the Air Force for the rest of his life. It was very possible to lose a plane on the way over to Africa. All the papers for that plane are in the brown military records paperwork envelope (FP-256-RH—pilot's name Lieutenant Horn; *Operations Order # 55 from Homestead Army Air Field, Homestead, Florida identify the plane as a B-26C serial no. 42-107730).* The plane was a big machine—the length was greater than the length of our ranch house in Orchard Park—and of course the wing span was much greater than the width of the house *(length: 51 ft 3 in.; span: 70 ft).*

They were required to check the new plane out. They checked it out at low altitude for about five days. It was the only place they were allowed to do low-altitude flying. It was the only time I flew the B-26 at 10 ft altitude along a railroad track that was marked and perfectly straight. Flying 50 ft altitude was reasonable, but 10 ft was pretty dangerous. I wasn't very comfortable with it. You flew out at 10 ft for about five miles, pulled up turned around and flew back the same way. They had a crew on board that checked the instruments during the flight. They hadn't figured out any better way to do a final check.

They used the straight line of the railroad tracks and the steel to do those final checks. It was a difficult and quite dangerous flight to handle.

We then moved from Hunter Field, GA to Homestead Army Air Field in Homestead, FL. We waited in Homestead to find out if we were going the northern route through Nova Scotia and Iceland, or the southern route through Brazil.

HEADQUARTERS
LAKE CHARLES ARMY AIR FIELD

Lake Charles, La
3 March 1944

SPECIAL ORDERS)
)
NO.........63)

E X T R A C T

. 1. The following-named O and EM comprising B-26 Crews are reld
fr asgd 336th Bomb Gp (M) and WP to Hunter Fld, Ga, via rail, TTG, so as to
report no later than 8 Mar 44, to Combat Crew Sec for asgmt to Shipment No
FM-420-CT. FCS.

CREW POSITION	RANK	NAME	ASN	MARITAL STATUS
		CREW NO. 1		
P	2nd Lt	JAMES L. BRESETTE	0687287	M
CP	2nd Lt	ALBERT P. CHUNIS	0813325	M
B	2nd Lt	ROBERT L. WILLIAMS	0760146	M
E	Sgt	Tony P. Deleo	33464403	
R	S/Sgt	Edward M. Shaffer	17167423	
G	Sgt	John L. Shearstone	33621402	
		CREW NO. 2		
P	2nd Lt	WILEY E. BURRIS	0686538	S
CP	2nd Lt	DAVID H. BUSS	0815826	S
B	2nd Lt	RAYMOND P. TOTTEN	0760169	S
E	T/Sgt	Arthur M. Shirey	6915870	
R	S/Sgt	William L. Sinkhorn	35090653	
G	Sgt	Richard L. Larson	19147590	
		CREW NO. 3		
P	2nd Lt	TOROLF H. BYLUND	0808366	M
CP	2nd Lt	GERALD B. LISZAK	0810184	M
B	2nd Lt	JOSEPH F. MIAZGA	0750089	S
E	Sgt	Alfred H. Bridge	11101024	
R	S/Sgt	Harold J. Shuck	35449031	
G	Sgt	John W. Davis	13108082	
		CREW NO. 4		
P	2nd Lt	ROBERT E. DINWIDDIE	0735538	M
CP	2nd Lt	RAYMOND L. ARNSDORFF JR	0813454	S
B	2nd Lt	HARRY C. HEPHNER	0749775	M
E	S/Sgt	Jones E. Booth	34076891	
R	S/Sgt	Heinz Thannhauser	31296512	
G	Sgt	Elmer W. Vicha	36741626	
		CREW NO. 5		
P	2nd Lt	RUSSEL E. BARRACLOUGH	0686881	S
CP	2nd Lt	JAMES E. ALLEN	0815267	S
B	2nd Lt	DOMINIC J. GERMANO	0750136	M
E	Sgt	David F. Huston	33152557	
R	S/Sgt	Joseph J. Forest	31265524	
G	Sgt	Francis M. O'Toole Jr	13098235	

(Over #1)

*March 3, 1944 orders (p. 1) from Lake Charles, LA for flight crew No. 12A
to report to Hunter Field, GA.*

```
                           R E S T R I C T E D

SO 63, Hq, LCAAF, Lake Charles, La    3 Mar 44 (Cont'd) Par 1 EXTRACT

                            CREW NO. 6
   P        2nd Lt    JOHN C. BLAKE               0686969      S
   CP       2nd Lt    ROY D. BASSETTE JR          0814630      S
   B        2nd Lt    JOHN E. TRUMPLER            0760139      S
   E        Sgt       Robert E. Irwin Jr          33179138
   R        S/Sgt     Thomas W. Powell            35582102
   G        Sgt       Robert (nmi) Paul           12130495
                            CREW NO. 7
   P        2nd Lt    ROBERT G. BORDEN JR         0750326      S
   CP       2nd Lt    THADDEUS F. BEDNARZ         0814633      S
   B        2nd Lt    ALBERT O. BULOW             0749809      M
   E        Sgt       Bernard J. Mauser           35389370
   R        S/Sgt     Clarion F. Snow             38414919
   G        Sgt       Donald J. Stone             39329951
                            CREW NO. 8
   P        2nd Lt    RAYMOND L. CONSTANT         0751987      S
   CP       2nd Lt    RAYMOND P. BRITTON          0816821      S
   B        F/O       SEYMOUR S. BASKOFF          T1931        S
   E        Sgt       John S. Albright            33362842
   R        S/Sgt     Andrew J. Rutherford Jr     33538600
   G        S/Sgt     Andrew (nmi) Wieczorek      12023520
                            CREW NO. 9
   P        2nd Lt    DOMINIC V. FLACCO           0687024      S
   CP       2nd Lt    RUSSELL C. KELLEY           0815152      M
   B        2nd Lt    THEODORE P. WITKOWSKI JR    0760148      S
   E        Sgt       Irwin W. Harder             17127154
   R        S/Sgt     John S. Slifka              13128784
   G        Sgt       Clive D. McCarty            33505385
                            CREW NO. 10
   P        2nd Lt    WILBERT A. HABEL            0808991      M
   CP       2nd Lt    ROBERT S. WOODHURST JR      0449790      S
   B        2nd Lt    LUTHER K. RITTER            0681762      S
   E        Sgt       Ellis R. Coffey             37003224
   R        S/Sgt     Charles E. Traweek          34586429
   G        Sgt       John P. Mole                32277284
                            CREW NO. 11
   P        2nd Lt    CHARLES J. WILSON           0686589      M
   CP       2nd Lt    GLENN E. MOORE              0755835      S
   B        2nd Lt    DONALD L. BREWER            0748863      M
   E        Sgt       Nelson W. Creeler           32626225
   R        S/Sgt     William F. Rhoads           19109307
   G        Sgt       William T. Cox              31140284
                            CREW NO. 12
   P        2nd Lt    LADD L. ECKY                0687598      S
   CP       2nd Lt    PAUL M. ROSEMAN             0755859      M
   B        2nd Lt    WILLIAM C. WEBB             0756087      S
   E        Sgt       Bernard Fineman             33586506
   R        S/Sgt     Barron E. Tupper            31181224
   G        Sgt       Harmon R. Summers           39288084

                            (Over #2)

                       R E S T R I C T E D
```

*March 3, 1944 orders (p. 2) from Lake Charles, LA for flight crew No. 12A
to report to Hunter Field, GA.*

RESTRICTED

HEADQUARTERS THIRD AIR FORCE STAGING WING (C-7)
Office of the Commanding Officer

SPECIAL ORDERS)   Hunter Field, Ga.
        :   11 March 1944
NO.   71)   E X T R A C T

        *   *   *

    6. Following B-26 Repl Combat Crews are asgd Shipment FP-256-AH (Project
90606R) and WP fr Hunter Field, Ga, immediately by air to either Homestead Field,
Fla, or Morrison Field, Fla, (instructions as to destination will be given crews
immediately prior to departure) rptg to CG ATC for temp duty pending further dis-
patch to overseas destination:

FP-256-AH-7A   P   2nd Lt ROBERT G BORDEN JR   0750326 Ap No. 42-107733
               CP 2nd Lt THADDEUS F BEDNARZ   0814633
               B   2nd Lt ALBERT C BULOW   0749809
               EG Sgt Bernard J Mauser   35389370
               RG S/Sgt Clarion E Snow   38414919

FP-256-AH-8A   P   2nd Lt RAYMOND I CONSTANT   0751987 Ap No. 42-107734
               CP 2nd Lt RAYMOND P BRITTON   0815821
               B   F/O SEYMOUR S BASKOFF   T-1931
               EG Sgt John S Albright   33362842
               RG S/Sgt Andrew J Rutherford Jr   33538600

FP-256-AH-9A   P   2nd Lt DOMINIC V FIACCO   0687024 Ap No. 42-107737
               CP 2nd Lt RUSSELL C KELLEY   0815162
               EG Sgt Irwin W Harder   17127154
               RG S/Sgt John S Slifka   13128784

FP-256-AH-10A P   2nd Lt WILBERT A HAMEL   0808991 Ap No. 42-107736
               CP 2nd Lt ROBERT S WOODHURST JR   0449790
               B   2nd Lt LUTHER K RITTER   0681762
               EG Sgt Ellis R Coffey   37003224
               RG S/Sgt Charles E Traweek   34586429

FP-256-AH-11A P   2nd Lt CHARLES J OLSON   0686589 Ap No. 42-107727
               CP 2nd Lt GLENN E MOORE   0758835
               B   2nd Lt DONALD I BREWER   0746853
               EG Sgt Nelson W Crisler   32626225
               RG S/Sgt William F Rhoads   19109607

FP-256-AH-12A P   2nd Lt LADD L HORN   0687596 Ap No. 42-107730
               CP 2nd Lt PAUL M ROSEMAN   0758859
               EG Sgt Bernard Fineman   33586506
               RG S/Sgt Warren E Tupper   31184224

FP-256-AH-13A P   2nd Lt WALTER F HOYER JR   0807446 Ap No. 42-107738
               CP 2nd Lt JOSEPH T TRAFF   0816181
               B   2nd Lt JOHN E BACON   0750111
               EG Sgt Leo R Green   17059675
               RG S/Sgt Lowell R Tillett   34721449

RESTRICTED
- 1 -

*March 11, 1944 orders from Hunter Field, GA for replacement flight crew
12A to report to Homestead Field, FL with B-26 No. 42-107730.*

Into Africa

The route Crew 12A used to fly to North Africa was the South Atlantic Ferry Route. Their original destination was Cazes Field, Casablanca, Morocco, but as you will hear, they ended up in Telergma, Algeria instead.

The dates for the transfer to Hunter Field, GA for the B-26 "pickup and testing" and then the transfer through Homestead Field, FL for departure to North Africa are very well established by Air Force orders and Bernard Fineman's flight log. The crew's orders from Lake Charles, LA dated March 3, 1944 were to go to Hunter Field, GA by train, to arrive no later than March 8th. Dad's processing papers dated March 8, 1944 were labeled Hunter Field, GA and we have papers verifying the completion of the processing for Crew 12A that are dated March 10, 1944. The orders that moved Horn, Roseman, Fineman, Webb, Summer and Tupper (Crew 12A) from Hunter Field to Homestead, FL for shipment overseas are dated March 11, 1944 (see previous page). Bernard Fineman, Dad's flight engineer, kept a detailed flight log and provided a typed copy for my dad after the war. If Dad moved to Hunter Field on March 8th, received orders to Homestead, FL on March 11th and the plane was tested for five days before they left Hunter Field, the timing would match perfectly with Bernard Fineman's flight log that states that they left for Homestead, FL on March 16, 1944. We also have orders from Homestead, FL dated March 15th that state that Crew 12A is to be part of a shipment overseas via the South Atlantic route. Crew 12A departed the US on March 18, 1944 leaving Homestead Field, FL for Borenquen Field, Puerto Rico based on entries in Bernard Fineman's flight log.

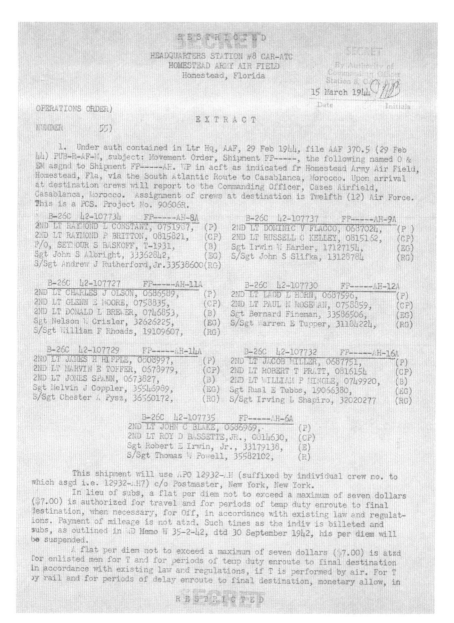

RESTRICTED

HEADQUARTERS STATION #8 CAR-ATC
HOMESTEAD ARMY AIR FIELD
Homestead, Florida

15 March 1944

OPERATIONS ORDER)

EXTRACT

NUMBER   55)

1. Under auth contained in Ltr Hq, AAF, 29 Feb 1944, file AAF 370.5 (29 Feb 44) PUB-R-AF-M, subject: Movement Order, Shipment FP-----, the following named O & EM asgnd to Shipment FP-----AH. WP in acft as indicated fr Homestead Army Air Field, Homestead, Fla, via the South Atlantic Route to Casablanca, Morocco. Upon arrival at destination crews will report to the Commanding Officer, Cazes Airfield, Casablanca, Morocco. Assignment of crews at destination is Twelfth (12) Air Force. This is a PCS. Project No. 90606R.

B-26C 42-107734   FP-----AH-8A
2ND LT RAYMOND L CONSTANT, 0751907,   (P)
2ND LT RAYMOND P BRITTON, 0815821,   (CP)
F/O, SEYMOUR S BASKOFF, T-1931,   (B)
Sgt John S Albright, 33362842,   (EG)
S/Sgt Andrew J Rutherford,Jr.33538600(RG)

B-26C 42-107737   FP-----AH-9A
2ND LT DOMINIC V FLACCO, 0687024,   (P)
2ND LT RUSSELL G KELLEY, 0815162,   (CP)
Sgt Irwin W Harder, 17127154,   (EG)
S/Sgt John S Slifka, 13128784   (RG)

B-26C 42-107727   FP-----AH-11A
2ND LT CHARLES J OLSON, 0586589,   (P)
2ND LT GLENN E MOORE, 0758835,   (CP)
2ND LT DONALD L BREWER, 0746853,   (B)
Sgt Nelson W Crisler, 32626225,   (EG)
S/Sgt William F Rhoads, 19109607,   (RG)

B-26C 42-107730   FP-----AH-12A
2ND LT LADD L HORN, 0687596,   (P)
2ND LT PAUL M ROSEMAN, 0758859,   (CP)
Sgt Bernard Fineman, 33586506,   (EG)
S/Sgt Warren E Tupper, 31184224,   (RG)

B-26C 42-107729   FP-----AH-14A
2ND LT JAMES H HIPPLE, 0608997,   (P)
2ND LT MARVIN E TOFFER, 0678979,   (CP)
2ND LT JONES SPANN, 0673827,   (B)
Sgt Melvin J Coppler, 35546989,   (EG)
S/Sgt Chester A Fysz, 36560172,   (RG)

B-26C 42-107732   FP-----AH-16A
2ND LT JACOB MILLER, 0687751,   (P)
2ND LT ROBERT T PRATT, 0816154,   (CP)
2ND LT WILLIAM P HINGLE, 0749920,   (B)
Sgt Rual E Tubbs, 19066380,   (EG)
S/Sgt Irving L Shapiro, 32020277,   (RG)

B-26C 42-107735   FP-----AH-6A
2ND LT JOHN C BLAKE, 0686969,.   (P)
2ND LT ROY D BASSETTE,JR., 0814630,   (CP)
Sgt Robert E Irwin, Jr., 33179138,   (E)
S/Sgt Thomas W Powell, 35582102,   (R)

This shipment will use APO 12932-AH (suffixed by individual crew no. to which asgd i.e. 12932-AH7) c/o Postmaster, New York, New York.
In lieu of subs, a flat per diem not to exceed a maximum of seven dollars ($7.00) is authorized for travel and for periods of temp duty enroute to final destination, when necessary, for Off, in accordance with existing law and regulations. Payment of mileage is not atzd. Such times as the indiv is billeted and subs, as outlined in WD Memo W 35-2-42, dtd 30 September 1942, his per diem will be suspended.
A flat per diem not to exceed a maximum of seven dollars ($7.00) is atzd for enlisted men for T and for periods of temp duty enroute to final destination in accordance with existing law and regulations, if T is performed by air. For T by rail and for periods of delay enroute to final destination, monetary allow, in

RESTRICTED

Orders (stamped "SECRET") dated March 15, 1944 for Crew 12A departure for Cazes Airfield, Casablanca, Morocco via the South Atlantic air route. Note that Crew 12A was flying B-26C 42-107730.

Dad's USAAF flight bag used for the trip to North Africa. Many of the documents in this book were stored in this bag. This picture was taken in 2022.

Bernie Fineman, my flight engineer, possibly taken in Homestead Florida. They issued these sheepskin flying jackets when we went, but then took them away when we got up to Sardinia. When it was winter in Dijon, France, we didn't have them to stay warm. It was good that we had them in North Africa because we slept in them because it got so cold at night.

B. Fineman flight log entry: "On 3/16/44 We picked up a new B-26 (Id #42-107730) straight from the assembly line at Hunter Field, GA. *(See the previous story entitled, "A New B-26C for the Free French Air Force")* We left Hunter Field, GA, and flew to Homestead Army Air Field, Homestead, FL."

B. Fineman flight log entry: "On 3/18/44 we were on our way! We flew from Homestead Field to Borenquen Field, Puerto Rico after about 6 h flying time. Magneto was repaired."

The following is my dad's oral story of the trip to the US Air Base in Telergma, Algeria and why they did not land at Cazes Field in Casablanca, Morocco.

As we were approaching Puerto Rico, I called in to the field, they cleared me and I entered the landing pattern as they instructed. As I turned into the downwind leg of the landing pattern for their field, the left engine quit. It shut down just as if you had turned off the ignition. I immediately called the tower for clearance for emergency single-engine landing and they cleared me. We went to working [*sic*] on the engine to see what was wrong. We checked switches, mixtures and throttles, pressures and everything looked right and we couldn't find anything. We moved everything and changed settings and just about when we were going to give up and feather it, the engine restarted. So, we actually landed with both engines running. However, they wanted to check the plane over and we had to lay over at the base. They changed the magneto and put on a whole new wiring harness even though it was all brand new to start with.

B. Fineman's flight log entry: "On 3/20/44 we left Borenquen Field, Puerto Rico and flew to Atkinson Field, British Guiana after about 6 ½ h of flying time."

In British Guiana, it was a big "fuss" because Eleanor Roosevelt decided that she should inspect the South American airfields to see if things were being handled properly there. (In other words, she went on vacation.) So, they made us park all our planes as far into the jungle as possible to "clean up the field" as much as we could so we didn't get involved with her inspectors. In the end, we were delayed a few hours while they inspected Atkinson Field.

There was no problem landing at Atkinson field, but once we landed, there was a problem. No one thought about the fact that the temperature was so high there that the fuel in the fuel lines would vaporize and we couldn't get the engines restarted. So, we couldn't leave when we were supposed to. The coolest part of the day was near morning and so Bernie went out sometime when it was the coolest and got the engines started the next morning. How they kept the engines so they would restart I don't know. The whole issue resulted in a delay of about one day.

B. Fineman flight log entry: "On 3/21/44 we left Atkinson Field and flew to São Luis, Brazil, about a 4 h flight."

B. Fineman flight log entry: "On 3/23/44 we left São Luis, Brazil and flew to Natal, Brazil. The total trip time was 7 h and 8 min, about the maximum flight time for a B-26 without a bomb load."

The main incident on that flight was that about half way to Natal a huge thunderstorm built up ahead of us. The area was known for its very bad thunderstorms and the military had restricted flying hours for the area around Natal because of them. This storm was very large and we were relatively low on fuel. So, we debated whether we should enter the storm or not. Our orders were to avoid these storms at all cost. But our fuel was so low that we couldn't go around given the large area of the storm. Together we decided that the B-26 was a "tough" plane and so we buckled everything down tightly (including ourselves) and entered the storm. We closed all the engine cowlings tight to keep the water out as much as possible thereby risking high engine temperatures (oil and cylinder). We no more than got into the storm and we hit almost a solid wall of water. The engine head temperatures went down almost to the bottom of the gauges and the engines went to running really rough just from the volume of the water going through the air-cooling system. After we made it through that first heavy water we entered up and down drafts that threw the plane around like it was a feather or balsa-wood glider. The rate-of-climb and descent gauges were hitting both ends of the gauge almost at the same time. You went from falling like a rock to being boosted up like you were on the top of an explosion. We really had some second thoughts about our decision to enter the storm, but we had made the decision to go in and now we had to keep going. Stuff started to break loose and fly around inside the plane even in the cockpit and the navigators' compartment and other places. We eventually broke out of the storm into nice weather and it was nice flying for the last small part of the trip into Natal.

A C-47 pilot that saw us enter the storm decided that he would enter too. He apparently decided that if we could enter, then he could too. He was transporting a load of glider winches for use in the upcoming glider assault that the Air Force had planned for Germany and Belgium. As he got well into the storm and hit the up and down drafts and other turbulence, the glider winches broke loose in the hold. As they broke loose they slid from side to side and up and down and they pounded the fuselage to bits. He was really scared because the winches were hitting the bulkhead behind him so hard that he thought they would break through and get him and his co-pilot. Amazingly his plane kept flying and he eventually landed it later that day in Natal. His plane looked like somebody had been inside pounding the fuselage outward with a sledgehammer. It was all lumps and cuts and stretched and deformed areas. I heard later that they scrapped that plane. They decided it was just not worth rebuilding.

At Natal during the first day that we stayed over, they posted a notice that if you went to a certain spot you could buy Natal boots at about $1 a pair (it wasn't over $2 a pair). A lot of the guys were saying that the boots were very nice and so I decided to go get some. I went to the spot where they had it roped off and they were selling them. All they did was bring a ten-wheeler truckload of boots and dump them in the ring. You sorted through for the color you liked and size that fit and you could take as many as you wanted. I only took one pair. They served me very well through all the rest of the war. We wore them for flying. The boots were on around 30-35 combat missions. They issued us regular infantry combat boots because crews that were getting shot down over Germany were taken on these huge long endurance marches and it seemed to be that the guys that were surviving were ones that had heavy duty hardware boots.

Dad's boots from Natal on a USAAF blanket. This picture was taken in 2022.

B. Fineman flight log entry: "On 3/25/44 we left Natal, Brazil and flew to Wideawake Airfield on Ascension Island in the middle of the Atlantic. Flight time was about 5 h."

Most of the supplies and parts were transported by C-47s (Douglas DC-3 basis) and C-46s. (Curtis plane—contracted earlier, but didn't get them completed because they were designed from scratch. They were the largest planes we had.) *(But,)* At Natal, Summer *(armorer)* and Webb *(bombardier)* were taken out of our crew because the plane was loaded too heavily. They took quite a few other things off the plane. The plane was filled with aircraft and machine gun parts for the free French. They gave me an Air Transport Command navigator.

In the next few lines Dad is talking about when he saw the plane before takeoff.

I was skeptical of the lift capability of the plane because I had been told of the effects of frost on the wings of the plane and how it affected the plane more than anyone had ever anticipated. We had been cautioned not to ever try taking off with frost on the wings in the colder climates. In Natal, the dirt, dew and dust looked an awful lot like frost except that the color was red like the dirt there. On our takeoff, I began to have doubts that the plane was ever going to get airborne. But we did get into flight just about the very end of the runway. The plane didn't want to climb or come up to cruising speed. I began to think that the dirt on the wings was having more effect than anticipated. I was holding the plane at full takeoff power and gaining no more than a few feet of altitude. The fuel consumption under those conditions was horrible. I began to think about turning around and going back in because we could never make our flight under those power conditions. That is when I spotted the cloud a few miles off in the distance that looked like it was dumping water. I told Paul Roseman *(co-pilot)* and Bernie Fineman *(engineer)* that the dirt was causing the problems with gaining altitude. So, I told them that if it *(the cloud)* was dumping water, I'd fly right into it and get the plane washed off. When we got to the cloud it was a heavy water cloud and was raining hard. We flew right into the middle of it even though we were quite low down. We no more than hit the water in the cloud than it felt like the plane had dropped a whole load of bombs and immediately started climbing normally.

We were just about at the point of "no return" *(to Ascension Island)* when the left engine quit. We were pretty concerned, I'll tell you! Just like the previous time *(see above in the description of the landing at Borenquen Field, Puerto Rico)* it just stopped like you had cut the power. I had left the cockpit and was on my way back to the navigator's compartment to have some lunch of sandwiches and coffee they had brought along. I was just ready to step through the bulkhead door into the navigator's compartment. Roseman was flying. He let out a screech saying, "Horn, you've got it!" So, I went back into the pilot's seat. Once I was buckled back in the pilot's seat, I jiggled all the switches, moved all the levers, adjusted everything and got set to feather. I didn't even run it through a restart procedure. I just left it "wind milling" and all of a sudden it restarted. Otherwise I would have gone through a full restart procedure. Roseman was still obviously very shaken. He was not keen on flying that plane on one engine, particularly over the mid-Atlantic. The engine kept running fine until we landed at Ascension Island. Nothing was done to the engine that time because they didn't have anyone or any place to repair it.

Our Air Transport Command navigator was navigating our course. However, as a pilot I always did navigation by dead reckoning to get an estimate of our location and distance to our destination. Well, sometime after the engine restarted we were getting beyond the time I had estimated for our arrival at Ascension Island. Our rule of thumb was that when you get beyond that time and you don't see your destination you start looking around and see if you can see something that indicates something about your location. I also called the navigator on the intercom and asked him for his ETA and correction and heading. He had a little bit longer ETA but he gave me a correction toward the north. And I got to thinking, every correction he gave me was toward the north. I knew we had a north-south crosswind but it shouldn't take that much to correct for it. So, I wasn't very satisfied with that and I decided the "look around" deal was the better choice. I started turning the plane in a large slow arc to the south planning to make a complete oval if I had to. As I got around about half way, way off, just about out of sight on the horizon, I saw a little white spec. I thought in this part of the Atlantic there are almost no clouds at this time of year and under these conditions. The only thing that would create a cloud would be an island. I called the navigator and told him that I didn't like his heading and that far to the southwest I could see a tiny speck. I was changing heading and was going to fly toward the speck I could see. After about 50 miles the speck was enough more visible that it did look like a little puffy cloud there. I couldn't see anything else anywhere on any horizon so I thought I should keep heading for that. After a while the cloud got bigger and I could see some interruption in the surface of the ocean down that way. My mind says; "That's it. That's the island. There are no other islands in this whole part of the Atlantic." I waited just a little longer and it became an island. I called Ascension Island on the frequency we had been told and after a couple of tries I got the tower. The guy said, "We were just starting to get worried about you. We hadn't had a call and you were off schedule." I told him we had spotted the island and were headed in from almost due North. He said according to his vectors I was still twenty-five miles out. I should just keep heading in and give him a call when I was close enough for him to give landing instructions. Somehow that seemed like a long twenty-five miles going in. He let me land straight in without going around the regular pattern, which was convenient. We were probably close to forty minutes *(off course)*. The navigator never said a word about being off course.

While I was in training, they made us do some takeoffs and landings at a place called Palestine, TX. They sent us there without telling us anything about the place or the field except that we were supposed to land there. When we landed there, we got a surprise because there was a lake and as you came over the runway, the runway went uphill for most of the runway and then went a bit downhill. It was surprising because that extra downhill required a lot of extra braking. I never knew why they made us practice landings there and they had us do quite a few. But when I came into Ascension Island I knew why they had us practice! The runway at Ascension Island ran the same way. The problem was you had to compensate for the uphill approach and the downhill required extra braking. The island was a single mountain peak that they had cut down. It was essentially a single mountain peak island that they had cut into two peaks with the runway in the bottom groove but they hadn't flattened it completely. It was tough on landing, but was a great boost for takeoff.

On these flights we flew at about 180 mph to conserve fuel.

B. Fineman flight log entry: "On 3/26/44 we left Ascension Island and flew to Robert's Field, Monrovia, Liberia. The flight time was about 4 1/2h [sic]."

Flying over to Robert's Field was a relatively short flight. It was somewhat relaxing. Nothing of any consequence happened on that leg of the journey.

B. Fineman flight log entry: "On 3/27/44 we left Robert's Field and flew to Dakar, Senegal. Flight time was about 6 ½ h."

This flight was normal and nothing unusual happened on the way.

B. Fineman flight log entry: "On 3/28/44 we few from Dakar, Senegal to Marrakesh, Morroco [sic] a flight of about 6 h."

The night before we left Dakar they told us how they were routing us up to Marrakesh, Morocco. They were sending us up through the western end of the Atlas Mountains. They looped us inland for a while, then north and then through the Atlas Mountains and into Marrakesh. They showed us movies of the mountains and flying through them. They wanted us to fly low through the mountains because they thought that the Germans had developed radar and were able to count our planes going up there. They thought that by flying low we would avoid the radar. Actually, the Germans hadn't developed radar that good yet. They just had a very good network of ground observers. The main reasons for the movies was that there are box canyons in the mountains in that area in particular and if you flew at the altitude that they wanted us to fly through, you would get boxed in and couldn't get out and it would result in an unavoidable crash. They ran the movie of the canyon we were to fly through and the pass we were to fly through so that the pilots could memorize the appearance and not get boxed in. Going up through there I followed the Air Transport navigator's headings and got to where we should be heading into the canyon we were supposed to use, but it didn't look like the movie we saw. So I questioned the navigator. He said, oh, this is the right canyon. This is the way to go. I've been through here before. So, I followed his headings for "a ways." The land looked stranger and stranger to me. So, I told Roseman, "Hey this is obvious to me that this is not the right route. We are going to get boxed in." I said, "I'm going against the navigator and I want you to help me spot the lowest point in any of these mountain ridges around here and we are going to head there and get out of here. I can already see its going to be close." So, we agreed together on what we thought was the lowest spot within our range of vision and we headed directly for it. I put the plane up to full takeoff power and flew it so we held the maximum reading we could get on the rate of climb. We just held the power and the direct heading for that point and Roseman turned to me and said, "You have had these engines at full takeoff power for five minutes already. You know the manual says you're not supposed to do this for more than two and a half minutes." I said, "I know that very well, but my plan is to get out of here alive. If we burn out the engines, so be it. We need to take the risk to get out." So, with the engines at that power and climbing at the maximum rate we could get, the ground kept coming up closer and closer and closer. Finally, that dip in the ridge was in front of us and we were barely climbing at the rate the ground was going up. At the last second we slipped over the ridge at what seemed like 10-feet altitude. It was probably forty or fifty feet but it sure didn't seem like it. So, I cut the power and nosed down and picked up normal cruising speed and plain as anything, there in front of us was the canyon we should have been in. Everything looked right. So, we dropped back to our prescribed altitude for the flight and got back on the proper heading for going up to Marrakesh.

When we called in to Marrakesh they told us we couldn't land there. When we pressed them for a reason, they told us that they had had a breakout of bubonic plague and that they had been closed down and no one could come in. They would not give us an alternate landing site due to air communication security. As soon as we found out that we couldn't land at Marrakesh, we turned inland. There were about twenty planes flying from Dakar to Marrakesh that day. I don't know where they all landed. I know one plane landed out in the desert and had a close shave on the landing.

Note: Dad and I had a lot of discussion at this point that I did not capture. The crew did not have orders to land at any other base than Marrakesh. What Dad remembered doing was turning inland and taking a line (northeast?) and telling his crew that they would eventually get to the coast and follow it. He told the crew that he thought that they would at some point be able to spot a US base where they could land. Dad was certain of one thing: that they eventually landed at a B-17 airfield near Tunis, Tunisia. When we looked at the map, a direct line flight to Tunis was around 1100 miles. That would have been in addition to the approximately 1,300 miles they probably had already flown from Dakar, Senegal to Marrakesh, Morocco. My dad was certain that they were not allowed to land at Marrakesh. Dad then did some simple mental calculations using fuel capacity, flying speed and approximate fuel consumption rates. At one point he said, "We must have landed some place, but I can't remember where." But, after a while he decided that they must have simply continued flying. The following is a summary of his thoughts in his words.

The flight to Marrakesh was about six hours. We did have two auxiliary fuel tanks with 250 gallons each in the bomb bay, so we could fly for perhaps just short of eleven hours of flying but that would be all if you were to have enough for an acceptable landing. *(Note: B-26 bombers would carry 1,000 gallons of fuel and then could add 250 gallons more in each of the two auxiliary tanks for a total of 1,500 gallons.)* The plane we were flying was heavily loaded with spare parts, but we were also flying so as to economize fuel. We were likely flying at about 220 mph that day and using an average of around 135 gallons of fuel per hour. At that rate, we would have had an approximate range of 2,400 miles.

Given the approximate range of 2,400 miles, it is actually possible that they flew non-stop for approximately eleven hours to get to the airfield near Tunis, Tunisia.

Final note on "Into Africa": The decision to fly through a rainstorm to clean dirt off the wings of their B-26 is also described by Bernard Fineman, Dad's flight engineer. (see below) Bernard Fineman's description is essentially identical to my dad's description of the event, except that the location is different. My dad believed this incident occurred when leaving Natal, Brazil on their way to Ascension Island. Bernard Fineman locates it as the flight from Ascension Island to Robert's Field, Monrovia, Liberia. Since my dad had a copy of Bernard Fineman's flight log, we discussed the discrepancy. The following are his words about the discrepancy:

I thought that the incident with dirt on the wings occurred at Natal, Brazil, even though Bernie's log says that it was at Ascension Island. My recollection, *(even)* knowing Bernie listed the event as being on Ascension Island, is that the runways at Ascension Island were all paved and that the field at Natal was all dirt except for the main runway, causing the dirt to build up on the wings. See Bernie's account which I believe is accurate, except for the location.

Bernard Fineman's account: "I must explain that the Ascension Island is a volcanic rock in the middle of the Atlantic Ocean and the wind blows in one direction and is used as a base for our aircraft. During the evening and early morning there was a dew on the wings and the sand caked on the wings. I know that this breaks up air foil [*sic*] on the wings causing a dangerous condition, and I know it must be cleaned off which I attempted to do. I tried everything in order to remove all the sand by sweeping, since there was no water available to me on the island. There was no way of getting down to the ocean to retrieve water—we were elevated by several hundred feet. This was extremely difficult to accomplish without water and there was still some sand remaining on the wings. I contacted Lt. Horn and advised him of the condition and he felt that enough sand had been removed and we probably would not have a problem. We then took off and were able to get to a proper altitude. He then found that the plane would not maintain the altitude on a lean fuel mixture and we had a distance to go to North Africa. He advised us if we lost altitude and the situation became critical we would have to stand by in the bomb bay to bail out. I was standing between the pilot and co-pilot checking all the instruments to make sure we were doing ok. Lt. Horn said he saw a black cloud in the distance and he was going to head for the black cloud, hoping that it would be a rain cloud."

"Stolen" Army Blankets

We landed at that B-17 base near Tunis, uninvited and unwanted because we didn't have any orders for anywhere else to go.

Note: Dad never gave me the name of the base near Tunis where they landed. However, given his description that they found it by flying along the shoreline, combined with his statement that it was a B-17 base and that it was near Tunis, Tunisia, possibly identify it as Bizerte Airfield. However, some sources say that the B-17 groups only used it until December 1943, three months prior to my dad's flight. Bernie Fineman's flight log simply says, "On 3/29/44 we left Marrakech[sic] and flew to Tunis, Tunisia another flight of about 6 h" and, "On 3/30/44 we left Tunis and flew to Telergma, Algeria. It took about 1 ½ h." Bernard Fineman's dates are not correct since my dad saved official orders from Telergma that date Crew 12A's arrival in Telergma as March 29, 1944. The March 29th date would be consistent with my dad's recollection of flying directly from Marrakesh to the base near Tunis and the following day flying back to Telergma, arriving on March 29th.

Well, they refused to feed us, they refused to service our plane and didn't give us a place to sleep. Not knowing what else to do we went to the radio communications tent (telephone and shortwave radio equipment). There was a fellow there who listened to what we were saying and he introduced himself and he seemed like quite a nice person in general. He told us, "Look, I'm the radioman that will be on duty tonight. It will be an all-night shift for me. If you want me to I'll try and get in contact with higher headquarters and see if I can get info on what you should do." We said, "Great!" But he said, "There is no sense of you waiting around because it will likely be four a.m. before I can make contact. I know how this radio stuff works." So, he said, "Why don't you find some place to sleep and I'll have the information for you in the morning."

So, as things went, they would not allow us any place to sleep because we weren't part of their outfit. *(It)* Didn't matter that we were from the same country, and fighting on the same side. So, we decided that maybe we could at least get some blankets and mattress pads from their quartermaster's supply warehouse for the base. Roseman and I and Bernie and Tupper went down there and went up to their counter and talked with the guys at the counter. "No, you can't have anything from here." So, it got to more and more talk and more and more argument and some of the other guys came over to see how this would come out. In the meantime, Bernie and Tupper shook their heads and went out—kind of faded out of the picture. They left Roseman and me talking. A little later Bernie showed up. He said, "Don't bother talking and don't waste any more time with these guys. It's a waste of time." When we got out of the building, Bernie said, "We could see you weren't making any progress. So, while you were talking, Tupper and I stole a jeep." We went *(with him)* down to the Jeep. When we got there, there was a bale of army blankets in the jeep— 40 army blankets. They said, "We can sleep in the plane tonight. While they were tied up talking with you, we went in the back door and stole a bale of blankets. We could hardly move them, but we got them in the jeep."

We all piled into the jeep on top of the blankets and wherever we could find a space. When we got to the plane we opened the bomb bay doors and working together, we were able to boost the blankets into the plane. There were five of us total (including the Air Transport man who was on as a navigator—usually on a lend-lease plane or short crew—he had been as far as Karachi, India delivering a plane) so we divided up eight blankets apiece. We made beds in the plane wherever we wanted. Tupper took the jeep back to where they got it. I had my eight blankets the whole time I was in combat and brought four of them home with me. They really came in handy!

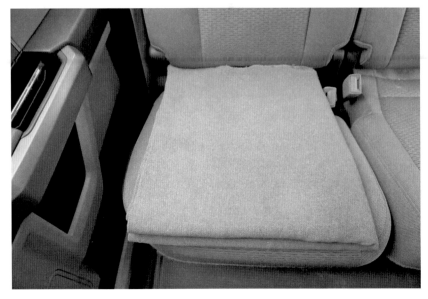

One of the "stolen" army blankets in my Ford F150 in 2022. Dad gave this blanket to me when I was in high school to keep in my vehicle in case I was ever stranded in a Buffalo snowstorm and it's still with me!

The reason they were able to steal that jeep was that, our fellows got so that they each carried a jeep rotor and points in their jackets or pants pockets for situations like this. Guys who parked jeeps usually took the rotor and points out so that they wouldn't be stolen. So, Tupper took the jeep back and took back his rotor and points for future use. The air transport guy likely sold his blankets on the black market somewhere.

I arrived in Telergma about the third or fourth week of March 1944 *(The actual arrival date was March 29, 1944 confirmed by the orders transferring Dad from Telergma, Algeria to Sardinia. see next page)* with my crew, turned over my plane to the Free French with what supplies were on board and, believe it or not, received a receipt for $350,000. I kept that for a long time but don't know where it is now. I was then assigned to the 17th Bombardment Group, 95th Squadron for combat duty.

BOMBARDMENT TRAINING CENTER
Office of the Director of Air Training
APO #762, U.S. Army

Date   4/4/44

SUBJECT: Non-Training Report.

TO   : Commanding General XII Air Force Training & Replacement Command
         APO #766, U.S. Army
      1. The following listed B-26 Combat Crew arrived at this station
March 29, 1944   from United States   , but received no tactical
training, and departed this station 4/4/44 per VOCG XII AF Tng. & Repl.
Command   , for assignment to 42nd Wing   .

         Pilot   Horn, L.L.   2nd Lt. 0-687596
         Co-pilot   Roseman, F.M. 2nd Lt. 0-758859
         Engineer   Finesan, B. Sgt. 33586506
         Radio Op. Tupper, B.B. S/Sgt. 31164224

                        For the Commanding Officer:

                                                 David J. Jones,
                                                 Lt. Major, Air Corps,
                                                 Director of Air Training.

Information copy to Squadron Operations Officer.

Telergma, Algeria arrival and departure "Non-training report" listing Dad's arrival in Telergma as March 29, 1944 and his departure and assignment to the 42nd Wing on April 4, 1944.

I didn't *(officially)* fly any missions out of Telergma, because I got there too late. *(Note: The North Africa Campaign, "Operation Torch," was essentially complete by May of 1943)* We flew some missions that we didn't get credit for. There were things that officially "disqualified" missions. Sometimes we didn't drop the bombs. Sometimes we missed the target.

WAR DEPARTMENT
A. A. F. Form No. 99
Revised May 14, 1942

WAR DEPARTMENT
ARMY AIR FORCES

~~DEBIT~~ *CREDIT

MEMORANDUM RECEIPT

No. 44-19

Station A.F. General Depot #1   Date 30 March 1944

Issuing organization Air Corps Supply.

~~xxxxxxx~~ } Horn, Ladd L., 2nd Lt., A.C.   (Ferry Pilot)
* Turned in by }

QUANTITY	UNIT	PART NO.	Class 01-A ARTICLE
1	ea.		B-26C Serial #42-107730 Project #90606R also turned
			in Air Corps Supply papers pertaining to it.
			LAST ITEM
			//

I acknowledge receipt of the above-listed Army Air Forces property:

(Signature with rank and organization)

MILTON L. GARON, 1st Lt., A.C.
Air Corps Supply Officer.

* Strike out words not applicable. (11-42) ☆ U. S. GOVERNMENT PRINTING OFFICE : 1942

Dad's receipt for B-26C Serial #42-107730, Project #90606 delivered to the Free French in Telergma, Algeria. The receipt was found March 9, 2021 in other military documents, almost four and a half years after Dad died.

"Dumpster Divers"

The 17th Bomb Group, 95th Squadron of the USAAF was initially stationed at Telergma, Algeria (southwest/inland of Constantine, Algeria) and ran their B-26 bombing missions from there. Water was scarce. There was a small stream that came out of the Atlas Mountains that ran through the base and could be used by the men. However, that stream also supplied the local town and surrounding area. The USAAF command was afraid the base would use too much of the water and that it would impact the town and surrounding area/people, so they limited each soldier at the base to one helmet's worth of water for washing and shaving per day and one canteen of water (probably about a quart) for drinking. The water was taken from the stream and run through a purification truck that then supplied the base. Even after purification all water still had to be treated with Halazone tablets. Initially the base had only one water purification truck but later this was expanded to three.

Supplies were, of course, scarce. But American ingenuity helped ease the shortage. The American forces seemed to use and salvage everything they could find that was abandoned by the German and Italian armies. They also found supplies in abandoned buildings or supply depots that were left behind during the German and Italian armies' retreat. They even scavenged things that had been bombed. This proclivity to scavenge and repurpose supplies and equipment was probably one of the things that allowed the American forces to get ahead of the German troops. While the 17th Bomb Group, 95th Squadron seemed to always have enough bombs (bomb-carrying ships traveled in multiples in case one was sunk), when a ship with food or clothing was sunk or delayed, there was no duplicate supply, leaving the crews without that particular type of supplies for several months. In these situations, and so many others, the Americans "scavenged" supplies from the battlefields across North Africa (e.g. Rommel's path) and their various abandoned supply depots. In many cases, unlike the American army, the other Allied armies and the German and Italian armies seemed to leave everything behind when they retreated or pulled out of an area. They would not only leave equipment on the battlefield (damaged weapons and vehicles), but they would also leave behind supply depots. The American crews would go out to the battlefield (it looked like a junk yard for thousands of miles) with trucks, tools and cutting torches. They would find abandoned jeeps *(usually VW rear engine cut down, imitation "Jeeps"; Kübelwagen—bucket-seat car)* or motorcycles (British and German) in an okay shape. These they would tow back to the base. They would also find other identical models that had been damaged. These they would strip or cut up for parts. The mechanics would then use the parts to convert the vehicles that were generally "ok" into running vehicles. Usually the teams would only require a few days back at the base to do the conversion. They would also scavenge German gasoline to run the "refurbished" vehicles (and even to heat their tents for the cold desert nights).

I was able to get a German military, Zundapp, motorcycle that had been rebuilt while I was in North Africa for $40.

In some cases, the base would send a crew out with one of the "war weary" planes (planes that could fly, but were damaged to the point where they could no longer be used in bombing missions) to scavenge supplies from abandoned supply depots. The American troops generally didn't abandon supply depots, but just once, my co-pilot, Paul Roseman, took one of the "war-weary" planes to an abandoned American supply depot. He came back with 5-gallon cans of ground coffee, sugar and cases of evaporated milk. We didn't turn them in to the mess hall, but instead stored them in our tent for our crew's use. Essentially all of the space under my bunk in the tent was filled with these supplies. These extra supplies really helped when there were ration shortages and they also helped to boost morale among the crew.

Me *[sic]* and my dog Madam (my mom called her "The Madam." For a while, she was the only female dog we had around.) The squadron commanding officer loaned me his jeep so I could drive to headquarters to serve as "officer of the day." The jeep drove forward in second gear and *(had)* no low, high or reverse. They didn't have parts or machines to make parts so you had to wait to get parts from another jeep. But it could get you someplace. As "officer of the day" you had to be in headquarters and answer incoming calls from other squadrons and pass on any orders. Note that I was combed and dressed nicely for the day. In Telergma, the non-commissioned officer of transportation always scrounged the North African battlefield for parts to keep our vehicles running. *This picture was taken in Sardinia.*

German military Zundapp motorcycle built from salvaged parts off the North African battlefield. *(This was)* My personal transportation while I was in Sardinia. The guys in North Africa scavenged the battlefield and assembled this motorcycle. I bought it from one of the mechanics for $40 so I didn't have to ride the 10-wheelers all the time. My dog Madam is on the motorcycle with me. This picture was taken in Sardinia in front of the "Marauder Mansion." *The motorcycle is a Zundapp KS600 worth about $20,000 today.*

It seemed that almost all of the American soldiers had some level of "dumpster diving" ability built into them but the same did not seem to be true of the other Allied armies, enemy armies or the local people. An interesting case was that of the local mothers with young children who were starving. The doctors at the base would save evaporated milk to give to them and they were always appreciative, but, surprisingly, none of them ever seemed to go out to the abandoned supply areas to pick up food for their children even though they knew about them.

It also seemed that few of the soldiers from the French or British armies scavenged supplies from the battlefield. The one exception I noted was the Free French who were being trained in North Africa. They did scavenge supplies, but mostly it seemed that they were only interested in finding parts to help them with the weekly motorcycle races they had set up at the base.

Similar "dumpster-diving" scenarios occurred as the 17th moved into Dijon France (after Sardinia and Corsica). Water was still short. The water purification truck came by the tent only once per week. My crew found an old P-30 drop tank that held perhaps 100–150 gallons that we could have filled by the water supply truck. We then picked up hydraulic lines from a wrecked B-26 and took the water from the drop tank into our tent. It was split into two lines and run to an old lavatory sink we had found in an abandoned building. We used stainless steel band clamps on hoses to act like faucets. The hot water line was wrapped around the 1-gallon stove we had for heating the tent. (We heated with scavenged German gasoline.) It didn't produce a lot of hot water, but would produce maybe a cup of hot water for shaving.

A couple of times we ran out of 50-caliber ammunition for our machine guns. The base would set up bins to collect the spent machine gun shells from missions and the ground crews would reload them. The machine guns then used sequences of three of these reloaded shells, one new shell and one tracer shell (these were also not re-loads) during missions.

One of the fellows in one of the tents across the street from us had a BMW motorcycle (German scrap off the battlefield) and he had problems with it so he got the other guy (one of the motorpool men) to help him. They have either the engine or transmission torn apart because of some problem. I had few problems with my Zundapp. I did have to make a new brush for the alternator to replace one that broke when I "jumped" a fence. *This picture was taken in Sardinia in the summer of 1944.*

The Horn, Ringo, Roseman, Miller, Olson tent in Dijon, France. Note the P-30 drop tank on the side used for their water supply. The gasoline stove Dad described is vented via the tall chimney through the roof.

The Move to Villacidro

The 17th Bomb Group and 95th Bomb Squadron had been moved from Telergma, Algeria to Sardinia, Italy in late 1943. My dad had been assigned to the 12th Air Force, the 42nd Wing as they entered Africa. Now Crew 12A was moved from Telergma, Algeria to Sardinia, Italy in April of 1944. The following is the only record I have of the transfer.

We went to Villacidro about the first week in April *(The official orders from Telergma assign the departure date as 4/4/44 but I do have letters that clearly were written from Telergma, Algeria dated April 6th and 7th 1944. Bernard Fineman's flight log says that they (Flight Crew 12A) were transferred to Sardinia on April 9, 1944 via an FC-47.)* and were assigned to the 95th but my bombardier, Webb, and tail gunner, Summers, were transferred over to the 320th Group because they were short on personnel.

The 17th Bomb Group headquarters' sign some way between Villacidro and Cagliari (Sardinia) because it covered all three groups that were under the 17th. All were B-26 groups; 95th Squadron, 219th and the 220th. (these *latter* two were not squadrons)

The 17ᵗʰ Bombardment Group is often referred to as having been "attached to" the 12ᵗʰ Air Force and from an administrative sense that is correct until sometime before June 4ᵗʰ, 1944. My dad's recollection is as follows:

At the end of the Rome-Arno campaign I was allowed a five-day rest leave to Rome because it had been liberated *(The liberation of Rome was on June 4ᵗʰ and 5ᵗʰ of 1944)*. At that time, I had to be issued 12ᵗʰ Air Force patches for that leave (Once we were separated from the 12ᵗʰ Air Force we were issued 12ᵗʰ Air Force patches for any leave. After the leave, they had to be turned in.) That means that the 17ᵗʰ Group, 95ᵗʰ Squadron was separated from the 12ᵗʰ sometime before June 4ᵗʰ 1944.

My dad was often adamant that the 17ᵗʰ Bombardment Group operated as a separate, "undeclared" or "stealth" unit to keep the German forces from knowing how many B-26s and flight crews were in Sardinia and involved in attacks on Italy and Germany. As a flight crew, they all had code names that they used on their intercoms (His code name was "Honk"; his tail gunner used his last name, "Summers"—in fact having used the code name for so long, Dad could never remember his first name, and I think that his co-pilot, Paul Roseman's code name was "Rosy".) Dad said that on the outbound part of missions their headsets usually filled with code-name chatter. He told me that even in London as he was headed home and on leave from the 17ᵗʰ Bomb Group, he was issued 12ᵗʰ Air Force insignia which he had to turn in after they returned to base.

A significant number of his missions were flown from Sardinia. However, he was also called back to Telergma multiple times both as a courier and to train pilots from France, Britain, New Zealand and Australia who were transitioning to the B-26s. The following six stories are from those times he was called back to Telergma.

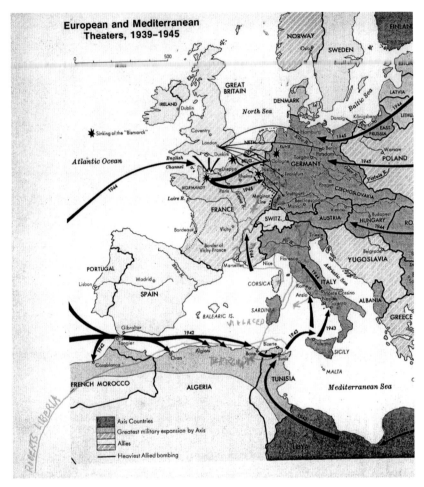

Dad's hand-drawn, generalized mission routes.

An Italian Janitor, Two SM-55s and Italo Balbo

This story was handwritten by my dad in 2007 (April 20, 2007). I did not discover it until this book was almost fully assembled as he had kept it in an Air and Space magazine (Air & Space Smithsonian, May 2005, pp. 28 ff.) that included a story about Mussolini and Italo Balbo. He had marked its reference to Italo Balbo, Mussolini's Minister of Air, on page 30.

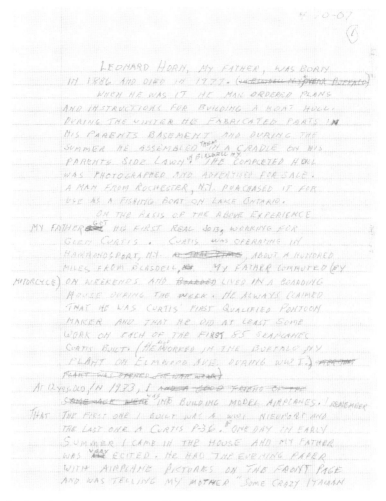

Dad's first handwritten page telling the story of the Italian janitor and the Savoia-Marchetti S55s in Cagliari, Sardinia.

L eonard Horn, my father *(my grandfather)*, was born in 1886 and died in 1977. When he was 17 [*sic*] he mail-ordered plans and instructions for building a boat hull. During the winter he fabricated parts in his parent's basement and during the summer he assembled them in a cradle on his parent's side lawn in Blasdell, NY. The completed hull was photographed and advertised for sale. A man from Rochester, NY purchased it for use as a fishing boat on Lake Ontario.

On the basis of the above experience my father got his first real job, working for Glen Curtis. Curtis was operating in Hammondsport, NY about a hundred miles from Blasdell. My father commuted (by motorcycle) on weekends and lived in a boarding house during the week. He always claimed that he was Curtis' first qualified pontoon maker and that he did at least some work on each of the first 85 seaplanes Curtis built. (He also worked in the Buffalo, NY plant on Elmwood Ave. during WWI.)

At 12 years old, in 1933, I was into building model airplanes. I remember that the first one I built was a WWI Nieuport and the last one a Curtis P-36. One day in early summer I came in the house and my father was very excited. He had the evening paper with airplane pictures on the front page and was telling my mother, "Some crazy Italian is going to try and fly 25 seaplanes across the Atlantic."

When I finally got the paper, there it was, "Italo Balbo Commanding a Squadron of 25 Savoia-Marchetti SR-55 *(S.55)* Naval Seaplanes Will Fly From Rome, Italy to Chicago, Ill. USA and Return to Rome." The paper further indicated their intended course would bring them either over or at least near Buffalo, NY.

A number of days later my father got the paper and became really excited. It seemed that Balbo's flight had passed over Buffalo without our seeing it but one of the planes needed service and it, along with another, had landed in the Buffalo outer harbor and taxied in to anchor. My father piled us into the old

Durant car he had and drove us into Buffalo to the harbour [*sic*]. The planes were there but anchored so far out that we couldn't see them as well as we had hoped.

At 22 years old in early summer of 1944 I was stationed at Villacidro, Sardinia with the 17th Bomb Group. Earlier that year I had flown a B-26 to N. Africa via the Southern Route and had been flying bombing missions over Italian targets. I had a day with no assigned mission and was sitting in front of my tent enjoying the leisure time when an orderly with a hand full of papers walked up to me and said, "Lt" Horn, there's a certificate in your personnel file that says you are a qualified B-26 flying instructor certified to train US and Allied pilots." I said, "That's news to me but if you say it's there I guess I'll have to accept that it is." He said, "On the basis of the certificate I have orders for you to go on detached duty at Telergma to train Free French and other pilots to fly B-26s. Pack up and catch the courier plane this afternoon for Telergma."

As part of my duty there *(Telergma)* I was assigned to fly the courier plane. One morning just as I was ready to climb into the cockpit, a GI came running out with a package wrapped in newspaper and tied with string. He told me I was to deliver this package to Capt Roberts who would be at the Cagliari Municipal Airport *(Sardinia)* at 2:30 waiting for it. He insinuated it would be as good as my life if I failed to hand it to him in person.

I stashed the package behind the pilot's seat and took off for Decimomanu, [*sic*] unloaded the stuff for there, picked up a few items for Villacidro and took off again. At Villacidro I visited my tentmates, ate lunch and headed back for Decimomanu [*sic*]. Once there I checked for passengers I was supposed to pick up and found a flight engineer waiting but was told a pilot I was to take wouldn't be available to leave until about 5:30. I asked the Sgt. Eng. [*sic*] if he would care to go over to the Municipal Airport with me and he said yes, so I packed him into the co-pilot's seat and we took off again. When we landed there, several miscellaneous planes were sitting on the apron in front of the administration building so I parked the "26" in the same area. I told the Sgt to stay with the plane and wait while I went in with my package.

```
                    TRAINING SQUADRON #1
             BOMBARDMENT TRAINING CENTER
                    APO #762

                                          8 May 1944.

OPERATIONS ORDER)
                 :
NUMBER . . . . 6)

            1.  The following named pilots are designated as
instructor pilots for the purpose of conducting transition for
Allied Flying Personnel in the B-26 type aircraft:

                    1st Lt. Hallman, Donald E.
        17th        1st Lt. Shively, Harold A.
        Bomb.       2nd Lt. Bylund, Toroff H.
        Group       2nd Lt. Horn, Ladd L.
                    F/O.    Johnson, William O.

                    1st Lt. Myers, Clell H., Jr.
        319th       1st Lt. Whitaker, Lewis G., Jr.
        Bomb        2nd Lt. Eddins, James A.
        Group       2nd Lt. Saunders, Maurice E.
                    2nd Lt. Wolfe, Lowell J.

                    Capt. Speegle, Charles P.
        320th       1st Lt. Oltman, Wilbert C.
        Bomb        2nd Lt. Clark, Norman B.
        Group       2nd Lt. Flake, Frank T.
                    F/O.    Richards, William F.


                              James N. Luttrell
                              JAMES N. LUTTRELL,
                              Capt., Air Corps,
                              Operations Officer.
```

Orders designating my dad as an "instructor pilot for the purpose of conducting transition for Allied Flying Personnel in the B-26 type aircraft."

Inside there were a number of GIs working at desks or roaming around so I began asking for Capt Roberts. No one knew him or anything about him. While I was standing, wondering who to check next, a little older Italian in janitor's garb came along pushing a broom and stopped next to me. He leaned on the broom, looked me over, and then in very broken English said, "I know who you are looking for. Capt Roberts has been delayed. He will be here a little after 5:00." He pushed away with his broom and I stood wondering what I should do next. While I was still pondering the Italian came pushing back with his broom and said, "Do you like airplanes?" I said, "Yes, otherwise I wouldn't be flying that B-26." He said, "Would you be willing to take a 45-minute walk with me? I will show you something very interesting." I thought, "Well I've got to wait all afternoon anyway." So I said, "Yes." (Then I thought—"What am I letting myself in for?")

We walked out to the B-26 and I told the Sgt he could do anything he wanted to for the afternoon as long as he was back waiting at the plane at 5:00 p.m. I stashed my package in the "26" and walked off with the Italian. We headed for a hole in the airport fence and followed a footpath heading generally south. After a ways, the path turned more toward the west and eventually joined a field road. Following the field road we came to a slight promontory that overlooked an inlet from the Mediterranean and a small bay that formed a sheltered harbour [*sic*]. Directly in front of us, down a slope, stood a large corrugated sheet metal building built over the water and supported by pilings. Blocking our way was an 8 ft high chain link fence with double swinging gates chained shut and padlocked with 4 or 5 padlocks.

The Italian came out with a huge ring of keys and eventually sorted out keys for the locks. He opened the gate enough for me to get through, stepped through behind me and immediately relocked the gates. The building had double steel doors also padlocked with multiple locks. After the same procedure as before the doors were padlocked on the inside behind us. During all this time he had said nothing.

There were no windows in the building and the only light coming in was through the water between the pilings. Coming in from bright sunlight I couldn't see anything until my eyes adjusted some and then I saw we were on a small platform overlooking the water and a narrow catwalk with a railing on one side only led off down the center of the building. As my eyes adjusted more I could distinguish the outlines of two large seaplanes tied up at the end of the catwalk.

My mind immediately went back to 1933 and the Buffalo, NY harbour [sic]. It looked like the same two planes.

The Italian motioned for me to follow him out the catwalk and as we neared the planes he began to talk and from then on he never stopped. I could only get about half of what he said but I could fit it together well enough to make sense.

The first plane we came to looked in good shape and he assured me it was fully airworthy but they had cannibalized the other one to make it so. He took me on board, showed me around, got me in the cockpit, made me sit at the controls, pointed out the instruments (not many), told which ones were missing and that it was impossible to get replacements.

Gradually I learned he was an aircraft mechanic, he had been a crew member on this model plane, he and a couple others had been working on it for many hours to make it airworthy, yes it was an SR-55 *(This should have been S.55.)*, the hulls were nothing but fuel tanks, it could travel great distances non-stop, the engines could be worked on in flight, etc. (My first thought when I saw the planes was "Is this guy Italo Balbo," but I remembered that Italo was killed in N. Africa after having a "fall-out" with Mussolini. Shot down by his own antiaircraft guns. [sic]) I can't help but feel this man was on that 1933 flight. (I never would have had the nerve to tackle the Atlantic in that plane, almost no instruments and not even a canopy or roof over the cockpit.)

We got back to the administration building just about 5:00 p.m. We stood by the same support column where I first connected with him leaning on his broom. He was completely silent now but he did tell me that when he saw Capt Roberts he would nudge me. About 5:10 p.m. an Air Force captain stepped in the back door. I felt a nudge on my right arm. The captain looked around and when he saw me with the package he walked directly to me and said, "I'm Capt Roberts." I was about to say, "Sir, I have a package for you." But before I could get it out he grasped the package, turned on his heel and headed back out the way he came in. No hello, no thank you, no good-bye. I turned to say thank you and goodbye to the Italian, but neither he nor his broom were anywhere to be seen. Even though it has been 63 years, I still sometimes see him and his plane in my sleep.

The Courier Flight

I made a courier flight one time from Telergma up to Sardinia and then back down to Telergma. (I'd been down there training a French crew.) It was an old stripped-out, war-weary B-26*(?)* *(I missed the specific model plane as Dad was talking and I never checked back with him on this detail. However, based on the issues the plane had with starting and comments Dad made about battery/starting issues that he felt caused the loss of B-26s at MacDill Field, Tampa Bay, this courier plane was almost certainly a B-26.)* I was flying, but the plane was in nice shape mechanically and flew well, partly because it was light. We took off from Cagliari *(Sardinia)* and headed for Telergma *(Algeria)* but when we tried to synchronize the props there was no way we could. Finally, we said, "Well, it's a short flight. Don't worry about it." Shortly though, we began to lose rpm so we put the props in fixed pitch. As time went by we lost more rpm so we tried to increase the rpm position but the props headed toward feather instead, so we quick [*sic*] went back to fixed pitch. We called the tower at Telergma and told them the situation and asked for suggestions. We had already tried everything they had to offer so we just kept adding more throttle with a rich mixture setting. We were starting to lose air speed now and soon started to lose altitude too. We nursed it along as best we could and called Telergma and said we were coming in straight, just watch for us. We came in on Telergma at about 50-feet altitude, full rich mixture, full throttle and about 800 rpm. We dropped the gear as we came over the end of the strip. The right engine quit as we touched down and the left about 600 ft farther down the strip. We rolled to a stop with both props feathered and the engines smoking. The crew chief and ground crew met us with a jeep and said they would take over from there and we could take the jeep in. One of the fellows in the ground crew turned out to be a fellow from my hometown that I have known all my life by the name of "Bud" Plarr. We had a great time together for the next few days including a trip in to Constantine. That was when I got the dog *(Mademoiselle; see the next story.)* "Bud" came back to the old hometown, but he died about a year and a half ago. *(Note: This piece was written between 1988 and 1995.)* When he came home he found his first wife dying of terminal cancer. She lived a few years, but they couldn't save her. The interesting thing is he married a second wife that looked and acted so much like the first one that she could have been her twin.

See Dad's story, "The Aborted Mission," for a potential explanation of the difficulties they had in synchronizing the propellers on this courier flight.

Mademoiselle

Constantine was the nearest large city to Telergma. At that time, it was built in two levels on a hill that looked somewhat like a butte. The top level of the city was about 800 feet above the desert floor and was built out to the edges with no railings or guardrails. The road "switch-backed" down the edge of the cliff to the desert floor and the upper- and lower-city sections were connected by elevators that were spaced about every city block. Below both levels of the city at the base of the hill, there was a water source that came out of the hill like a small stream. The city had built a park around the water source and had developed ponds and swimming pools and walkways. During the day, you could always find people congregating in the park, talking and hanging out together. It was a way of life there.

Evenings, it seemed that all of the people of Constantine and the surrounding areas gathered on the upper level of the city. The throngs of people who gathered there would walk in groups and would move together through the rest of the crowd. Over time, patterns would develop with groups and lines of people slowly shifting and flowing from area to area. It was fascinating. If you looked at it after the pattern had formed, you would have thought that it had been planned ahead of time. This was where all business for the city was carried out. People bought and sold land, clothing, food and all other products as they walked and discussed the news and business.

One evening, "Bud" Plarr from Blasdell, NY ("Bud" lived down the street from me in Blasdell, but I didn't know him until he met me at the base in Telergma), went into Constantine and to the upper level of the city. An Arabian man was working the crowd trying to sell some puppies. Some of the puppies would walk behind him and others he would carry. When he saw us he immediately came over to try to sell us one. (Americans must have money!) He showed us the dogs and told us that he would sell us one for $10. Luckily

"Bud" Plarr had been at Telergma for a while longer than I had been and was more familiar with the area, the customs and the city. He bargained with the man and eventually we bought one of the puppies for around $2.00 to $2.50. Some French pilots came along after us and bought another one for about the same price.

Later, with the puppy in hand we caught a cab down the hill. If I remember right, the cab was a 1925 Essex. As we started down the "switchback" road toward the bottom, the driver picked up too much speed for our comfort. He seemed to only use the hand brake to slow the vehicle and it didn't seem to slow enough for the sharp turns and the steepness of the road. When we asked why he didn't use the regular brakes he simply told us that he didn't want to wear them out. It seems like it would have been more prudent to use the real brakes than to crash! In spite of his "conservation of the brakes," we made it down without mishap.

We named the dog Mademoiselle, which over time was shortened to Madam. She was a cute pup. She looked like a German Shepherd but was about the size of a toy poodle. When we got back to the base we treated her with the standard Air Force "bug bomb" for fleas. After we had sprayed her, she stood there for a minute, got a funny expression on her face, then her body started to shake. Fleas fell off that dog like coffee grounds. The sand around her was covered in what looked like a pound of coffee. I'm sure glad we treated her. I didn't want those fleas in my bed!

Mademoiselle, "Madam"—born in Constantine, Algeria but travelled the world.

Dad with Mademoiselle in Sardinia.

Mademoiselle at home in Dijon, France.

Mademoiselle took her place alongside the other two 95th mascots named Falstaff and Stud. She loved to fly, and if I got on a plane you couldn't keep her off. She'd jump up on the navigator's table and sit so she could see out the navigator's window. She would sit there for the whole mission. She eventually got in seven missions. On the seventh mission while she was looking out the window a burst of flak went off straight out in front of the window. She took a flying leap off the table and crawled as far under as she could get and huddled in the corner against the bulkhead, trembling and whimpering for the rest of the mission. You couldn't get her back on a plane after that except by brute force. It was a real problem when we moved her up to Corsica and eventually Dijon, France.

Three of the squadron dogs—Madam, Stud and Falstaff. The one with the curled up tail is Madam. Madam was one of the only female dogs around. She had one pup that was born dead while I was there.

I would sometimes walk outside the Telergma base and there I would sometimes meet an old shepherd. He only spoke a few words of English (though he was learning more words daily) and I didn't speak any Arabic. He loved Mademoiselle. He would pick her up and cradle her in his arms for the whole time I stayed with him. He wanted me to sell Mademoiselle to him, but I didn't really want to give her up. Sometimes I wonder if I should have given her to him.

Dad's mother (Freida May [Wenz] Horn, my grandmother) wrote the following poem about Mademoiselle:

"Mademmoiselle" [*sic*]

She's an "Air Way" Dog
With a "Special Log,"

Is Mademoiselle, Petite,

She has missions galore

Chalked up to her score,

And a rough "Air Sparc" as a treat!

The GI Diet has no food appeal

To this faithful canine

Attached to your heel

But talk about garlic, or break an egg,

And Mademoiselle will sit up and beg!

Mademoiselle is loved right well,

Stories of her affection many can tell;

When she's sassy, she's scolded,

But she doesn't fret,

Isn't she 1st Lt. Horn's PvT. [*sic*] PET?

She's pretty, she's tiny

She's quick, she's discreet,

She's happy, she's loving,

Even rides in a Jeep!

And she's just enough fun

To make life complete

For the Boys at the sticks

In the 95th Squadron and the B-26.

—*Composed by Mrs. Leonard A. Horn, Oct. 12-1944*

Dad's mother, Mrs. Leonard A. Horn (Wenz), wrote numerous poems and songs about Dad and his time in the USAAF. Her other poems are gathered in Appendix 10.

The Most Fun I Ever Had With a B-26

The most fun I ever had with a B-26 was while I was training a French crew down at Telergma. The captain *(French; Dad was helping them transition to flying B-26s.)* who was to be the first pilot was snooty, stuck-up, stubborn, difficult to teach anything and treated his crew like he was somebody but they were nobody. I couldn't help but dislike him although I am not usually of that nature. I don't even remember his name. When it came to flying, he was awkward and stiff as a stick at the controls. His co-pilot, whose name was Cornu, was just the opposite. His *(Cornu's)* rank was apparently the equivalent of Master Sargent [sic] and the Captain let it be known that Cornu came from a poor ghetto family and didn't deserve a higher rank.

Cornu was a relaxed, pleasant fellow and a born pilot. He followed instructions, learned quickly and just loved the B-26. He also had a feeling for the machine, its capabilities and its limitations. I had to hold Cornu back so the Captain could be the first to make a solo landing (I honestly didn't think anyone would live through it).

We were just ready to come back in from a training session one day and I had just buckled into the pilot's seat with Cornu as co-pilot when one of the P-39s from a training base in the vicinity decided it was going to make a mock attack on us which was quite common as the boys liked to get in some realistic practice. I asked the flight engineer who was also the crew chief and was kneeling between Cornu and myself if he cared what I did to his plane. (He spoke Cajun French and was from Louisiana. I used him as my interpreter for teaching.) He said, "She's due for engine changes and complete overhaul when we get in so I could care less." I said, "Then watch this, but keep tabs on the instruments and if anything gets too far out of line, let me know." At that point, I firewalled everything and put the nose down just a little. The P-39 was flying a trajectory to make a pass at our right rear quarter so I started a turn to the right and as we picked up speed I began to tighten the turn. At first the P-39 was gaining on us but after a little bit he was only just holding position. Pretty soon he was falling back some so I racked up [sic] the B-26 right up on her wing tip and came around in a near-vertical bank. Pretty soon I was closing on the rear quarter of the P-39. When he saw this, he put his nose down and dove for the deck. I went right after him and followed him move for move. Cornu was jumping up and down in his seat, grinning from ear to ear and shouting in French as well as shaking his fist at the fighter. The crew chief gave me the high sign and I bored right in on the other plane. As we leveled out on the deck we passed that fighter like it was standing still. I hadn't watched the air speed except to note at one point it had gone way beyond the red line. As I pulled up it was all I could do to control myself not to slow roll that B-26! We were back up to 5,000 feet before I could get throttled back and normal settings on everything. I wish Rosie my co-pilot had been along. He was a P-40 fighter pilot before they assigned him to B-26s. He would have loved the whole deal. It was sort of the end of the world for him when he was transferred to bombers. He considered it truck driving.

I don't know for sure what speed we hit, but the higher the speed got the smoother and nicer that plane flew. I know we must have passed the 400 mph mark because the one time I looked the needle was way beyond the 356 mph red-line. The crew chief swore we hit 492 mph just before we leveled out.

For some time before we throttled back, the *(French)* Captain had been pounding on my back and yelling at me in French, which meant nothing to me, so I asked the crew chief what it had been all about. He said the Captain had been yelling at me, "Didn't I know how many pilots had been killed doing foolish things like that?" only not in that nice a [sic] language. There's always someone around to spoil the fun. So, what did it matter? The next mission out I might get hit right in the middle with an 88 mm. How many pilots got killed that way?

Telergma Crash

The following is Dad's official pilot's/instructor's report on the B-26 crash that he survived in Telergma, Algeria. The full report (Accident Report 440522-504) is in Appendix 5.

1st Bombardment Training Squadron

Bombardment Training Center

APG 762, U. S. Army

24 May 1944

S T A T E M E N T

To Whom It May Concern:

In the crash landing of B-26 type aircraft #41-17900 on the date of May 22, 1944 I was acting as instructor pilot and flying in the right seat of the aircraft. The student, Lieutenant Overed, RAF, was receiving transition training in the B-26 and was in the process of shooting what would have been his fourth left seat *(Pilot's seat)* landing in that type aircraft.

We turned on to the approach for a landing from west to east on "This Year" strip. His air speed was 150 MPH [*sic*] as he rolled out level on the approach and dropped his flaps. About 1/3 of the way down the approach his air speed dropped to a little below 145 MPH [*sic*]. I cautioned him about the low air speed and as we were definitely not undershooting he dropped the nose of the aircraft to regain the airspeed rather than adding any more throttle. This resulted in a rather steep but not abnormal descent. At about 45 to 50 feet in the air, just short of the end of the runway, he started to flare out. The air speed at this time was just under 150 MPH [*sic*], probably about 148 MPH [*sic*].

About 1/3 of the way through the flare out I started to reach over to put my hands on the prop pitch and cowl flaps to be ready to adjust them when we touched down. Just as I leaned slightly to the left to reach them more easily, I felt the plane sort of settle or start to mush. I made a wild grab for the controls and glanced toward the air speed. Just as I touched the controls of the plane, the aircraft stalled completely and we fell the rest of the way to the runway. The airspeed at the time I first glanced at it was reading about 137 or 138 MPH [*sic*]. As the plane stalled onto the runway the air speed was still reading slightly over 130 MPH [*sic*]. I judged the altitude where I first felt the plane mush to be about 20 to 25 feet and the completely stalled condition developed between 12 and 15 feet in the air. As the main gear of the aircraft struck the runway there was a sharp report and it felt as though the right tire had blown out. Overed immediately cut the switches and I cut the mixture controls. Just as I cut the mixture the right gear collapsed completely and the plane veered to the right off the runway. As the plane came to a complete stop I unlatched the hatches and climbed out. I jumped down off the right side of the nose and saw that a small fire had already started in the right engine nacelle apparently around the fuel strainer or the fuel line coming to it.

Ladd L. Horn

2nd Lt., AC,

Pilot.

Ladd L. Horn

Exhibit "A"

The following are notes typed from discussions of this crash with Dad in 2016 after we had obtained and read the official accident report.

I was the pilot who was training two New Zealand pilots because I had a pilot training certificate for B-26s. The day of the crash I was flying in the co-pilot's seat while one of the inexperienced New Zealand pilots was flying as the pilot. This accident report has always made me a bit angry. While the report (440522-504) assigns the accident as 100% pilot error *(assigned to Dad since the pilot, Lt. Overed, RAF, was inexperienced in this type of aircraft and Dad was the instructor)*, there are some backstories that show it was not my fault:

1. On the prior practice landing the New Zealand pilot had brought the B-26 in hard and had blown a tire on the side the landing gear broke during the crash. After that landing, the ground crews simply brought out a new tire, put it on and sent us back out. I suspect that there was damage to the landing gear from that hard landing since during the crash the tire on that side didn't blow (tires always blew before the landing gear broke), and

2. After the crash and the mandatory "no fly" period, I went out to the wreckage and checked it over. I found that the plane had been hit by flack on a bombing mission and that a repair had been made to the wing on the pilot's side (the side opposite the damaged landing gear). When they had patched the wing, their high-speed drill had punctured

the pitot tube and so the air speed was not registering correctly. *(Dad told me that when they were on approach the day of the crash, he felt that the speed was too slow and yet all instruments seemed to be reading an appropriate air speed.)*

As the stall occurred, I took the controls and applied full throttle. I managed to keep the plane straight on the runway so that it didn't spin or cartwheel.

Interestingly, a piece of the prop broke off and went through the fuselage without hitting me or any of the other crew members. However, it did cut off the serial number plate (they were riveted into the fuselage on the flight deck). I picked it up before exiting the plane and have it somewhere in my military stuff. *Note: As of the writing of this book, we have not found that serial number plate but we did find a metal plate from that plane in his letter of May 24, 1944. The plate says "Replace all screws in this panel before flight."*

Also, the report (440522-504) says there was no injury to personnel. This is technically true. However, the first person out was the flight engineer. He exited the top of the aircraft, climbed onto the wing, saw the fire at the engine cowling, calmly walked down the wing, jumped over the fire and walked off the end of the down wing without any injury. However, one of the New Zealand pilots climbed out of the top, saw the fire, got scared, ran up the opposite wing, jumped to the ground from the wing tip and broke his leg.

Additional notes from conversations in 2016:

I started training French pilots first, but then was asked to train pilots from New Zealand.

I feel there are some things wrong with the accident report (440522-504):

1. We lost the left landing gear and left engine, but the report says the right side and the pictures show the right side. I think the pictures were printed backwards and then the report was "fudged" a bit to fit the pictures. (*Note: Dad was likely incorrect here. If his thoughts were correct, all pictures in the report were printed backwards from the negatives and all mentions of the damage and wings have been changed to say "right side" including the right-side references in my Dad's statement of May 24, 1944, Lt. Overed's statement, and the statements of the tower personnel as well as the description of the accident. I also note that in Dad's statement #2 above, he refers to the pitot tube being on the pilot's side and being "...opposite the damaged landing gear.". This would mean that the right landing gear broke and the right wing was down as in the report.*)

2. There are also too many of the New Zealand personnel listed in the report (some weren't actually on the plane) and it leaves out some other personnel that actually were on the plane.

Cockroach Mess Hall

I went into one mess hall on a training mission in Telergma, Algeria. I had moved to Sardinia but was called back to Telergma to train pilots for flying the B-26s. These were men who were pilots but who had never flown a B-26. Not only were these a new plane to these pilots, but the B-26s had some unique flying characteristics that you needed to be prepared for. I was called back from Sardinia several times to train pilots from Australia and France on the B-26 because I had the flight hours and held a trainer's certificate. The mess hall at that time in Telergma was a barracks-like building with windows along the wall. I looked over at the windows and saw that the windowsills looked like rough-hewn lumber. But that seemed puzzling to me because the rest of the building was made from smooth-sawn lumber. I went over and looked and what I thought was "rough-hewn lumber" was really cockroaches lined up all along the window sills. There were so many that they lined up body-to-body on an angle to fit in. I talked to one of the guys who worked in the mess hall. He said that if you were the first one in the mess hall in the morning and turned the lights on, you could hear the "rustling" and "scurrying" as the cockroaches scrambled off the tables and ran for the windowsills. Of course, the tables were really clean every morning. Not a speck of food was left.

About then the Air Force came out with "bug bombs" with a really powerful pesticide. We used them to spray the dogs we had as mascots. When we would spray one, it would take a minute, then the dog would shiver and shake and the fleas would fall off like coffee grounds all around the poor dog.

Crews

Flight crews had been established during training (e.g. my crew was Crew 12A leaving from Homestead, Florida), but flying crews didn't stay together. Some were broken up before they reached their bases in Europe and Africa. My crew was such an example. Leaving Natal, Brazil, our plane was loaded too heavy [*sic*] with repair parts for airplanes and machine guns destined for the Free French army. They split our crew up with Tupper and Summer being taken off our crew and shipped via boat to Africa. Even if a crew made it to Europe or Africa "intact," as missions started, crews had to be reorganized to match the skills needed on each flight. If a man was sick or if he was injured or killed in action (KIA), replacements had to be moved into the crew. In addition, as some co-pilots became more proficient, they were then checked out as pilots and after testing, assumed the role of pilot on another crew.

Flight crews were not placed in the same tent. The Air Force did not want friction to develop within a crew by spending too much time together. Flight crews for the day's mission were assembled overnight and posted on sheets outside the mess hall. So, you never knew who you would be flying with that day. Similarly, planes were assigned at the last minute based on which planes were in flying condition and had been tested—often having been repaired and tested overnight. Therefore, you did not know which plane you would be flying until very close to the time of the mission.

Ground crews were usually teams of about five men. They were assigned to a specific plane and it was their responsibility to keep that plane flying. When planes returned from a mission with damage, the crew immediately started to work. They would repair the damage, fix or replace engines, and go over the plane mechanically, often working all night. Once repairs were done, the plane had to be test flown to be sure it was mission-worthy.

Tentmates were chosen from different crews. Generally, someone from the tent became the "head of the tent." No one elected them, but somehow, they just seemed to emerge as the leader of the tent.

Paul and I became tentmates which was quite unusual based on Air Force policy.

Three of Dad's tentmates. Left-to-right: Paul Roseman, Robert Ringo and Paul Martinson. We were still tentmates with Paul Martinson, but it wasn't long before he split for the "higher level" with the commanding officers. I printed this picture, but it wasn't taken with my camera.

When you transferred from base to base or back to the USA, you could only take with you what you could carry for some distance on your back. When our tent leader had completed his last mission and his service duty was complete and he was being transferred back to the USA, he "willed" his extra stuff to me. One of the best things he left for me was an Air Force sleeping bag. It was such luxury. I could put four or five of the army blankets I had under the bag, slip into the bag and pull several more army blankets over top of me. It was wonderful.

The "Aborted" Mission

I completed all missions to which I was assigned as pilot or co-pilot except for one. On this particular day, the plane I was flying was overloaded. In addition to full fuel tanks, a bomb bay filled to capacity and as much ammunition as could be included; we also had a full crew and a photographer. The plane's load was close to 5,600 pounds, putting it at close to 800 pounds over the maximum load capacity for the B-26.

A typical crew of six before a mission. Donald Burnett (Chuckie) was flying first pilot and Roseman *(Dad's co-pilot from Crew 12A)* was flying co-pilot for him because he was young and didn't have the experience yet. Chuckie stayed in the Air Force and flew Douglas B-26s in the Korean War. The Douglases were designed as A-26s, but it was so close to the B-26s that they started to call the Douglas A-26s, B-26s. Martin stopped manufacturing the B-26s to manufacture the B-29s. One of the air magazines has an article on Burnett. I have a copy somewhere here in the house. I presume this is the plane they were flying on that mission. *The picture was taken in Sardinia, Summer 1944. Donald Burnett is on the far left and Paul Roseman is second from the left.*

A partial bomb load. [*sic*] Picture taken in Sardinia on the flight line. Paul Roseman's *(Dad's co-pilot from Crew 12A)* gift to Hitler for his young nephew, Pennrod. He was always after Roseman to address bombs to Hitler for him.

This is a 1,000-pound bomb.

We taxied onto the runway, and slowly picked up speed on the runway under full throttle. Having used much of the runway, we were finally airborne. As we gained altitude, turned and moved away from the base, we began to work to synchronize the props. Everything we did just resulted in the props moving into feather position. Standard settings didn't seem to work and so we continued to search through throttle and rpm conditions while working to stay with the other planes. After minutes of searching and not finding conditions that would synchronize the props, I called in to the tower to request a return to base. The call in to request a return was not done lightly. In fact, past experience weighed heavily in the decision. On a recent short courier run I had had a plane where my crew and I could not synchronize the props. We had worked at synchronization throughout the entire flight. We had even called in to the tower on that flight and asked for any suggestions from other pilots who had experience in difficult synchronization situations. On that flight, we never were able to synchronize the props. The result was a close call, coming in toward the base with no more than about 50-ft altitude, landing after a short flight under full throttle and having the engines quit part way down the runway.

The tower approved the return. We circled the runway, sat the plane down and taxied in. The crew chief inspected the plane and said that nothing was wrong mechanically and declared it just to be a case of "cold feet."

The issues with prop synchronization on this mission and the courier flight seem to be linked with something that occurred at the training base in Tampa Bay, Florida *(MacDill Field)*. Many training missions took off from the air base at Tampa Bay. They lost so many B-26s because they were "ditched" in the bay that a saying developed around the base—"One a day in Tampa Bay." I am not sure if the true cause was ever determined, but some evidence points to the fact that those whose engines were repeatedly started using batteries only (vs. using the runway generators) could not correctly synchronize their engines and would lose power and altitude. Their pilots would then have to ditch them in the bay. On the courier flight, there were multiple short flights among bases *(Villacidro, Sardinia to Telergma, Algeria; Decimomannu was another stop but, at this point, I did not get the names of the other air bases that Dad mentioned.)* At each location, the plane was restarted from battery packs. The total restarts via battery pack would have been about five. The difficulty synchronizing the props occurred after the last of those starts.

Takeoffs are Dangerous Things!

While most people think of landings as being dangerous (and they are), many planes and men were lost on takeoff. At the time of takeoff B-26 bombers were loaded to their maximum, around 34,000 pounds. The fuel and bombs made any accident incredibly dangerous. In addition to 700 gallons of fuel in the two wing tanks, they carried two 121-gallon auxiliary tanks. (Note: They could also carry up to four 250-gallon transfer tanks in the bomb bay.) A normal bomb load was two 2,000- or 1,600-lb bombs, eight 500-lb bombs, sixteen 250-lb bombs, or thirty 100-lb bombs. Crews were usually six to seven including pilot, co-pilot, *(flight engineer)*, navigator, bombardier, and a beam and tail gunner. The engines were R-2800-41s on the B-26B-2s and generated 2,000 hp each on takeoff.

Missions were composed of planes in groups of six (six, twelve, eighteen, twenty-four…) with three lead planes—lead and two wing planes followed by three more bombers in the same group of six. The wing planes flew at higher altitude than the lead plane on either side (right/left) and the second group of three flew with the same pattern, but all at a lower altitude than the lead planes. To get all planes for the mission in the air and in their position in the formation in the minimum practical time, all planes lined up on the runway and taxiways in lines. The planes were spaced, so that on takeoff, they could be released on fifteen-second intervals. The fifteen-second spacing was only enough time for you to start your plane moving, turn your plane onto the runway, and give it full throttle to start down the runway.

(The) 95th Squadron planes lined up for takeoff. Lineup for takeoff for a mission from Sardinia. This was taken through the windshield of our plane with the Sears and Roebuck camera that used 127-mm film. It was a half-frame camera taking two pictures per frame. This is the same camera that the guy from S2 wanted to buy from me so badly. You had fifteen seconds between planes for takeoff. One plane would be just lifting off when you would put full throttle to yours. It was all you could do to get that plane moving, turn into line, and give it power to take off. Usually you had two planes on the runway at a time. Once in a while you had three. Sometimes to get more planes in the air faster you would have two lines of planes one in each direction. You would come head on toward each other. At the point where you come together you would turn and take off at the right spacing. In the early part of the war, this could be one of the most dangerous parts of the mission because if a German fighter saw you, he could strafe and bomb the whole row.

This straight-line, ground formation and the close spacing was very dangerous. First it was dangerous because of the short distances between planes and the condition of the planes under full throttle while fully loaded with fuel and bombs. But, second, it was also vulnerable to enemy attack. If a German fighter came in on a takeoff formation, it could strafe and bomb the formation on the ground and damage many planes simultaneously. The tight fifteen-second takeoff spacing was designed to spend the minimum time necessary to get all planes into the air.

Planes flew many missions, typically being retired due to damage or after a large number of missions *(My recollection is that he told me over a hundred missions if they could still be repaired.)*. Many pilots and crewmembers did not like to fly planes that had flown over ninety missions as they had been repaired many times and were also worn and had much higher risk of component failure. Unfortunately for the crews, these war-weary and repaired planes under full throttle and full load would sometimes catastrophically fail. Planes would explode while under full throttle on the runway or just as they lifted off. Mercifully many of these disastrous explosions were so violent due to the nearly 1,000 gallons of fuel and the bomb load that they were carrying that there was almost nothing left of the plane. The crew would be killed instantly leaving few or no remains. It was not unusual to find a crater seventy-five feet wide at the point of the explosion. However, perhaps about forty percent of the fires and explosions did leave seriously wounded survivors. Once in a while a crew escaped unharmed. It was rare, but was the best of all results.

Two examples that happened in Sardinia may help to illustrate the magnitude of the problem.

One day at our base in Sardinia, I was in our tent. It was located about five miles from the runway. We heard this huge, huge, blast. After a few seconds, the tent billowed out and then caved back in on itself. We quickly looked out to see what had happened and saw a huge black cloud on the runway. Knowing it was an explosion of a plane on takeoff, we got in an armored carrier that someone had parked near our tent and quickly drove to the runway. Even though it took us several minutes to get to the runway, when we got out, there were small parts of the plane and bits of parachute cloth still raining down on us. The plane had exploded on the side of the runway. It left a crater perhaps over seventy-five feet across and there was little-to-nothing left of the plane. Fortunately, the crew had escaped unharmed. When they had discovered something was wrong on takeoff, they had pulled to the side of the runway and exited the plane before it burst into flames and exploded.

Another day we were heading out on a mission from the Sardinia base. I was in line for takeoff and was scheduled fifteen seconds behind the plane in front of me as was standard procedure. The plane in front of me was piloted by two pilots named Hornberger. The two were not related to each other, but when they found out that they had the same last name, they had teamed up on many missions, partly for the fun of it. I had gotten to know them because alphabetically their names appeared near mine (Horn) and I would see them on the mission crew lists that were posted outside the mess hall on mornings of missions.

That day the Hornbergers' plane was at the point of lifting off the runway and I already had our plane moving on the runway at full throttle to maintain our required fifteen-second takeoff spacing between planes. The moment the Hornbergers' plane lifted off, something went wrong and the plane exploded in a huge black ball of smoke and fire. It would seem like we should abort our takeoff and clear the runway, but, regulations did not allow pilots to abort takeoffs. Once you were in line and moving out, you were required to proceed. At the point the Hornbergers' plane exploded in front of ours, you can't imagine the powerful emotional feeling I had to pull back on that throttle and to abort the takeoff. In any civilian situation people would be frantically calling for you to abort and to do anything in your power to prevent an accident, to clear the runway and to not risk crew members' lives (to say nothing of your own life). But regulations required me to take off and so I kept full throttle on the plane and we took off right through the huge black cloud left from the Hornbergers' plane. We simply continued on and completed the mission.

Accidents like this took their emotional toll on the crews. First, there was the realization that men you knew—sometimes well—sometimes tentmates or co-crew members had been killed. Second you realized that it could have been you or one of your crew. But then there was another emotional aftereffect. Every day that there was a mission, crews would be formed and posted on a board outside the mess hall. The crews were assembled overnight based on the availability of men and allowances had to be made for men who were sick, injured, or killed. The emotional impact on the men when they came out of the mess hall and saw those lists was profound. They would see the list, check for their names to see what crew they would be with for the day, and at the same time would see that men they knew were listed as KIA (killed in action). As the reality of it would set in it would once again overwhelm them. It was quite common for men to see the lists and the names of those killed in action and throw up outside the mess hall.

After the Hornberger plane exploded, at breakfast on the following mission day the Hornbergers and their crew members were listed as KIA (killed in action).

Monte Cassino

The battle for Monte Cassino, was actually a series of assaults on the old monastery that occurred in January, February, March and May of 1944. Dad arrived in Sardinia in April of 1944 and participated in the final, or fourth, battle that took place from May 12, 1944 to May 17, 1944. This successful assault paved the way for the liberation of Rome on June 5, 1944.

The following comments refer to events before the main battle for Monte Cassino.

The problem in the Allied command between Britain and the US troops— sad story—is that they made a good landing up there and were all set to move out and had surprised the Germans and could have moved in as far as their objectives if they moved right then. But they put the troops under a British commander. He would not move until he had a direct command from the British higher officers and until he had the backup troops at the level he wanted. The delay gave the Germans time to move about four times the number of troops into position and they almost wiped out the troops on the beach. *(I believe this reference is to the Battle of Anzio.)*

I believe the following story occurred during the fourth assault on Monte Cassino.

Right in the middle of the most severe fighting, along came an Italian peasant woman with a child who was perhaps about four or five years old. She walked right through the middle of the battlefield. She first walked right through German lines and then across the American line. When she went through the American line, the men stopped firing and stood there amazed that she made it through. She moved on to a small town that the Allied Troops held. Apparently, her home was in the German-held portion of the battlefield and she did not want to abandon her home.

The bombing that we did at Monte Cassino was what the 17th Group and the 95th Squadron had been designed for. Americans had attack bomber forces, heavy bombers (strategic), and we did tactical bombing. Each type of force had different bombing strategies and procedures. While the "heavies" would focus on taking out factories and industrial centers and did bombing intended to discourage the general populace, our bombing gave immediate help to the troops engaged in battle. We carried as many bombs as the heavy bombers but bombed with a bit different strategy. We did horrific damage in some locations. At Monte Cassino, the bombing we did was typical tactical bombing.

In about the second wave of bombing we did there, one of our planes was shot down. We went in fairly low there—quite a bit lower than we normally did. *(Name?)* his plane was shot down. He bailed out and made it down alive and was not injured. He didn't know what happened to his plane and his crew. There were more waves of bombers coming in and he is on the ground with Germans and bombs coming down. Along came a Catholic nun with young kids. She was escorting them through all of this stuff. When she recognized him and that he was American she told him in good English to come along with her. He helped her with the kids. They went into one of the main buildings and they went through passages and down stairs and way into the bottom into some form of a bomb shelter that she knew but the Germans didn't. He survived with her and the kids for a long time. Eventually she slipped him out of there and he made it back to the squadron. I didn't know him personally and don't have many other details.

Bombing the Brenner Pass

As Dad was telling this story he was looking at the following picture of the Brenner Pass from Wikipedia: *https://en.wikipedia.org/wiki/Brenner_Pass* . *The picture is a view from the southwest across the town of Gries am Brenner toward the top (northern opening) of the pass.*

Brenner Pass view from the southwest. Author: Sönke Kraft aka Arnulf zu Linden under the
https://en.wikipedia.org/wiki/en:GNU_Free_Documentation_License

Note the saddle in the mountains from the picture—there is a second one to the right but hidden in the picture. We approached the pass through this second dip on the right (behind the hill on the right) and the second we broke over into the valley we turned to the north and east and paralleled the cornice because that was what we wanted to bomb. This gave more time to the bombardier—more time than a west-to-east pass as described by others *(see story from the 17th Bomb Group website entitled, "Brenner Pass" https://sites.google.com/site/bombgroup17/brenner-pass)*. We found out right away that coming straight in here, you'd slam your bombs into the wall of the pass above or below it. By making the turn as we came in we got the bombardier more time and set the course more parallel to the railroad on the wall (now it is both a railroad and a highway). The only highway at that time was on the valley floor.

The main purpose of the mission was to block the passage of supplies through the pass. To do that, the main idea was to knock the cornice off the mountain. We bombed it with a combination of 1,000-lb demolition bombs and 1,100-lb naval armor-piercing bombs. Many of the demolition bombs had timed fuses so that they would continue to blow the thing apart long after the mission.

Not in the Brenner Pass, but we bombed several similar cornices in the High Apennines and we used that same method there (bomb combo). In one of my missions we flew back over one of the cornices we had bombed a few days earlier. The Germans had a literal army of POWs and slave labor from various camps on site repairing and rebuilding the cornice encircled by German troops with machine guns. Apparently, if anyone balked at working in those areas with the timed bombs, they were shot. I assume that they used the same method to repair the cornices in the Brenner Pass because they always got the railroad up and running faster than you could think. I never got close enough in the Brenner Pass to see anything similar, but I think that was the method they used.

One other mission we went to the northwest side of the Brenner Pass (not through it, but close to it) we went into Austria and as far as Oberammergau *(Germany),* then returned to bomb a location between Bolzano and the Brenner Pass. That was the farthest we ever went into Austria.

Once we bombed the railroad we very shortly made a turn to the right which took us to the east side of the mountains through another small dip in the valley sides. Immediately after we were out of the pass, there was quite a high mountain. We flew our whole formation around that mountain in a clockwise fashion. We then came back across the valley opposite where we entered the pass coming in and went straight across. That exposed us for only about 15 seconds to the antiaircraft fire. Once we were across the pass, we headed southwest toward a point a little below La Spezia. Going back to Sardinia we flew directly over La Spezia. It was a very long route—quite a long mission. About six hours was the longest missions we went on. Fuel economy on the way out, fully loaded, was much poorer than once you dropped the bombs. They figured that an average mission was 1,500 miles and we stretched them to beyond 1,800 miles. Especially in Dijon, we pushed the limits and were often "sucking the vapors" from the tanks. Everyone would be calling in asking for first priority to land because they were out of fuel, but it was against the rule and so you took your chances. They *(The B-26s)* consumed 160 gallons of gas per hour over the full mission; 6.5 hours was about the maximum length mission you could do. One mission coming back to Dijon all of our fuel gauges were reading empty for the last 3 minutes of the flight. Bernie Fineman was on his knees in front of the pedestal timing it with his stopwatch.

Sometimes flight engineers were "toggaliers"—that meant that they could turn on the bomb sights and flip the toggle switch and release the bombs. If a bombardier was out of commission then the "toggalier" was in charge. Often, they timed the release of the bombs by the release of the bombs from the lead plane in the formation (of course these were not sighted bombings, but general drops).

The 17th Bomb Group is known as the only group to have a pilot who flew under the La Spezia bridge. His plane had been hit and was losing altitude. As it did, he dropped into the ravine and eventually was so low he went under the La Spezia bridge and ditched in the harbor. He and his whole crew lived through it. They had notified the Navy PB2Y that patrolled the coast. They *(The PB2Ys)* patrolled day and night which was for rescue work in that area. They saw him ditch. The navy pilot came in low, skipped the plane over the submarine nets, *(and)* he swung the PB2Y next to where they ditched. They had been loading into a raft. They went from the raft to the PB2Y, he hit the throttle, and skipped over the submarine nets again. He took off with the German shore patrol boats firing on him. He made it.

Flying co-Pilot for Paul Roseman

Regular procedure after a co-pilot flew enough missions that they thought he could possibly fly as first pilot he would be sent out as pilot with an experienced first pilot flying co-pilot for him. If he did okay on that flight, he would then be sent out on a first mission with his original first pilot flying as co-pilot for him.

Paul Roseman in San Antonio Rose. This was a fairly old plane, one of the early models. It has the opening on the left side for the fixed machine gun—even though it isn't mounted. It also has half the package guns removed. We removed the fixed machine guns as they weren't much use and were considered excess weight. Very heavy dividers in the cockpit windows date the model. *Note: The plane is serial number 42-107539, battle number 56.*

Paul Roseman, my co-pilot, completed his first mission as a pilot. Per procedure, he and I were assigned to a mission where I flew as his co-pilot. There were eighteen or twenty-four planes that day—three or four sixes together. We often did these missions "in trail" (each group of six following another, i.e. in a line).   This mission from Sardinia was to fly South of La Spezia (the normal path for missions through the Brenner Pass into Germany) through the High Apennines *(Northern or the Tuscan-Emilian Apennines)* into the Italian Alps with a turn-around in, or just before, Germany, with the bomb drop being on the start of the return trip homeward. The target was a highway bridge at Bolzano, Italy used for supplies for the German forces. This bridge was noted for being the highest highway bridge in the world at that time *(Note: The height mentioned is the altitude at which the bridge was built, not the mechanical height of the bridge.)*

The following paragraph is from the same story written in Dad's, "Recollections of 95ᵗʰ Squadron Activities; Sardinia, Corsica, Dijon; 50 Years After the Fact".

This day we were briefed for a mission over Northern Italy above the Po River Valley. As we were still flying out of Sardinia this was a very long mission. They indicated heavy flak was to be expected and had routed us over a gunnery school where the Germans were training Italians to man the German 88 mm Ack Ack guns. They considered this to be safer than flying over the regular gun positions (they assumed the students would be inaccurate, but overlooked the instructors). We were instructed on breakaway to fly down the center of a long narrow lake and that would put us just out of range of the gun positions on both sides of the lake.

At this point the oral story from 2016 restarts

Note on back of picture written by Dad's mom: "Roseman at stick. Rec'd. Aug. 28–44."

We started out on a beautiful summer afternoon. Roseman was a good pilot and had no problems. We followed the prescribed route that had been set up at the briefing before the mission. We were to fly from Sardinia across to Italy near the upper end of the Apennines where we entered enemy territory. The first part of our flight was up at around 16,000 to 18,000 ft at the edge of the Po River Valley. We went past the big mountain face that borders the Po Valley on the northern end of the Northern Apennines. It is one of the biggest mountains of the Apennines and is absolutely gorgeous *(Dad never identified the mountain by name, but it is almost certainly Monte Cimone which at*

7,103ft, is the highest peak in the Northern Apennines. It would have been on their right as they headed on a straight line from south of La Spezia to between Modena and Bologna.). On that day, the view was spectacular. It was the same view that was used as the frontispiece of *Italy From the Air* (a book published in 2007). We enjoyed the first part of the trip as if it were a pleasure trip. There were no enemy fighters and no anti-aircraft fire. We went across the Po Valley in the same direction normally taken to the Brenner Pass. The idea was to make the Germans think it was a routine Brenner Pass bombing mission. As we neared the Brenner Pass, we turned left and went up the valley just short of the pass (one valley West of the Brenner Pass). We continued up in beautiful weather still with no fighter planes and no antiaircraft fire. We went all the way up to the German border (possibly the route included a short sweep into Germany). We then made a U-turn and headed slightly southwest down another valley at an altitude of 18,000 ft headed for the location of the highway bridge just before the town of Bolzano. (*Note added by Dad at a later date:* The highway bridge that we bombed was not in Bolzano. It was due *(on the)* north side of Bolzano coming in from Germany. We then passed Bolzano on the west side. The highway bridge was higher than any of the bridges in Bolzano and was at a much higher elevation than the bridge in the town or the railroad tracks in the town.) We bombed the bridge rather effectively. There were still no fighters and no anti-aircraft fire. As we went southwest from Bolzano we went over the Fineilspitze where they found Otzi, the Iceman, or the Tyrolean Iceman. (*Note: the Fineilspitze is northwest of Bolzano, but southwest of Brenner. One of us likely made a mistake typing/speaking, recording it as southwest of Bolzano.)* The mountain scenery was still gorgeous. Per our mission flight plan we went down the valley where Lago di Garda is located. (For those from New York State, Lago di Garda is a lake about the size of Lake Chautauqua, though perhaps a bit wider.) We were to follow the center of the lake down toward the Po Valley and to slowly lose altitude so that we didn't suffer too much from lack of oxygen which we didn't carry. According to the briefing and the regular routing, by flying down the center of the lake we were supposed to be just out of the range of the large number of anti-aircraft guns located down each side of the lake. As it turned out, by going down the center of the lake we were just within the range of those guns and the guns opened up on us with heavy fire. Shortly the air was full of small bits of shrapnel. We could hear the small bits of flak rattling off the plane like hail off a tin roof. That day they were small enough that they didn't penetrate or puncture.

As we continued down the center of the lake, the small flak continued to rain down on us constantly without damage. But then, all of a sudden, we took one larger piece of flak straight through the center of the windshield shattering the plexiglass and creating a hole. *(Right where Lago di Garda widens out is where they got the hole in the windshield.)* Instantly, the subzero air came in through that hole, whistling and roaring at close to 300 mph and millions of plexiglass splinters and chips came into the cockpit. The sunlight in the west struck those chips and glittered so that we couldn't see anything. In addition, the cold air and the expansion of it through the hole in the windshield created a fog that also inhibited vision. We could neither see outside landmarks nor see our instruments. Between the two of us we could only just about hold the plane level. We did the best we could to hold the plane normal but couldn't tell how well we were doing except that we seemed to maintain speed and altitude. After a while the cockpit air cleared so we could see. When we looked around, there were no other B-26s in sight and the flak had stopped. Roseman turned to me and said, "What are we going to do? We can't see any other planes to join up with." Based on the situation, I instructed him to take a direct heading to home base. *(Note added later by Dad:* Somewhere near the northern edge of the Po River valley *{is where}* Roseman said that he couldn't see any other B-26s or fighters. We came down and stayed between Modena and Parma. Once we got to the Northern Apennines we took a heading straight to the field on Sardinia.) Because it was mid-summer, as we continued to drop in altitude it gradually warmed up in the cockpit. We flew at a good cruising speed toward home losing altitude, going back to our original "sightseeing" mode. Luckily, we saw no fighters.

As it warmed up, Roseman turned the controls over to me and started taking off his flight clothes. Off came the parachute harness, a Mae West, a flak suit, his flying jacket and shirt. I thought he had gone "batty." He continued to take clothes off and to look at his skin. As he got stripped down to the waist, he brushed himself off, looked at himself and let out a sad statement, "All this and no purple heart!" He had always wanted a purple heart and was hoping the plexiglass had cut him enough to warrant it. He got re-dressed and we continued home.

The flight was uneventful except that about two-thirds of the way home another lost, lone B-26 pulled in on our right wing and stayed in position with us until we went into a landing pattern at Villacidro.

Heading home from a mission along *(the)* Italian coast, Sardinia 95th.

We made it back to Sardinia without any fighters attacking us or without experiencing any additional anti-aircraft fire and landed about 10 minutes later than the main mission arrived. I got out of the plane and was welcomed by a fellow I knew from home. He was from a church connected to ours in Blasdell, NY—Assembly Hall in Buffalo. He had found out that I was stationed in Sardinia and he just been stationed there as an antiaircraft (Ack Ack) gunner to help protect our base.

No one considered the hole in the windshield even worth mentioning which made Rosie more disgusted than ever.

Notes:

1. *The flight path for this mission went from Sardinia toward La Spezia fairly close to the coast. They went south of La Spezia and then flew east/northeast through the Po River Valley, between the two towns of Modena and Bologna (both were heavily protected by antiaircraft gunnery). They then traveled to the east of Lago di Garda toward the Brenner Pass.*

2. When pilots completed their required number of missions (64), they were given three options: return to the US which brought with it the risk of being assigned to the Pacific theater, or serve as a pilot to fly officers around Europe, or to sign up for the Air Transport Command and be guaranteed not to fly any additional combat missions. When Paul Roseman completed his total required missions, he made the choice to join the Air Transport Command and apparently was killed while serving with them. I do not have any other information about him other than that he was known deceased.

Dad sent a piece of that plexiglass windshield back to the USA in a letter he sent to my mother—see his letter, Villacidro, Sardinia, June 19, 1944 in

"PART II The War Through the Lens of Love."

The Zundapp (Model, KS600)

Me *[sic]* and Madam in Sardinia on my motorcycle during the one or two days I had after my hospitalization for hepatitis. *This picture was taken in Sardinia looking out from Dad's tent, the "Marauder Mansion" in early August 1944.*

The only time I ever saw him *(Paul Roseman)* more disgusted was the day when he borrowed my liberated German Zundapp motorcycle and drove about 20 miles north of Villacidro. He had just turned around to start back when the cycle stalled and wouldn't restart. We were beginning to get worried about what might have happened to him when late in the day he showed up at the end of a long rope being towed by a ten-wheeler he had flagged down. The only things showing through the half-inch of highway dust covering him were his eyes and mouth. He, the motorcycle and the road were all one color. He was spitting dust for two days after and wouldn't even speak to me. He told me later what happened.

In the meantime, I cleaned up the motorcycle and found the generator had stopped charging due to a cracked brush and the cycle had run until the battery was dead and then stopped. I took an old aircraft generator brush and ground it down to size by rubbing it on a hard rock, installed it in the generator, got a hot charge on the battery down at the motorpool and the cycle was back in running shape.

Paul Roseman. He trained with me as my co-pilot *(Crew 12A)* and flew quite a few times as my co-pilot on missions. He was a good co-pilot and so they moved him up to pilot. Paul is on my motorcycle. Paul made First Lieutenant before I did because I was in the field hospital and missed my promotion.
This picture was taken in front of Dad's tent, "Marauder Mansion" in Sardinia in the summer of 1944.

I originally brought the cycle up from North Africa and everybody told me it was no good, but everybody also wanted to borrow it until the requests became an unmitigated nuisance. One fellow I wasn't even acquainted with was after me continually, always telling me how he had ridden cycles back in the States, etc., etc. [*sic*] Finally, I had had enough of this and so said, "OK, come down to the motor pool and I'll check you out and you can take it for a ride."

I showed him how to start it and how to shift gears. I cautioned him that the clutch and throttle levers were on opposite handlebars from an American cycle. All the while he was telling me he knew all about it and didn't need instructions.

Robert Ringo and Mademoiselle on the left, Barnett on the right.

I then told him to start it and take it around the motorpool a couple of times easy until I see how you are doing and then take it down the road. He went around the pool once with no problems and the second time around I took a picture of him, which I still have even though I don't think I ever knew his name *(His name was Barnett. Dad remembered his name when we were reviewing the pictures in his photo album.)*. As he completed the circle he pulled up beside me and was going to stop. That is when I should have taken the picture. Instead of de-clutching as he intended, he hit full throttle. The dirt and gravel flew, the cycle popped a wheelie, and he rode it for about 6 feet on the rear wheel like he was riding a bucking bronco at which point the torque from the transverse mounted engine threw him sideways with the front wheel up in the back end of a parked weapons carrier. He parted company with the cycle, which immediately stopped as he let go of the throttle lever. He picked himself up out of the dust, looked himself over real well, and walked away. He didn't even say thanks for the ride. I never saw him again that I can recall. I sold the "no good" cycle just before we moved to Corsica for more than three times what I had paid for it. The fellow *(who bought it)* felt he had made a good buy.

Barnett… He wanted his picture taken. So I took the picture while he was riding a large circle around the motorpool…

The US Army Diet

We never ran out of bombs and gasoline. Bombs and gasoline were shipped over and always sent in duplicate so that if one ship was destroyed by German submarines or planes, the other one would most likely get through. No duplicate shipments of food were arranged, so if a shipment of food was lost, it could be weeks or months until the next shipment got through.

While in Sardinia we ran low on food. The cooks were out of everything except canned bacon that came in cans about 6 inches thick by about 2 feet long and maybe a foot or foot and a half wide. They also had a few canned hams, though not very many. We were even out of coffee and the dried skim milk and other rations they normally provided. There was also little food available in the countryside as the cooks had already depleted most of the local supply.

However, about the time we were running short of food, they did find a good supply of escarole. The cooks made up a good bacon dressing using the canned bacon and we had escarole salads for about two weeks. As the escarole was running out, the cooks asked every man in the squadron for any liquor or other alcoholic beverage they might have saved. They asked the officers' club for their liquor as well. There was a liquor that was given out after missions. Each man who completed a mission was offered a shot. I never even tasted the stuff, but even those men that drank regularly said it was awful. The cooks even collected that. They then took a truck filled with all of the alcoholic beverages they had collected up to the northern end of the island where there were fishing villages and bartered for what food they could find. That day the cooks came back with a full truckload of rock lobsters! So, we went from eating nothing but escarole salads with bacon dressing to eating boiled rock lobsters! It was a great feast for everyone except the men who were allergic to shellfish! The cooks did find some chickens for those who were allergic. You really had to prove you were allergic to shellfish in order to get in the chicken line at the mess hall. It wasn't long after the rock lobster feast that a new supply ship got through and we were back to standard rations.

Standard rations included little that was very good. There were powdered eggs that when cooked, yielded a gray, almost porridge-like substance that didn't taste anything like eggs. Then there was the powdered skim milk that tasted awful. You might as well have been putting dirty dishwater in your coffee! They also provided powdered "ice cream mix" that you were supposed to use along with snow to make ice cream! Imagine that. Use snow from North Africa or Sardinia to make ice cream! There was no snow in North Africa and there was none on Sardinia except on the top of the only mountain on the island that was outside our camp. Only once did we have snow on the ground around our camp. It was the only time that I ever saw snow on the ground with orange trees in blossom. The sea breeze coming in that time to the island of Sardinia passed over the mountain *(Possibly Punta La Marmora—6,017 feet)*, cooled and dropped about two inches of snow. Of course, the temperature never got below about 32 degrees, the snow melted quickly and the orange blossoms survived. Eventually the guys found that if you mixed the ice cream mix with the powdered skim milk, you got something that was good enough for coffee even though it didn't taste like ice cream! They would mix the stuff up 40 gallons at a time.

The Tent "Crew"

Ladd L. Horn pilot

James Miller—a younger, relatively lesser-experienced pilot

Ollie Olsen—a relatively inexperienced co-pilot

Bob Ringo—bombardier (we called him Little Bobby Ringo—he was not very big)

Paul Roseman—co-pilot

Paul Roseman and I were the only ones that flew together. Normally tent "crews" were made up of guys who did not fly together. It was only by chance that Paul and I were in the same tent. Paul and I were originally put in two different tents with total strangers.

Every tent chose or developed one man who became tent leader. Paul was in a tent with a nice tent leader. He liked to hike when he had time. He found an old abandoned US ammunition depot. He would never tell anyone where it was, but anytime he wanted he would take a hike and come back with .45-caliber ammunition by the satchel full. We used that ammunition for practice. We had had almost no practice with the .45 automatics. This let us get some real practice.

One day Paul Roseman's tent lost one guy and had an empty bed. Paul's tent leader told Paul Roseman that he wanted Ladd Horn, his pilot to fill the spot. He sent Paul Roseman up to my tent quite a ways up the line of tents. Paul found me and told me that his tent leader wanted me to be in his tent. He told me to pack up my stuff and that he would carry anything I wanted down to his tent. I packed my stuff and went down to his tent. The tent leader told me that I should move in. He told me that the officers respected him and that it would be ok. I moved in. It was very nice because I now had a cot. That was such a relief after having slept only on straw before. And so, from then on Paul and I were tentmates as well as flight-crew members.

I'm not sure why that tent leader liked me and favored me, but he was a very nice man. When his missions were up, he appointed me as the new tent leader and from then on everywhere we went, I was the tent leader. I chose how the tent would be set up and the men in the tent followed my orders. When the previous tent leader left, he gave me a lot of his stuff. One of the best things he gave me was a sleeping bag. Once I put that sleeping bag on the cot, I had a great bed! One thing he gave me that I wish I had today was a pair of "Arabian" shoes. They were made of soft leather in a Middle Eastern style. They were nice and I wore them some while in the USAAF. When I got home my dad "appropriated" them for himself and wore them so much he wore them out. It made me kind of mad. I didn't think he should have been so quick to take them for himself. Usually I didn't let anything like that bother me, but that one thing did.

Luigi's Mother's Laundry Service in Sardinia

While on the base in Sardinia our laundry was done by one of the local women. I don't know her name but she had three sons and a daughter—all half sisters and brothers and her oldest was Luigi. I'll call her "Luigi's Mother." Some of the women didn't want their pictures taken and they all had their own stories as to why, but Luigi's Mother was open and pleasant with us but her own personal story was a very sad one. Luigi's mother is the one on the left in album Picture #60 delivering laundry to us. (note the woman on the right hiding her face.) Even though it was warm summer weather, all of the women seemed to wear black clothes and a long black coat. The kids usually wore coats as well. In contrast, Luigi's little sister always was dressed in a puffy, white dress.

The woman on the left is Luigi's Mother delivering laundry.

Luigi's Mother married an Italian soldier at the end of the Italian war in Ethiopia but unfortunately, he was killed in service. Luigi was his son. She then married a second Italian soldier who was also killed in action. She had one son by him, Luigi's first half-brother. She then married a third Italian man who was inducted into the Italian army. He was killed in action some time at the start of WWII when Hitler and Mussolini took their first actions together in the war. The son by this man was Luigi's second half-brother. All her husbands were nice, but all were killed in action and she was now widowed with three sons to care for. At this point she decided that she had had enough of marrying soldiers, so she married a seventy-two-year-old Italian man. She had one child by him, a cute little girl. Now the job of supporting the whole family fell on her under very bad conditions. She made her living by doing laundry for the guys on the base. Her children all helped her. They were all good and never gave any trouble. They worked hard, carried laundry, collected the money, and were totally responsible. In the picture you see Luigi and his half-brothers playing on a jeep owned by the squadron commander (That old jeep only had second gear and no reverse so you parked it so you could always get going forward.). The kids were good and so no one cared about them playing on the jeep. In the picture, Luigi is the oldest child in the middle.

Luigi and his brothers (half) by a 95th Squadron jeep (the one that had only second gear.). Luigi is in the center—the biggest one.

One day I drove Luigi home on my motorcycle with his load of laundry. He rode on the fender packed in with the clothes because there was no extra seat. He and his family thought that was the greatest thing that had ever happened to their family. An American had given their son a ride home on a motorcycle! How could it get any better than that?

It was a long way to his house. I estimate that it was about 3 or 4 miles, but those kids walked it every day with the big loads of laundry on their heads. In album Picture #53 you see some of the kids carrying loads of laundry. When they walked, they didn't touch the clothes. They had them perfectly balanced; however, as soon as they stopped walking, they had to reach up and stabilize the load.

This is Luigi in front of his house on the main street in Villacidro, Sardinia...
Note the woman carrying the jug of water on her head. All the water in the
village came from a gasoline pump less than a block from Luigi's house.

Luigi and his oldest half-brother picking up laundry from the 95th Squadron.

Luigi's little sister would carry loads of laundry from her house to us (maybe 3 or 4 miles). One day I lifted the load of laundry she was carrying. I think the load of laundry was heavier than she was. You see Luigi's little sister carrying that load of laundry in album Picture #58.

Luigi's little sister carrying laundry.

Paul Roseman (Dad's co-pilot Crew 12A) "hamming it up" with Luigi.

Crying Over Lost Men

Today when I think about the Air Force I break down crying when I think about what happened to so many of the men during the war. I never cried before, even though I cared and felt very badly for them and their families. But now, it hits me very hard.

We had a saying in our group—"Only pilots are brave enough to cry." Pilots felt an awful heavy responsibility for the men flying with him [*sic*]. A pilot could make one small wrong move and the whole crew would be lost. It always weighed on their minds.

I went all the way through training with him *(Dad couldn't remember the pilot's name)*—right from cadet through to the end. We were in the same training at the same time because his name started with an "H" and came close to mine in the roster. He was in our group and he was still in it when we went overseas. I don't know the mission we were on, but we were likely flying out of Sardinia. We were carrying four 1,000- or 1,100-lb bombs (in any case heavy bombs). He was flying a plane and he passed the "initial point" (the point where the bombardier picked up his first sighting of the target—and then you started the bomb run). Somewhere between that initial first sighting and the start of the bomb run, his plane was hit heavy [*sic*] by flak. The plane was flyable, but losing altitude fast and he knew it was going down. He called all his crew members and told them to bail out because the plane would never make it. He told them he would hold the plane for them as long as it was flyable and he would not bail out until he was sure they were all out. The crew members all bailed out and their chutes all opened. He made sure they were all out and then he bailed out. About a second or second and a half after he bailed out the plane exploded. His chute opened, and he came down only a little way from where his men had landed. They all got together and went over to check on him before any of the German cleanup crews got there. They looked at him, he had no face, no hands, no feet and was "clobbered up" in between. *(Note: at this point he was still alive)* They *(the crew)* walked away from him and stood there until the Germans got there. The German officer and his cleanup crew were pretty good to Air Force personnel. The pilot's crew told the Germans that the pilot was a short way away and they would take him over to him. The crew member who told me about this said that that was the closest he came to seeing a German officer crying when he looked at a dying enemy. The German officer looked for a few seconds, came out with his pistol, and looked over to the crew members. He said in English, "My inclination is to shoot him. What should I do?" None of them answered him verbally, but they all nodded, "Yes." The rest of the German crew led them away and they heard the shot.

Dad also told of a co-pilot who was hit in the neck by a piece of flak while returning from a mission. The injury opened up the carotid artery on the left side of his neck. The pilot was able to reach over and hold pressure on the artery, slowing the bleeding. The pilot held the pressure on his co-pilot's neck until the final approach to the home base runway. At that point, he required the active use of both hands to successfully land the plane. In the few minutes that he released the pressure on the co-pilots neck to land, the co-pilot bled out and died. In 2013 when my mother was critically ill with a tumor-strangulated intestine, my dad and sister had to make a decision to give the surgeon permission to do the surgery. There was high risk to the surgery at her age (ninety-two), but without the surgery my mother would have died within hours. My father used the story of this pilot's response to his co-pilot's injury as part of his decision to go ahead with the surgery. He asked us, "If someone is injured, don't you do everything in your power to save them even if they don't make it? Why would we not try the surgery?" (My mother returned home after the surgery and lived for five more years!)

Fred Harms

I entered the army in July of 1942 and was picked up by the USAAF in August of 1942. Fred Harms entered the USAAF in August of 1942. I met Fred Harms when we were in the San Antonio Aviation Cadet Center *(SAACC)* in September or October of 1942. He was a class behind me (they were graduating a class every month at that time). In October of 1942 I was in the hospital for an injury received in training for nearly a month and as a result I was moved back one class, thus joining Fred Harms' class. From then on Fred was always in the same class with me and we were always placed in the same class because of the proximity of our names when placed in alphabetical order. We continued together always in the same Air Force class until we both graduated from cadet training at the San Antonio Aviation Cadet Center. From there we went on to primary training, basic training and advanced twin-engine pilot training. We both completed advanced twin-engine pilot training at Goodfellow *(Dad misspoke; it was Ellington.)* Field, Houston, TX and graduated on July 28th of 1943. We had both selected twin-engine bombing as our next stage of training. We both were shipped at that time to Dodge City, Kansas for B-26 twin engine bomber transition training. We completed transition training in mid-October of 1943. At that time, we were both shipped to Lake Charles Louisiana for combat crew training in the B-26. We completed combat training in mid-February. *(Following)* Completion of the training there, I was shipped to near Augusta Georgia to pick up a new B-26 bomber for transport to overseas combat. My plane was scheduled for lend-lease delivery to the Free French Air Force. (That was the first time I ever signed for $350,000. I was responsible for it if I lost it! That was no joke! It was a big concern. I knew a guy who lost something like that, and he was in the Air Force for many years until he paid for it out of his salary. It never made sense to me because it was a loss to the enemy that could not be avoided.)

Immediately following the pickup of the new plane, I received new orders handed to me as I left the field in Georgia which, when opened, ordered me to Homestead, Florida. The continuing orders ordered me to fly to North Africa via the Southern Atlantic route. Apparently (no proof), Fred was also ordered to Homestead, Florida, with his plane. He was ordered to fly to North Africa via the same route to join up with the 17th Bomb Group which was active in North Africa at the time. I arrived in North Africa on March 11th of 1943 *(Dad made a mistake here. The date for arrival in Telergma, Algeria was March 29th of 1944)*. I am not sure when Fred arrived. The French accepted my plane and gave me a receipt for it so I was free of my $350,000 debt! I was immediately transferred into the 42nd Wing of the USAAF. They in turn put me into their 17th Bomb Group which Fred Harms was apparently already in. The 17th Bomb Group assigned me to the 95th Squadron which was then flying out of Sardinia. Fred Harms was in that squadron as well. *(He may have been in the 17th Bomb Group but the 34th Squadron)* The whole time I flew in that squadron we were familiar with each other, but not regularly together as close friends.

About the time that Rome was taken by the Allies *(June 4, 1944)* and the Allied lines moved up enough to include Naples, Fred started talking about and being quite concerned about his family because of the loss of his two brothers *(we believe Don R. and Herbert—see Appendix 6)*. He also started talking about Hitler and that Hitler would suffer for the loss of his siblings and he was going to make it happen. About then he got word that his sister had been shipped overseas and was stationed in or near Naples as a nurse in the USAAF. He became quite excited about this and decided that since it was so close to where we were stationed that she should be able to come and visit. Somehow he got in contact with her and he informed her that we had courier planes flying quite regularly between Naples and Sardinia because they were sending Air Force men over to Naples on rest leave. She apparently was able to contact our courier planes and find out when one was going from Naples to Villacidro where we were based. He was very excited when he got word that she would be on one of the planes coming in from Naples and was excited that he would see her in Sardinia. The plane that she got on, by the word we received, very shortly took off from Naples, the pilot called in 10 minutes out from Naples and said everything was ok and that they were on target for Sardinia and he would not call in again. That was the last word ever heard from that plane. They immediately started an extensive air search for the plane hoping to find wreckage or find it "ditched." After a reasonable amount of searching they decided that they had to give up on it. They ruled that all on board were assumed to have been lost and presumed dead. Fred flew on a number of the search planes and even flew some of them. When they received orders that the search should be ended, he tried to keep them searching—to prolong the search—which they did for a day or two. However, regardless of the amount and the expanse of the search, no sign of the plane was ever found. This was not only very disconcerting to Fred but also to all our flights and squadrons in the area because there should have been at least some kind of distress call or radio contact from that plane before it was actually down. Some people were sure it was some unanticipated enemy action because this was still a combat zone. Fred insisted that he was not going to give up bombing Hitler until he was dead. He said even though he was coming up on enough combat missions to be shipped home to the US, he was not going to accept going home. He would stay until the end of combat.

I fulfilled my missions on March 11th *(1945)* and returned home to the States. Fred stayed over there even though he was up to around eighty missions (sixty-four completed your duty). The rest of what I know about Fred I received from fellows that wrote to me or had some kind of contact with me afterwards. The word that I received was that Fred was leading a three-plane chaff mission flying out of Dijon, France ahead of one of our regular missions when his flight was attacked by a flight of ME-262 fighters commanded by Adolph Galland. The ME-262s were so fast compared to the B-26s he was flying that they basically had no chance. Galland himself shot down Harms. One of his wing planes shot down another of the B-26s. One of the three B-26s escaped and made its way safely back to the base. The action occurred over either the extreme northeast corner of France or the extreme northwest corner of Germany. I never received clearer information on exactly where he was shot down. Fred's death occurred one or two days before the end of action. *(Honorstates.org lists a Fred Harms from the 17th Bombardment Group whose date of death was April 24, 1945. Incident location: Germany.)*

I always felt this was one of the saddest stories I had out of the war because the Harms family who were very patriotic and nice people from all I had heard about them, lost all four of their children, Donald, Herbert, Joyce and Fred.

See independent information about the Harms family in Appendix 6.

Robert Ringo; Tentmate and Friend

Ringo was around fourteen when several friends from the group he ran around with enlisted in the Army Air Force and received great praise from family and friends for their patriotism and their willingness to fight for the country. I think Ringo saw that and wanted that same praise. In any case Ringo decided to enlist…

Robert G. Ringo enlisted in the USAAF at age eighteen on February 23, 1943 in Santa Ana California. He was assigned to his B-26 flight crew on April 2, 1944, and became my father's tentmate in Sardinia in the summer of 1944. He received the Air Medal on August 12, 1944.

From the time he got in training, Ringo was always getting into trouble. He simply acted like the kids he had hung out with before he enlisted and now he was with a tougher crowd. He was trained as a bombardier, but since he was always getting into trouble he was still only a warrant officer when he was shipped out to Africa…

Flight crews were changed on a regular basis. New crew combinations were made up each night by a young officer in the 95th (I believe he was twenty years old) and there were many factors that influenced the crew makeup. Each crew was usually made up of a pilot, co-pilot, flight engineer, bombardier, a radioman and an armorer. Sometimes others were added, up to eight for special operations (e.g. official photographers). So, the crew members were decided on the basis of which men in the squadron were healthy and free of serious injury. Each position was filled on the basis of how many men were available and skilled in that position. Decisions were also made each day on how to best replace those killed in action (KIA—to this date I can't look at a KIA car without thinking about those killed in action), those who were sick and those who had met their total points and had been shipped home (points were assigned on a complicated basis based on number of missions, success of missions, injury, and etc.). The result was that flight crews didn't always have enough time together to build rapport and camaraderie. Therefore, at each air base, the tightest bonds among men were often formed among those in your tent. Tentmates bonded and tended to help each other out. Even the Army Air Force recognized this since when they moved from base to base, they moved the men on the basis of tents instead of by crew.

Rest leave in Naples. Bob Ringo and a crew that Bob Ringo knew—all officers. This was after Rome was recaptured and they then took a while to get up to Naples to get that area cleared. We had special orders not to bomb any of the buildings with architectural and historic value. In Rome we didn't damage any building that was historically significant. The few buildings we did damage were damaged because the Germans took them over for protection for their own troops—they were "safe havens" for German troops. Then at Monte Cassino they eventually decided that they had to bomb the historic monastery in order to get by the German defense. The man down low in front is Bob Ringo. They were on rest leave. Probably on one of the fronts of the government buildings. The picture was taken with my camera. Bob Ringo probably had it and had someone take the picture. Picture taken in Naples, Italy.

Bob Ringo on the bombsight in a B-26. It was in one of the planes sitting on the line and showed his position in the plane. The inspectors shouldn't have let this picture through the mail because the Norden bombsight was still high secret. The teams that checked pictures and other information being sent home didn't stop this picture. *The picture was taken in Sardinia.*

Ringo was one of my tentmates (he had the cot next to mine) and he was one of the best bombardiers in the whole 95th Squadron. He was very accurate. To this day, he tells of how he and Duensing were able to bomb a German artillery nest that had been placed next to the Monte Cassino monastery without doing any damage to the monastery, and how he had been able to bomb German sites adjacent to the Leaning Tower of Pisa without damaging it.

Robert Ringo with the Italian crew of an Italian tank. This tank broke down
in the driveway into our tent. That is where it remained for quite a while.
Eventually it was repaired and moved on. It was just prior to the invasion of
Southern France while preparations were being made. It was in Sardinia. The
Italian tanks wanted to be part of the invasion force. So they moved up to the
north end of Sardinia under their own power, but so many broke down and
fell apart that they decided that it was hopeless to put them into battle. They
had been through North Africa and everything else so it was no wonder they
were beginning to break down. The Italian forces were very enthusiastic
allies once they were captured. *The Italians called Bob Ringo the "Bambino
Lieutenant."*

Ringo leaning on the Marauder Mansion sign, Sardinia.

Robert Ringo, bombardier, mid-summer in Sardinia laying [*sic*] in a makeshift hammock made from a shelter half (half a pup tent). Everyone wanted to use it because we had no soft places to lay down. We had some cots but they were hard. We also had straw-filled mattress covers. Good idea but they don't work.

Ringo 95th bartering for watermelon. Sardinia

Bob Ringo (on left) and James Miller (on right) writing home in Dijon, France. Miller was noteworthy for bringing a plane home that the ground crews said had approximately 3,000 holes in it. They bellied in to a farmer's field in France, but all the crew survived. They got so low going over the front that the German soldiers and officers were shooting at them with their side arms. This is part of why they had so many holes in the plane.

Bob never flew as my bombardier because he was almost always paired with Duensing (pilot) and Roy (co-pilot). The two *(three)* of them had been recognized as being a very good team and especially accurate in their bombing runs and so they were not often separated. Gunners on Bob and Duensing's crew included gunners Muskovis and McCluskey who are well-known for their miraculous survival after their plane was shot down. *(See the story, "Greater Love Hath No Man" by Charles O'Mahoney, 441st Bomb Squadron.)*

Bob's standard routine before each bombing run was to get up and eat breakfast at the mess hall. But, then on the way out of the mess hall, he would throw up his breakfast. He would then go to the tent, get a "handful" of aspirin and swallow them with about a half cup of water from his canteen. He would then say something to the effect, "There, now we're ready to go." Several of us became worried about the amount of aspirin he was taking and went to the flight surgeon to tell him about it. His response was, "Where do you think he gets that aspirin?"

Robert Ringo in Dijon, France.

...After a number of bombing missions in which he had done some particularly accurate and effective bombing, he was promoted to 1st Lieutenant *(on October 30, 1944).*

Expert bombardiers were vital as they were in primary control of the plane for a brief time while locking in on the target and releasing the bombs. There were instances in which they made split-second changes during that time. In a few cases the decisions they made resulted in serious unintended consequences. My dad told one such story.

…we were sent to bomb a specific target in *(location not recorded)*. There was a factory in the same town as the target. On that mission, we were given very specific orders to only bomb the target and not the factory. The rationale was that after the Allied forces captured the town, they would want to use the factory to advantage in their effort against Germany. That day as… *(the bombardier's)* plane approached the target,… *(he)* identified the target and began to prepare the bomb sight. But, then he saw that it already had been totally destroyed *(by the preceding planes)*. Not a part of the target was left standing.

…*(The bombardier)* did not want to "waste" the bombs the B-26 was carrying that day and so he looked around for another good target. That's when he saw the factory. It had a large chimney that was most likely from a large steam boiler that powered the factory. So,… *(he)* adjusted the bombsight, locked it in on the factory and dropped the bombs…One of the bombs actually went down the factory chimney and the rest went into the plant operations buildings in a neat row, leveling the entire plant.

Unfortunately, the Allied forces had sent word to the town and the factory through the resistance fighters before the mission that the bombing run was only going to target military operations and that the factory would be spared. The message said that they should not evacuate the factory during that bombing raid… *(The bombardier's)* last-minute decision to bomb the factory killed 1,800 people who were in the factory because they had not fled due to the promise that they were not going to be a target that day. When he returned to base,… *(the bombardier)* was demoted to warrant officer. I am shocked that the punishment was not more severe.

Test Flight of the San Antonio Rose

The San Antonio Rose, a B 26C, had been badly damaged by flak and had been repaired. She was ready for a test flight. The pilot who was assigned the job of test flying San Antonio Rose that day was mad about the assignment. He had just test-flown a repaired plane a day or so before and thought that he shouldn't be assigned to test fly this one. Someone else should be assigned the test flight.

His anger apparently boiled over on the test flight. As he took off he gave the bomber full power and left the power on full. When he got to about 10-feet altitude he took a left turn over the armament tent (where they loaded all the .50-caliber shells). His prop wash wiped the tent out completely (We're talking a tent the size of an average size ranch house). He held the plane at that altitude and held it in that turn, just clearing the tops of tents and trees. As he completed the U-turn he came down through our residential tent area at full takeoff power. From there he continued on at low altitude and took the brick chimney off the remains of the German bakery. This took part of the bottom off of the left wing. He completed the U-turn at ground level and landed back on the field where he started. There were some very unhappy high-brass people on the field after that test flight. Normally he would have been severely punished, but because he was a good pilot and they really needed pilots, they couldn't give him a punishment that would take him off flying duty. I'm not sure what they charged him with, but his punishment was to re-erect the armament tent singlehanded. It was an impossible task, of course, but he worked on it the rest of his time on the island other than when he was flying. I think Paul Roseman, my co-pilot, took the picture with my Kodak Box Camera. We always had a camera set up on a desk in the tent so anyone could quickly grab it to take a picture if something different or unusual happened (of course we didn't always have film).

San Antonio Rose? She went back to "repair" again and she was sent back out flying missions. Of course, the next time someone else had to test-fly it.

Album Picture #52 San Antonio Rose B-26C-45 (#42-107359) on that fateful test flight.

Toulon
August 1944

Toulon—the French Navy had 17-inch guns on their ships. These were the most accurate and longest-range guns available in any of the Allied navies. When the German troops captured the French Navy ships, they pulled the guns off the ships and put them in 200-foot-deep silos along the shore in the South of France. These guns then had a range that was perhaps three miles longer than any gun the US Navy had.

Given the range and accuracy of these guns, the US Navy didn't want to go up against them. The 17th Bomb Group was assigned to take them out. They tried to bomb the guns several times. But the guns being in these deep silos were basically impervious to even armor-piercing bombs. In the multiple bombing missions the 17th Group made against these guns, they only ever put one out of commission—and that is an interesting story.

Bobby Ringo was the bombardier who put that one gun out of commission. He was one of (or perhaps, the most) accurate bombardiers that the 17th Bomb Group had. He was a tentmate of mine. In spite of his skill, Bobby Ringo never made a higher rank than "flight lieutenant" because he was always pulling some crazy stunt and getting into trouble. However, on one of the Toulon bombing raids Bobby Ringo managed to put one armor-piercing bomb right down the muzzle of one of the 17-in. guns. The armor-piercing bombs the 17th Bomb Group was using were a longer and somewhat slimmer bomb than any of the standard ones. Being slimmer the armor-piercing bomb that Bobby Ringo dropped actually fit in the barrel of the gun and took it out. Had it not been for a reconnaissance photo that day that captured the bomb going into the gun barrel—half in/half out—the story would have been questioned and contested to this day.

Toward the end of the war the 17th Bomb Group used quite a few of the

Navy armor-piercing bombs.

Given the incredible silos and protection the Germans had for these guns, at some point the 17th Bomb Group gave up on bombing the guns/silos with the intent to knock them out. In order to make it safe for the Navy to approach the beach a new strategy was needed. The new strategy that was devised was to sprinkle the entire beach with hundred-pound time bombs that were to go off erratically from the time they were dropped until a few minutes before the Allied troops came ashore. This did about as much good as anything the Navy could do by shelling the beach. Of course, simultaneous with the dropping of the time bombs, the 17th Bomb Group *(1st Tactical Air Force Provisional)* also bombed the German troops behind the silos.

With this plan in place, the US Navy agreed to come in and attack the shore and land troops. This invasion of Southern France *(Operation Dragoon— August 15–18th of 1944)* has not been talked about as much as the invasion of the northern beaches in France by the British and US troops in Operation Overlord (Normandy; D-Day) which had occurred two months earlier, but it was a very significant invasion, nonetheless.

The German troops *(German Army Group G—eleven divisions to hold France South of the Loire)* only held out four or five days and then backed out. The 1st Tactical Air Force Provisional *(the 17th Bomb Group that my father was in was assigned to this Air Force once they moved into France)* bombed them mercilessly and the Allied fighter squadrons strafed them as well. The German General in charge *(Johannes Blaskowitz)* had been a leader in WWI as well as WWII and had never before ordered a retreat. He was very disappointed to have to retreat, but there was no choice given the intense bombing effort of the Allied troops and Patton's army. The German troops left their dead, their wounded and equipment behind as they retreated to the Rhine. It was an incredible trail of strewn equipment and men.

Toulon: A Right-Wing Plane is Lost

From "Recollections of the 95th Squadron; Sardinia, Corsica, Dijon; 50 Years After the Fact"

(This incident occurred on August 20, 1944. See, "Greater Love Hath No Man," by Charles O'Mahony, 441st Bomb Squadron, 320th Bomb Group.)

During the sixty-four missions I flew as a pilot while in the 95th, there were three times that the plane immediately to my right was lost due to enemy action. The first time I was flying co-pilot for a man that was a relatively new pilot in the 95th. (He had flown a few missions as co-pilot.) I did not know him well and cannot remember his name. We were flying #77, a rather worn, old, olive-drab Marauder with blue-gray belly camouflage. Our position was on the left wing of an almost-new, all-bright-aluminum plane.

The target was Toulon, France (harbor installations, I believe). Going in on the target, we hit moderately heavy flak that was fairly accurate. Spent pieces of flak rattled off the skin of our plane, but neither we nor any other plane in our flight seemed to receive any serious damage. We dropped our bombs and broke away from the target heading generally southward toward home. The flak stopped, there was no indication of fighters, and everyone was starting to breathe easy [*sic*]. The pilot was complaining that our plane couldn't keep up with the speed of the flight on the breakaway and we fell back a little out to the side. I was just debating increasing engine rpm a little when a few bursts of flak appeared well off to the right. This drew my attention and just as I looked, four bursts went off essentially in our flight path. One was outboard of the right-wing plane, one was a direct hit in the right engine of the silver Marauder, the fourth [*sic*] *(third)* burst was just left of the silver Marauder and the fourth burst was in front of us and to the left.

The silver Marauder's right engine was completely severed from the plane and went off on its own almost like a helicopter. The wing instantly burst into a huge ball of flame and the plane started a slow roll to the right. As the plane started its roll, a waist gunner on the right-wing plane took a picture (which has been published numerous times) that shows the engine falling away and the plane in flames (most of the published pictures have been cropped, but a contact print, un-cropped, is more revealing in some ways.)

Picture taken from the plane on his right from the waist window. It was the first aerial photo the cameraman had ever taken. I was in the plane on his left in the picture in plane #77. I was the co-pilot and could see the damage and watched the plane go down. This was the plane that Moscovis and McCluskey escaped. See the story "Greater Love Hath No Man." You see the flak smoke as the smudgy "clouds" in the background (We had gone out and were now coming back toward the base.) The black spots just ahead of plane #77 are four 88 mm cannon shells exploding. The Germans were set up to fire four guns at the same time. We had fallen back because the old #77 plane could not keep up with the formation. My pilot was complaining about not keeping up. But it was a good thing because if we had been in position those shells would have been right on us. *Note: the writing on the back of the picture says,* "You can't see plane #77," but that is incorrect. The small plane in the back is #77. The reason this pic looks different than some of the others is because S2 (Air Force intelligence) loaned me the original negative so that I could make this contact print of the picture. I wanted a contact print because all of the other pictures were cropped or expanded. This is an unretouched/not tampered with negative. S2 handled all the official photography and all of the crew debriefing so they got all of the information first hand. Moscovis pushed McCluskey out of one of these waist windows. It doesn't show in the picture, but a hole about 4' x 8' was blown out of the left side of the fuselage from the nose cone back to the leading edge of the wing.

Cropped picture from the contact print (see previous picture).
As the plane was in the process of rolling over, I could see a large hole in the fuselage reaching almost from the nose cone to the leading edge of the wing and at least about 2' high. The plane continued the roll until completely upside down and then went into a spin. We watched as far as we could see the plane and saw no chutes. The plane in the background of the picture is old #77.

Later we learned that two crewmen escaped but their chutes had opened so close to the ground that they weren't noticeable to us. I believe it was the waist gunner and tail gunner that got out. I have pictures of them, one *(Moscovis)* in a walking cast as his chute opened so close to the ground that it did not fully break his fall and he received a broken leg. Within about two weeks of being shot down they were back with the 95th (Ron Macklin has their pictures and their stories would be worth getting. I'm sure there are people still around that have a record of their names.)

George Moscovis who was shot down over Toulon in plane SN 42-107735, a B-26C. His cast and cane are both German. *Note that this picture was mislabeled. The note on the back of the picture reads:* Picture of McCluskey in left leg cast. *This label was incorrect and caused some significant debate in the 95*[th] *Squadron Newsletter. However it is in fact, a picture of George Moscovis. Dad and I both knew the note on back conflicted with the identification in the story "Greater Love Hath No Man." The picture was eventually shown to George Moscovis and he identified it as a picture of himself. The picture was taken in Sardinia, around September 1944.*

These were 5 tentmates who lived. Moscovis is in the crew with the cast on his left leg (note this may be in disagreement with the story "No Greater Love") *(This title is incorrect. See, Greater Love Hath No Man" by Charles O'Mahony)* McCluskey is also in the picture, I think. This was taken with my Sears and Roebuck 127-film camera (split-frame). This is after the Toulon raid where Moscovis and McCluskey were shot down. Both men got back to the base within a day of each other in-spite of all they had gone through.
Picture taken in Sardinia around September of 1944.

Moving to Corsica

We moved up to *(Poretta)* Corsica from Sardinia on September 21st 1944. We only stayed in Corsica from then until a week before Thanksgiving—maybe about six weeks. Bernie Fineman and I didn't fly any missions together from Corsica.

Corsica. "Shanty town" where we lived while on Corsica. The first larger tent with the shack on one end and the gas drum up on the platform was the headquarters for our 95th Squadron.

This is the orderly tent. All orders came through here. This was essentially the headquarters. That is where you went if you were looking for a higher-level officer. All orders that came in were posted on the front as well as distributed to the men they affected. When we moved into a spot, a whole village that looked like this would spring up in a day or overnight. There were around 1,200 flying crew members. The town would be far bigger than this.

Washing clothes on Corsica. He was a Captain and a pilot. He was very nice. He later took on the command of the 95th. Boiling the clothes in a half-drum using German gasoline... We had plenty of water in Corsica so that got all the washing going. The guys would leave the clothes in for about a half day *(and)* go back and slosh them around. If the water didn't look too dirty someone else would use it because it was already hot.

Bob Ringo (bombardier) doing his laundry on Corsica. Note the white laundry hung out on the lines. No white laundry could be hung out until we got up to Corsica because it could be too easily spotted by observation planes. You could only hang out olive drab laundry until then. Observation planes—up until that time in Corsica we would be observed every afternoon by a German observation plane (a stripped down Ju 88). The Ju 88 was a stripped-down bomber. They had pulled out all of the armor and everything else of any weight so they could fly it high and fast over our bases.

Chow call at the dining tent on Corsica with the guys coming to the meal. This is where the day's roster would be posted on one of the poles. It would give all the KIAs, the new crews... Flew many missions from Corsica but was only stationed there a short while. I arrived in Corsica in October around the second week. I left Corsica the week before Thanksgiving. We were only there about six weeks.

Flying with Schoeps—Told Twice

From the written story, "Recollections of 95th Squadron Activities; Sardinia, Corsica and Dijon; 50 Years After the Fact."

With high certainty, this is 1st Lieutenant Joseph T. Schoeps—see Appendix 7. (Note that one of the following stories says Joseph Schoeps and Dad were flying from Corsica and the other says they returned to Sardinia. I've simply marked them to indicate the uncertainty as I have been unable to independently identify the base they were flying from.)

At either Dodge City or Lake Charles, there was an instructor whose name was Schoeps. A while after I was assigned to the 95th, he showed up overseas in the same squadron *(95th Squadron)*. Because of the large number of hours he had in B-26s, he was almost immediately made a flight leader. He was an excellent pilot, but shortly became known as a "flak magnet." Every mission he went on he came back with his ship full of holes. Once while we were flying out of Corsica *(Sardinia?)* I was assigned to fly co-pilot for Schoeps on a mission well into Northern Italy, in the general area of Brenner Pass. We had a nice, almost new, silver B-26. Going into the target we hit flak like you couldn't believe—that is, our flight did. They must have used our plane as an aiming point. We made it through, dropped our bombs and started to turn around and head back out. The flak was right on us. There were bursts all around and in our flight. I vowed right then that I would never fly with Schoeps again. After several minutes of this our left engine suddenly started shaking as though it was going to shake itself right off the plane. Schoeps yelled over to me not to feather it, but play with the RPM [*sic*] and power settings to see if there was a condition where it wasn't vibrating so badly. Oil pressure, cylinder temperature and fuel pressure were reading normal so I tried making adjustments. After what seemed like ages, I found a setting around 1800 RPM and about half to two-thirds throttle, where it ran reasonably smoothly. Schoeps yelled, "OK, leave it right there." We actually were still maintaining nearly normal cruising speed. The flak had stopped and I now had a chance to check around us. We didn't seem to have any serious damage, but there were no other planes in our flight. I asked Schoeps what had become of them and he just shrugged and shook his head.

Schoeps tried to add more power to the left engine, but it immediately began to shake so he cut it back to the setting I had determined. The engine continued running and it wasn't long before we were over water headed for Corsica *(Sardinia?)*. After some time, a lone B-26 pulled in on our right wing and the pilot waved to us. He wasn't one of our flight. Looking over at him we could see that the outboard wheel door was completely missing from his plane. The tire on the left main gear was in shreds and there were wires, tubes and aluminum pieces dangling all over. We tried to radio him but got no answer. Finally, by hand signals, he got us to understand that he could hear us but couldn't transmit. We described the condition of his left gear to him and told him to plan on a belly landing when he got in. He looked serious, then got a big grin, and acknowledged he heard us. When we got near home he left us and headed for an auxiliary field. We went in for a normal landing and our left engine was still running when we parked. On inspection, we found that an 88 mm shell had come in at an angle such that it either came through our propeller or behind the propeller and hit the valve push rods on one cylinder and then took the cylinder head completely off the adjacent cylinder. The engine ran that way for about an hour and a half. Say a prayer for Pratt & Whitney. God help them to build more engines like that one.

Over a period of the next half hour, all five of the other planes of our flight straggled in, all crippled to some degree, but all made normal landings with no losses.

Not long after this mission (I wasn't flying co-pilot for him), Schoeps was shot down and killed on a mission over Kaiserslautern, Germany *(January 1,*

1945. See Appendix 7). I believe he was flying *New York Central (actually New York Central II)* at the time. I received a letter from a fellow in the mid-West who was collecting B-26 WWII pilot memorabilia. He wanted to know what I could tell him about Schoeps, as he had his pilot's wings, ribbons, medals and some of his printed orders and awards. He said that he bought them from a bartender who wasn't sure where they had come from.

Dad actually told this story again orally in 2016. This version tells a few details not in the earlier written version in, "Recollections of 95th Squadron Activities; Sardinia, Corsica and Dijon; 50 Years After the Fact."

Flying with Schoeps—The Oral Story from 2016

Next few missions after the one with Roseman where we got the hole in the windshield. [*sic*] These missions were the same general-type mission and in the same general area, but not so far up (north and northeast). We followed about the same route that Roseman and I did coming home.

On the one *(mission after the mission flying as co-pilot for Paul Roseman)* I was flying co-pilot for a squadron leader named Schoeps. He had been a B-26 instructor in the USA at the same schools I had attended. He got tired of teaching combat crews and applied for a transfer to combat for himself. They took him up on it and shipped him over to us and he was in the 95th Squadron with me. Because of his many hours of flying time they almost immediately put him in as a flight leader. This mission that I was flying with him was a rather mild mission, no great antiaircraft battles or fighter battles or anything, but we followed about the same route coming home over the Po River. Just as we were coming out of the mountains south of La Spezia, we suddenly caught antiaircraft fire from an obtuse angle firing at us head-on. The first few rounds were close and we got a couple of rattles of small shrapnel hitting our plane.

And then an 88 shell came at an obtuse angle right up through our right *(left?)* propeller and took the top center cylinder head right off the engine along with a chunk of cowling. It should have exploded but it didn't (Note: 88 mm shells were very good equipment and very rarely didn't explode). The engine immediately lost power and ran extremely rough. It was shaking our plane like a bulldog shaking a rat. I immediately prepared to feather the engine and stayed poised waiting for the pilot's instruction. He stayed very calm, maintained control of the plane somehow and after a few seconds thought, he told me, "Not yet." He said, "Play with it a while and see if you can get smoother power under some other set of conditions." I tried various rpm, power settings, mixtures and whatever I could and I eventually got the engine running at a reasonable power output but at a low rpm of about 1,800. He said, "That's not too bad, let's try it for a while." So I told him, "Ok" and I watched the instruments carefully. Meanwhile our whole flight had vanished out of sight somewhere. We immediately took a heading directly for the Sardinia airbase *(Poretta, Corsica?)*. We were gradually losing a bit of altitude, but not much and flying at quite a low speed. But we decided we could keep going like that as long as nothing more happened to the engine.

The engine continued running although quite rough all the way home to the base and we maintained enough altitude to not be in serious trouble. We landed at the base and parked the plane in its regular slot. The ground crew chief was very glad to see us. They had about given us up as we were very late because of running at low speed and power. The crew chief was enthused that he had his plane home in one piece and not in too bad a shape even though he had an engine change ahead of him.

About two weeks later I was assigned as first pilot with the same plane (didn't have a name) on a similar mission. At the end of the mission we came home with no serious events and the plane was running well. We landed, and pulled into the parking space for that plane; the crew chief motioned to me to open the pilot's window and that he wanted to talk with me. He came out and got as close to me as I could when I leaned out the window. He called up to me and said, "Schoeps bought the farm today." We both knew he was flying lead in *New York Central II (42-43308)*. We had no further conversation. That made me feel bad and the crew chief felt very bad.

There was quite a bit of confusion about what plane Schoeps was flying. Some thought it was *New York Central I*, but *New York Central I* had been shot down quite a while before Schoeps got overseas and I knew that personally.

New York Central II that Schoeps was shot down in and killed. I don't know who it (the pilot) was, but when I took one of these pictures it was usually one of our people. *New York Central I* and *II* were supposed to fly forty missions each and then they were to come back to the US to sell war bonds. They were donated to the Air Force by the employees of the New York Central RR [*sic*]. The employees took up donations to buy them. Neither plane made 40 missions. Note that the engines are [*sic*] running when I took the picture. The cap shows that this was a commissioned officer flying that day.

95th Klyne Beaumont and Thomas Eichler with the *New York Central*.

Moving from Corsica to Dijon, France

Dad was only stationed in Corsica from September 21, 1944 until the week before Thanksgiving, 1944, i.e., approximately seven weeks.

The Dijon, Longvic Airfield had been abandoned by German forces on September 10, 1944. B-17 and B-26 groups had bombed the field multiple times in 1944 leaving many destroyed planes and buildings. The Germans destroyed much of what was left as they retreated.

We moved from Corsica directly to Dijon France. The way we moved to Dijon was in groups of three or four planes at a time by tent and crew so that each group included only those men who were associated with each other. After the first group went, a day or two later that many more planes and men would go. A few days later another group would go. The first guys who arrived worked to get the Dijon airbase organized for the rest to come.

95th Squadron pilot Pagett moving from Corsica to Dijon. They gave us short notice. They told us to be down at the field. We had a fairly nice day that day in November. To move quickly they loaded stuff on the cot and carried it down to the field. Pagett had three wives. They caught up with him when the Italian girl put in a complaint that she didn't get her funds/payment as a wife. By that time he already had a French wife. He had a full Catholic wedding with all of the trimmings in Italy. I'm not sure what they did with him. He was a good pilot. We had one plane that the guys loaded without any concern for the balance. It was ok on the takeoff when filled with fuel, but when they got to Dijon, France, the fuel weight was gone and after they pulled out on the taxiway, the plane's nose went up in the air and it sat on the skid on its tail. Everyone stood around wondering what to do with the plane.

95th Squadron area, Dijon, France, likely November 1944.

95th *(Squadron)* Headquarters, Dijon, France.

First aid medical building 95th*(Squadron)*, Dijon, France.

Quartermaster building 95th (*Squadron*), Dijon.

The single biggest issue with the Dijon airbase when we arrived was the runway. The only runway in Dijon was the runway that the Germans had used. At the time we arrived, the bomb craters had already been filled in, but the runway was only about 5,500 feet long. This meant that we could land the B-26s with a light load, but once we landed, we could not take off again. The runway was too short. So, there were no missions flown out of Dijon until the army engineers got into Dijon and extended the runway with metal mesh. They must have added around 4,000 feet. It took them perhaps two to three weeks to finish and since they didn't get started until after Thanksgiving we didn't start flying missions until about a week before Christmas. We preferred to have 10,000 feet of runway, but the approximately 9,500 feet we had with the combination of the German runway and the metal mesh the army engineers had added was ok. Once the runway was completed, we started flying missions out of Dijon.

Left to right—Crew chief of the plane, Paul Roseman, Duensing, Bob Ringo (short one on the end). The buildings in the background are the remains of the German buildings. The tower without a top is the German Tower. The Germans had enclosed hangers, typical towers, etc., while we had nothing of the sort. Of course the German ones were bombed out by the time we got there, so we got no benefit from them. Mid-December 1944.

Tower ruins on the Dijon-Longvic Airfield in Dijon, France.

Ruins on Dijon-Longvic Airfield

Part of Dijon-Longvic Airfield

Ruins at Dijon-Longvic Airfield, Dijon, France.

Ruins of German planes on the Dijon-Longvic Airfield. *The man in the two pictures on the preceding page is pilot, James Miller*

The following series of six pictures were taken at the Longvic Airbase in Dijon, France. They appear to be buildings abandoned by the Germans when they evacuated on the 10th of September 1944. Multiple pieces of wall "art" are shown. The last picture in the series shows an artist's rendering of the bombing of London with three German bombers (Junkers Ju 88s?) and the London Bridge showing through a break in the clouds. My dad took these pictures sometime between December 1944 and April 1945.

The Second Right-Wing Plane Lost *(First account)*
Mission Details—Out of Dijon

Dad told this story twice. Each has a few different details. Rather than attempt to make a composite, both are reproduced here.

We were on a mission well into central Germany and we had to do a turnaround because of *(the)* weather and do a second pass on the target. Halfway through the turn-around, one of the gunners called and said, "There are three German fighters following us way high up." and he pointed them out as little specs high up behind us.

I was flying co-pilot for a squadron leader. I was in the right-hand side of the cockpit. I looked up where the gunner said and I could just spot them up there. They were high up and they were passing us obviously getting ready for a head-on attack. After about 5 minutes the German fighter leader peeled off from the three-ship flight and started a gradual "U-turn" to the left at a fairly steep downward angle so he could get up speed and get set up for the attack. He completed the "U-turn," and as he completed it he lined up right square on our nose knowing as flight leader we couldn't do any evasive action without causing trouble in the whole formation. As soon as he got his sights lined up on us he started firing even though he was well out of range. He was closing on us at a rate of nearly 600 mph considering our speed and his speed. Their fighters at that time were carrying 30-mm cannons so their rate of fire was a lot less than a .50-caliber machine gun—but much more effective too. We could see his shells exploding coming straight at us. His sights were dead on us. Each shell burst closer, headed right for our nose. When it looked like the next shell would explode right inside our cockpit I prayed a quick silent prayer. I prayed, "Lord if you want me right this instant, here I am." I then waited for the explosion. To my surprise the shell burst in the left-hand, auxiliary fuel tank of our right-hand plane. I could actually look across to the pilot of the other plane and see the consternation in his face. The explosion formed a ball of white vapor composed of aviation fuel from the tank which ignited almost instantly and made a huge ball of fire which then streamed back of the plane to their rear. I immediately changed my prayer. I said, "Lord, why them? Why not me? I said, I was ready. I don't think they were." The pilot of the plane recognized immediately that just about any action was futile but he pushed his plane down and out to the right so it wouldn't interfere and cause a mid-air collision. The last I saw they were headed down at about a 45-degree angle in a huge ball of fire. I never saw anything more of that plane or any of the crew members from it.

The Second Right-Wing Plane Lost *(Second account: Dad's written account in, "Recollections of the 95th Squadron; Sardinia, Corsica and Dijon; 50 Years After the Fact.")*

During the sixty-four missions I flew as a pilot while in the 95th *(Squadron)* there were three times that the plane immediately to my right was lost due to enemy action…

The second time a plane was lost in that same position, I was flying out of Dijon as co-pilot for a flight leader. Our target was well into Germany but I don't remember the name of it. We came off the target, made a wide turn to the left and took up a heading for Dijon. We were a ways northeast of Kaiserslautern if I remember correctly, when the gunners called on the intercom that three ME-109s *(Messerschmitt Bf 109s)* were attacking. I looked around but I could only see one. He was at 2:00 o'clock [*sic*] high when I spotted him making a diving turn down to his left. As he swung around he came straight in on our nose. He started firing immediately even though still out of range but he was closing fast. He apparently had time-fused 20-mm shells *(Note that Dad refers to 30 mm shells in the first telling of this story and*

20 mm in the second. This discrepancy is likely because the Messerschmitt BF 109 armament was being changed in 1944 from 20 mm cannons in the G models to 30 mm cannons in the K model. Which model fighter was attacking is uncertain.) because they started popping well out ahead of us. Each one burst closer and he was lined up perfectly with our cockpit. The last shell I saw pop looked like it was about 20 ft in front of our windshield. I cringed in my seat and could literally feel the next shell bursting in my chest—but nothing happened. He apparently veered just a bit and that next shell burst in the auxiliary fuel tank area of our right-wing plane. There was a ragged hole in the wing with white smoke vapor trailing out.

In the meantime, the ME-109 *(Messerschmitt Bf 109)* rolled over and did a split S. He came under through our plane belly up and I could see tracers bouncing off his underside but they seemed to have no effect on him. He completed his split S and came back up under the tail of the crippled bomber for a rear attack but by now the left wing of the bomber was a ball of fire and it was sliding away rapidly to the right and starting to roll with the burning wing high. The fighter broke off his attack and made a further attempt to approach our flight. I could only see the bomber for a short distance as it moved down, back and under our plane so my view was blocked. I know nothing of that crew's final fate.

The Third Right-Wing Plane Lost *(First account: Dad's*
written account in, "Recollections of the 95th Squadron; Sardinia, Corsica
and Dijon; 50 Years After the Fact.")

Dad also told this story twice. Since each has a few different details, both
are included.

The loss of the third plane was the most spectacular that I saw during my tour of duty. Once again, I was co-pilot for a flight leader and the target was in the same general area of Germany as before. We had just come off the target and completed our breakaway when an ME-109 *(Messerschmitt Bf 109)* attacked us head-on. However, either his aim was errant or his guns were malfunctioning because his fire was going all over the place and nowhere near us. He broke off his attack early, did the customary split S, and came back up for a rear attack. He came right up close but he wasn't firing. He came boring right on into our flight and the gunners were all screaming and cursing on the intercom because they couldn't fire on him either because our own planes would be in the crossfire. He pulled into position between our plane and our right-wing plane. He was so close I could see the expression on his face. His total attention seemed to be focused on our wing plane and as I watched he eased gradually to the right and down a little. As his position became right, he pulled his nose up, slid more to the right and let his propeller rip into the bomber just to the rear of the waist gun door. There were chunks of plane flying back in the slipstream as his propeller cut in like a buzz saw. I could see the tips of his propeller bend back and then the propeller came to a sudden shuddering stop and he fell away dropping down into a nearly vertical dive.

The bomber was still holding position in our flight but more and more chunks of plane were tearing away in the slipstream. Within a few seconds the fuselage began to buckle and then suddenly the entire empennage broke away. The forward portion of the bomber stayed in formation for a much longer time than I would have thought possible, but it soon fell completely out of control. I could see it from my position no more than a few seconds.

The Third Right-Wing Plane Lost *(Second account)*

Two or three missions after the one when I was flying co-pilot *(for Paul Roseman)* they had me flying co-pilot for squadron and group leaders. This time we had a very similar situation develop but the fighter attacking us from the front fired about four shells and stopped. He then fired two more and stopped. He was still coming at us fast, but then he rolled over and went under us on his back and did a split S and started an attack from the rear coming back up under our tail. As he got close our gunners were all swearing and hollering on the intercom because they couldn't fire on him with their machine guns without endangering our own planes which would be within their trajectory. He kept coming up closer and closer and closer without firing which I somewhat expected because I suspected he had gun problems which is why he had stopped firing on us from the front. He kept coming up closer and closer because he was sheltered by our own planes. He kept coming until he was between our plane and our right-wing plane at which point he eased his plane to the right at the location of the waist window. Using his propeller as a buzz saw, he proceeded to saw right through the adjacent plane at the weak point where the window was. As he got pretty well through the plane his propellers bent back and his engine stopped. When he did, he dropped out of our formation nose first, straight down. I could see that his own or another fighter field *(was)* straight below us. The plane on our right continued flying for probably 15 to 30 seconds. Then the empennage began to flutter and break off. As it broke off completely, the plane nosed down out of control. I followed the plane as far as I could see it. It was just in a tumbling fall headed for the ground. I don't recall that we saw any chutes out of that plane, but it would seem that there should have been some. Once again, I never heard anything more of that plane or crew. When we landed, as was common they picked up the pilots for debriefing. When I got back to the headquarters they took me into the debriefing room. The officer debriefing me instead of asking questions and asking for descriptions and information, said, "I want you to know there was no such thing as a "ramming" in our combat mission today." He then dismissed me. I gathered from that action that I must not tell anyone about the incident. Many others had seen the incident. Any others that saw it probably received the same treatment.

Ramming was outside the international protocol. They didn't want any commotion or rumors and wanted to keep it out of the higher command.

Head-on attacks were fairly common because they were very effective. The other most common type of attack we received from the fighters was a sweeping diving turn by a fighter coming in on our right or left rear quarter.

I received a very nice commendation from that squadron leader for my performance on that flight. He said he had never flown with a co-pilot with that many combat missions that was as calm, collected and with that degree of competence. Most of the high-mission pilots that flew with him were so jittery and so disconnected or uncollected that they were essentially worthless as a co-pilot.

Squadron leaders were picked by coolness under combat, capable flying, and the ability to fly a real-good bomb run with their bombardier. The actual bomb run took some meticulous flying if you wanted to do accurate bombing. You had to respond meticulously to the commands of the bombardier and the Norden bombsight. Once you went into the bomb run the plane was under command of the bombardier until the bombs dropped. The instructions from the bombardier and the bomb sight came up on instruments in the cockpit. They indicated exactly what altitude, speed, etc. that could affect the trajectory of the bombs.

I believe the same story was reported in The Coeur d'Alene Press, Monday October 15, 1979 by Reporter Tim Hanson apparently after interviewing Van Dusen, 17th Bomb Group photographer who was flying in Gorgeous Betty *that day. The bombing mission was December 23, 1944 from Dijon, France. The target was the ammunition dump at Siegelsbach, Germany. My dad told of how the shock waves from that explosion shook the B-26s violently and, at ground level, broke windows 80 miles away. Dad's flight records show that he was flying a B-26 C45. The mission lasted five hours and twenty minutes.*

Gorgeous Betty

Long Mission to Central Germany

Essentially a mid day mission leaving Dijon, France with good weather. [*sic*] I don't remember the city in Germany, but it was well into the middle of Germany. When we arrived there, the conditions had changed and we couldn't see the target. The leader called in and was told that the clouds would likely move out within a half an hour and so they should try a second pass at the target. We were thirty-six planes and so the turn would require something like 30 miles across. Essentially, at the midpoint of the turn, we were met by German fighters and they attacked us. We continued to turn and completed the circle. The attack seemed to be relatively ineffective. I did not see any planes shot down even though I saw the attacks. When we got back over the target, the clouds had moved out and our bombardiers locked in on the target and dropped the bombs. We headed home. But because of the extra fuel consumed and the extra time, everyone went to reduced throttle and leaned out the mixtures to conserve fuel. The only thing on the radio was pilots lamenting about the low level of fuel. We continued. We made the flight back to Dijon without incident, but as we approached Dijon, everyone was breaking silence and crying that they didn't have enough fuel to make it. So, my flight engineer, Bernie, looked the whole plane over and came up front to the cockpit and reported to me. He said, "We're pretty x#! shot up, but everything is working pretty well. Even the alternators are paralleled." Then he went over the engine instruments on the pedestal and he very earnestly looks up at me and says, "Lt. Horn, all fuel gauges are reading empty." I replied, "Bernie, they have been for quite a while already." He just looked at me with no comment and went back to perusing his instruments. It was against the rules, but many pilots were calling in to land at an emergency field or land early at the base. No one got preference. It was absolutely against the rules. We stayed on course and got in to the base and got into the field in our flight order with all fuel tanks reading empty. It looked like it was going to be an uneventful landing as long as the fuel held out. I made a normal turn onto the final approach—wheels down, flaps down, everything set for a normal landing. We were just starting to feel a little bit comfortable when the plane ahead of us crash-landed on the runway. We "upped" our wheels, flew full engine power, made as hard a turn to the left as we could, milked the flaps up, and proceeded to make a second run. I tried to judge it so that we would land just as they cleared the runway. We made our second approach. As we were getting ready to touch down the other plane was just being cleared, in fact, its tail was still on the runway. There were crash trucks still on the runway that were scattering as fast as they could. It looked like we might just have clearance so we touched down. The last vehicle just barely got off the runway for us. We cut off on the first taxiway we could and headed for our parking area. We swung our plane around into the slot where it was normally parked. The crew chief was signaling us in. Just as I set the brake, the right engine quit. The co-pilot cut the ignition switch on it. I went to cut the ignition switch on the left engine but the engine quit just before I cut it. We were all in a cold sweat. For some unknown reason the ground crew started cheering and throwing their hats in the air. Then they cheered some more. I was filling out the paperwork that pilots were required to fill out after a mission like that. I was too shaken to do the job. I handed the form to the co-pilot and told him to complete it if he could. I told Bernie to get out of the plane and find out what all of the yelling was about. Bernie got out and when he did, he too started yelling and throwing his hat in the air. I motioned him back to the cockpit. He came back to the nose wheel door and stuck his head back up in. He said, "An 88-mm shell had gone through our wing just outboard of the right engine and had taken off the main wing spar. There is a hole in the wing you can throw your hat through." (Note: 88-mm shells were very good equipment and rarely failed to explode on contact). At that point, I admit that not only was I in a cold sweat, but I was shaking. The weapons carrier that took the pilots to the debriefing area arrived at the plane at that moment. I climbed in and went along.

The fact that we survived that mission and that I survived I credit directly to the Lord's direct intervention. The same is true of the mission I flew with Schoeps where the 88-mm shell took the engine head off. I survived, but **not by chance!**

James Miller's Landing in a Farmer's Field— 3,000 Holes and Counting

James Miller was a tentmate with me most of the time I was overseas.

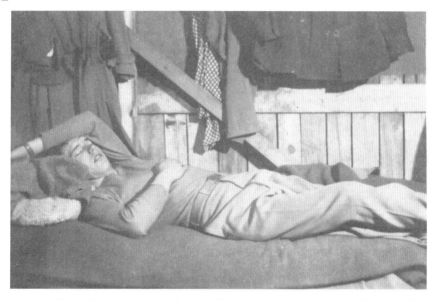

James Miller taking a nap (real nap). He was noted for that typical position. If you went in the tent he would be lying there like that. The tents had wood sides. They were made from German supply skids/pallets that were left in the area because they had been bombed and strafed out.

James Miller was on a mission from the Dijon air base fairly far into Germany. His plane was hit by flak and in spite of still having both engines running, could not maintain altitude. He turned toward home, kept working the controls, and headed toward France and the Dijon air base. He kept losing altitude, but kept working to get back into Allied territory in France so if they went down, they would at least be where they could be rescued. They made it to the main front, but were at maybe only 50-ft altitude. As they went over the German front, the German officers and infantrymen turned their attention to the plane. The officers pulled their pistols and began firing at the plane. The infantry men did the same. Since it was small arms fire, most did not penetrate the plane's inner armor. As they passed over the Allied front, they were still losing altitude and eventually they went belly in on a farmer's field. When they landed, they were all amazed *(that)* James Miller and every member of his crew were alive and okay. The French farmer came out and asked what he could do to help the crew. They said, we are far from the Dijon Air Base and we don't know how we can get back there. He said, I have a car in my barn that I have kept hidden from the Germans, but I don't have any fuel. They said, well, we should have some fuel left because both engines were still running when we bellied in. So, they drained some of the 100-octane fuel from the B-26's tanks and put it in the farmer's car. I'm not sure what it did to his engine, but he drove them back perhaps 200 miles to Dijon. When the ground crew went back out to the plane, they carefully began to account for all of the holes in the plane. They had a sort of contest to see which plane had the most holes. They got to 3,000 holes before they quit. Thankfully most were just the small arms holes.

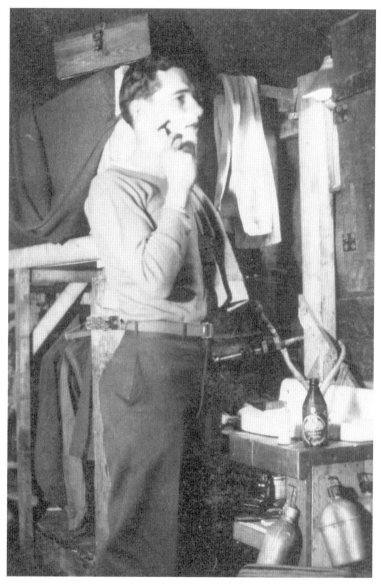

James Miller shaving in Dijon, France.

Note on back of picture: James Miller, Dijon. Had to develop in mess kit under blanket. No darkroom here.

Kaiserslautern

With the start of the Rhineland campaign, we started flying missions that generally were over Germany (not all). One of the first ones we flew was to Kaiserslautern, Germany, The Germans were using Kaiserslautern as a "rebuild/re-equip" site for troops coming back.

The idea of the mission was to stop them from re-equipping troops and getting them back to the front so early. To accomplish that *(the re-equipping)* they had a big set of barracks for housing the troops while they were re-equipped. They had a very busy RR [sic] yard with a roundhouse and locomotive repair equipment. The main center part of the city had become a major crossroads for military traffic to and from the front and from the industrial inland for these troops (three-way intersection). So, the aim was to knock out the railyards, especially the roundhouse, block the traffic through the center of the city, *(and)* destroy the barracks and as many of the troops *(as were)* congregating there.

The troops had all of this old crippled equipment coming back from the front. There was a large area in front of the barracks. They were on a hill with a large slope down away from the barracks and away from the city. As the equipment came in the German crew decided whether the equipment was salvageable. If it was salvageable, they pulled, pushed or towed it into a large parking area. If not, they aimed it down the hill, pushed it over the brink and let it roll however far it went. The bottom of the hill was nothing but a big junkyard.

I actually went there on two missions. Generally, they sent out groups of twelve planes in each group. On the first mission our target was the barracks. It looked like we took out a whole row of the barracks. It looked like the bombs hit square on that row. By the time we got home, they had reconnaissance photos that showed we had just nicely missed the whole row. So, no one was very happy. They immediately started planning a second mission.

As we went out there were thirty-six planes—three groups of twelve each. A different group was assigned to bomb the barracks this time. We were loaded with a combination of demolition bombs and large magnesium incendiary bombs. I don't know the weight, but they were definitely big. Our target was the main intersection in downtown Kaiserslautern. The third group was assigned the railroad yards.

We left Kaiserslautern with the downtown in the largest inferno, demolished buildings, fires like you couldn't believe—I don't know how to describe it—that I ever saw in my life (I never saw anything like this before or since). The barracks and railroad yards no longer existed. Those large magnesium bombs were still burning like photo flares.

Surveillance photo, Kaiserslautern after bombing. Note on front says, Kaiserslautern Barracks Germany.

We returned home with no significant events. We essentially considered it a "no-loss mission," but there was basically no true "no-loss" mission (just a couple—but not many). Someone was always injured, killed, planes lost...

K-Rations, Mac and Cheese & Christmas Ham

On the base at Dijon, France I was known for making mac and cheese. I think it is the only thing I ever cooked while in the Air Force and the story of how I got there is kind of interesting. It all started after we moved to Dijon in September of 1944.

We essentially always missed lunch when we were on a mission. The only way we would get lunch on mission days was if we were sent on a very early morning or late afternoon mission—and those were rare. So, the Air Force gave us K-rations to "eat on the mission."

K-rations were packaged in a cardboard box that looked something like a Cracker Jack box. The box was coated with an olive-drab, waxy coating that made it waterproof. Only a bureaucrat sitting behind a desk could have made this up because only someone who had never flown a mission could have thought that you would have the time, or luxury, to eat while on a mission. There was just too much to do, too much tension and too much enemy fire to stop to eat lunch.

K-rations had very little that was edible in them. Every box had a hard "chocolate bar" filled with "vitamins and minerals and other nutrients." But, they were so hard that you couldn't eat them. We tried taking those chocolate bars and putting them in a can with water and leaving them to simmer on the gasoline stoves in our tents to try to soften them up. After heating all day on the stove, you would still be left with a hard "chocolate bar" in the bottom and some slightly brown water. You just couldn't eat it. We tried breaking them into pieces and soaking and simmering them too, but nothing we did gave us anything we could eat.

In addition to the so-called "chocolate bars," K-rations had some crackers. They were actually C-ration crackers. They were round and about the size of Ritz crackers, but had little to no flavor. Then there were the cans that looked like tuna fish cans, though made a bit smaller to fit in the K-ration box. You never knew what might be in those cans. Sometimes they had processed American cheese that was actually pretty good. It seemed to can well and had enough flavor to be edible. Then there were the cans that were filled with some processed spread that was supposed to be "butter." The butter-like spread was meant for the crackers, but, it didn't taste like butter and had a faint flavor similar to the processed cheese. Since there was no way we could eat the K-rations while on a mission, we would just collect them and save them for later. We would eat anything in them that was edible as a snack.

The mess hall never made mac and cheese. They sometimes got a little macaroni, but there was never enough to make a meal for the guys. Over time the guys learned to ask their parents and girlfriends to send them macaroni and spaghetti noodles in packages. Even if you had no flavoring, you could still cook up the noodles and eat them. It was still good food! So, through a combination of picking up macaroni from the mess hall and getting some in packages from home we would have some macaroni.

One day I was in the tent at Dijon and decided to cook some macaroni I had. I had an empty institutional-sized can that I could cook in, but, having no experience cooking macaroni and being short on water (we had very little water at the base in Dijon), I added only about enough water from my canteen for the macaroni to absorb it all—but no extra. I put the can on to simmer and pretty soon the water was mostly gone, so I added a little more from my canteen. Soon that water was gone too. I couldn't spare any more water from the canteen, so I looked around for anything that had enough liquid to finish cooking the macaroni. I found a can of evaporated milk and added that. Then I added a can of the processed American Cheese from a K-ration can and stirred that in. Then I added a can of that butter-like substance from the K-rations. About that time some of the guys came in from a mission. As soon as they entered the tent, they started saying things like, "What is that good smell?"

and "What are you cooking?" I told them that I was cooking macaroni with some of the K-ration cheese in it. Well, they tasted it and from that time on, any time I made mac and cheese I had to hide it if I wanted to have any for myself.

Paul Roseman (my co-pilot) had been a short-order cook at a restaurant in Washington, DC near the Capital building. At lunch hour, many of the senators and congressmen would come to the restaurant he worked at. Paul would search for meat everywhere we went and whatever he found he would cook it on the gasoline stove in our tent. He would cut the pieces of meat he found into small steaks or "top round-like cuts" and simmer them until fully cooked. He would usually come up with pretty good-tasting meat that way. So, Paul became known for "great" meat and I for mac and cheese.

We never had stoves in our tents until we got to Dijon. The Air Force provided a few tent stoves earlier than that, but there were so few that they only issued half a stove to each tent. We usually looked to find a "top half" because it had a top that could work as a burner plate and it had the connection for the chimney. The bottom half was good if you needed a door into the stove. The stoves were small, maybe 10 gallons, with a chimney the size of a gutter downspout on a normal house.

We used German gasoline in those stoves. In fact, we used German gasoline for a lot of things. There was always a good supply of German gasoline around. The Germans had abandoned jeeps and trucks and other machinery on the battlefield and we would get the gasoline out of them. We also had captured German supply depots that had lots of gasoline. At some points, there was enough around that we actually used it in our jeeps and other vehicles. The German gasoline was a low-octane synthetic gasoline, but it was good fuel. To run our vehicles with it we just retarded the spark so the engines wouldn't knock. And, we used German gasoline in our tent stoves.

In order to use gasoline in our tent stoves we would put a can of gasoline outside our tents so we could gravity feed, or siphon, the fuel through hydraulic lines we had pulled from planes that had crashed. We would have one section of rubber hydraulic tubing somewhere in the line and we would control the flow of gasoline through the line using a screw-type, "pinch" clamp. Using the screw clamp you could adjust the flow so that a single drop of gasoline at a time would come out of the end of the tubing in the stove. We learned that once the fire was going, that the heat from the fire would vaporize the fuel in the line and allow for a steady stream of vaporized fuel to come out of the tube. We would run the pipes underground, under the tent and bring them to the surface under our "top half" cook stove. We would first prepare the stove site by burning any paper we could find. We would leave the ashes where we were going to put the stove and bring the hydraulic line up through the middle of the pile of ashes. Usually we would run two or three coils of the hydraulic tubing in the ground below the ashes and bring the end up through the ashes so that the heat would vaporize the fuel in the coils under the ashes. By controlling the screw clamp you could then adjust the flow of gasoline so that it would maintain a uniform flame. The heat from the flame warming the coils and vaporizing the fuel in the line would generate a flame that was a lot like a natural gas flame. Once you got it right, you could get a smooth, steady and quiet flame. But, if you didn't adjust it correctly, the flame would start, go "whoosh" and then stop, only to restart again and go "whoosh" again. The quiet flame stoves were nice to sleep by; the "whoosh" stoves—not so nice.

About two months before Christmas, Paul Roseman (Rosy) and Bob Ringo started talking about getting a ham for Christmas. While those of us from the North would think about having a turkey for Christmas, the guys from the Southern states thought about having ham. Now, we had tons of canned bacon in the mess hall. In fact, there was so much that they couldn't use it all. I guess someone thought that all servicemen needed bacon and eggs for breakfast every day so they shipped tons of canned bacon to us but there were no fresh eggs. We only had powdered eggs. None of the cooks knew how to cook them or the canned bacon to make something edible. You would get chunks of fried stuff that didn't look or taste like real eggs. Well, "Rosy" and Ringo didn't think the canned bacon would do for Christmas. They had their hearts set on finding a ham. We told them that the French probably didn't even know what a ham was so they would be out of luck.

About two days before Christmas, "Rosy" and Ringo were sitting around and they decided that not having a ham on Christmas Day just wouldn't do. They decided to take action. At that time of year, it would get dark around 5:00 p.m. and so, around 5:00 p.m. as it turned dark, "Rosy" and Ringo set off in search of a ham. We didn't hear anything from them the rest of that evening until about 11:00 p.m. when out of the dark we hear voices and sure enough they were back. And, they had a big ham! Where and how they got it, is still a mystery to this day.

The next morning, Paul Roseman started cooking that ham. He slowly turned it on that small gasoline stove all day. On Christmas, we gorged ourselves on ham!

Paul Roseman—likely location—Sardinia, Summer 1944.

Christmas in Dijon, France. The door to our tent. [*sic*] The other fellows put
the "KITCHEN" on the door because I cooked mac and cheese and Paul
Roseman and Bob Ringo had a ham. We were the last tent in the line.

My Sixty-Fourth and Final Bombing Mission

Pilots who completed sixty-four missions were considered to have completed their full foreign service for the US Army Air Force and were then moved back to the USA unless they "re-upped" for additional service in Europe. My sixty-fourth, and last, bombing mission left from Dijon France and flew into Germany.

As background, my 17th Bomb Group, 95th Squadron was attached to the 12th Air Force when in North Africa at Telergma, Algeria. However, later we were separated from the 12th and flew as a secret force. This occurred about the time we were moved to Sardinia (in mid-April of 1944; *early-to-mid* Rome-Arno Campaign). When the 17th was separated from the 12th Air Force they became the 1st Tactical Air Force, Allied. At this point in the war, the Allied command did not want it known that there was an Allied Air Force that incorporated British, Kiwi and French crews. The 1st Tactical Air Force, Allied, of which we were part was kept secret. We used code names in all radio communication so that the Germans would not know the names and number of crew. My code name was Honk and then crewmembers were Summer and etc. On missions, the airwaves would be filled with these code names.

At the time of the invasion of southern France, Eisenhower and the other Allied commanders created the 1st Air Force Tactical (Provisional) to link the US Air Force with the Air Forces from New Zealand, Australia, Britain and France. This Air Force was to provide support for the invasion against the German 19th Army who was protecting the coast. The 17th Bomb Group, 95th Squadron supported the invasion of southern France from Corsica (about 100 miles from the point of invasion at Hyeres.). Later they were joined with the 1st Air Force Tactical (Provisional) and stationed at Dijon, France. The 1st Air Force Tactical (Provisional) should not be confused with the 1st Tactical Air Force which patrolled the US coast for subs.

We supported the invasion of Southern France *(Anvil-Dragoon)* and then provided protection and advance support for Patton's troops as they moved from the southern coast of France up to the Rhine River. The combination of Patton's troops and the support bombing by the 1st Air Force Tactical (Provisional) decimated Germany's 19th army. The German Army's retreat left a path of equipment from the southern coast of France all the way to the Rhine. The Germans of the 19th were so destroyed by the bombing that they left their dead unburied and even left their critically wounded as they retreated. The German General over the 19th *(Johannes Blaskowitz)* said that he had been part of two wars and had never ordered a retreat, but in this case, he had to and was very disappointed about it. He desperately tried to get his troops back to Germany, but very few made it.

It was from Dijon, France that I flew my last mission *(March 1, 1945)*. On that 64th mission I flew as co-pilot with a squadron flight leader (I don't remember his name). I had logged more flying time than he had. Flight leaders were pilots who over time were selected because they were very "stable" and predictable. These selection criteria were important because it was critical for the flight leader to set a flight pattern that was stable and that all moves and maneuvers would be clear to all others in the group. It was the only way to maintain flight formations and for all other pilots and crews to be able to follow their lead.

Dad (second from right in the light-colored jacket) and crew just before takeoff on his last mission (sixty-fourth) with the 95ᵗʰ Bomb Squadron, Dijon, France. The plane is Old Faithful. *The picture was taken March 1ˢᵗ, 1945.*

Dad told me that he flew the B-26 named, Old Faithful *(41-35031), twice.*

He told me that the second time he flew it (his last mission), it had already been on over 96 missions (Note that the bomb markings in the above picture appear to show that the number of missions was actually well over 100). In general, the crews did not like to fly planes that had anywhere near 100 missions. They figured they had been damaged and repaired so often and they had been stressed to their limits so many times it was inevitable that your chances of being shot down or crashing were very high compared to flying a new plane or one with only a few missions.

There was nothing remarkable about that last mission. We flew into Germany (not particularly far as I recall, though all missions into Germany tended to be long enough to test the limits of the B-26's air time). I don't remember the target for that mission. The only thing I remember is that the flight leader (pilot) remarked that he had never had a co-pilot who had flown as many missions as I had and yet was as stable, clear and sane. In order to understand the compliment contained in his remark you have to understand what happened to many pilots as they racked up missions and time in the war zone.

Flying bombing missions took their toll on pilots and their crew. The danger, intensity, conditions, their health, the fear, death and overall pressure of the war and flying led many to use alcohol to "survive." The US Army Air Force unofficially recognized that many of the pilots were psychologically or "chemically" impaired at least to some extent. From time to time the local command would make accommodations for pilots who had issues and were near the end of their maximum total missions (sixty-four). They would let them fly on missions that were routine and not as sensitive. Sometimes they even would be sent on a mission but not in any actual crew member spot. I knew one pilot that was most likely an alcoholic. Near the end of his total missions, he would fly, but the crew would have him ride in the rear of the plane behind the second bomb bay doors. He would somehow smuggle alcohol on the flight and drink while in flight. This would have been inconsequential as the rest of the crew was handling the plane, except that when the bomb bay doors would open, he would throw his empty bottle out. While the heavy bombs that were released would fall away at the speed of the plane through the slipstream, the bottles would not. As soon as they hit the slipstream they would become projectiles in the plane of the formation. All following planes were then at risk of damage.

The Trip Home

Due to a hospital stay and a period of assignment back at Telergma, I didn't complete my sixty-fourth mission until March of '45. I flew that one in #96, *Old Faithful*. It was a "milk run." A few days later I left for London and good old USA. At the time I left Dijon, there were three survivors from my original crew, we thought—Bernie Fineman, Paul Roseman who had been transferred to ATC after sixty-five missions and myself. I found out years later that Warren Tupper had survived after spending time as a POW.

My arrival in Telergma was on March 11, 1944. [*sic*] (this is either the arrival date or the day that I left for Telergma *see note below)* It was April 22, 1944 *(actual transfer was April 9, 1944—see note below)* that we moved up to Sardinia. My full time overseas was only one year. (I had two years of training.) I arrived back in Boston April 22nd, 1945.

The March 11, 1944 date does not match the Telergma, Algeria orders for departure to Sardinia which lists their arrival date in Telergma as March 29, 1944. Dad was remembering the date they received their orders at Hunter Field, Georgia to move to Homestead, Florida for their departure overseas to Casablanca, Morocco.

The April 22, 1944 date for their move to Sardinia does not match with Dad's statement of "first week in April" in his story titled, "Dumpster Divers." A review of the official orders from Telergma, Algeria shows that they were ordered from Telergma to the Villacidro air field, Sardinia, on April 4, 1944. Moreover, Bernie Fineman's flight log shows that though the orders came on April 4, 1944, they actually were transported to Sardinia on April 9, 1944.

It took twenty-two days to come from Southampton, England, to Boston, MA. I left Dijon, France on March 13th. When we got to London, we got the first decent food we had had in a year. The Air Force had taken over several of the large hotels in London and they had a very good supply of food ingredients. Once the army cooks had good ingredients they made very good meals. We left England around April 1st after a break of about five days in London and around two weeks in Scotland. The boat we took was about the size of the Crystal Beach Boat (a Buffalo area passenger ferry boat named the Canadiana) at about 40' beam and 350' long. It seemed like it "stood on end" for about halfway across the Atlantic. A North Atlantic hurricane had stirred up the ocean with waves that were about 40 feet high. Something like three waves in a row would hit, lifting the bow of the boat continuously higher and on about the fourth wave, the boat would crest the wave and sit there on the peak like a teeter-totter and finally drop over and head down. The deck was off-limits for most of the trip. The storm made things interesting. Once as I was heading down the stairs to a lower deck, my first step was the only one I needed. As I took that first step, the ship simultaneously rose so rapidly that I missed the entire stairs and landed standing up on the deck below. I had missed all the other steps on the stairs.

R E S T R I C T E D

HEADQUARTERS AAF REDISTRIBUTION STATION NO. 1

SPECIAL ORDERS)
     NO. 133)   E X T R A C T   Atlantic City, N.J.
                                                             26 May 1945.
              x   x   x
8.   DP each of the fol named Off's (White) asgd AFPDC 1010th AAF
Base Unit Sq H (Redistribution) this sta is reld from asgmt and dy
thereto and WP his home or unit rendezvous as shown via Separation
Center listed for TDY as required for processing revert to inactive
status under RR1-5, par 4 not by reason of physical disability.
Terminal lv and WD AGO Form No. 53-98 auth. CO Separation Center
will issue orders specifying amt of terminal lv, date of release
from Separation Center and date Off reverts to inactive status.
AUS apmts held continue in force during the present emerg plus
six (6) months unless sooner terminated DP. AUS-AC apmts terminate
on EDCMR date. FCS. TDN. TPA. 5C1-31 P 431-01 C2 03 07 08 212/
5C425. Auth: TWX Hq AAF 10 May 45, RR1-5 Par 4 and TWX 1201002 Hq
AAFPDC 12 May 45 and WD Cir 485, 44. (O-1948) (O-1944). (O-1945).

TO: 1st SvC Fort Devens Separation Center, Fort Devens, Mass.
EDCMR and reporting date 6 Jun 45.
       #   Each Off auth ten (10) days delay enroute.
#CAPT   (1035) WILLIS E COBB   0711341   AC   Hardy Hill, Lebanon
                                                    NH
#CAPT   (1035) PETER T NANOS   0688754   AC   305 Hubbard Ave,
                                                    Stamford, Conn
 1ST LT (1051) RUSSELL H TABER   0800965   AC   293 S Mammoth Road
                                                    Manchester, NH
#CAPT   (1081) WILLIAM R CUTLER   0790804   AC   97 Summit Ave
                                                    Wollaston, Mass
#1ST LT (1035) NORMAN A FAGERQUIST   28 Andler St,
                                     0717767   AC   Worcester, Mass
#1ST LT (1035) EDWIN T MacBRIDE   0766306   AC   380 Cushing St,
                                                    Hingham, Mass
 1ST LT (1034) DANIEL H SALTZMAN   0722368   AC   107 Tyndall Ave,
                                                    Providence, RI

TO: 2d SvC Fort Dix Separation Center, Fort Dix, NJ.
EDCMR and reporting date 4 Jun 45.
       # Each Off auth eight (8) days delay enroute.

#1ST LT (1034) JAMES B KANE JR   0723370   AC   20 Navejo Parkway
                                                    Buffalo, NY
 1ST LT (1035) EDWARD D GRZEGORZEWSKI   1022 Landsdown Ave
                                     02057752 AC   Camden, NJ
#1ST LT (1035) JOHN J DEVINE JR   0752323   AC   263 Second Ave
                                                    Albany, NY
#1ST LT (1035) RICHARD McCOMB   0722514   AC   4295 Napier Ave,
                                                    New York, NY
 1ST LT (1034) RICHARD D DORION   0703965   AC   805 Linden Ave
                                                    Ridgefield, NJ
#CAPT   (1091) NORMAN COSBY   0441727   AC   161 Elk Ave,
                       R E S T R I C T E D   New Rochelle, NY
                             - 1 -

*Page 1—Orders to the Fort Dix separation center to report on June 4, 1945
with eight days of travel time.*

R E S T R I C T E D

Par 8 SO #133, Hq AAFRS No. 1, Atlantic City, NJ, 26 May 45 Cont'd

#1ST LT (1034) RAYMOND L BECKER	02060456 AC	28 Haverford Road Runne Mede, NJ
#1ST LT (1034) JOSEPH A CAMELIO	0691718 AC	38 Tilden St, Rochester, NY
#1ST LT (1091) EDWARD J GEHL	0826916 AC	644 St Mary St, Bronx, NY
#1ST LT (1035) LEON SHEWELOFF	0765850 AC	2754 Bronx Park E Bronx, NY
#1ST LT (1082) CHARLES F GLOCK	0816294 AC	6 Fairview Ave, South River, NJ
#1ST LT (1035) DOMENIC J GERMANO	0750136 AC	360 6th St, Rochester, NY
#CAPT (1035) JOHN S JACYNA	0749717 AC	26 Vanderveer St, Amsterdam, NY
#1ST LT (1034) NEIL W JOHNSON	0718327 AC	458 Prospect Ave, Mt Vernon, NY
#2D LT (1035) JOHN D W LAMPHEAR	0668972 AC	RD #2, Rome, NY
1ST LT (1051) ROBERT A CLEMENT	0694123 AC	242 Oxford Ave, Buffalo, NY
#1ST LT (1054) ROBERT C COTTRELL	0801799 AC	1129 79th St, Brooklyn, NY
#1ST LT (1034) MORTON S KLAYMAN	02060440 AC	532 Summit Ave Schenectady, NY
#CAPT (2162) ROBERT J LYNCH	02040747 AC	566 4th St, Brooklyn, NY
#CAPT (1091) WILLIAM D LAWSON	0758585 AC	777 Webster Ave New Rochelle, NY
#1ST LT (1035) HAROLD L GLASSER	0716724 AC	661 Willoughby Ave, Brooklyn, NY
#1ST LT (1082) LADD L HORN	0687596 AC	54 Salisbury Ave, Blasdell Branch Buffalo, 19 NY
#FLT O (1026) JAY KATTELMAN	T802 AUS	522 Spruce St, Philadelphia, Penna

TO: 1st SvC Fort Devens Separation Center, Fort Devens, Mass.
EDCMR and reporting date 5 Jun 45.

1ST LT (1082) WILLIAM A HAHN JR	0815689 AC	North Woodbury, Conn
1ST LT (1034) WINFIELD J MEANS	02061114 AC	165 Clifton St, Portland, Me

x   x   x

BY ORDER OF COLONEL SNYDER:

FREDRIC P AMELI
Major, AC
Adjutant

OFFICIAL: *[signature]*
FREDRIC P AMELI
Major, AC
Adjutant

R E S T R I C T E D
- 2 -
SSN as shown are primary and shipping SSN. (AAF Ltr 35-10 C).

Page 2—Orders to the Fort Dix separation center to report on June 4, 1945 with eight days of travel time showing Dad's name.

Army separation qualification record issued June 24, 1945 prior to Dad's discharge at Fort Dix.

LIBER 17 PAGE 173

Army of the United States

CERTIFICATE OF SERVICE

This is to certify that

FIRST LIEUTENANT LADD L. HORN O 687 596 AIR CORPS
17TH BOMB GROUP 95TH BOMB SQUADRON EUROPEAN THEATER OF OPERATIONS

honorably served in active Federal Service

in the Army of the United States from

29 JULY 1943   *to*   3 JULY 1945

Given at SEPARATION CENTER, FORT DIX, NEW JERSEY

on the 3RD *day of* JUNE 1945

FOR THE COMMANDING OFFICER:

CHRIS S. SCOTT
MAJOR, INFANTRY

Certificate of service issued at Fort Dix, NJ prior to discharge. Note that the 29 July 1943 date is the day after he graduated from Ellington Air Force Base, not when he entered the service.

MILITARY RECORD AND REPORT OF SEPARATION

LIBER 17 PAGE 174   CERTIFICATE OF SERVICE

1. LAST NAME - FIRST NAME - MIDDLE INITIAL		2. ARMY SERIAL NUMBER	3. AGE, GRADE	4. ARM OR SERVICE	5. COMPONENT
HORN, LADD L.		0687596	1ST LT.	AC	AUS
6. ORGANIZATION		7. DATE OF RELIEF FROM ACTIVE DUTY	8. PLACE OF SEPARATION		
17TH BOMB GROUP 95th BOMB SQUADRON EUROPEAN THEATER OF OPERATIONS		3 JULY 45	SEPARATION CENTER FORT DIX, NEW JERSEY		
9. PERMANENT ADDRESS FOR MAILING PURPOSES		10. DATE OF BIRTH	11. PLACE OF BIRTH		
54 SALISBURY AVENUE, BLASDELL BRANCH, BUFFALO, 10, NEW YORK		28 JUL 1921	TOWN OF HAMBURG NEW YORK		
12. ADDRESS FROM WHICH EMPLOYMENT WILL BE SOUGHT		13. COLOR EYES	14. COLOR HAIR	15. HEIGHT	16. WEIGHT	17. NO. OF DEPENDENTS
SEE 9		BLUE	BROWN	5'11"	160 Lbs	0

18. RACE		19. MARITAL STATUS		20. U.S. CITIZEN	21. CIVILIAN OCCUPATION AND NO.
WHITE NEGRO OTHER (specify)	SINGLE MARRIED OTHER (specify)			YES NO	
X	X			X	MAINTENANCE MAN 5-83.64

MILITARY HISTORY

SELECTIVE SERVICE DATA	22. REGISTERED YES NO	23. LOCAL S. S. BOARD NUMBER	24. COUNTY AND STATE		25. HOME ADDRESS AT TIME OF ENTRY ON ACTIVE DUTY
	X		OSCEOLA FLORIDA		SEE 9

1945 JUL 16 PM 3 23

26. DATE OF ENTRY ON ACTIVE DUTY	27. MILITARY OCCUPATIONAL SPECIALTY AND NO.
29 JULY 1943	PILOT B-26 1082

28. BATTLES AND CAMPAIGNS
EUROPEAN THEATER OF OPERATIONS   ROME-ARNO   SOUTHERN FRANCE GERMANY

29. DECORATIONS AND CITATIONS
EUROPEAN AFRICAN MIDDLE EASTERN THEATER CAMPAIGN RIBBON AIR MEDAL WITH 9 OAK LEAF CLUSTERS CROIX de GUERRE AVEC PALME

30. WOUNDS RECEIVED IN ACTION
NONE

31. SERVICE SCHOOLS ATTENDED	32.	SERVICE OUTSIDE CONTINENTAL U. S. AND RETURN	
ADVANCED TWIN ENGINED FLYING, ELLINGTON FIELD, TEXAS B-26 (*)	DATE OF DEPARTURE	DESTINATION	DATE OF ARRIVAL
	16 MAR 44	EUROPEAN TH.	23 MAR 44
33. REASON AND AUTHORITY FOR SEPARATION	6 APRIL 45	U. S. A.	23 APR 45
WD. CIR. 485 1944 RR 1-5 DEMOBILIZATION			

34.	CONTINENTAL SERVICE			FOREIGN SERVICE			35.	EDUCATION (years)		
YEARS	MONTHS	DAYS	YEARS	MONTHS	DAYS		GRAMMAR SCHOOL	HIGH SCHOOL	COLLEGE
0	9	27	1	1	7		8	4	0

INSURANCE NOTICE

IMPORTANT IF PREMIUM IS NOT PAID WHEN DUE OR WITHIN THIRTY-ONE DAYS THEREAFTER, INSURANCE WILL LAPSE. MAKE CHECKS OR MONEY ORDERS PAYABLE TO THE TREASURER OF THE U. S. AND FORWARD TO COLLECTIONS SUBDIVISION, VETERANS ADMINISTRATION, WASHINGTON 25, D. C.

36. KIND OF INSURANCE	37. HOW PAID	38. Effective Date of Allotment Discontinuance	39. Date of Next Premium Due (one month after 38)	40. PREMIUM DUE EACH MONTH	41. INTENTION OF VETERAN TO
Nat. Serv.	U.S. Govt.	None	Allotment	Direct to V.A.					Continue	Continue only	Discontinue
X			X		31 MAY 45	30 JUN 45	$ 6.50	X		

42.	43. REMARKS (This space for completion of above items or entry of other items specified)
RIGHT THUMB PRINT	(*) TRANSITION, DODGE CITY, KANSAS
LAPEL BUTTON ISSUED.
Supplemental Final Payment of $74.30 pd on you # _____ July 45 B/o of R.M.FIX, Major FD, Sym #211-948 Ft Dix, N.J.

STATE OF NEW YORK
ERIE CO. CLERK'S OFFICE

ERIE COUNTY CLERK'S OFFICE

44. SIGNATURE OF OFFICER BEING SEPARATED	45. PERSONNEL OFFICER (Type name, grade and organization - Signature)
Ladd L. Horn	GEORGE GELARDI 2ND LT., AUS George Gelardi

WD AGO FORM 53-98 1 November 1944   This form supersedes all previous editions of WD A(G) Forms 53 and 280 for officers entitled to a Certificate of Service, which will not be used after receipt of this revision.

Certificate of service issued at Fort Dix, NJ prior to discharge. The dates are incorrect. First, note that the issue date is June 3, 1945, more than a month before his discharge. The final service date of July 3rd is incorrect. Compare this certificate with the letters Dad wrote from NJ (see "PART II The War Through the Lens of Love") in which he says that his discharge was delayed until after July 9th due to administrative delays at Fort Dix. Dad wrote on the envelope containing this document that the correct date for his last day of service was July 11, 1945 and that at one point it had been "officially corrected" but still showed up wrong in documents.

PART II

The War Through The Lens of Love

Dad's Letters

From July 11, 1942 when he left for Fort Niagara as a draftee, to the day he was discharged, July 11, 1945, Dad wrote faithfully and often to Ethel J. O'Neil (his girlfriend at the time, future wife September 15, 1945, and my mother—see Appendix 1). Mom kept three hundred thirty-nine of those letters in two boxes in their attic. The following are excerpts from those letters arranged in chronological order (with two key exceptions). They are the real-time, "unfiltered" thoughts and emotions of a twenty-one to twenty-three-year-old trainee and pilot. In a single letter he can talk of what they had for dinner, loss of men in his group in training camp, severe injuries and major operations he faced, or later, of surviving particularly dangerous missions or squadron or crew members who died that day. The excerpts I have chosen are ones that tell the human side of war—the people, emotions, and life experiences that are particularly hard to comprehend if you have never lived in war. Though typed and excerpted, I have tried to be faithful to the originals, only changing minor style errors or mistakes and even placing the valedictions in the locations they are found in the originals. They begin with his entry into the Army at Fort Niagara, Youngstown, NY, then on to his training at multiple USAAF ground- and air-training bases in Arkansas, Tennessee, Texas, Kansas, Louisiana, Georgia and Florida (see Appendix 3 for his training camps and dates attended) through his trip to North Africa via the South Atlantic Air Ferry Route to Liberia, Sierra Leone, Morocco, Tunisia, Algeria and on to Sardinia, Corsica and Dijon, France and they end with his return to the USA.

The letters are still in excellent condition. The following three pictures give you a good sense of what they are like. Some were airmail, some V-mail and all but one were handwritten.

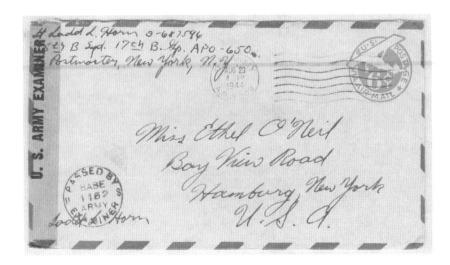

Airmail letter written from Villacidro, Sardinia, August 22, 1944 in which he told of the loss of two of his crew members.

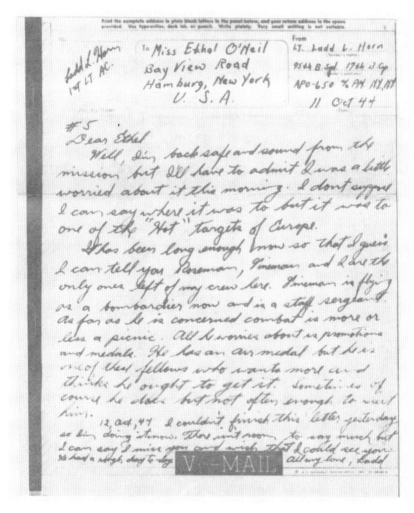

V-mail letter written from Corsica October 11, 1944

The first two excerpts from Dad's letters (see below) are out of chronological order. They are placed first because they are so typical of his expressions of love for Ethel. Other excerpts of letters will be of camp life, war and planes and people. While those letters are excerpted and may not include anything about his love for Ethel, he essentially never failed to include something about his love and desire for her, and his devotion to her, in every letter he wrote.

Bruce Field, Ballinger, Texas January 30, 1943

"Dear Ethel,

I feel terribly lonely for you this evening. I'm writing in the hope that it will sort of bring you nearer to me for a few moments while I am writing…

I've been thinking so much about you lately. If I pass all my checks and tests perhaps at the end of about 5 more months I will be able to get 10 days to come home and see you. I had hoped that perhaps we could see each other before then but it doesn't look as though it will be possible. It is about 6 months now since the last time that I saw you at Fort Niagara. Ethel, it seems as though it has been years to me. When I think of having to wait at least that much longer and even then perhaps not have the chance to see you it makes me feel rather forlorn to say the least. I can't help but remember and think of what a wonderful thrill it was to feel you nestle close against my body and how sweet and tender the feeling when we kissed.

Ethel, I don't know how to say it, but honey, don't break faith with me, don't ever let your love for me grow cold, because I love you so. Whenever I think of how sweet and lovely you are and how good, pure and wholesome I feel a thrill and a pang of desire for you all through my body. Perhaps I'm old fashioned for wanting a girl who is pure and virgin but if that is being old fashioned then I think it is the best way to be.

Darling, we may have to be apart now and suffer heartache and longing for each other but if we wait patiently the time will come when we will be together again. When we are I'll enfold you in my arms and press you close to me and all those longings and heartaches will be dispelled just by the thrill of each other's nearness and our kisses and caresses will seem all the sweeter because of the separation we have suffered now.

There is a new song just becoming popular here now:

When the war is over and all the world is free,

This earth will be a heaven, darling, for you and me.

I hope it will be that way for us. Don't you, Ethel?

Love

Ladd"

Bruce Field, Ballinger, Texas January 27, 1943

"Dear Ethel…

Nothing in this world is nearly so precious to a young man as his girl back home, that is of course if he loves her truly, and you will find that everything he feels, thinks or does depends an awfully [*sic*] lot on her and how she feels toward him.

I have to tell you too, Ethel, that I am proud of my girl and the more I see of other young women the more reason I know I have to be proud of you. I pray that you'll always love me and that God will help me to be a young man whom you cannot only love but whom you can always be proud of too. Darling, I love you so much there's no way I can tell you in words how precious you are to me. Yours truly

Ladd"

The following letters are in chronological order.

Fort Niagara, New York, July ?, 1942. *Welcome to the Army!*

"Dear Ethel…

On my last card I told you that I would possibly leave here by the 29th, but no information that you receive here is very definite. Almost all of our group left except 6 of us. 1,200 men were processed and shipped within the last 18 hrs. This is a new record for the U.S. Army…

To give you some idea of the kind of days we are having I will give you a short account of my activities today. 3:00 a.m. got up, washed, dressed, shaved, made bunk, straightened locker. 3:20 a.m. fell out for reveille, drilled a few minutes, roll call, received orders, dismissed for mess at 3:30 a.m. 4:00 a.m. got ready for K.P. and reported to cook orderly for directions. 5:00 a.m. Sergeant took us to mess hall #12 for duty. 8:00 a.m. relieved from duty and reported to examining board. 8:30 a.m. returned to barracks and drilled in rain then reported for detail duty to QMC, "Quartermaster Corps." 11:30 a.m. dismissed for mess 8 ½ h after breakfast. Off duty till 12:30 Then report for roll call and then back to QMC until 4:00 p.m. got cleaned up and changed to uniform. 4:15 "retreat" some drill and more orders, dismissed for mess about 5:30. 6:00 lucky me is off duty for evening unless something special shows up. Usually you don't get a chance to go to bed until about 11:00 p.m. Most of the men are about half dead. Incidentally I fell asleep on my feet in the mess line today at dinner. The men however receive very good treatment outside the strenuous routine. Our meals are very good…"

Fort Niagara, New York, August 5, 1942
"Dear Ethel…

A new man landed in the bunk beside me last night and landed in the brig today, such is life in the Army…

Yesterday I started training with "Section B. Paratroops". The training for a Pilot is the same as theirs for the first 8 wks. The only good thing about it is that I probably won't be getting K.P. (at least not very often).

Yours

Ladd"

Camp Mills, Mitchell Field, Long Island, New York, August 12-14, 1942
"Dear Ethel,

From worst to worster [*sic*] seems to be the order of the day. I guess I just don't have any luck.

I arrived here at Camp Mills, Mitchel Field on Monday morning at 11:25

O'clock [*sic*] in dark drizzly weather and we pitched a tent in muck, mud and water and finally got cots and 2 blankets and went to bed. Sheets and linen are out of the question, everything is sloppy and muddy and you can't keep clean. I guess the sun never shines here. The ground is low and mosquitos and knats [*sic*] are terrible. Today I got a little drill and some brushing up on math...

Aug. 13, Well it's still raining today as it has been ever since I got here. That morning sun is something I haven't seen in a week. There is about 2 inches of water under my cot today. All the fellows in my tent have coughs except me. This morning we built a clothes rack in the tent and then had a lecture on meteorology until dinner.

...We have foxholes dug all over the place and we're supposed to get into them if enemy planes come over. If we did get in it would mean certain death by drowning. It has been raining until they are all full of mud and water...

They say that New York is the soldier's town but when they charge the poor soldier boy 10 and 11 cents for ice cream suckers and 20 cents for a hamburger or hot dog he can't understand very well where the name came from.

It seems funny, in some places when a soldier comes along in uniform everything is free for him and in other places the price doubles immediately...

Aug 14 I'm all packed and have orders to leave for Blytheville, Arkansas. I don't know what it's all about but I will probably find out...

Yours truly

    Ladd"

Blytheville, Arkansas, August 18-20, 1942

"Dear Ethel...

    "Monday morning I reached Blytheville training field...

We have lost four boys already and at that rate our entire group will be gone before we complete our training. I guess it's a case of the survival of the fittest and that after the weaker ones are gone the rate will decrease. Three of the boys went crazy and the fourth we lost with a burst appendix. In addition to those four a fifth went "over the hill" on the trip out here. They have a new name for that now. They say that the man "Goofed Off."

They claim that you learn to like the army after a while but the longer I am in it the less I find I like about it…Just to show you something of what it is like we are cursed continually all day by the officers for everything we do whether we do it right or wrong. This afternoon when we fell out for formation we were marched to the orderly room to receive our orders from the top sergeant. His exact words to us were, "You're here for four weeks of hell and your instructors have orders to give it to you. If any man sounds off we'll make it really hot for him."

I might add to what's gone before that it is so hot here that if you walk on the asphalt you sink in over your shoe soles. When your [*sic*] out in the sun every time you wink your eye a little shower of sweat sprinkles off. We have to drill 8 h a day in that. You will sweat right through your clothes until they are soaked just sitting still in the shade. Most of the men go naked in the barracks…

Love

Ladd"

Blytheville, Arkansas, August 24, 1942
"Dear Ethel…

I'm not sure now whether I told you or not that I received my pay which amounted to $10 by the time it reached me…

We had a new man come in here from Tenn. He was telling me about some of the draftees from the Tenn. Hills. They had never worn shoes or store bought shirts until they got in the Army. Most of them tried to take their shoes off and go barefooted in ranks. When one of them signed on the payroll he put XX for his signature. The paymaster jumped him and said he would have to put another "X" for his middle initial. When he heard this he said, "Aw Shuckins, ah nevah did learn to make but two o' them thar things."

Most of the officers and men here are from the southwestern states, they call us "blue bellies". That's left over from the Civil War yet…

Love

Ladd"

Blytheville, Arkansas, August 27, 1942

"Dearest Ethel…

Well, I finally got to church once since I've been in the Army. You'll never realize how little there is in life to live for when you don't have your liberty unless you once have to live under conditions like these, but after all this is to preserve that liberty for those we love. So far I haven't found one Christian young man in our group, but there is a new man *(who)* just came in who I've noticed reading his Bible quite often although I haven't had a chance to get acquainted yet. Some of the men read their Bibles at night but during the day they curse and smoke and drink the same as the rest so I can't seem to really consider them as Christians….

You couldn't conceive the wickedness that goes on around a camp like this unless you saw it yourself. The relations between the young men and women are terrible. I couldn't tell you in here how bad.

Right at present about 75% of the men in the barracks are engaged in a "crap" game and a "Black Jack" game. In the morning about half of them find themselves broke and if we get passes the other half will probably be drunk...

Ladd"

Blytheville, Arkansas, August 30, 1942
"Dear Ethel...

I have your wings for you now and I am going to enclose them in this letter, also the pass which enabled me to obtain them. It might make a sort of souvenir, at least you will be able to see what one is like, take note of the beautiful signature. After looking at it I don't think you can find any fault with my writing.

The wings that I am sending you are the ones for the left lapel of the top coat. There are two other sizes that are identical in design. One size is the same as those printed at the top of this page

and one is worn on the left side of the shirt collar and another on the left front side of your cap. A fourth size has a span of about 3 inches and is worn on the front of your cap.

The actual Air Corps insignia that you spoke of is a smaller set of wings the same design but superimposed on a round gold button that exactly matches the regular U.S. Army insignia that is worn on the right side of the collar. The shoulder insignia is a round ultramarine blue patch with two golden orange wings attached to a silver star. The star originally had a red center but just recently this has been done away with. The silver wings are still a question mark. Up until August 7th when a man became a full-fledged pilot he received not wings but 1 gold bar. All those becoming pilots after that date (among whom I will be included) will receive instead an ultramarine blue sphere with a fine gold hairline around the center, similar to the emblem of the regular U.S. Army Warrant Officer. I will not be known as an officer as heretofore but rather as "Mister" and any officer no matter how high in rank he might be must call you "Mister" or it will be too bad for him…

Yesterday we had our barracks all clean and neat for inspection at 2 p.m. but by midnight the place was a pigpen. About half the fellows came in stewed, potted or whatever you want to call it. One fellow across the aisle from me threw up all over the bed, floor and everything. A few of the others came through and turned the place topsy-turvy. They put fellows' shoes to bed, filled some of the beds and shoes with gravel, short sheeted some and just tore up others. One Arkansas boy across from me had a quart and a pint of different kinds of liquor and drank most of it himself. I have to give him credit though because he could still talk sense and still navigate. Two of the eastern boys got hold of a pint of Ark. Peach whiskey and that really finished them off short. This state is supposed to be dry and you are not allowed to drink anything stronger than beer in public, but there is more whiskey for sale than I have ever seen.

Quite a few of these same boys got up this morning and went to church. I felt so disgusted that I couldn't go with them. I don't know as you can understand that, but you could if you were here…

Yours
Ladd"

Blytheville, Arkansas, September 7, 1942

"Dear Ethel...

I am still in what they call basic training, following that I will be assigned to duty for a while as they call it. This is to acquaint me with guard duty, line work and etc. The second period of training you go into is called "Primary," the 3rd is "Pre-Flight," 4th is "Flight" and following that you are probably assigned for a short while as instructor or on patrol duty until you build up some extra flying hours and then you are given combat duty...

I am taking it pretty well. Nevertheless from my point of view it is a "rotten" life just the same. You understand that it isn't I *(or)* the Army drill or routine that makes it so, but rather the actions and the wickedness of the men.

Yours truly

Ladd

(Shh, this is a secret/ you can get gas here 4 gallons for 50 cents and all that you want.)"

Nashville, Tennessee, September 9-14, 1942

"Dear Ethel...

I signed the pay roll again but so far my first 10 dollars is all the money I have seen and I am afraid that now I won't ever see what I had coming...

I am going to tell you another thing that you probably don't know and may not believe even if I tell you and that is that you should never drink any Coca Cola or other Coke drinks for two reasons. First they contain a percentage of alcohol and second they are a drug that will throw your heart way off. One bottle of Coca Cola is too much for a pilot to drink before tests or flights because it affects his heart and blood pressure too much for safety's sake. The ruling here is "No Smokes and No Cokes." Cokes do pick you up only it is too much of a pickup.

It evidently won't be much longer now until I will be flying a plane if things go alright, perhaps not more than five or six weeks but I can't be quite sure yet whether I will be pilot, navigator, or bombardier…

Love

Ladd"

Nashville, Tennessee, September 12, 1942

"Dear Ethel…

On Wed. I was moved and assigned to the 700th Squadron for active duty as I told you I probably would be following basic training…

I am going to speak too of another thing I perhaps shouldn't but it will show you how careful those of us must be who wish to keep our self-respect and especially to keep ourselves clean for the sake of the young women we love.

You may know that we in the Air Corps are examined every two weeks for venereal diseases and every morning when we work on cadet mess. In spite of these precautions the government claims that one man out of every ten catches syphilis which as you know is considered the worst of these diseases at present. Two men were taken from our ranks this morning. It can be caught through a handshake, through the mouth, or through the feet… *(Note that the modes of transmission are not correct as a result of their still limited knowledge of the virus.)*

As far as those silver wings and commissions are concerned, the cadets received them who had started flight training before August seventh I understand. Flight officers still wear wings and glider pilots wear silver wings with a disc in the center. The insignia that I will receive if I pass everything has been changed again to a maroon-brown bar with a silver stripe in it. Also the Air Corps officers now will wear their insignia on their collar rather than their shoulders as they did previously…

Yours truly

Ladd"

SAACC (San Antonio Aviation Cadet Center) San Antonio, Texas, September 25, 1942

"Dear Ethel,

Well, it looks like I am going to spend a good part of my life in the Army Air Force on railroad trains and Army trucks. So far I have spent 10 days of my life on trains and I'm a long ways from home.

I passed all my tests and made my classification as "Pilot" at Nashville and was shipped out here for assignment to classes in ground work, theory of flight and general aircraft information etc…

The field is truly enormous in proportion to any others I have seen. It is as big as a large city. We have beautiful large two story barracks that hold 50 men each. They have automatic gas heating and air conditioning units and each man has a closet and table for his own use, but true to Army style you have no chairs…

No. 1   Home   "A" Flight Barracks

The "A Flight" Barracks that my dad stayed in at SAACC, San Antonio, Texas from September 1942 to January 1943.

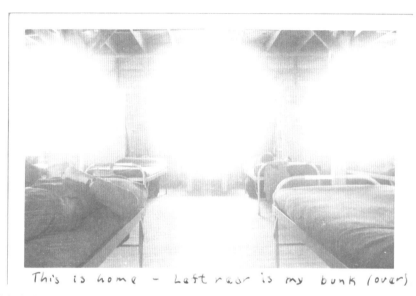

This is home — Left rear is my bunk (over)

This is home—left rear is my bunk. Look at the negative, it is better than the print. The canvas bags at the front of the beds contain gas masks. The camera I have has no time exposure. I sat it on a table and clicked it twenty-four times to get this picture.

Fall out for guard duty, see you later. (Interval of 27 hrs.) I've finished my tour of guard duty now so I guess I can continue with my writing. I had 24 hrs. guard duty and have caught about 3 hrs. sleep and a hot shower, now I am one of 3 men in the barracks who are up and moving, the rest are all asleep. Out of those 27 hrs. I went 17 without anything to eat and the meal I had before that wasn't much. They've been giving us very good food only not enough of it…

Yours truly

Ladd."

A not very impressive guard

Dad with his rifle at the SAACC, San Antonio, Fall 1942. Note the barracks in the background.

SAACC, San Antonio, Texas, October 2, 1942

"Dear Ethel

...The wings at the top of the page are Pilot's wings,

but it will probably be a long while yet before I can give you a pair of those. Right at present after much *(change)* of regulations and type and position of insignia they are giving practically everyone on flight duty silver wings. That includes not only "Flight Officers," which I will be when I graduate, but observers, gunners, navigators and bombardiers. Up until recently, Kelly Field, which is known as the "West Point of the Air" was the only field to give silver wings to its graduate pilots. That accounts for some of the controversy over them. I will receive both wings and a brownish maroon bar with a gold stripe in the center to wear on the right side of my collar.

This next paragraph is a reference to President Roosevelt's inspection of SAACC at Kelly Field on September 27, 1942. Dad included a news clipping from October 2, 1942 that described the visit.

I am going to enclose a news clipping that will tell you something of what happened here last Sunday. The report is rather vague. One thing that I will have to add to it that isn't told in the clipping is that the highway into camp was guarded by a man every 40 inches for as far as you could see. I was one of the men in that guard. Pictures including movies were taken, some of them included me but evidently none of the pictures have been released to the press.

Yesterday we had open post, that comes about once in 6 weeks. I was in town all day and my trip cost me just $37 when I figured it up today. I could stand it pretty well though because I have taken in 85 dollars in the past 2 weeks. I still have 1 month's back pay coming but I don't know when I will ever get that and too, it is not at all definite when I will get paid again.

I bought a $1.50 camera and took three rolls of pictures of San Antonio and those that come out good I will send home. My folks will show them to you. I don't know how much I can expect from the camera though, but I think the pictures will be passable."…

Yours truly

Ladd."

SAACC, San Antonio, Texas, October 4, 1942

"Dear Ethel...

In one of my other letters I told you that we weren't getting hardly enough to eat. That condition has been remedied but now they are cutting down some on our milk. There was a notice on the bulletin board that the reason for the shortage was that the Army camps and air fields around here use more milk than the entire output of the local dairies combined. I might add that San Antonio has a normal population of 500,000 people. That means that these camps are using more milk than the city ordinarily would use. That should give you some idea of the number of men around here.

From one who loves you dearly.

Ladd"

This is "Mess F." This dining hall could feed 2,900 men at a single seating. The milk crates and boxes piled in front represent milk, apples and oranges for one meal.

Dad included the following drawing of the pilot's insignia:

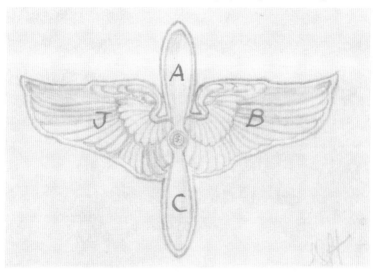

Each base had different insignia. Dad included pictures of the insignia from the bases he had been at in a letter dated October 3, 1942.

SAACC, San Antonio, Texas, October 6, 1942

Dad included the "Cadet Creed" in this letter.

"My bearing is along a course directed toward the accomplishment of a high mission, that mission being to raise my earth-born self into the blue above, to develop honor, self-discipline, and strength of character in myself so that when I am called upon to defend these principles I will neither disgrace my country, my duty, nor myself. To this end I will strive diligently, honorably and hopefully."

SAACC, San Antonio, Texas, October 8, 1942
"Dear Ethel…

You have perhaps seen some of these Army camps beautifully landscaped and having not a pebble, twig or blade of grass out of place. I will be sending home some pictures that will show you how they came to be that way. That is what becomes of what would otherwise be our spare time. They don't allow us to use modern methods because then you could get it all done and they wouldn't have a way to rob you of your time and keep you continuously tired. I'm going to send pictures showing men paving streets pebble by pebble, picking them up and laying each one in place by itself, also a ditch graded dug and stoned up practically by bare fingers alone. They are liable any time to have you mow or clean up a whole acre or so of yard just by pulling up a blade of grass at a time with your fingers. I've had to do that more than once…

A never ending job - picking up stones

IT Might be exasperating but it's good For You

Somebody decide it would be fun to throw at the Guard.

I was wondering if you would care to sort out enough colored pebbles to make a design like this, and lay them in place too.

Since I last stood guard they have changed the orders and you have to stand guard now with fixed bayonets. We have been using 1917 model Eddystone and Winchester rifles. The one I had the last night I was on guard you couldn't have fired if you wanted to. You could cock it, pull the trigger and the hammer wouldn't even fall because the spring was so weak. I had orders if a car came down the road and wouldn't halt for me to throw the rifle through the windshield…

Some things that make you wonder though are the fact that we have to put in 50 cents a month to feed 12 Great Danes that they keep at the field and $2 a month to keep up the Cadet Club in San Antonio. That sounds reasonable enough at first thought but when you multiply 10,000 cadets times 50 cents it makes $5,000 to feed a dozen dogs, likewise $20,000 to keep up a sort of educated cocktail lounge. We would kind of like to know who gets the money…

Yours

Ladd."

SAACC, San Antonio, Texas, October 10, 1942

"Dear Ethel…

I had some portraits made in town and I'll send you one when I get them if you want it. I am afraid though that I'm not much to look at and that a picture of me is even less to see.

Yours truly

Ladd"

SAACC, San Antonio, Texas, October 15, 1942

"Dear Ethel…

The song Evelyn wants to know.

> Into the air Army Air Corps
> Into the air pilots true
> Into the air Army Air Corps
> Keep your nose up in the blue.
> When you hear our motors singing

And the steel props start to whine

You can bet the Army Air Corps

Is on the firing line

That is about the favorite, but I'll send others if I get the chance…

Yours truly

Ladd"

SAACC, San Antonio, Texas, October 18, 1942
Preflight School Group I, Squadron II, Flight A

"Dear Ethel…

You asked about the other fellows; for the most part I haven't stayed with the same men for more than a week or so at a time, you get so that you don't really make any friends because you know that in a few days you will probably be separated again. Some of the men washout, some get sick, some are transferred, some are sent to different classes, some receive "CDDs" which stands for Certificate of Disability Discharge and others receive "GDOs" which stands for Ground Duty Only because of physical defects that show up or for marked nervousness or inability. The result of all this is that the men you are with are constantly changing…

I might give you some idea of the schedule we follow at present.

6:00 Reveille

6:05 Roll Formation

6:20 Breakfast

7:00 Clean barracks, make beds, shave, wash, scrub and mop floors

7:45 Police Call—clean up yard and area

7:55 Class Formation

8:00 Class in sanitation and medical care

9:00 Class in mathematics

10:00 Organization of ground forces

11:00 Radio Code

12:00 Dinner

13:00 Drill

14:35 Physical training

15:35 Take shower and then dress for retreat parade

15:50 Form for retreat, march to parade grounds, pass in review, have inspection and etc.

17:00 Wash and get ready for supper

17:15 Supper (chow call)

18:20 Return to barracks, take off class A uniforms and shine shoes, clean rifles, polish our brass and 101 other small things.

20:15 Call to quarters—in other words do your homework and don't talk, visit, make any noise or anything but study and I do mean study.

21:30 You are free for the rest of the day which is from 9:30 until 10:00. During this time you may write, clean your teeth, take a shower or anything else you want to do but you must be in bed and lights out by 10.
I might say that from 6 in the morning until 9:30 at night you cannot lay [*sic*] down or sit down even if you do get a few minutes free. You may sit only for classes or study…

I am going to enclose a copy of a code sheet just so you can see something of what it is like. If the sheet looks sloppy you must remember that all this has to be done very rapidly. This is a practice sheet of course and that accounts for the repetitions in some places. I might also say that each letter can mean a full word or just a single letter…

Yours

Ladd"

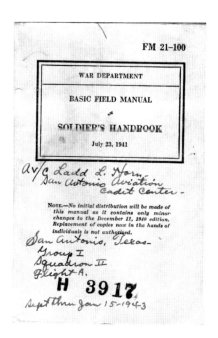

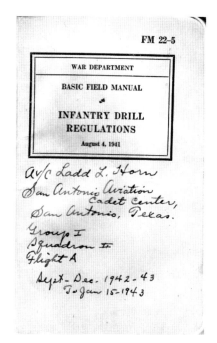

Dad's field manuals while stationed at the SAACC from September 22, 1942 to January 15, 1943. Both manuals show his assignment to Group I, Squadron II and Flight A.

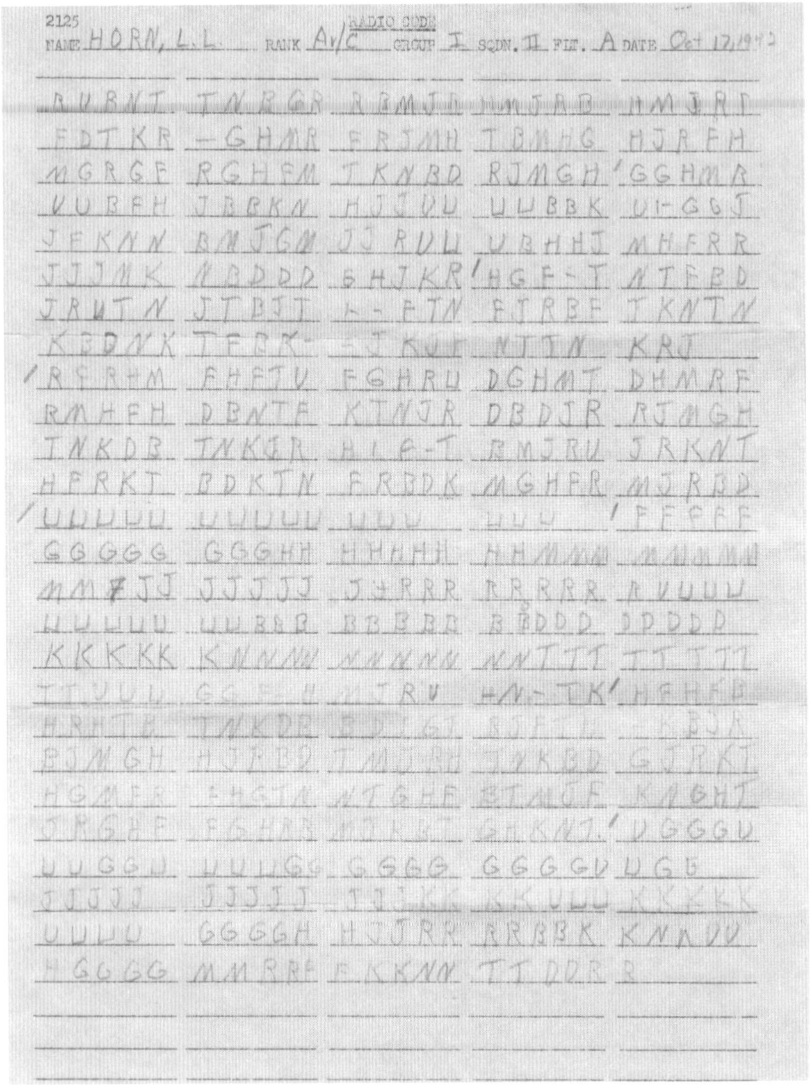
2125
RADIO CODE
NAME HORN, L.L. RANK A/C GROUP I SQDN. II FLT. A DATE Oct 17, 1942

Code sheet.

School rooms—2nd from left is Code. Notice the plane, it happens to be a "consolidated B-24" one of the largest bombers we use. Notice also the checkered water tower so that planes won't hit it.

SAACC, San Antonio, Texas, October 19, 1942

"Dear Ethel…

You may not have known or realized that I am in the Gulf Coast Air Force. I was originally in the Northeastern, following that I was in the Southeastern and now I was transferred to the Gulf Coast when I came to San Antonio.

P.S. It might interest you to know that there are 7 distinct U.S. Air Corps; Navy, Marine, Coast Guard, Northeastern Army, Southeastern Army and Gulf Coast Air Force."

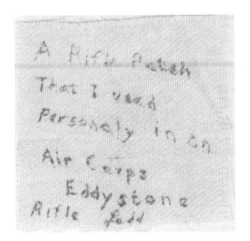

SAACC, San Antonio, Texas, October 26, 1942

"Dear Ethel…

These are some of the biggest favorites among the songs we sing.

"Two-Pence Song"…'Oh happy is the day when the airman gets his pay, as we go rolling home.

"Stout-Hearted Men," by Sigmund Romburg, "I've been Working on the Railroad" and also the Air Corps song once in a while. The "Two-Pence Song" is really more the Air Corps song than the official Air Corps song, at least it's more popular. "Stout-Hearted Men" is *(the)* Flight A song.

Yours

   Ladd."

SAACC, San Antonio, Texas October 25, 1942

"Dear Ethel…

Yesterday I made a bum landing from a "high jump" and got to the hospital as an emergency case. They X-rayed me twice for a broken right leg, but it showed the bone O.K. and they decided it was only ligaments and cartilage that was injured. They taped me up and sent me back to the barracks where I have to hobble around the best I can until it gets better. Of course that leg ached so that it meant the loss of another night's sleep, the only good about it is that I received a Medical Excuse from all drill, parades, calisthenics and etc. so perhaps I'll get a little chance to rest up some at least I hope so. [*sic*] You'd better not tell my folks or let them know anything at all about it because my mother especially will worry about me even though it isn't anything.

By the way, I took my first set of exams here and I don't know whether I did what you could call good or bad. I received 100 in math, 100 in ground forces and failed my code. I think I got about 32 in that. When we're not having a test I can get it perfect but when the test started my mind just seemed to go blank and I couldn't think what anything meant…

I am enclosing a test for colorblindness which might be of interest to you…

Yours truly

Ladd."

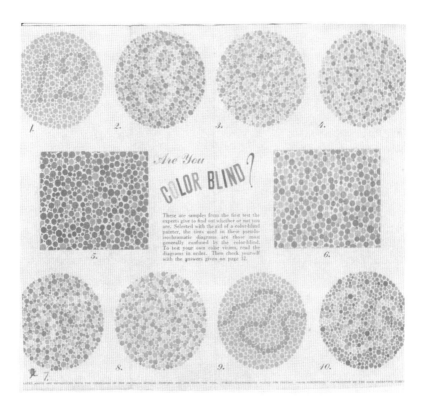

SAACC, San Antonio, Texas, October 30, 1942

"Dear Ethel…

I have some other news that I don't know whether is good or bad and that is that within the next four days I have to go to the hospital for an operation that will lay me up for about 6 weeks, perhaps even longer depending on how I come out of it. They're going to go to work on my leg for a ruptured cartilage, a semi-lunar cartilage I believe they call it. I can walk on it fairly well now but they claim it won't ever get really better without an operation. It feels about like a perpetually bad toothache at present. Don't let my folks know because they will worry if they find out…

Love

Ladd."

SAACC, San Antonio, Texas, November 2, 1942

"Dear Ethel

They actually have me in the hospital now, I was admitted yesterday. This morning they started getting me ready for the operation, checked my blood type and count and took the other tests that come before an operation. Following these they shaved my body from the hip down, washed me with alcohol, ether and then wrapped me in face towels to make sure I am well sterilized. Tomorrow I will get the ether and alcohol again and then Wed. morning I go on the operating table. Right now my leg is bandaged from my hip all the way to my ankle bone. I guess they are going to practically cut my leg off and then sew it back on again. I don't care, much, as long as they do sew it on, I don't look like much of a soldier, though, getting laid up before I even get in the fight…

Love

Ladd."

SAACC, San Antonio, Texas, November 5, 1942

"Dearest Ethel

When you look at the appearance of this letter you will have to consider the conditions under which I am writing. Honestly I never knew it was possible to suffer the pain I am in at this time. I asked my mother to write and tell you how I was but I have to write now myself to try to keep my mind occupied. *(His mother and father were there on a planned visit, but not because of the surgery.)*

They operated on me yesterday morning. They took me in the operating room at 7:35 a.m. and I got out at 9:05 a.m. The doctor was cutting for 30 minutes. True to Army style they left me conscious for the operation, I was able to watch everything that went on and talk with the doctor too. They gave me three hypodermics of morphine by 11:30; that should give you some idea of what I was up against. Today the pain is very severe and I don't get anything more to stop it. Several times in the night I wished I was dead rather than to suffer any more…

Love

Ladd."

SAACC, San Antonio, Texas, November 6, 1942, Station Hospital

"Dear Ethel…

I don't know how much my mother wrote you but I guess I might as well start at the beginning and tell you what they did to me. I haven't been able to see myself yet to know just what size incision they made but the general idea is that a cut was made straight up the front of my right knee, curved in an arc to the left of the knee cap and then straight on for a ways up the knee. Following this the knee cap was laid back much as you would open the cover of a book and the cartilage under it were [*sic*] removed. Next the main joint of the knee was bent and opened and the cartilage removed from there leaving my lower leg held to my body only by the two large cords at the back of the knee and the thin layer of flesh at the sides of the joint. After that the joint was fit together again, sewn up and taped in place. You can understand that in removing those cartileges [*sic*] they were working practically on the bones themselves, that accounts for the very severe pain following the operation. They have continued to give me two shots of morphine a day, every other day they eliminate one shot and give me pills instead… I may have a stiff leg for the rest of my life. I thought it best to tell you this now rather than have it brought home to you as actual fact a little later on.

However, it is possible too that the knee will heal and be practically as good as a normal knee. If the former should be true though we would have to forget some of the dreams we have had in the past. The very fact that I love my girl makes it impossible that I should ever have her for my own with such a condition existing. All we can do now is wait and see how things turn out.

Honey, please pray for me.

Love

Ladd"

SAACC, San Antonio, Texas, November, 10, 1942

"Dear Ethel…

In four more days it is time for the stitches to come out, but my leg is still entirely helpless… When it gets so that I can lift my heel from the bed then I will be getting better. That is the main sign that the doctors use…

They give you good care here and you have the care and opinion of many doctors rather than one as you do in civilian life. I was examined by 6 doctors before I was operated on and I have been looked at by about 25 others since then. Between the bunch they ought to know what they are doing.

Love

Ladd"

SAACC, San Antonio, Texas, November 12, 1942
"Dear Ethel…

The week following the operation was a week of misery for me but I am feeling a lot better now. At first when my leg hurt the worst if I just took a swallow of water or fruit juice I would throw it up almost the moment it hit my stomach…but this morning I got up and walked around some on crutches and sat on the porch in the sun which felt good after being in bed for twelve days. Afterwards I hurt so badly though that I almost wished I hadn't, but if it's sunny tomorrow I'm going out again…

Lovingly yours

Ladd"

SAACC, San Antonio, Texas, November 14, 1942
"Dear Ethel…

The operation is one that for years our best surgeons have been afraid to tackle and have tried everything to avoid but still without results. Up until the present a very large percentage have been unsuccessful…It takes about two months to recover to a point where you can get around in an approximately normal manner and about 14 months for complete recovery…

Yours

Ladd"

When I was in my teens, I heard this story of Dad's knee operation several times. The following are my recollections of the circumstances surrounding his injury and operation. In pre-flight training (SAACC, San Antonio Aviation Cadet Center), they had Dad and the others doing basic physical training. One day while running hurdles, the hurdles were set in the high position. As Dad ran, he hit the top of the hurdle with his foot. His leg went through the hurdle and his knee was badly injured when he fell with the hurdle around his leg. He was taken in for surgery after it did not heal on its own. They did not have enough medical personnel and so a young recruit had been trained to give spinal injections. As Dad told the story, that guy put one knee on his back and "rooted around" with that needle until it finally went in. Until the day he died, Dad had a lump the size of a small tangerine on his back where he was given that injection. While Dad's knee was repaired sufficiently for military service, he always had problems with it. It was operated on at least twice more (once by the surgeon for the Buffalo Sabres) and then a total replacement was done when he was in his early seventies. Dad was initially given a 100% military disability when he was discharged, partly as a result of the damage to that knee but the disability was reduced to 10% over time.

SAACC, San Antonio, Texas, November 16, 1942

"Dear Ethel…

It's nearly two weeks now since the operation and I can get out of bed and take four or five steps without crutches but I don't think you could call it walking. It is some sort of crab hop or something…Most of the Army jokes I have found run toward extreme foolishness such as; What is the difference between a duck? One of its legs are both alike…

Perhaps you would care to know something about the hospital anyway. It is composed of 100 buildings connected by covered runways, each building about 3 times as large as your house and completely self-contained. Each building has two offices, one room for serious cases, a completely equipped kitchen, small laboratory for drugs and bandages etc., latrines, shower and washroom, linen room, sunporch and open porch. It can care for about 43 patients and is practically a hospital in itself. Each building has a staff of 4 doctors, 4 nurses and six 6 ward-boys who have specialized in the type of cases that it cares for. My ward of course is the orthopedic ward…

Yours truly

Ladd"

Dad's cartoon drawing from the letter.

SAACC, San Antonio, Texas, November 20, 1942

"Dear Ethel…

You may be surprised when I tell you that I was on K.P. today. After all, you know this isn't a civilian hospital and just as soon as you are able to stand up even if it is with crutches, you have to help make beds; when you can stand without them you go on K.P. and wash dishes and when you can put one foot in front of the other you become a tray carrier. While you are still flat on your back you fold paper ashtrays and similar things…

While I'm talking about this I might fill in with some slogans that are floating around. "Earn you wings by taking a few pings at those dictator things." "Go Bye Bye in a PBY." "Cool your pate in a P-38." "Japs don't thrive on B-25." "Make Hitler sore with a B-24." "Bonk Benito on the bean from a B-17." "Have fun in a B-1."

I just happened to run across that sign and I couldn't help but think about one of the boys in the hospital here with me. He got mixed up in a propeller and nearly lost both his hands, they were so mangled that the doctor couldn't even set the bones of his hands or forearms, but he taped, stitched and wired the flesh together, gave the boy shots for gangrene and blood poisoning and left [sic] him lay here in the hospital. He has been lucky and is starting to regain some of the use of his hands. Any place but the army they probably would have amputated just the same as a civilian hospital would have put my leg in a cast for 6 weeks…

…some of the expressions we use that are different from what you ordinarily hear. A poor pilot or we might rather say a dumb pilot is known commonly as a "knucklehead." Something rather poor or we might say rotten is spoken of as being "ronchy" while the exact opposite is "spoony." A "yellow peril" is a plane flown by a beginner which has its wing and tail surfaces painted yellow so that other pilots give it a wide berth."…

Love

Ladd"

SAACC, San Antonio, Texas, November 26, 1942

"Dear Ethel…

I am out of the hospital now and I really got a better deal of it than I expected. I was released yesterday and was marked quarters for only one day. This morning I received a medical excuse from all drill, calisthenics and formations but I have the privilege of leaving my barracks and attending classes if I so desire…

I feel entirely disgusted with a life like this. They teach us nothing but hate and discipline and all that kind of goes against my grain, not that discipline isn't correct in its place but the term can be exaggerated and misused. It boils down to hypocrisy more than anything else the way it is used here. It's just an outside show and everything underneath is evil and wicked more than you will ever know…

Love – Ladd"

SAACC, San Antonio, Texas, November 27, 1942

"Dear Ethel…

Please excuse the many mistakes, I'm feeling kind of disgusted this fine day. I spent most of this Thanksgiving morning standing in line for clothing shortages. There is a cold north wind blowing and we nearly froze to death. When we got all done waiting they didn't give us anything. At noon I did get a sliver of turkey, 1 glass of apple cider and one tablespoon of cranberry sauce.

What became of the rest of it I don't know. When we asked for more we got bread, ice water, and cold pork shoulder. Just found out too that this afternoon they have the rest of the boys out picking up stones from the gully back of the barracks. This morning they had the enlisted mans [*sic*] detachment out there throwing stones down into the gully. They wanted to make sure that there would be enough work for everybody. All in all it's a very enjoyable Thanksgiving day.

I have to be thankful though that I am alive and that I can walk and without crutches too.

They did pass out a half pound box of candy to everyone for Thanksgiving but that was as the compliments of some candy company in San Antonio. At least we weren't forgotten…

Yours

Ladd."

SAACC, San Antonio, Texas, November 28, 1942

"Dear Ethel

What kind of Thanksgiving did you have? Ours wasn't so bad but it wasn't so good either. They stretched our Thanksgiving dinner to make two meals which meant neither one was too good. That box of candy was really good…

I forgot to tell you in my last letter that I am an upper classman now, I no longer wear a red name tag, but rather a blue one. I guess I can send the old red one to you and you can see the little thing that makes so much difference in one's status around here.

HORN, Ladd Leonard

Yesterday morning I watched the sunrise and, oh! I wished so you could have been here to watch it with me. The sky here in the early morning is the clearest most brilliant blue you ever saw and as it changed to gold, orange and then crimson it was so beautiful that watching it one could hardly think that almost the whole world was at war…

The boys were paid while I was in the hospital and the result wasn't very satisfactory. One of the boys received 4¢ while our flight lieutenant signed the payroll only to find out that he owed his full month's pay to the government, all of next month's pay and $10 from the third month. The thing is that you can't figure out what the deductions are for and no one can tell you. I have $260 coming to me on Dec. 9. When I figure up the deductions that I should have it cuts it down to about $150 and what I will probably receive will be around $50 if I am lucky. What becomes of the rest nobody knows. The worst part is that I have to pay income tax on the $260. I think they take out $4 a month for tax and then we will have to up whatever is the difference at the end of the year out of our own pockets…

Yours

Ladd"

SAACC, San Antonio, Texas, December 4, 1942

"Dear Ethel…

Another thing you might be interested to know is that we have a young man in our group who has photographed nearly all of Germany since the war started. He made a map of Germany accurate enough for all military purposes. They flew over the country and photographed it and then dropped parachutists with portable radio sets which were used to find the exact location of the photograph on the land and then radio that location back to the plane which would still be within range of the set. The parachutists were then left to dispose of their equipment and get out of Germany as best as they could. It is needless to say anything about what happened to those who didn't get out…

They have just lengthened our training by 30 flying hours so it will even be a little longer now before I will go on combat duty. It looks like I will still have about 7 months training to go through or perhaps even 9 before I will be signed to duty…

Love and best wishes

Ladd"

SAACC, San Antonio, Texas, December 5, 1942
"Dear Ethel…

It looks right now as though I am going to be moved within the next 8 or 10 days possibly even sooner…

The reason for moving is that I have been recommended for advancement even though I have only completed about half of my ground work. I was recommended by all four flight lieutenants, by the acting first sargeant [*sic*] and by the group commander. I have an interview coming up now with the squadron commander. If I get through that alright I will be shipping out pretty soon. I can't tell where but two possibilities are Vernon, Texas and East St. Louis…

I found something out the other day that you wouldn't believe possible. In a class on navigation the instructor drew a line on the blackboard and then asked us to estimate its length. Of course no one could guess it exactly except by accident and if anyone did guess it correctly they had no way of knowing that they were correct. Do you know how to find the length of that line exactly without measuring it? It is really very simple. You take about 50 persons of average intelligence, have each one estimate its length and then average their estimates. The answer will be the length of the line. If you want the length very quickly you just take the largest and the smallest estimate and average them and you will probably have the length within an eighth of an inch. That is the law of averages in action. If you think about it for a while you can easily see why it works although it seems impossible at first...

Love

Ladd."

An Army Air Corps patch worn on the left shoulder was included in the letter.

SAACC, San Antonio, Texas, December 8, 1942

"Dear Ethel...

I haven't been able to find out anything more about whether or not I will be moving. I do know however that if I do go I will be going this Sunday... Whatever happens I don't feel like staying here much longer. You can get terribly sick of this kind of place. As one of the boys put it the other day, "If I never see this place again except through a bombsight it will be alright with me as long as I have plenty of bombs that one time."

My knee is pretty good now, I can nearly do a deep knee bend and I can start to run a little bit.

...I finally received the clothing that I waited in line for on Thanksgiving day...

That insignia I sent you in my last letter is the kind I wear on my left shoulder. The black one I sent before is the one that I wear on my right sleeve. 4 1/2" up from the cuff to be exact.

I finally have been able to get one of the U.S. emblems that match the first pair of wings that I sent you...

Lovingly

Ladd"

SAACC, San Antonio, Texas, December 11. 1942

"Dear Ethel...

I thought yesterday morning that I knew quite certainly that I would be going only to have my plans all upset again last night...

Love

Ladd

(over)

Right now it looks definitely as though I am not going anyplace. The shipping orders just came out and my name isn't on them. That means I'll be hanging around here for a while yet."

SAACC, San Antonio, Texas, December 13, 1942

"Dear Ethel...

This letter is to let you know that it appears definite now that I will be here for another month. Probably until sometime around the 16th of January...

Yesterday we had a sham battle or maneuvers or whatever you want to call it. I was left out because my knee isn't good enough yet, our side won though just the same so I guess they really don't need me very much. The real reason why we won though is that the enemy planes accidentally gassed their own troops.

They spray scented molasses from the plane to simulate mustard gas or Lewisite. For the lacrimatory or sturmutator gasses [*sic*] they use the real thing so you have to be quick with your gas mask or suffer for it.

I don't know whether you know it or not, it may be the word "gas" has confused you, but mustard gas and Lewisite gas are thick sticky liquids and not vapors as you might think. They go by the name of "vesicants." Their effect is to penetrate your flesh and they burn you horribly.

Everyone was in pretty good spirits when it was over due to the fact that the officers got most of the molasses that was sprayed. You can imagine the kind of mess it would make and everyone always feels good when the officers get in a ridiculous position...

Love

Ladd"

SAACC, San Antonio, Texas, (December 12, 1942?)

"Dear Ethel...

I'll copy down a few things under the heading of "Pilot Tips and Pilot Taps" that might be of interest. *(Note: I've kept inappropriate racist language as it is part of the historical experience. See my Father's reaction to these in the note below.)*

<u>Pilot Tips</u>

Whenever some Jap plane gets naughty

Depend on dives speed and fire power

They're your best bets in your P-40

Use them—you'll make the slant eye cower

The aerobatics you can master

Like a demon—know your place

The Jap planes can do them much faster

What's more, my friend, in much less space.

If Jap is near, ere bailing out

Take time before you open chute.

If Japs around, the Nippon Lout

Will train his gun on you and shoot.

Pilot Taps

A very hot pilot was Henry Hightowers

Who boasted of having some 300 hours

He dove on his girlfriend's house one day

They would have been married the 15th of May.

And so it goes on and on and more and more and day after day and week after week and month after month and course after course and more and more and harder and harder and faster and faster until someday perhaps you're a pilot until some Jap is a little quicker on the trigger than you are... *Note: my dad was quite critical of the U.S. Army Air Forces' propaganda and hypocrisy and multiple times sent propaganda items like this that he personally could not stand just to let my mom know what he was going through.*

Love

Ladd."

SAACC, San Antonio, Texas, December 15, 1942

"Dear Ethel...

I'll have to tell you about one of the fellows here. He had been receiving letters from his girlfriend right along telling him how much she missed him and how much she cared etc. For about two weeks he didn't receive a letter and then finally one came. He opened the letter and started reading, for about two minutes all was quiet and then he let out a yell and nearly hit the ceiling. The reason? She was very sorry but she had been too busy to write to him. She married a sailor last week and they were on their honeymoon in Jacksonville, Fla. That was the first chance she had to write.

He read the letter to us afterward, while it wasn't at all funny to him the rest of us couldn't help ourselves and we just roared. The poor fellow's life was utterly miserable all the rest of the time he was here. Whichever way he turned somebody was teasing him about how fast the Navy could work. While it did seem funny to us I can imagine how one of the rest of us would have felt in the same position.

I don't know as I told you what my job as Officer of the Guard consisted of Sunday. I had to keep about a thousand cadets and their visitors in line. In general to see that none of the rules of the post were disobeyed was my job and if you don't think that is a job you have another think coming. I was just about dead by night.

Ladd"

SAACC, San Antonio, Texas, December 20, 1942

"Dear Ethel

Well, its five months today since I left home to go and live with my rich uncle who is I guess somewhere around $80,000,000,000 in debt by now. I may be wrong about that number but I think it is somewhere around that. They tell me that by next July he will have spent about $27,000 on me alone. Just to educate me. That being the case I've been wondering just how much a good education would cost.

In three more days I go back to full duty. That means physical training again…

I hope Ethel, that you have a nice Christmas. Here it is no different from any other time of the year. Most of the boys will have to study and drill just the same as any other day…

"Merry Christmas"

Ladd"

SAACC, San Antonio, Texas, December 23, 1942

"Dear Ethel

Drawings Dad included in sections of the letter.

I have just been studying ships and how to recognize them. We have to know a ship well enough so that we can look at it from 5,000 ft away and be able to say, that is the *Washington*, the *Long Island*…the *South Dakota*…If all its 16" guns were fired at once 20 tons of steel would leave the ship at one shot. If the ship were sailing forward at 30 knots and all the guns were fired forward at one time the ship would not only be stopped but would be moved about 25 ft backward by the recoil from the guns… I'll explain what is meant by a 16" 50-caliber gun just in case you don't understand. It means that the "bore" is 16" in diameter and the barrel of the gun is 50 times as long as the diameter of the bore. In other words the guns on our more modern battleships are about 70 ft long and can shoot accurately up to about 23 miles…

If everything goes according to schedule I will be sent sometime in August or September of 1943. Right about then is also when the big push will be made to beat Japan…Right now we couldn't make any real push because our naval Air Force has been knocked down <u>to three aircraft carriers and two aircraft escort vessels. Perhaps there are only two carriers now</u> but we are hoping that it was one of the escort vessels that was sunk instead of another carrier. After the first of the year however we <u>will be commissioning about one carrier each month which will make us about 10 by next Aug.</u> considering that no more are lost in the meantime. <u>10 makes up the number that would be necessary to do much damage to Japan in the east.</u>

That is official and it would be best if you didn't talk about the underlined sections in public…

About that gasoline situation, they have quite a racket down here. You just go to a garage and rent a car with the tank full of gas. They have "T" ration cards with the cars that are rented and can get practically all the gas they want. If you can't get enough that way you can at least get enough to drive to the Mexican border and buy all you want on the other side…

Love

Ladd"

SAACC, San Antonio, Texas, December 25, 1942

"Dearest Ethel…

We have so many classes to learn now that they just get to swirling around in your head with the result that we all get acting foolish about them. We decided we were going to have the stacks come out of the bottom of the ship and create an underwater smoke screen so that the submarines won't be able to see to torpedo the ship...

Dad's drawing about preflight training.

Love

Ladd."

SAACC, San Antonio, Texas, December 27, 1942

"Dear Ethel...

Christmas day we had a very nice turkey dinner with all the trimmings. It was really good which is a bit unusual...

You say that it has been hard to get butter at home, well, we haven't been having any butter either. Once in a while though, we have been getting Oleo. We're not getting ice cream very often either anymore but lately we have had a little extra milk to make up for it…

What is worse than that is that some of the people up in Mass. And Conn. Don't have fuel enough to keep warm in the cold weather that they have been having. One of the boys from Boston received word from his family saying that they all had to sleep in one room because they only had fuel enough to keep one room in the house warm.

I took a test the other day and received 100% again. That was in physics too. It's getting to be a habit with me but once in a while I miss…

Lovingly

Ladd."

SAACC, San Antonio, Texas, December 31, 1942

"Dear Ethel…

Perhaps you have seen these colored designs made of candy that they use to decorate cakes and etc. for Christmas. The cakes we had for Christmas were decorated with them and of course everybody made a grab for the pieces that had the decorations on them until someone picked one off and looked at the backside of it. They all had "made in Germany" printed on the backside which was pressed into the frosting of the cake.

By the way, I made that 100 in Physics also 100% in maps and charts yesterday. The more they throw at me the better I am able to learn it, it seems…

Love

Ladd"

SAACC, San Antonio, Texas, January 1, 1943

"Dear Ethel…

We had a surprise yesterday. They have been getting more WAACS and etc. around here all the time, first they started taking over office jobs, then staff car jobs, after that taxi, ambulance and truck drivers' jobs. Yesterday they really hit the top. "Guess what?"; female athletic instructors. What next? Personally I don't think they can go much farther than that. You can imagine what it is like for a class of 500 men to be out on the athletic field taking calisthenics from a pretty girl in red shorts and a white sweater. They were taking pictures of one of the girls instructing a class. I imagine they will use them to get more young men to enlist in the Cadets, young men who don't realize that a girl can practically kill them when it comes to calisthenics. Especially when she can rest for the rest of the day and they have to give all they've got from morning until night.

The girls do a good job as far as their work is concerned but most of them are so immoral that it makes any decent man feel disgusted with them. You might not realize what it has been like but it is bad enough that the government has had large posters made and put up all over the place which say, "Girls! Take a tip," and then list about 20 "don'ts" for the girls on the post...

Love

Ladd"

Picture from PM's Daily Pictures Magazine that Dad included in the letter.
It shows SAACC Cadets in formation for General Arnold. The formation
covered 10 acres. Reported December 24, 1942

SAACC, San Antonio, Texas, January 8, 1943

"Dearest Ethel…

I'm sorry that I wasn't able to write but it was impossible. I've been forced to make up physical training that I missed besides doing my regular work every day. I took physical training for 4 ½ hrs. yesterday. That was possible due to the fact that I have finished up my academic subjects. My average in Physics was 99% which isn't bad considering that most of the fellows have to sweat to even pass it.

The man the arrow points to is the only one in the picture I know. His name is Hare. Notice the mixture of uniforms. We still don't have enough of one kind for the men to be dressed all alike. We have been issued 3 different types and color tones in blouses alone.

Gym — Just completed

The newly finished gym at SAACC, San Antonio, TX, 1942.

Athletic   Field

The athletic field at SAACC, San Antonio, TX, fall, 1942.

Not Pajamas, Not Long Underwear (over)

A cadet wearing the standard athletic uniform. Dad wrote the following on the back of the picture: Not pajamas. Not long underwear. This is what the Air Corps calls an Athletic Uniform. It is heavy woolen goods lined with fleece. You don't know what it is to sweat until you wear one of them on a hot day.

SAACC postcard entitled, "War Games - S.A.A.C.C.," San Antonio, TX 1942." Note on back from Dad: Remember one of the pictures I sent you that showed a young man in an athletic uniform standing on the porch of our barracks. Here he is again. The one on the right. [*sic*] Posed picture by aviation cadets. [*sic*]

A picture from the middle of the cross country course at SAACC, San Antonio, TX—picture #11 from a series of fifteen pictures Dad took of the course.

No. 14. The last big hill. It doesn't look like it in the picture but this hill goes up at an angle of better than 70°. When you have been running for 2 miles before you come to it, it is just about enough to break your heart.

That song about Texas has been popular here for quite a while. It fits most of us pretty well. I certainly have too much of Texas in my walk…

…these will probably be the last pictures I can send to you for a while because they took my camera away from me again. Everywhere you go they decide to do that after a while.

Love

Ladd"

SAACC, San Antonio, Texas, January 10, 1943

"Dear Ethel…

I expect to leave here about Thursday morning. That is not official, I am just reading the signs as you might say. I don't have the least idea where I am going as yet but just as soon as I find out I will write and let you know…

Lovingly

Ladd"

SAACC, San Antonio, Texas, January 13, 1943

"Dear Ethel

I'm shipping out for sure now. I am leaving 4:30 Friday morning for Harmon Flying School, Ballinger, Texas…

…If you searched those pictures for me you were out of luck because I wasn't even in the bunch that listened to him speak *(referring to General Arnold)*. I was on guard duty that day at the Service Club. I didn't miss everything though because I stood at the door at attention while General Arnold entered with his staff to inspect.

Ballinger, where I will be going now, is you might as well say the very heart of Texas. If you look it up on a map you will find it is located about in the exact center of Texas. I might as well say too that there isn't any chance that I will be shipped nearer home for any of my training…

Love

Ladd"

SAACC, San Antonio, Texas, January 14, 1943

"Dear Ethel…

I am all packed and just waiting now for 4:45 a.m. to come around and then I will leave…

I said before that I was all packed, in fact my baggage is already gone. When I leave in the morning I hope it will be the last I see of S.A.A.C.C.[*sic*] for a long time unless it should be in peace time…

Love

Ladd"

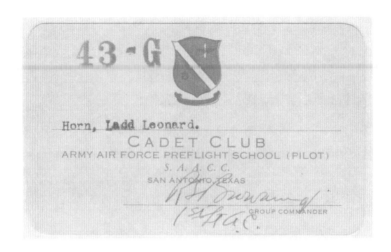

Bruce Field, Ballinger, Texas, January 16, 1943

"Dear Ethel,

I arrived here last night at 8 o'clock. I can't describe the country round about except to say that if you can imagine utter desolation this is it.

When we came into these parts and saw what it looked like we gave up all hope. We pulled into a station without even any electric lights in a town that at night appeared very much like some of the towns you see in some of the western magazines. Practically no lights were lit any place and things really looked dreary.

The country here is all flat plains as far as you can see except that some are raised up about 2-300 ft above others just like large flat table tops perhaps 10-20 miles each way. I can't describe it very well but I will draw a picture of the way the land lays.

These plateaus have almost an absolute straight drop down to the lower level. Just as straight as it shows in the sketch I drew. [*sic*] The slanted line shows the way the roads go up onto them.

When we arrived in the station we were met by buses and loaded onto them. We started up a road then onto one of these plateaus, it was a road that would almost take a mule to go up. The buses went up this road in low and second for about 3 miles and needless to say most of us felt pretty forlorn and disgusted with the place before we even saw it, especially considering that we had had one scant meal in 18 hours of travel with nothing in prospect but a few cold cuts and some cheese when we did arrive which is what the Army always gives you when you arrive at a camp at a time other than a regular meal time.

We finally reached the top of the plateau and then ----- we arrived at paradise.

The field is built up like some high class country club. It was arranged like a large tourist court with nice lawns and shrubs. There are sidewalks all around and everything is meticulously clean and neat. The barracks inside are finished in knotty pine, each man has a large locker for himself and there is a desk for every two men with individual desk lamps for each.

As soon as we arrived we were taken to a mess hall finished like and furnished like a high class cafeteria, in fact even better. They had hot roast beef, hot biscuits, pudding, hot coffee, milk, tomatoes and lettuce salad ready and waiting for us. As soon as we had eaten they issued us blankets, sheets and pillows and put us to bed in ¾ width beds with coil springs and good thick mattresses. They felt better than anything I have been in in a long time.

To show you something more of what it is like we have bathrooms all furnished in white, refrigerated drinking fountains, venetian blinds and a negro porter.

The surprising thing is that this is all done at the same expense per man as it was in the other camps where I have been. That shows what can be done under efficient management.

Another good thing is that our schedule is just as efficient as everything else. Everything is done correctly, in order and on the exact second. If our whole army was run as this one small field is the war would have been over already.

Our training will be tough but when everything else is good it makes it an awfully lot easier.

Almost every place I have been the arrival of men at a camp was always accompanied by confusion, disorder and mix-ups. Here everything was taken care of, our orders and records checked and all equipment issues made in just a few minutes. Everyone knew what needed to be done and did it. In the U. S. Army that is unusual. It was so different that I haven't been able to get over it yet.

From those that I have sent you, you have a pretty good idea of the technical manuals that we study from. I'm going to list some of the others that I have to study and more or less absorb. Those that I sent you of course are just basic military principles while these are more technical.

Air navigation, 2. Theory of flight, 3. Aircraft engines, 4. Weather, 5. Aircraft electrical systems, 6. Airplane inspection, 7. Aircraft propellers, 8. Airplane hydraulic systems, 9. Aircraft engine operation, 10. Aircraft induction, fuel and oil systems, 11. Airplane structures.

You see that as a "Flight Officer" I have to be a lot more than just a pilot. Flying is one of the lesser jobs in a way. As flight officer you are head man over the entire crew and you have to be a little bit of everything. You have to be bombardier, radioman, gunner, and everything else. You even have to be somewhat of a mechanic. In case of emergency you are supposed to be able to take over any man's job in the crew.

I'm hoping that I will be able to make it all the way through the course. I'd hate to wash out after what I have gone through so far. However, whatever training I do get through is worthwhile knowledge to have.

We are allowed to take pictures here so perhaps I will be sending you some more one of these days. We have to have our pictures and films censored though so I don't know how much of a picture they will allow us to send home…

Love

Ladd"

Dad also sent a thorn—about 4" long—in the envelope with the comment that "these grow everywhere around here."

Bruce Field, Ballinger, Texas, January 19, 1943

"Darling…

This is the nicest place I have been at so far. I don't enjoy being away from home but as long as I have to be away I can't expect anything better than this.

I might say that women are getting into this war more and more. We have women mechanics here…

Yours truly

Ladd"

Bruce Field, Ballinger, Texas, January 21-24, 1943

"Dear Ethel…

I didn't fool you any this time and stay at San Antonio. I moved out just about the time that I expected. I was set back some by being in the hospital but I am still ahead of some of those who started out with me.

…I'll have a few more *(pictures)* that I took myself to send to you one of these days. I said that I took myself, I meant pictures of myself that someone else took. I don't know how they'll turn out as yet but I'm hoping for the best. They were taken while I had my flying clothes on. Even if they turn out good I don't think you will be able to tell that it is me.

a.

b.

a. …a winter flying suit for the open cockpit planes we were training in at Ballinger Texas. Picture taken in front of barracks at Ballinger, TX. b. …the winter flying suit for the open cockpit planes we were training in. Goggles down and collar up. In front of the barracks at Ballinger, TX. You felt bundled up, but those suits were warm. The gloves were really nice.

I'm going to enclose a couple of pieces of one of the planes that one of the fellows handled a little bit roughly. The thin plywood piece is a splinter of the covering that is placed on the wings and forms the outside contours. The little piece of stuff like tinfoil is the aluminum skin that in turn covers the plywood. It may not seem possible but that little thin layer of aluminum increases the strength of the covering about three times and the wood and metal together are stronger and a lot lighter than sheet iron.

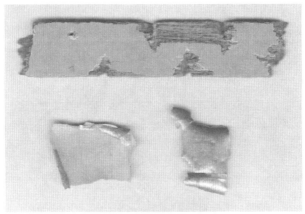

January 24, 1943

...I decided to enclose those couple of pieces of that plane because I thought it might be kind of a thrill to you to own a couple of pieces of a cracked up U.S. Army plane. I may be flying that very plane any day because it has already been rebuilt and is in use. Cracking up a plane doesn't mean much to us, we only cracked up six in one day not long ago. That doesn't mean much, they only cost $12,000 apiece.

Life isn't without its funny moments even here. One of the boys went up and forgot to buckle his safety belt. After he was up awhile he decided to do a loop with the result that when he reached the top of the loop he fell out of the cockpit. He landed ok with his chute but the poor plane leveled out and flew cross country on its own until it finally connected with a mountainside farther west of here.

One of the boys quit the day before yesterday. His plane fell into a spin and he tried everything he knew to pull it out without any success. Finally he remembered that these planes fly a level course of their own accord at 2100 revolutions per minute and let go of the controls. After falling about a mile the plane leveled out. He landed the plane and went directly to headquarters and told them that he was no longer a pilot. I don't blame him much because you don't know what a sick scary feeling is until after you have been in a spin. If you ever spin close to the ground that is the end right then and there and it is the only thing a pilot worries much about…

The planes that we are flying here have a takeoff speed of 94 miles per hour but when you get them in the air you can't coax them up to more than about 130 at the most. They are "red-lined" at 220 mph but you would have to point them straight down with the throttle wide open to get them to go that fast. We're flying them on practically kerosene. We are using 65 octane gas. You can ask your dad how his car would run on that. I don't think he would care to use very much of it even with gasoline being rather scarce…

Love

Ladd"

Bruce Field, Ballinger, Texas, January 27, 1943

"Dearest Ethel…

I will be here for about 8-9 weeks then I expect to go to San Angelo, Texas. That is not at all official but I think that is what will happen. That is also if my flying continues to please the Army. This flying is different from civilian flying. We do all what is known as precision flying. It would take a lot of paper to describe completely the difference but I will try to give you some idea.

When I put a ship into a spin I don't have to just put it in and pull it out as a civilian flyer would. I have to clear my area with two exact 90° turns first and then go into the spin from a certain definite direction, allow the ship to turn a certain number of times, pull it out in an indicated direction determined beforehand with the engine turning over a certain number of rpms. To do that would make a lot of civilian pilots sweat blood but still they are good pilots. Another thing that is different is our landings. We have to make perfect 3 point landings every time. Even the Navy Air Corps allows so called wheel landings but they're not for us.

For two days we couldn't do any flying here. We fly in almost any kind of weather but the day before yesterday we had a blizzard and yesterday it was so cold that the wings and propellers of the planes collected so much ice that they couldn't stay in the air but a few minutes at a time. It was beautiful to see a plane flying though. The hot exhaust would condense and freeze and leave a silver trail for a couple of miles behind the plane.

To show you the kind of weather we have here—one day last week it was -4°, the next day we had a dust storm, the next day it was 85°, the afternoon of the next day we had a blizzard, the next day it was so cold the planes collected too much ice to fly and the next day, which was today, it was like a warm balmy day in June at home. All this happens within 200 miles of San Antonio where it is warm summer nearly the whole year. They claim Amarillo, Texas is the coldest place in the U.S. I can believe it after being here.

If you want to know where I have been doing most of my flying, it has mostly been over or within sight of the Colorado River.

I did pretty well with my flying according to my instructor this morning. I ended up in the hospital though just the same. I had a slight case of sniffles and I went up pretty high to practice some spins. I made out ok as far as the flight was concerned but the high altitude raised Cain with my ears, nose and sinuses. This afternoon I came over to see the doctor and he took one look at me and said go get your toothbrush and come visit me awhile. I hadn't expected him to do anything more than give me a few nose drops or something so this was rather unexpected but if he wants me to be in bed I'm willing.

At one of the training bases (Likely either Ballinger or San Angelo, TX) many of the cadets got some flu-like sickness. My dad eventually got it as well and had to go into the health center. After the doctor checked him over, he placed an order for bed rest and ordered him to take so many medications, that my dad simply described the number of pills he had to take as, "hands full." My dad did not want to take that many pills and asked the doctor to confirm that he had to take them all. The doctor told him, "'yes, it is the best thing we have found for this flu, so take them." My dad did, but after taking them for several days and recovering his strength, when he got up, he had very bad "vertigo" and had trouble feeling things with his fingers (neuropathy-like symptoms). He knew that with the vertigo he could not fly all maneuvers, and if he was too bad, he would be taken out of flight training. He hid the symptoms as well as he could, but on his next flight training day, he still was unable to fly. His flight instructor recognized he was having problems. He finally told Dad to get in the seat and they would simply fly without maneuvers of any kind and he would give him credit. The "vertigo" symptoms decreased over time and Dad was able to control it well enough to continue flight training. Dad suffered from both symptoms ("vertigo" and "neuropathy") the rest of his life.

349 Let The Kicking Mule Kick
348 Let The Kicking Mule Kick

I think I told you one of the guys quit because he was scared by a spin. Yesterday we had another fellow quit because of the same reason. I don't know whether I am too dumb to be scared of one or what but I am getting to where I get a big kick out of doing one. All it takes is a little will power to keep control of your senses so that you remember and know what to do and it becomes a thrill to do it. If you once get rattled or just kick the controls around then it is all off. It seems funny but just by will power you can learn to force yourself to retain consciousness under twice the strain that would cause a normal person to lose their senses or "blackout" as a pilot would say.

I told you once before I think, that I thought I was being trained for combat in the far east. I am led to believe that is true more than ever due to the fact that we have Chinese pilots for instructors here. The one I have *(Young G. Wong)* speaks English very well but some of them speak quite brokenly. My instructor is only just about 5 ft tall so you can imagine the kind of appearance we make.

The ships we are flying are supposed to be some of the simplest that there are but I counted up and there are 25 instruments that you use at least once each flight; 7 of them you use continuously in flight and most of them are used at least several times…

Yours truly

Ladd"

Left: Cadet, Bennett, from Endicott, NY; Right: Young G. Wong, Dad's Chinese instructor at Bruce Field, Ballinger, Texas 1943. Dad moved to Ballinger on January 15th of 1943, so this picture was taken in the spring of 1943.

Bruce Field, Ballinger, Texas, January 30, 1943 *(See also the excerpt of this letter at the beginning of "PART II The War Through The Lens of Love.")*

"Dear Ethel...

I'm going to enclose a picture of one of the planes that we fly here. It's just one that I tore from a magazine but it shows pretty well what the planes are like. To give you a method for estimating the size the vertical fin is about 7 ft high and the fuselage would be a little longer than your house. It has about the same weight as your dad's car and gets about 5 mi to the gallon of gas at the most economical speed. It is redlined at 220 mph. Your car I guess is redlined at about 35 now...

Love

Ladd"

Bruce Field, Ballinger, Texas, February 2-3, 1943

"Dear Ethel...

I bought something for you yesterday that I am going to mail as soon as I get the chance...It is a silk scarf made from a strip of a parachute. The material of course is about 5 years old but you will find that it is about the best silk that there could possibly be and extremely durable for being silk. New silk of course is rationed and they can barely get enough to even patch the chutes that we are using here. The old silk of course is never used to patch a new chute...

…These authors and reporters seem to be able to take a few facts and fill an awfully lot in between. A lot of it is just purposely for the public to swallow.

Just the other day I was reading in the Dallas paper. There was an article there going into a lot of detail explaining the Jap "0" wasn't such a wonderful ship after all. When it ended up it said that recent tests had shown that at least one of our fighter ships was superior. It didn't go on to say that that one ship isn't in use yet. That's the trouble, they write everything up so that it sounds big. The ship they meant probably was the new model of the North American Mustang which at present is supposed to be the best fighting ship in the world. That is according to the Army.

You asked what it felt like to fly. I can tell you that if you ever want to fly with me you will have to be able to stand a lot more than that large "Rolly [*sic*] Coaster" at Crystal Beach. The feeling is a lot on the same principle only stronger. The ride is smoother though because after all it is cushioned on air…

I'll have to warn you though not to be too surprised if I should be kicked out of the Air Corps one of these times. There are only about 20% of us that make it all the way through and that's not much of a margin to work on. The boys around me are getting E rides as we call them right and left every day. That E doesn't stand for Excellence.

Love

Ladd"

Bruce Field, Ballinger, Texas, February 2, 1943

"Dear Ethel…

You asked me to take it easy on my plane. Well I did, but one of the other fellows took it up three mornings ago and he didn't. The last I saw of it they were picking up the pieces from one of the auxiliary fields and loading them in the back of a truck. He flew the plane right into the ground. The wheels and landing gear were ripped off, the engine was torn out, the left wing was broken completely in two and the right wing was torn from the plane. He sat in the middle of the wreck with pieces laying all around and nothing more wrong with him than a bloody nose.

We had two more crackup yesterday and one so far this morning. Out of 101 ships we only have 81 in flying condition now. If we keep it up in a few more days we will have to be flying kites instead of planes.

One of the boys from our bay came in for a cross wind landing yesterday and the wind caught his plane sideways and knocked one wing into the ground and then the other. After bouncing around along the ground for a ways he succeeded in getting the plane clear of the ground and into the air again. He went up into traffic and came around again for another landing but by the time that he got ¾ of the way around the traffic pattern his plane was falling apart under him from the beating it took when he came in the first time. He got it in alright though minus a strip of one wing and a few other small things.

It has got to where a crack up is the only excitement that we have around here…

I'm not doing so well with my flying lately. I don't know just what is wrong but for some reason or other I just can't seem to judge distance from the air. I have good depth perception and on the ground I can look across country and tell very well just how long or wide a certain field is and how far it is to it but when I get in the air and look straight down I can't judge the distance at all. In a forced landing I will pass up a large field and try to set the plane down in a small one. If I can't overcome that some way I won't last long as a pilot. It bothers me even coming into a marked air field because I can't judge where my traffic lanes are, due to the same reason.

Well, since I started this letter I was up for an hour and just came down again. I couldn't seem to do any better today either. I think the ship that I am flying is jinxed. It happens to be ship no. 13. There's nothing I can do about that though.

The crackups for today number 3 now. We've smashed up so many ships that the officers are having a meeting of some kind to see if something can be done about it. It will probably mean that an awfully lot of us will be washed out.

I hadn't told you before but there are only 206 of us that came here to start with. We're leaving now at the rate of about 6 a day. I've been going over to the flight stage every day expecting to see my name up on the bulletin board but so far it hasn't been up there. All I can say is that if you want me to make good in this you will have to pray that I will be able to do better from now on. If I should wash out after going this far I would feel so ashamed of myself that I couldn't hold my head up…

Love

Ladd"

Control tower at Bruce Field in Ballinger TX. The guys waiting are waiting for the previous guys to get back with their plane so they can take their run.

Bruce Field, Ballinger, Texas, February 9, 1943

"Dear Ethel…

Well, I think that I have made the grade today. I improved some on my flying yesterday and today I didn't do good but I didn't do too terribly bad although after two of the landings I made my instructor said I'm getting out, if your [*sic*] going to fly it that way you can fly by yourself. I'm not going to ride with you. When I came in today though he told me to fill in the IA form of the ship and put S.P. in the box provided for it. S.P. stands for Senior Pilot so that means I can wear wings on my Flight Cap now and also that I can sign a ship out and OK it as far as flight is concerned. Before this my instructor has always had to OK the ship and sign it out for me.

I think I have one of the forms that are used on every plane and I'll enclose it so you can see what it is like; also a dispatcher's clearance slip such as you have to turn in to the control tower of an airport before you can take off. It may be of interest to you to see what they are like.

I wish that I could take you up with me and show you what it is like. My instructor swears that I am going to stall or spin in and break my neck one of these days though so maybe you are lucky that I can't take you up.

We fellows are a little too tough for some of our instructors. Two of the fellows have blacked their instructors out or caused them to lose consciousness by pulling their planes out of dives too fast for the instructor to stand it. I wish you could hear one of the fellow's version of it. We call him "Hoiman the Goiman from Joisey" and he can really tell it. He went into a spin and then pulled out of the spin in a dive. He looked at his altimeter and found he was down to 900 ft so he decided that he had better start going up so he pulled back on the stick. He claims that he didn't feel anything at all but the first thing he knew he couldn't see the instructor in the front cockpit anymore. He leveled out and flew straight for a while and pretty soon the instructor's head came up above the side of the cockpit, he kind of shook himself a little bit, rubbed his head and then turned around slowly and looked at "Hoiman" and said take this thing in and land it. To hear "Hoiman" tell it you couldn't help but burst out laughing. He puts in all the actions that go with it.

We have another boy here who is an exact living replica of "Mortimer Snurd." His voice even sounds exactly the same. He is about 6' 2" tall very thin and gawky, has brilliant red hair and the dumbest expression on his face that you ever saw. When it comes right down to it though he is very brilliant. If you ever heard him say just 3 words you would swear that it was Mortimer Snurd and if you saw him you would know that it was except that he is life size and very much alive rather than made of wood.

If this letter seems to have a lot of light brown dust and grit in it, it is because we have been having another dust storm. Along the road to town the dust has drifted and been ploughed off just like snow. It was piled 2 to 3 ft deep along the road in some places Saturday and fresh dust had already drifted across until the pavement was covered.

Ladd"

Flight report showing aircraft inspection data Ballinger, TX.

*Typical flight report Young G. Wong, instructor, and Ladd L. Horn, pilot
Ballinger, TX.*

Bruce Field, Ballinger, Texas, February 11, 1943

"Dear Ethel…

For some reason or other I haven't been flying too well lately. I improved some today but not much. I have some days when I can fly very well and then other days I can't seem to do anything right. I'm only just making it and that's all. I have already outlasted almost all the fellows that I started training with so that is some consolation. I'm going to hang on just as long as I possibly can but I don't know as I have much reason to hope that I can make it all the way through but no one can say that I didn't try.

They held a special meeting the other night and told us that the training program has caught up with the number of pilots that are needed and from now on only the quality of the pilot counts. That is the reason for the terrific number of washouts that we have had. There is a whole list every day. We had 19 leave the other day.

One of the men we had with us was from the R.A.F. He joined up when the war started and asked to be transferred to the Army Air Force last summer. He had had 2,000 hrs. of combat flying in a Spitfire over England, the Channel and France. A couple of days ago they washed him out. He couldn't fly one of these trainers well enough to suit them. That shows you something of what we are up against. You almost have to have the ability to fly born in you if you are going to pass the tests. If I get washed out though it looks as though it will be for dangerous flying rather than inability. I just don't have enough sense to be scared I guess. My instructor keeps telling me time after time that I am going to break my neck. Both me [*sic*] and my instructor were reported today I think for dangerous flying. Ship no 13 is too easy to remember. It seems when anyone sees that number on a plane they automatically remember it…

Love

Ladd"

Bruce Field, Ballinger, Texas, February 13, 1943

"Dear Ethel…

…there are only 15 of us left in our bay. There were 28 to start with.

They claim that probably one man out of each 10 will get through to go to basic training. That will mean that in the end there will probably be about 25 of us left out of the 206 that came here originally.

I don't know how much you understand about the training but I can give you a brief outline of the four stages.

1. Pre-flight of course gives you the groundwork for flight. Elementary navigation, physics and mathematics of flight.
2. Primary is to teach you to fly a plane the Army way whether you have never flown before or if you have flown thousands of hours. Along

with it you receive the basic groundwork for instrument flying.

3. Basic training is to teach you instrument and formation flying.

4. Advanced training then comes along and you have to learn transitional flying. That is you have to learn to go out and fly a pursuit ship, an Attack bomber or a B-24 without it making any difference to you. The idea is to get you so trained that you can get into a Piper Cub or a B-17E and feel just as much at home in one as the other and be able to fly your best in either.

I'm still hanging on as far as my flying is concerned. I have improved some and am starting to regain hope again that I can make the grade. They only give you three grades in your flying; failing, passing and OK. They put a line --- for failing, a check for passing and OK for good. The reports my instructor turns in on me are all check marks.

I'm going to enclose a snapshot of myself in a flying suit…

I just figured out that when I am up in the air flying one of these planes around there is $50,000 flying around with me.

In case you are interested the other boy who is shown in the picture looking toward the camera is Edward Hoey usually called, "Hooey." He is from Boston, Mass. He weighs about 200 lbs. and is Irish through and through. He is the only man left who started flying in ship no. 13. He is also the only one I know of who has gone up for an "E" ride and survived…

Love

Ladd"

Ladd L. Horn *(right)* and Edward Hoey *(left)* at Ballinger Field, Texas.

Bruce Field, Ballinger, Texas, February 15, 1943

"Dear Ethel…

…Don't think that just because I told you I might wash out that I was quitting or that I had any superstition about the number 13. The thing was that for all of one week and part of the next my flying was so close to the edge of failing that it wasn't at all funny. It wasn't at all that I can't fly it is just that I have to rank in the top 10% in order to get by and I have the best men in the country to compete against. That doesn't make it easy to rank that high. Many of the men have flown for several years before and those of us who haven't have to fly just as well as they do in the few weeks of flying that we get here…I have improved enough in the past few days though so that I think I can make it. I'll have to continue this later because I have to get ready to go up right now.

Since I stopped writing I have been up for 1:53. I didn't do too badly this afternoon. I had to shoot 5 landings first because I was being graded on them today. The first one was good but the others were just average. I'm gradually getting better though. After that I went up for an hour by myself. That's the only time that it is really any fun but even then you have to watch your step every minute. I had an old ship that is just about completely worn out instead of my regular 13. It was spitting oil and I got a pretty good dose even in the rear cockpit. The first cockpit was all spattered with oil. Its ceiling was only about 10,000 feet. I put it in a spin and it took me five turns to pull it out. Your [sic] not supposed to spin over 3 turns with these ships so technically I should have bailed out but I pulled it out and brought it in. What someone else doesn't know won't hurt them.

You asked me about the kind of camera that I have. It is an Eastman Baby Brownie that takes 127 film. You can't change the focus, shutter speed or lens opening of it so the whole secret of getting good pictures lies in using the correct film…

Those monkey suits are brilliant blue with wide gold braid stripes down the sides. They are just like you see the monkeys dressed in at the circus or the fair. The boys saw the similarity immediately and they were dubbed "monkey suits" from the time they were first issued.

The reason I mentioned the Colorado River was because I figured that if you looked Ballinger up on a map you would see the river and be able to judge just about where I was doing my flying. If you get that map out again look for a point where the Concho River flows into the Colorado then follow up the Colorado for about 40 miles taking in a strip about 15 to 20 miles wide and you will have the area that we are flying in most of the time…

…A good many of these boys have wives and children at home that they are trying to support and how they possibly do it is beyond me. I'll enclose one of my pay envelopes so that you can see what we get. Our pay isn't too bad to start with but after the deductions are taken out we don't have much left. That "Escrow" marked on the envelope is what we call "The Mexican General We Support." Perhaps you get the idea. What it really is, is washout insurance so that the government won't lose if we should washout. Besides what shows on the envelope I have to pay for laundry and dry cleaning about $6 a month and then Pilot's log and also for having our barracks cleaned. On top of that they have the nerve to ask us for donations to the Red Cross, Army and Navy War Relief and a lot of others. We kind of feel that those things ought to be up to some of the others at home to take care of…

Love

Ladd"

Pay $126.58 — Class "A" allotment $16.35 Your Check $ 110.33
A/C   Horn, L.L.

Balance Due	
Board and Room	35.88
Coupon Book	
Laundry	
Barber Shop	.70
Bus Ticket	.24
Class Party	
Escrow	20.00
Telephone	
Photograph	
Class Book	
Red Cross	
Other	
Total	57.48
Balance $	52.85

Bruce Field, Ballinger, Texas, February 21, 1943

"Dear Ethel…

You asked about how much flying we have to do before we can go up alone. You have to do from 8 to 16 hours of flying before you can go up alone. If you can't fly a plane by yourself in 12 hours though you have to be pretty good in certain ways or you will be washed out. Sometimes you can fly allright [*sic*] all except for one thing such as landing, taking off, keeping a normal glide or something similar. If that is the case they will allow you as many as 17 hours to overcome that inability, that is if you show continued improvement. If that improvement doesn't continue though you will find yourself washed out so quickly that it will make your head swim…

Ladd"

DATE	MAKE OF AIRCRAFT	CLASS	TYPE	CERTIFICATE NUMBER	MAKE OF ENGINE	H.P.	REMARKS OR INSPECTOR'S SIGNATURE CERTIFICATION NUMBER AND RATING
2/21/43	Fairchild		PT MA	U.S. Army	Ranger	175	
2/22/43	"	"	"	"	"	"	
2/23/43	"	"	"	"	"	"	
2/24/43	"	"	"	"	"	"	
2/25/43	"	"	"	"	"	"	
2/26/43	"	"	"	"	"	"	
2/27/43	"	"	"	"	"	"	
3/1/43	"	"	"	"	"	"	
3/3/43	"	"	"	"	"	"	
3/4/43	"	"	"	"	"	"	
3/5/43	"	"	"	"	"	"	

I HEREBY CERTIFY THAT THE FOREGOING ENTRIES ARE TRUE AND CORRECT.

SIGNED *Ladd L. Horn*

FROM	TO	INSTRUMENT RADIO OR HOOD	DUAL AS INSTRUCTOR	DUAL AS STUDENT	SOLO DAY	SOLO NIGHT	DAILY TOTAL TIME
Ballinger, Texas	Local			40	1 45		2 25
"	"			55	1 00		1 55
"	"			42	55		1 37
"	"			55	40		1 35
"	"			1 00	40		1 40
"	"			45	25		1 10
"	"			55	1 25		2 20
"	"			10	1 45		1 55
"	"			1 05	45		1 50
"	"				2 00		2 00
"	"			30	1 35		2 05
	TOTAL			7 37	12 55		30 32
	AMT. FORWARD			15 38	7 00		22 38
	TOTAL TO DATE			23 15	19 55		43 10

Dad's pilot's log book used during his training at Bruce Field, Ballinger, TX.

Bruce Field, Ballinger, Texas, February 27, 1943

"Dearest Ethel…

You asked in one of your letters what I meant by an "E" ride. The "E" stands for "elimination" and this boy who sleeps under me is the only one I know of who had one and wasn't actually eliminated. I'm afraid though that he will be put up for another one this coming week and perhaps me with him.

I had two check rides last week and failed my first one but passed my second one. I've been trying to do the best that I possibly could but I'm still afraid that that might not be good enough to suit the Army. I do know though that I can fly better than the average civilian pilot by far or they never would have kept me this long. We have to learn twice as much in one third the time that a civilian pilot has and everything has to be perfect…

Right at present I have to try to master "Chandelles" and "Lazy Eights." To do them the way they want them are some of the hardest maneuvers that there are. You find too many pilots who do just an imitation of them and that is as far as they get. Even now I could give most of the "Barnstormers" that I have seen a pretty good run for their money…

I'm wondering if you can read code like this, we have to learn several different kinds that are similar. There are more than a hundred characters in each and we have to learn to read them in about three days as though they were regular English.

RJ SPL E50 0/0 62L-121/ / →/ 12+/989/FEW/200
RANDTBRONO ICGIOVC TOVC 8 tHSDMSL FCST PLPN +

The first line says that according to a special report published at the regular time there is an estimated ceiling of broken clouds at 5000 ft at Buffalo, New York. There are high broken clouds above 10,000 ft and some scattered clouds at 2,000 ft. Visibility is six miles and there is a light freezing drizzle. The barometer stands at 1012.2 millibar, the temperature is 31° Fahrenheit and the dew point is 32°. The wind is west southwest at 12 miles per hr with strong gusts now and then. The altimeter setting is 29.89 Hg. The radio vane is not in operation nor is the broadcasting station.

The second line is just some of the abbreviations that we use. You can try to figure them out if you want to but I don't think you will have much success…

Lovingly

Ladd"

Bruce Field, Ballinger, Texas, February 28, 1943

"Darling…

I have to try to pass that check ride someway. If I shouldn't pass, it doesn't necessarily mean that I will no longer be a Cadet, but it does mean that I won't be a pilot. If I should fail they will probably try to make a navigator out of me.

I can fly pretty well and get the maneuvers that they want fairly well only I can't seem to learn them quite quickly enough for what they want. I could evidently make a good pilot but whether I can do it in the time that they allow is what is bothering me right now.

I believe that the only thing that passed me this last time was the kind of landings that I made. Most of the students have trouble with their landings but both times that I was up with the check pilot I made good landings. The second time that I was up with him I made such a perfect landing that you couldn't tell the wheels touched the ground. One second the ship was still flying and the next it was rolling on the ground and it happened so smoothly that there was no way you could tell definitely when the change took place. He tried to get me to admit afterwards that my landings were luck but I didn't give him any satisfaction on that point. He is used to jack rabbit landings and everything else from students and I guess a couple of good ones seemed kind of funny to him especially when my flying in the air wasn't good enough for what he wanted…

You spoke of an Air Corps Officer in one of your letters recently who wore and emblem of a three-bladed propeller. I imagine that this is the kind of emblem he wore

If that was the case he wasn't in the Air Corps at all or the Army either but is a CPA pilot. I imagine he wore a forest green shirt and pinkish gray trousers and a pair of small gold wings. The CPA is made up of pilots who for some reason or other are unable to qualify as Army pilots. They fly their own planes for the Army and any kind or make from up-to-date planes to some that are practically antiques. They are responsible for the patrol of the coast and many other duties. Their planes while many of them are nothing more than Piper Cubs are armed and carry a few bombs and can deliver a very unexpected sting due to their rather peaceful and helpless appearance…

Yours truly

Ladd"

Bruce Field, Ballinger, Texas, March 1, 1943

"Dear Ethel

Just a couple of lines to let you know that I am thinking of you, still a cadet, still in the Air Corps, still flying and O.K. Still flying good in some ways bad in others, close to being washed out but not quite a goner. Six more of our boys were washed out today, one of them a boy that I thought surely would make it. That fat Irish boy was almost washed out again today but is still with us for a couple more days.

My engine quit on me once today but I got it running again ok. I thought for a minute I might have to make a forced landing.

I only burned up 70 gallons of gas this afternoon, I suppose you wish that you had some of it.

I passed another spot landing stage today and if I can just pass my check tomorrow I'll be alright for a while. I only have two more weeks to go through but they will be tough weeks. Perhaps I can sweat it out though.

Last spring if you had told me that I would risk my life flying a plane like the one I was in today I would have told you that you were crazy. Both landing struts were cracked, the engine was knocking, the oil temp was out, the front tachometer was out and the rudder would turn only partway to the left. To top it all off I was doing Chandelles and spins with it with full throttle most of the time.

Love

Ladd."

Bruce Field, Ballinger, Texas, March 2, 1943

"Dear Ethel…

We just found out today that they have raised the requirements for our flying and they expect to wash out more than half of the few of us who are left. That doesn't sound very good for me but I'm going to keep on trying and see if I can stick it out. It's only two weeks more and perhaps I can but it is a slim chance. Every man that went up for a ride yesterday was washed out so you can see what they are doing to us. Today the weather has been too bad to fly so we have had one more day of grace.

I don't know as I told you what happened to me the other night. We had an officer in charge who thinks he really is somebody big although he is only a

2nd Lt. The fellows have a name for him that I wouldn't dare mention and when he was making his rounds at night inspecting the barracks he found a couple of boys who were out of bed. He made them put on their pants and go run on the ramp. Some of the other fellows woke up and asked what the commotion was and he sent them out too. We were wakened by all the running outside and began to wonder what was going on. The head of my bed comes right to a window so I opened the venetian blind and looked out. Some of the other fellows wanted to know what was happening so I told them. Several had various comments to make on the situation and while they were still talking the lights were suddenly turned on. This officer had slipped into the other end of the barracks and listened to what everyone had to say. The result of course was the we found ourselves outside running along with the others who were already there. I'm telling you it is rather a shock to be yanked out of bed in the middle of the night when you were all warm and cozy and have to go out in the cold and run until you felt as though you were ready to drop. That bed felt awfully good though afterwards.

We received a lecture too of course to the extent that if we weren't tired enough to sleep at night they would see to it that we were in the future…

Lovingly

Ladd"

Bruce Field, Ballinger, Texas, March 3, 1943

"Dearest Ethel

Well, I don't know just how to feel about it but I passed my check this afternoon. They got the Irishman though and almost got another one of my buddies. They didn't get him today but I am afraid they will Friday on the recheck.

Passing this check today means that I will probably get in at least 15 more hours of flying without worry of washing out. Don't expect me to pass the next one though because it is almost an impossibility. I don't much care now though because I will have enough time in and be a good enough flyer to get a license without much trouble if I should want to when I get out of the Army. However, I would like to get through, more because you would like me to I guess than for any other reason. Perhaps then you could witness one of those presentations that you spoke of in your letter. If I don't make it as a pilot you may have the chance though anyway because I believe that I would have a better chance at the navigator's wings than I ever would at the pilot's. That was what I wanted to be when I first started out anyway.

I've learned since how to get to be a pilot if you really want to. Being a civilian though I didn't know the tricks of the trade, for that matter neither did the other boys from the old Army that I have with me. All you have to do is apply for O.C.S. school. That is officers candidate school where you will receive 90 days training and then just as soon as you receive your commission you apply for pilot training. The boys who were wise enough to do that are the ones who are becoming pilots. I have never known one of them to be washed out. We have several with us and one of them is just as dumb as they make them but you never hear of him failing anything. He asks such dumb questions sometimes that the rest of us can barely keep from laughing right out but you don't dare because after all he outranks you.

If any of the rest of us get through it is mostly luck or else pull. One boy got through although they actually admitted that he couldn't fly very well. His grandfather had something to do with the founding of Randolph Field so they couldn't wash him out because it wouldn't look right...

...They tell us that any of us who are left now are crazy so it doesn't matter anyway. I'm beginning to believe they are right. Tonight an old 1st sergeant who is here with me was standing by his locker pounding his head against it saying over and over again, "Primary doesn't affect me any."

If you were to see me right now you would see one of the most haggard looking young men that you ever saw in your life. I'm getting such rings under my eyes that you will soon be able to use me to shoot basketball. I've got so that I have to force my nerves to hold steady when I go up through sheer will power alone. The doctor here a while ago fed me 40 aspirin in 5 days and then I wouldn't take any more. My knee that they cut around on at San Antonio works fairly well now but I can't bend it all the way and never will be able to. I can't kneel on it even yet, not even on a bed where it is soft. I've got through calisthenics somehow so far and I haven't complained about it but I am still afraid that they may wash me out because of it if they don't for some other reason. At present I could never pass the entrance exam for the Cadets and if they should examine my eyes again I am afraid that would be my finish right then. I'm getting so that I can't see too well at a distance especially with one eye. A couple of times I have come into the airport and was unable to see which way the traffic tee was set. I had to let them think that I didn't know where the traffic pattern is for that setting. When I am up alone it is alright because I can hover in the let-down area until I see another plane go in for a landing and then I can determine the setting by the way he went in and go in myself. If I try that when the instructor or a check pilot is with me he wants to know what I am doing of course and all I can do is let on that I don't know. Most of the times so far though there has been enough planes coming in at the same time when I was on a ride that I could just follow them in. Today my check pilot had me come in at 500 ft so that was alright but normally I have to come in at 1,500 ft and about a half mile away at the least so that makes it a lot harder to see…

In one of your letters you spoke about chewing gum to keep from getting sick but I can tell you that it doesn't help much. It will help relieve the effect of altitude on your ears and sinuses though so most of us chew some when we are flying. As far as gum itself is concerned I don't care for it but do chew it for that reason.

If I ever get the chance I am going to take you up and put you in a real spin and let you know what it is really like to feel sick. You would like it though after you once got over the sickness…

Love

Ladd"

Bruce Field, Ballinger, Texas, March 7, 1943

"Dear Ethel…

I had a rather mean trick pulled on me yesterday though. I just finished one Army check Wed. and yesterday they gave me my next one. You are supposed to have about 20 hrs. of flying in between to learn Chandelles, lazy eights, steep turns and several other maneuvers. I had four hours. They seem determined to get rid of me some way or other but I think I beat them yesterday. I won't know for certain though until tomorrow…

They just lengthened the training period for the new Cadets by five more months…

Did you know that I was a weatherman now? I received a grade of 99 on my meteorology test the other day. I wonder if you know what a "theodolite" is…its use is to measure the velocity of wind aloft which is another headache that we have to contend with. I hit one at 5,000 ft the other day that blew me about 15 miles down the river so quickly that I could hardly realize what had happened to me. I headed my plane directly into the wind and flew for 7 minutes and only gained about a half mile of distance on the ground so I went into a dive and got down out of it. You hit some so strong sometimes that you can actually fly your plane backwards. Just a few weeks ago a pilot flew across

Great Salt Lake in his plane. There was nothing unusual about that except that he flew all the way across the lake going tail first.

By the way, I made another perfect landing for the check pilot the other day. You could barely feel the plane touch the ground and I made it in a strong wind too. Most of the fellows were either stalling them in or making wheel landings…

Someday I would like to take you up in a plane with me and show you that I can really fly whether they wash me out or not. It is a lot of fun and a thrilling sensation even though you do get sick sometimes from certain maneuvers, high altitude, rough air, etc. You never become entirely immune to that sickness either. I'm not bothered very much but I got the ship into a rather peculiar attitude the other day and in less than half a minute I was as sick as I have ever been. The two worst things are changing from a steep dive abruptly into a steep climb or the reverse of that. If you change the direction too suddenly you not only get sick but you lose consciousness until your body accustoms itself to the change…

…It has certainly been cold here. A couple of nights ago I even had my Army overcoat on the bed trying to keep myself warm. When I went out for reveille I had my leather flying jacket on with my overcoat on top of that. Even with that I almost froze before the formation was over. I haven't felt so cold in a long time…

Ladd"

Bruce Field, Ballinger, Texas, March 10, 1943

"Dear Ethel…

I don't know whether I told you in my last letter or not that I had passed my next check…The check pilot pulled almost any mean trick that you could think of and some too that you never would think of but I managed to out-do him somehow and passed O.K.

One of our boys cracked up yesterday. His engine stalled in a loop and he had a plane that was brand new with the result that his engine was so stiff that he couldn't start it again by diving the ship. He was over cultivated land that was full of fences, ditches and trees. When he saw what it was like he got rattled and tried to land the plane down wind. He just cleared three fences, tried to bounce the plane over a fourth and left his landing gear behind in a ditch, clipped a fence post and left most of his propeller behind, next came in contact with a mesquite tree and left one wing behind and finally ended up with the engine and fuselage in the middle of a ploughed field. Somehow he came through with nothing more than a few cuts around his forehead and face. He said, "Well, at least he brought the tail down in one piece if all the rest was smashed." It wasn't all loss though because after all he did get his name in the paper…

You know I'm the youngest man that is left flying out of the bunch that I came from pre-flight with. Most of the fellows range from 3-6 years older than me. More of them are nearer six than three years older. All the 18–19 and 20-year-olds have been washed out, also all but one of the married men. I'm beginning to wonder how they decided which ones to wash out anyway.

Saturday afternoon I expect to fly to Abilene and Sweetwater and then back to Ballinger…

Mar. 11

They gave me another check today. Again I should have had 20 hours between and I only had about 5. I don't know what the idea is but I think that I got past it all right…

I expect to leave here on the 20th if everything goes alright. I don't know where I will be going though. Waco, Greenwood and San Angelo, Texas are all possibilities but I can't be sure of any of them. My next period of training will cover heavier planes, night flying, instrument flying, and radio range flying. About the only daylight flying I will be doing will be formation flying.

I'll get a lot more instruction in code and radio operation also blinker code I imagine…

> Lovingly yours
>
>
> Ladd"

Form 06

STUDENT'S SOLO LOG

NAME _MORN, LADD L A*C_ NAME OF INST. _WONG, Y. G_ DATE _3-10-43_

DURATION OF FLIGHT FROM _10 45_ TO _11 40_ TIME _255_

PLANE NO. _13_ REMARKS ON CHARACTERISTICS OF PLANE _NONE_

- ✓ Landings & Take-offs
- Normal Glides & Gliding Turns
- ✓ Normal Climbs & Climbing Turns
- ✓ Medium Turns
- ✓ Coordination Exercises
- ✓ Steep Turns (1500')
- ✓ Stalls (Recovery Not Below 2000')
- ✓ Spins (Recovery not Below 2500')
- ✓ Rectangles & "S" Across Road (500')
- ✓ Elementary 8's (500')
- ✓ Chandelles (1500')
- ✓ Lazy 8's (2000')
- ✓ 90° Approach
- ( ) 180° Approach, Side-O'Head *
- ( ) 360° Approach
- ( ) Aerobatics (Recovery Not Below 2500')

STUDENT'S CERTIFICATE

I certify that I have practiced the maneuvers checked here on AND NO OTHERS, and at an altitude not lower than that specified.

Signature of Student: _Ladd L. Horn_

*Line Out One

(Over)

Form 22

CLEARANCE SLIP

CLASS _43-G_ DATE _3-10-43_

NAME _HORN, LADD L. A*C_ SHIP No. _13_

TIME _1345_

DUAL _____

SOLO ✓

WONG, YOUNG G.
Instructor

Bruce Field, Ballinger, Texas, March 13, 1943

"Dear Ethel…

…On top of that I am O.D. for tomorrow and Monday morning. That means I am going to be mighty busy. O.D. stands for "officer of the day" so that means that I will be running the whole place here for that period of time. It's too big a job for one man to handle steady so one man is appointed to take over for about a day at a time. It is sort of a case of playing nursemaid to everyone on the post for a day…

March 15, 1943

…I flew on a short cross-country trip today. It was fun for a change. We don't have too much to worry about now about getting through all right and everybody just went for a joy ride. Some of the folks in the small towns along the way saw a show that would have cost them a dollar at least any other time.

Ladd Horn ready to take off on a solo training flight in a PT-19 at Bruce Field, Ballinger, TX. Dad flew this plane on the day of his graduation, March 17, 1943. Note on back of photo: This is me ready to take off on my last flight on graduation day at Ballinger. The aerial picture in the group was taken from this plane on this flight *(Rowena, TX aerial picture)*. The plane was brand new, just delivered a few days before. 36' wing span 32' fuselage plane stands 9' high 7' propeller 175 horsepower.

Rowena, Texas 1 mile down and 5 miles away as seen from ship #20 on my graduation day at Bruce Field. Colorado River in foreground Ballinger-San Angelo highway runs diagonally across center of picture.

Continued again March 16, 1943

I was flying at a higher altitude than some of the fellows and had less headwind so I caught up with 3 other fellows over a small town. They were fooling around and doing some spins and stuff along the way. We got to flying side-by-side about a quarter of a mile apart and first one would do a snap roll, then the next one over would do one and so on down the line. Next one of us would do a loop and it would go on down the line the same way. For about 20 or 30 miles along the way everyone was doing snap rolls, slow rolls, loops, chandelles, flying upside down and everything else that's in the book. When I made my next change in course I lost the other fellows though.

One of the boys and his Chinese instructor got lost. They got so far off their course that they were out of the area shown on their chart. When they got all done the instructor had to give the plane to the student who had finally recognized a town that they passed over. The student brought the instructor home ok but they were about 3 hours late. Before they got back though they had all the faster planes at the field out searching for them. They had the ambulance and doctors waiting at the operations office for the first word that might come in about them. When it got so late and no word had come in about them everyone began to consider that they had probably crashed someplace out in the Texas "Bad Lands" as they speak of them. When they did finally come in it was sundown and their engine was about ready to quit from lack of oil.

They asked the Chinaman where he had been. He said "You ask me where I been?" "I ask you," "You tell me where I been."

Well, Ethel, tomorrow I graduate, parade and everything. At 2:30 I go out and fly for the last time at this post and come down just in time to change clothes for the graduation parade. The public is invited and I wish that somehow you could be here…The girl mechanics were allowed to watch us parade last week. Most of them laughed right out at some parts of the ceremony…

For a while I never expected to get this far but I have a good chance of getting all the way through now. There will still be some pretty tough going though for a while, especially learning this night flying.

Continued 6:20 a.m. Mar. 17, 1943

I had to go on hanger duty last night and was unable to get this letter finished for that reason. The duty consisted of draining the oil from three or four planes.

Well, this is the big day for me, not as big a day as that final graduation will be for me though…

Ladd"

Cover of "The Cadet," the graduation book for Class 43-G of Bruce Field, Ballinger, TX, March 1943.

Inside cover of "The Cadet," the graduation book for Class 43-G of Bruce Field, Ballinger, TX, March 1943.

Dad's picture (top right) in "The Cadet," the graduation book for Class 43-G of Bruce Field, Ballinger, TX, March 1943.

Goodfellow Field, San Angelo, Texas, March 20, 1943

"Dear Ethel

Well here I am in San Angelo but not to stay as yet. We had the day off so I got a pass and hitch-hiked over here for the day just to look the place over.

It seems like quite a nice town but what the airfield will be like I don't know. From what we hear it is pretty rugged I guess.

Coming over was the first time that I had ridden in a car in nearly 7 months. It seemed funny and more scary riding in that car than it ever does in one of the planes. When we would pass another car or one coming toward us I would jump more than I would if my plane engine had quit. It seemed more dangerous than a plane ever thought of being. There are certainly a lot more safety measures taken in a plane than there is [*sic*] in a car...

...I'll be coming down again in the morning by train to stay for a while. I may possibly stay here until the completion of my training which should be in about 19 to 20 more weeks...

...The Cadets wear the same insignia no matter where they are stationed and both the Army and Navy Cadets wear the same uniform now. When a Cadet graduates and receives his commission he will wear the standard Air Force insignia which is a white star with white wings on an ultramarine background. To make it a little simpler we might as well say just plain blue. At that time if his squadron that he is assigned to has a special insignia or symbol of its own he will probably wear that on the left front of his shirt beneath where he wears his wings...

You'll notice one boy's picture with an ink line under it *(in the Ballinger class book Dad sent to Mom)*. He is just about my twin. Some of his friends mistake me for him and I don't know what they are talking about when they speak to me until I realize the mistake that they have made. You may see some of the resemblance in the picture...

Lovingly

Ladd"

Picture of another cadet, Clarence T. Matlock, from Dad's class (43G)—
Dad's "twin." This guy's friends would mistakenly identify Dad as him.

Goodfellow Field, San Angelo, Texas, March 23, 1943 *(In this letter, Dad*
proposed again to Mom. He had proposed before he left for the Army, but she
had said, no, not until she knew he would return from the war.)

"Dear Ethel

Well, here I am at another field for a little visit. I'll be here about 10 weeks I guess if I don't wash out before then.

It's really rugged living here and tough going. We have regular Army barracks again now with no tables, chairs or anything else. They gig you for practically nothing [sic] and if you don't get many letters from me for a while you will know that it is because I have practically no time to myself and that I am probably walking the ramp in what little time that I do have.

After the first few weeks we will be doing night flying and then have to get up and go through a regular daily routine just the same. To top that off I will have to take another 64 examinations within a few days and whether or not I will still be able to pass it or not is questionable. I'm afraid that they might catch me on my eyes even if they don't get me on anything else. We have one consolation though and that is we have good food so far and if it continues the same it will be a big help…

Perhaps you will be a little surprised at the rest of this letter. It concerns something that you probably considered completely settled long ago but for some reason or other I just had to bring it up again. I guess it is because I have been so lonely for you and thinking about you so much lately.

Ethel, just before I left home I tried to have you accept a ring from me. Perhaps I wasn't very diplomatic about it at the time, but sweetheart, I believe that you do care a lot for me and while I realize that I have many faults and that there are many ifs and many doubts in any plans that we could make at this time, still, I wish that you would accept an engagement ring from me as a token of the love that we feel for each other and of the hope of the things that we desire when this time of separation is past. For some time past you must certainly have realized and understood that something more than anything else in this world, I wanted you to be my wife.

Ethel, would you accept the ring from me now? I love you and desire you with all my heart. Could I possibly give you a better reason than that?

Honey it hurts to have to write to you about something like this instead of being able to take you in my arms and hold you close while I talked to you about it, but there is no way that we can be together and I just have to ask you again…

All I can say for now is "you'd be so nice to come home to."

Lovingly

Ladd"

Dad—likely location Goodfellow Field, San Angelo, TX

Goodfellow Field, San Angelo, Texas, March 28, 1943

"Dearest Ethel…

It is Sunday but we will fly just the same. I will have to be on the flight line from 1 o'clock to 6:30. Don't ever think that isn't a long time. Your nerves are strained to the very limit the whole time and when 6:30 comes around you feel like just laying down and letting them cover you over never to get up again.

I've never seen a more discouraged or more utterly miserable group of men in my life. Several of the fellows have quit the last few days. Even a week of it was too much for them. I feel terrible myself and wonder if it is worthwhile to stick it out. I knew that the place had a bad reputation before I came here but I didn't half realize what it was…I would never go through it again for anything but I don't feel that I could quit this far through either. Besides, quitting doesn't sound good to me in any language.

I can't seem to get away from the number 13. I'm flying Vultee B-13s now. They're heavy, all metal ships and riding in one is just like an old Hamburg bus. They're just as well worn, just as clumsy and bump and vibrate along through the air the same way. The feelings are almost identical. One of the fellows hit a description of how they fly. He says that they fly "solid" and that's the only word that comes anywhere near it. We have about 60 instruments, gadgets and controls to fool with now. To make it worse we are operating from a very large airport with four control towers and radio controlled traffic. It's just one complicated mess and I don't mean maybe.

Dad standing on the wing of a Vultee BT-13 Valiant basic trainer.

The instructors take the attitude you're a Cadet and I'm an officer, therefore your [*sic*] dirt under my feet and I don't care how much I step on you. There are three boys walking up and down past my window right now in class "a" uniform wearing gas masks and white gloves. They'll be walking there about all day probably just because some officer found some dust under their beds or some of their clothes unbuttoned or some similar small misdemeanor. I've never seen anyone in my life who could be meaner than an Air Corps 2nd Lieutenant. One of the boys said the other day that if he ever had a son who took his first step on his left foot he would kill him. That sounds rather coarse but I know how he felt and what he meant…

…Keep praying sweetheart, it does help and our God does answer prayer and you'll know that I'm praying too and someday everything will be different again.

Love

Ladd"

Goodfellow Field, San Angelo, Texas, April 4, 1943 (Mom gave Dad a very careful, "no" to his proposal and dad is responding in this letter.)
"Dear Ethel…

Ethel, I realize that the letter I sent you was hard for you to answer, I can understand just how hard it would be and how difficult to know what to say. You should know, even just by what I said in my letter, that I couldn't be angry with you for the kind of answer that you sent me. Don't worry at all about that. Don't think either, Ethel, that I haven't thought about the same things that you mentioned or that it wouldn't hurt me not to have the priviledge [sic] of placing the ring on your finger…I suppose the one thing that you can't understand is that even though I tell you that I considered the same things that you did, still I asked you again.

Before you could ever understand that you would have to know the mental, nervous and physical strain under which we are living and also a good many other things that I don't feel that I could write to you but which I perhaps can tell you someday…

I feel sorry many times that as long as you do care for me that I'm not more handsome or that I don't have a more pleasing personality, that may seem to be a peculiar thing to say but I cannot help but feel that a girl as good and as lovely as you are should have the best kind of young man that there could possibly be. This I can say though, "Honey, I love you."...

A picture of a Vultee BT-13 Valiant. The propellers were 9' long and about 900 lbs. The engine was about 450 hp.

Yesterday we had four planes crack up and five the day before. That isn't too good for morale especially with the other things that we have piled on us besides. One of the boys got into a spin and couldn't pull out. My instructor and one of my flying partners circled the plane as it spun down and watched it crash. The Cadet who was flying it got free and landed alright with his chute. Two cowboys picked him up and brought him in. Some of the other boys weren't so lucky. These planes are just like some wild animal that has been tamed but suddenly turns on you and tries to kill you...

...don't worry about what I asked you or how I might feel about your answer. I can understand how you feel and it's only natural and right.

Love

Ladd"

Goodfellow Field, San Angelo, Texas, April 7, 1943

"Dearest Ethel…

…It just happened that I hit a class that was all old service men. Most of them are sergeants of some grade or other who are trying to become pilots. One man who was with me until a while ago had even been a Lt. [*sic*] in the Marines. Some are commissioned Lts. [*sic*] from the infantry and artillery. One of the men has more service stripes on his sleeve than any officer that I have seen, they reach from his cuff to his elbow without a break. Several of the men have already seen foreign service in this war but most of the bunch were stationed in Panama up until the time when they became Cadets.

This afternoon I was flying in a light thunderstorm and had a bolt of lightning strike the lead-in wire on the radio aerial of my plane. It didn't hurt anything but I heard a terrific crash in the headset and for a few seconds I could see blue fire and sparks shooting all over.

I don't know how much longer I can stand the grind. I'm getting so tired both physically and mentally that I don't know whether I am coming or going. The other day I fell asleep flying the plane. My instructor didn't know what had gone wrong with me for a while and finally grabbed the mike and started yelling loud enough so that it woke me up…

Love

Ladd"

Goodfellow Field, San Angelo, Texas, April 8, 1943

"Dear Ethel…

They have started thinning the class out a little more, a boy or two seems to be leaving us each day. I don't know how much longer I will last. It seems impossible that I should go on very much longer without washing out…

One thing that makes things worse for me is that me [*sic*] and the Air Force can't seem to agree on some things very well. I stand for some things a little different than what the Air Force practices and being a Christian I don't feel that I can conform to a lot of things. That makes it doubly hard for me…

…One of our flight lieutenants just today received ten gigs just because he made a slight mistake on a report. That means ten hours for him on the ramp…

Love

Ladd"

Official photo of a Vultee BT-14 built for the Canadian Air Force as a trainer. I think that the Canadian Air Force rejected them because they were too obsolete at the time they received them. They wanted a more advanced trainer. They were diverted over to US trainers.

Goodfellow Field, San Angelo, Texas, April 11, 1943

"Dear Ethel…

…Monday I start on night flying, about every other night I will get 7 h sleep and the nights in between I will get about 4 if I am lucky. Our day schedule goes on just the same as ever so I don't know how well I will be able to take it. I can fly when I am wide awake but when I am so tired I can't do anything right. You don't know what it is to be tired until you have lived as we do here.

I have a 20-h check in the morning whether or not I can pass It I don't know A lot of the boys have failed and washed out. It doesn't look to me as though hardly any of our class will ever really be Army pilots. They took the boys from 5 different primary schools and only had enough of us left to make one class here. By the looks of things they will be able to take all the men left from 5 Basic schools and form one class at an advanced school someplace.

It doesn't hardly seem possible but I only have about 15 weeks left to go if I can last it out, until I will get my wings. Even so 15 weeks is a long time…

I'm glad those pictures turned out good…I didn't even think that I could get those aerial pictures at all because after all a baby brownie wasn't made for aerial photography. I tried to take those while I was flying the plane and that didn't help but the main thing that I had trouble with was the vibration of the plane itself. There was no way that I could hold the camera steady enough to take a good picture…

That little Chinese boy that you got the big kick out of happened to be my instructor. He is the one who taught me just about all that I know about flying right now…

The planes we are flying now weigh nearly 5,000 lbs and have 450 horsepower, considered on the same rating as your Dad's car they have 15 times the horsepower that it has. That means you really have quite a piece of machinery to handle when you go up in one…

…It only took me 5 ½ h to solo one of them so I don't consider that too bad…

Love,

Ladd"

Two pages from Dad's pilot's log book at Goodfellow Field, San Angelo, TX, May, 1943. Total flight time upon completion was 86 hours and 18 minutes.

Goodfellow Field, San Angelo, Texas, April 13, 1943

"Dear Ethel

I'm writing from the flight line while waiting for my ship to come in…I said that I was writing from the flight line, to be more correct I should have said the parachute room…

I grow so tired and nervous with all this stuff day after day that it doesn't help my flying out one little bit. I haven't ever pulled any real boners yet or made any bad mistakes but I can't tell you when I will…I can't seem to stomach a lot of the evil that goes on around me. It is one of the things that makes this harder for me than anything else does, living around it every day gets on my nerves more than anything else and there is nothing I can do about it.

4-14-43

Dear Ethel

Am continuing letter from the cockpit of a BT-13 on my way to Sweetwater. Am in ship 162 at 4,500' cruising at 132 mph. Just passed my first check point Robert Lee on course. Everything *is* going smoothly.

Just checked in at Sweetwater 10:15 a.m.

Left Sweetwater 10:18 headed for Abilene course 82°

I am passing through a light rainstorm right now at Merkel, Tex. Carburetor is icing and engine running rough, not serious as yet.

There is a large building on fire at Merkel. It must be blazing up 200 ft high

---

Cleared Abilene OK, out in sun carburetor ice cleared up. Just past Winters, Texas on return course for Goodfellow Field.

I am now crossing Colorado River. I can see Bruce Field from here. I can't help but think of old times and how many times I have been glad to see that field under my wing.

…Several of the boys got lost on that trip today…

Love

Ladd"

Dad sent a small piece of parachute cord in the letter.

Headquarters Building

Nerve Center--Goodfellow Tower

Picture copied from the "Goodfellow Field, Army Air Forces Basic Flying School, A Pictorial Review," San Angelo, TX March–May 1943. Dad wrote on that page, We have four radio control towers. The only time that I call this one is on Cross Country flying. My station is DR21.

Likely location is in front of the Headquarters Building at Goodfellow Field, San Angelo, Texas.

Goodfellow Field, San Angelo, Texas, April 18, 1943

"Dear Ethel…

…In a couple more days I expect to fly to Harpersville, Texas then to Curtis Ranch, Texas and back to Goodfellow. That is about a three hundred mile trip and will take us a little better than 2 hours to fly. We'll probably have boys scattered all over Texas before the day is over. A couple of classes ago one cadet ended up in the middle of New Mexico. He got to his destination alright and started back. Just a little way along he met a formation of advanced bombardier training planes headed in about the same direction. He took them to be planes from Concho Field which is just about 4 miles from Goodfellow so he just tagged along with them and figured it would be a simple way to get home. The next they heard of him he had run out of gas still following the other formation. He was somewhere in New Mexico then…

…One boy just got 16 gigs yesterday for little things not nearly as bad as that. That means 20 hrs. for him to walk on the ramp just for dust on his locker, dirty shoes, sheets folded improperly and a few other small things like that…

Love   Ladd"

Goodfellow Field, San Angelo, Texas, 4/22/1943

"Dear Ethel…

I've been up and going since five thirty this morning. I did 3 hours of instrument flying this morning besides some contact flying. I left the flight line at 1:15 ate dinner and then came to school. Its 3:10 now and I have an hour and 15 minutes more of school and then I will have to go to physical training class. We call it physical torture, especially on a day like today when it is 94° in the shade. I'll get through with that about six o'clock eat supper and then report back to the flight line at 7 for an hour and a half of lecture and then go to Lane field for 2 hours of night flying and more instruction. It will be about 2:30 or 3 a.m. by the time that I get back from Lane field and go to bed. By 5:30 I will be awake again. I'll have to clean my barracks polish my shoes and etc., then eat breakfast and change to P.T. clothes for an hour of torture and then I'll be ready to go back to school.

The following night I will be allowed 7 ½ hours of sleep to catch up some. As far as I am concerned 7 ½ hours regularly wouldn't be enough. A 20 hr. day one day and a 16 hr. day the next is no cinch when they follow week after week.

I completed navigation with a 97. I see they have my probable average as 93…

Ladd"

Goodfellow Field, San Angelo, Texas, Easter Sunday, April 25, 1943

"Dear Ethel

Here it is, Easter once again, and once more the world is so full of sin, hatred and misery that it seems impossible to realize what the meaning of

Easter really is. Man seems to have forgotten entirely the one who died and rose again, who purchased such a wonderful salvation at such a terrible price for those who will only believe, no matter how undeserving they might be.

I often wonder what the other men in the flight think of me when I don't smoke, or drink or swear or do any of the things that they do. They can't seem to understand it at all and don't know what to make of it.

This was an official USAAF picture of my training mates at San Angelo, TX. The uniforms in this picture were blue. They were in the process of changing over to regular army olive drab. Goodfellow Field, San Angelo, TX. *Dad*

started training at Goodfellow Field San Angelo, TX on March 21, 1943 and completed this stage of his training on May 24, 1943. Dad couldn't tell me the names of the guys in the picture.

Out of the five men assigned to our instructor we have just lost one because of venereal disease. In the Cadets we have been losing 3% a month because of that. That is about 25 or 30 men out of a hundred in the space of a year. That is one of the things that seems to me to be more of a disgrace to our American people than anything else could possibly be. If our young men who are supposed to be the smartest and best aren't good enough to keep themselves above such things I don't know what kind of a country we can expect to have after this war is over…

You asked in your letter about us keeping track of our flying time. We have to keep a log in accordance with the regulations of the C. A. A. I have about 100 h or a little over now in regular time and about twenty hours of instrument time. That perhaps doesn't sound like very much but it is quite a bit to the person who has flown it. When I graduate I should have about 240 to 260 hours of logged time altogether…

I put in nearly three hours of night flying last Thursday night. I like to fly at night only we lose so much sleep because of it. You might not believe it but at night from a plane it is possible to see highways, streams and lakes just from starlight although it seems to be pitch black to you when you are on the ground…

I'm still wondering and worrying about whether or not I will get through this training. I don't know as it really matters whether I do or not but still I go on worrying about it. We had another boy quit a few days ago and another boy was washed out in our flight. He just accidentally taxied into a boundary marker on the field and that gave them excuse enough to get rid of him. He was watching another plane so that he wouldn't bump it and he bumped the marker instead. He was almost standing still when he hit it but that didn't make any difference to the Army. When a man has gotten so far along with his training and has done well you would think that they would have to have some real reason to wash him out but instead they wash out men every day, even some who are halfway through advanced training just because they say that the man has the wrong attitude or some other silly little thing like that. It's almost impossible to win in this game. If an accident doesn't get you it seems some officer who is feeling ornery does. I saw an officer put a man on the ramp today just because he happened to be whistling in the mess hall…

> Love
>
> Ladd"

Goodfellow Field, San Angelo, Texas, April 30, 1943
"Dear Ethel…

I only have about 2 ½ weeks of flying left to do here but whether or not I can make it I still don't know. We are doing mostly instrument and night flying now. The night flying doesn't bother me at all but the instruments do. I can fly instruments pretty good in a link trainer but I'm not doing at all good on them in the plane…

…Most of the fellows are willing to swear that our Commandant is crazy. He acts just as though he is drunk a lot of times even though he isn't.

They tell us now that this is the biggest and best flying school that there is. I'd hate to be in one that was even a little bit poorer…

> Love   Ladd"

Goodfellow Field, San Angelo, Texas, May 2, 1943
Darling…

You remarked about that Chinese instructor of mine looking young in one of your letters. He is about 5 years older than me I think but you can't tell much about the age of those Chinese. You seemed to have the idea that the instructors were all officers. That isn't true. The only officers we had at Bruce Field were check pilots and even some of the check pilots were civilians. Most of the instructors are civilian pilots who are too old or who cannot pass the physical exam for Army pilots. Others are men who are exempt from the draft because they are working as instructors for the government and wouldn't want to change because they are getting more money as it is than they would as an officer and can live at home at the same time.

My instructor here is a commissioned 2nd lt. He is about 5' 3" tall or maybe just a little bit more. I doubt that he is more than 27 years old but he is listed as a service pilot. They consider that he has already past [sic] the time when he would be very good as a combat pilot. They consider that an Army pilot lasts only 4 years as a combat pilot. This instructor of ours actually froths at the mouth when he gets mad. We call him old "Diddle-dy-spits" among ourselves but of course he doesn't know that...

The last couple weeks I have been shooting night landing stages. At first we had floodlights on the runway and then just our wing lights on the plane. Our next stages now will be without lights. You just let down slow toward the field and hope that you hit easy.

I don't know whether I told you in my last letter or not but we had one fellow run off the field and hit a horse in a pasture outside the boundary—Result—"Hamburgers" and $23,000 worth of airplane ready for the junk heap. I'm pretty sure we ate that horse the next day at mess so perhaps it wasn't all loss after all.

Perhaps you have heard of black light. That is what we use to light our cockpits at night. We have a fluorescent bulb about ½" in diameter and 6 inches long. It makes a buzzing sound when it burns and gives off a deep purple light. This bulb is inserted in a tube of jet black glass of some kind. In the daylight you can hold your fingers tight against the back side of that glass and try to see them through it and you can't see a thing. Light doesn't seem to pass through it at all but still at night when it is turned on it will cause objects in the cockpit of the plane to sort of glow just enough for you to see them. You can look right at it though and not see a bit of light coming from it and a person looking at the plane cannot see any light at all in the cockpit.

The last part of this week I will start my course in formation flying. That is the most dangerous flying training that I will have to go through. We have to fly close formation with our nose 3 ft behind the wing tip of the leader and our wing tip 3 ft out from his tail. It doesn't take but the slightest slip to cause an accident when you are flying that close. You have to fly your plane entirely by feel because if you take your eyes off the leader for just one second it will cost you 50 cents or five stars even if it doesn't cost you an accident. I don't know whether I told you before or not but every time we forget something or make a mistake we get a star and each star costs us 10 cents. It isn't at all hard to get a bunch of stars…

Love

Ladd"

Goodfellow Field San Angelo, Texas, May 7, 1943

"Dear Ethel…

Yesterday it rained for the first time in 7 weeks, it seemed to relieve everyone a whole lot and make them feel refreshed…

I started in today learning to fly a radio range. It is quite a bit of fun but it keeps you pretty busy. I have a little better than 30 hrs. on instruments now. The day before yesterday I took off and landed for the first time on instruments. The instructor complained because I took off with one wing a little low. I was glad to get the plane in the air even without cracking up. It seems kind of funny at first to be traveling at better than 100 mph and not be able to see anything at all.

I was night flying last night shooting landings without lights. I don't know how I did it but out of 6 landings five were perfect. On one landing I bounced about 6 or 8 inches and then sat down perfectly smooth. That isn't bad for a night landing when you can't see the ground…

Love

Ladd"

Goodfellow Field, San Angelo, Texas, May 9, 1943

"Dear Ethel…

…I've never bounced so badly that I had to go around although I have overshot the field that I intended to land in and had to try again because of that.

We had one cadet at Bruce Field who tried four times and then landed on his nose the fifth time he tried. He did make a pilot after a while though…

I expect to go to Harpersville and Curtis Ranch, Texas on Tuesday… Sometime this coming week I expect to go to Sweetwater, Abilene, Harpersville and back to Goodfellow Field at night. Both those trips are about as far as from Buffalo to New York City. It only takes us about 2 ¼ hours to fly it though…

I think perhaps when I get out of here I am going to be sent to a twin engine school. I'll be getting into some pretty good planes then…

Love   Ladd"

Goodfellow Field, San Angelo, Texas, May 13, 1943

"Dear Ethel

Well, I'm almost through here now. My flying will be finished by next Wed., all that I have left to complete is 4 hours of formation flying and some cross country.

Friday night I have about a 300 mile night flight and then one high altitude flight after that. On the night flight they are going to let us land at Sweetwater.

They never will let us land there in the daytime because they have a class of girl aviation cadets there. They know that the first second a cadet from Goodfellow got on the ground there they would have trouble. Both groups are worse than a bunch of wildcats as it is…

Postcard "High in the Clouds Over Goodfellow Field" postmarked May 13, 1943. A/C Ladd L. Horn Cadet Detachment Class 43-G Goodfellow Field, San Angelo, Texas. Dear Ethel, This is what I will be doing from now until next Wednesday. My flying here will be completed by then. I don't have the least idea where I will be going but I think it will be to a twin engine school. I'll probably leave here a week from Sunday. Ladd. Ethel J. O'Neil Bay View Road Hamburg, N.Y.

I'm pretty sure that my instructor has recommended me for twin engine training and while that doesn't automatically mean that I will get it I still feel quite sure that I will because I have a fairly high average and that gives you some choice in the matter. The twin engine training will give me a lot more useful experience than single engine advanced would…

Someone wrote on the wall the other day in one of the flight rooms, "After the war Texas will be the most hated state in the union, 2,000,000 G.I's can't be wrong."…

Love

Ladd"

Only one or two of Mom's letters to Dad have survived. The following is a short excerpt from one of those few.

Miss Ethel O'Neil, Bay View Road, Hamburg, New York, May 14, 1943

"Dear Ladd,

How were your two trips that you told me you expected to take? I was saying that I wouldn't mind going along with you. I don't know how crazy I'd be about the flying, but I know I'd like the riding with you…

In one of your other letters you were telling me about radio and instrument flying. I bet a person does get a strange feeling the first time he takes off "blind." I suppose you feel as though the plane is doing all sorts of tricks…

With love

Ethel"

Goodfellow Field, San Angelo, Texas, May 15, 1943

"Dearest Ethel…

It seems good to think that I only have 9 more days and I will be leaving here. I don't know just how things will work out for me though, I can't seem to fly very well when I have a check pilot in the rear cockpit. I only have one more exam to take in ground school, my average right now isn't a 99 but I am one of the highest in my squadron. I believe right now it is about a 94 without the last exam in radio procedure.

The last week of flying is just like the last week of regents exams used to be back in school. These checks really make you sweat though. I never worried much about the exams in school. I like the flying itself but I have got so that I don't much care whether they make a pilot out of me or not. The more I see of this the more I think that the regular G.I. soldier has the best deal after all. The training in this is good but the rest of the stuff is terrible...

Darling I love you very much. Ladd"

Goodfellow Field, San Angelo, Texas, May 16, 1943

"Dear Ethel...

The hot weather and short sleeping hours have me just about licked. I don't know how I can keep going for this week. With the heat and not much sleep I get indigestion after almost every meal and when the time comes that I can lay down I can't sleep...

To top it all off I have a check Mon. and an instrument check Tuesday that I have to pass... I know I can do all that's required only the thing is can I do it with a check pilot in the rear cockpit. That is the thing that gets me, especially when I feel the way I do right at present...

I don't know whether I ever told you or not but our squadrons are divided up according to height. We have one squadron that we call the "Gremlins." They are all about 5' 2" tall and it really looks funny when you see one of the squadrons of tall men march past them. We have one bunch who are all about 6' 4" and when you get the two together it really is funny...

We had some hard luck yesterday and lost one boy and perhaps another and his instructor. A BT-13 had a collision with a BT-9 and the 9 exploded on contact with the 13. The cadet flying it was killed instantly. The 13 seemed to be in pretty good condition yet so the instructor and cadet in it tried to land it but the plane was so wracked [*sic*] from the shock that it disintegrated when they landed it and both were nearly killed. The doctors don't have much hope for either of them to live. It probably would be best for the Cadet if he did die although I suppose that is an awful thing to say. He has both legs broken, both hands crushed and one eye and his nose missing. That should explain why I said what I did. I suppose I shouldn't have even told you about that but we have to live with and be able to stand a lot of things like that in days like these…

Yours truly

Ladd"

Curtis BT-9 at San Angelo, Texas. Not many were built. The guy crawling out of the service door has been inside the plane repairing it. The space inside was pretty tight. Picture taken by the small plastic "broken" camera. *(Some pictures like this one were taken by my dad to the local photographer who enlarged them to standard size.)* I never flew one of these in spite of the fact that it was parked outside my barracks. You were assigned to a specific plane.

Goodfellow Field, San Angelo, Texas, May 20, 1943

"Dear Ethel…

In about another two hours I'll be going on a night cross country flight. It's about a 300 mile flight and the ceiling is almost closed in but I think they will send us out anyway. We are supposed to have a ceiling and visibility unlimited for night cross country but we are behind schedule so I imagine we will fly it if we just have 500 ft. 500 ft [*sic*] is just enough to see land.

I haven't been able to dig up any real information as to where I will be going from here but it looks as though it might be Ellington Field, Texas of course…

They called a special new formation for those of us who fly at night and I was just interrupted due to the fact that they called it earlier than usual. I came back to the barracks and was just going to change to flying clothes when they announced over the P.A. system that flying had been called off.

In case you wonder what I had for mess it was macaroni and cheese, mustard greens cooked with chicken and ham skins, I mean just the chicken skins, not the meat and then pumpkin pie, fruit jello, ice cream and sweet pepper salad to top the meal off. It was a rather peculiar mixture to have but it tasted pretty good to me…

Love

Ladd"

Goodfellow Field, San Angelo, Texas, May 21, 1943

"Dear Ethel…

It looks fairly definite now that I will go to Ellington Field, Texas. That is near Houston and almost on the Gulf of Mexico. I'm not entirely certain of that though. There is a possibility that I will go to Mission, Texas.

I still have some flying left to do here. I have an instrument check to try to pass yet, a night cross country flight and some formation flying and landing stages. I'll have to fly all day tomorrow, most of tomorrow night and part of Sunday. Monday I should be leaving.

I flew formation above the clouds for almost two hours this afternoon. It's really beautiful up there. I wish that I could have had you with me. Perhaps someday I will be able to…

Please, honey, don't ever forget me.

Love

Ladd"

Goodfellow Field, San Angelo, Texas, May 22, 1943

"Dear Ethel...

I finished up my flying here for today and for good about 11 o'clock this morning....

They finally definitely made up their mind to make a bomber pilot out of me. I leave Monday afternoon at 4 o'clock for Ellington Field. I understand that the way they are teaching you now you have to fly AT-6s for a week or so then BC-1s for a little while and after that twin engine AT-17s. The BC-1s were built as combat planes but weren't quite good enough for what they were supposed to be so they are being used as training planes. The idea of the two single engine planes for a while at first is to get you used to the extra horsepower and extra speed although the twin engine planes won't be very much faster than the planes we are flying now. We fly these planes for all that there is in them. There are times when every instrument will be to the end of its dial.

These planes are red-lined at 230 miles per hour and you aren't supposed to slow roll them at more than 160. The other day though one of my flying partners slow rolled our plane and when he pulled out the airspeed indicator read 280. That shows what we make these poor planes do...

Love

Ladd"

Class 43-G graduation book, May 24, 1943. Dad's picture is on the top right. Note: CAVU stands for "Ceiling and Visibility Unlimited." The term was used at Goodfellow Field because of its clear skies and open land without mountains.

Note from Dad to Ethel J. O'Neil on the inside cover of the CAVU graduation book for Class 43-G.

Ellington Field, Houston, Texas, May 26, 1943

"Dear Ethel

Well I'm in advanced training now. It doesn't hardly seem possible but still it is true.

This seems like a pretty nice post, the food is very good and the tactical officers aren't at all bad. They seem to be able to act human at least.

We have three types of planes that we will fly. AT-9s and AT-10s for transformation training on twin engines and AT-6s which are single engine planes which we will use mostly for gunnery practice and tactics. The AT-9s are about the fastest, most maneuverable and nicest planes of the three. They are just two large engines a cabin and a tail like a fish. The AT-10s are more of a regular transport type plane…

I have caught up with almost all the fellows who washed out of my class along the way. They have classes of Navigators, Bombardiers and Gunners here. Almost all those boys washed out *(as)* pilots from class 43-G—boys that we thought we would probably never see again. I was talking to one of the boys last night and he says that the bombardier training is so easy and simple beside the Pilot training that there is no comparison whatsoever. That fat Irish kid that was pictured in one of the snapshots I sent home a while ago is here training as a navigator and he says that it is easy too. They all seem glad to see us again and want to fly with us.

We will have a pretty good chance to choose what we will go into when we leave here and I think I will try to get in the Air Transport Command. There doesn't [*sic*] as much glory go with that as some of the other services but I think it will be the best thing in the long run. I have to play for a lot better and higher stakes than glory anyway. I believe that I would rather drop supplies or reinforcements to troops than to drop bombs on a city and perhaps kill a mother or her child even though they are enemies technically.

Truly yours

Ladd"

Ellington Field, Houston, Texas, May 30, 1943

"Dear Ethel…

This place is an awfully lot different from Goodfellow. The country at Goodfellow was just bordering on the verge of desert. Here everything is wet and it rains practically every day. The field is right on the tip of the Gulf of Galveston. One of our auxiliary fields is on a little peninsula that sticks right out into the water. You don't dare overshoot or undershoot or you'll have a bath for sure.

I have only put in an hour and a half so far on one of these planes, that was in an AT-10. Most of my time so far has been taken up by lectures, orientation, more physical and eye exams and etc. My eyes have improved again. The way that they grade your eyes in the army they start at 0 and go down to 32. 0 of course is perfect, anything beyond 32 is failing. When I first came in my eyes were graded as 6, when I left primary they were graded as 24. That's quite a drop and don't think that I couldn't notice it. Yesterday they examined my eyes again and gave me a grade of 10. I still have a sort of blind range though. I can't see good [sic] at a range of about 1,500 ft. Beyond that and nearer than that I can see good [sic].

These planes we have now are so full of instruments and gadgets that it is pitiful. You never fly them solo, the reason being that it is about impossible for one man to do it. You fly always with a copilot and the copilot really has the most work to do. These planes are nasty to fly though. They are restricted for everything but stalls and gentle turns. They're nothing but a big crate full of instruments. You only have a hundred controls, switches and instruments to keep track of and keep in the right position. To help make things worse they are all left handed beside the other planes we have flown. I have to learn to fly now with my left hand and take care of my instruments and switches with my right hand. It seems terribly awkward to me after flying the other planes. That is one thing wrong with our planes, they are not standardized whatsoever.

Every time that you change to a different make of plane you practically have to learn to fly over again. Not only that but doing something that is correct procedure in one plane is enough to cause you to crack up in another.

We just had a B-26 try to land here a few minutes ago. It is raining and visibility is practically 0. He must have come in on radio and made an instrument let down. He tried to make it twice but couldn't see well enough so headed on for another field. I pity him. You don't feel very good flying in a thunderstorm with it getting dark, your gas getting low and visibility so poor that you can't see to land.

I am really getting a dose of ground school now. I have 28 text books to work from covering almost anything you can think of. We have to learn to recognize aircraft in one seventy fifth of a second. They are starting us out at one tenth of a second and will gradually decrease that time to 1/75. We only have 43 planes to learn to recognize that quickly though…

Love

Ladd"

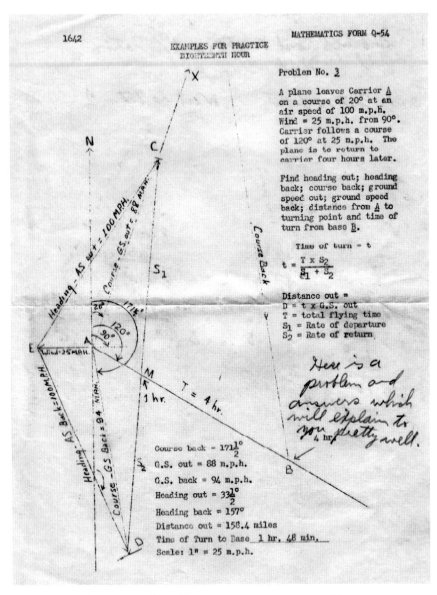

1642

Problem No. 3

A plane leaves Carrier A
on a course of 20° at an
air speed of 100 m.p.h.
Wind = 25 m.p.h. from 90°.
Carrier follows a course
of 120° at 25 m.p.h. The
plane is to return to
carrier four hours later.

Find heading out; heading
back; course back; ground
speed out; ground speed
back; distance from A to
turning point and time of
turn from base B.

Time of turn = t

$$t = \frac{T \times S_2}{S_1 + S_2}$$

Distance out =
D = t x G.S. out
T = total flying time
S_1 = Rate of departure
S_2 = Rate of return

*Here is a
problem and
answers which
will explain to
you pretty well.*

Course back = $171\frac{1}{2}°$

G.S. out = 88 m.p.h.

G.S. back = 94 m.p.h.

Heading out = $33\frac{1}{2}°$

Heading back = 157°

Distance out = 158.4 miles

Time of Turn to Base 1 hr. 48 min.

Scale: 1" = 25 m.p.h.

This is one of Dad's navigation practice problems.

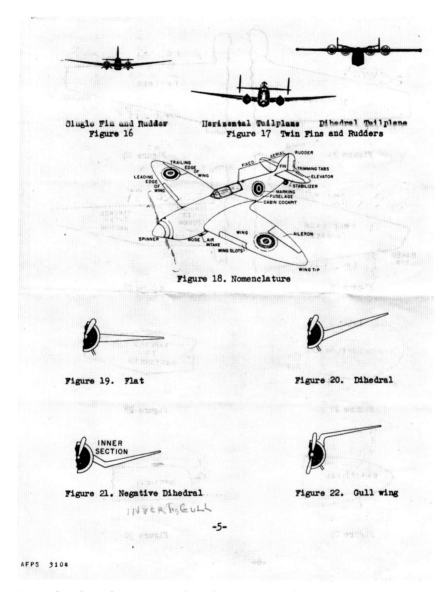

Aircraft tail- and wing-type identification page that Dad used in training.

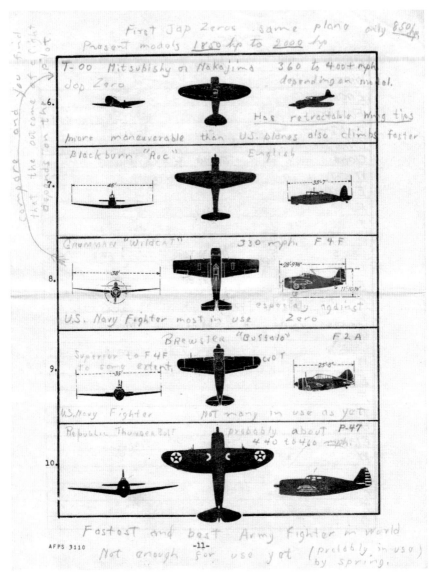

Aircraft identification training page including Dad's notes.

This is a sample of the kind of propaganda the Air Force plagues HATE YOUR ENEMY *us with. It doesn't quite go [ ] with me.*

When John Dillinger was Public Enemy Number One, the American people had no personal hatred for him. He was impersonal in their minds as Jesse James or Robin Hood. So long as he let them alone, they were not concerned. But the Federal Bureau of Investigation agents, and the police, hated John Dillinger. Their own friends had been shot down by him. It was not only that he was a law breaker, and it was their business to capture him. It was much deeper than that. There was not a man in the F.B.I. who would not have been supremely happy at the opportunity of filling Dillinger's body with lead.

Because they hated him, their efforts to corner the bandit were intensified. They finally killed him like a mad dog in a Chicago alley---and were happy in his death.

That's the way you've got to feel about the Germans and Japanese and Italians.

War is a business of killing or being killed. Those enemies of ours don't fight by the book. They have brought a brutality never known before into warfare. Remember what the Goering's bombers did to Warsaw and Rotterdam, when those cities were helpless to defend themselves? Suppose your wife or mother or children had died in the blazing ruins. You wouldn't think the war was impersonal then, would you? Suppose your family had been in Lidice, when Hangman Heydrich killed everyone, and left not even a stone of the town standing. Wouldn't you be in a mood to bathe a bayonet in German blood?

The atrocities of the Japanese have filled columns in the newspapers. When they took Singapore, they tied prisoners in bunches and bayonetted them to death. They raped American and British nurses--- the filthy yellow devils---and then cut their throats. Doesn't the thought of that stir your pulse?

An eye for an eye, says the old Mosaic Law, a tooth for a tooth. The hell with that! Two eyes for one. A whole jaw for a tooth. Our enemies taught the world a savagery that most of us thought had died with Attila, the Hun. They must be paid for it.

The man at the front soon develops a personal hatred for the enemy. All you have to do to learn that is to lie in a fox-hole for half an hour while dive bombers come over, and machine guns chatter. The only thing that counts after a little of that is to get out of that fox-hole, and kill the men who are trying to kill you. No, war isn't impersonal. It is the most deeply personal thing that can come to you as long as you live.

Just because you are on this side of the water don't feel that the war is far away, and the dead and maimed are only rows of names in a newspaper. Before they died, those men found out what sort of dirty swine we are fighting. You'll find out, too, before the last shot is fired. Then you'll hate them, as everyone who has gone into battle against them, hates.

-1-

Page 1 of USAAF propaganda Dad sent home to Ethel J. O'Neil. Dad hated it.

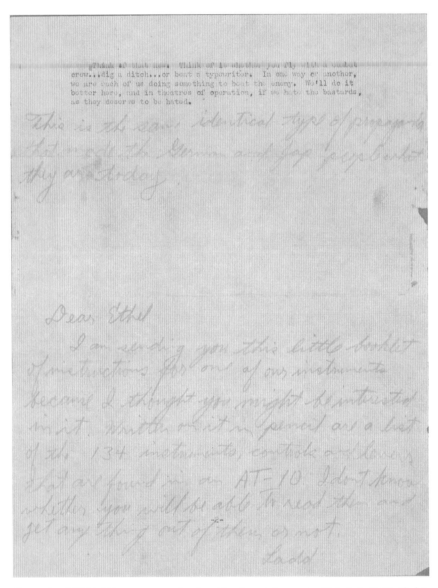

Page 2 of USAAF propaganda that Dad sent home to Ethel J. O'Neil, his girlfriend. My dad hated it. You can get a sense for how he felt by two of his handwritten notes on these pages. The third note is about a booklet he sent home that showed all of the instruments on an AT-10. It goes along with the previous letter.

Ellington Field, Houston, Texas, June 3, 1943

"Dear Ethel…

I'm going to try to answer your questions first. Yes, we did fly some with another Cadet as our partner in Basic. The one about miles per gallon of gas is a little harder to answer. We figure gas consumption in gallons per hour because weather, altitude, temperature and everything affects the mileage too much, however, the plane will always fly about the same length of time on the same amount of gas. Our BT-13 used about 29 gallons per hour. At 10,000 ft on a normal summer day you would probably average about 5 miles to the gallon. The transport type planes that I am flying now would probably average about the same in miles per gallon but they use about 34 gallons an hour. A B-26 uses about 215 gallons an hour and would get about 1 ½ miles per gallon or a little less. Our largest bomber can carry about two tank cars of gas or about 8,000 gallons. 1,200 to [sic] 1,500 gallons is normal for a medium bomber, 4,000 gallons for a heavy bomber. Three-quarters mile to the gallon would be about normal mileage.

Perhaps you have heard of the new YB-40, It is a Flying Fortress that has been made over into a four engine fighter plane. They took a regular Fortress and covered it with armor plate. The weight of the armor plate makes up for the bomb load the plane was originally built to carry. Then they added two extra gun turrets and a crew of 8 gunners. The plane flies over enemy territory and the enemy seeing a lonely heavy bomber sends about 30 fighter planes up after it thinking they have some easy meat. The fighters try shooting it down and when they find their shots seem to have no effect they move in a little closer and then the fortress cuts loose and shoots down 10 to 20 at one crack. They are sending flights of 8 Fortresses and one YB-40 out now. The planes all look alike and the enemy fighters don't know which one to steer clear of with the result that a lot of them get shot down…

Love, Ladd.

"Dear Ethel

This is one of the landmarks around here. We have to watch out for it because it is in the traffic pattern of one of our fields. It stands 600 ft high and when you fly the pattern at 800 ft the top looks pretty close to you."

Ellington Field, Houston, Texas, June 6, 1943

"Dear Ethel

I'm trying to write to you but I don't know really what to say. There is so much I want to say to you and still it seems so futile to write when what I really want is to see you and talk to you.

Darling, I miss you so very much. It's impossible for me to tell you how much I long for you or how much my heart aches because I can't see you or be with you. I'm so lonely and life seems so empty without your presence. As day after day goes by without my being able to see you I realize more and more how much you mean to me and how much of the happiness in my life has been because of you. Ethel, you're so precious and it has been so very wonderful to me to have you close to me in the past, just the memory of a kiss from your lips makes my heart thrill and brings new hope of a day when we can be together again in peace and happiness…

…Some of the things that I used to do seem so far away from me now that it doesn't seem as though they were real or that I ever did do them…

…When I go to sleep at night though my last thoughts will be of you and when I awake in the morning my first thoughts will be of that one lovely girl who means more to me than all else this world might have to offer. Please remember me and think of me too.

Ladd"

Ellington Field, Houston, Texas, June 13, 1943

"Dear Ethel…

I flew as co-pilot for an officer yesterday in a flying review that we had here. We had a formation of about 120 planes that came over the field in 12 plane echelons. We came over just about level with the control towers.

I finally soloed one of these planes Thursday. It took me longer to solo here than any place so far. I say solo but I had a student co-pilot with me. Any time that you fly without an instructor in these planes it is considered solo.

It might interest you to know that a co-pilot is called a "Sand Bag." I guess that name came from the fact that Sand Bags are used for ballast and the Pilot considers the co-pilot just some extra "ballast." Nevertheless he has a lot of work to do in a large plane. I imagine that I'll have to fly co-pilot for a long time after I graduate before I ever get a plane of my own.

I just received a letter, just yesterday in fact, from Charles Goodier. He evidently is getting along alright now although he was pretty worried about washing out. He says they washed out 69% of his upper class at primary alone. He ground-looped and wrecked a wing of his plane a couple days before he wrote to me but came out of it alright.

Just to show you that this isn't any sissy flying that we do here, from Jan.

1 to Feb. 3 in one class here 54 cadets were killed *(graduation class sizes were approximately 300)*. The first day that we met in our flight room here the Flight Commander told us that on the average 9 of us would be killed before we graduated but if we were careful perhaps we could cut that number down some. Needless to say something like that makes you feel kind of funny inside.

The weather here is awful. It is terribly warm and on the average it rains about every three hours. It rained yesterday morning, yesterday afternoon, yesterday evening, last night, this morning and it is getting ready to rain right now. The rain really comes down for a little while and then the sun comes out hot enough to cook you alive…

…Ethel, if there's any way possible of sending a kiss to you then you'll know that there is one sealed in this letter, for you. Whether you can find it or not you'll know that it is here wrapped up in heart-felt love for you.

     Ladd"

Ellington Field, Houston, Texas, June 16, 1943
"Dear Ethel…

I don't know as I told you before but it might interest you to know that most of our instructors here are R.A.F. pilots who have been sent to this country for rest periods. They don't get much rest out of it but the idea is that it gives them a rest from combat and at the same time their talents are put to good use.

I've worn blisters on my left hand and then worn blisters on top of the blisters trying to fly these planes. It's hard work flying these large planes especially in this hot weather. The weather is so poor and the ceiling so low here most of the time that we can seldom get up high enough to get cooled off. My co-pilot is 6' 4" tall and not wide. The sweat just pours off from him. This morning I thought there wouldn't be anything left of him by the time we got back down. He's so thin you'd think he would just shrivel away to nothing. The way he is built I can't help but think of a grasshopper or katydid whenever I look at him…

They are teaching me and all the Cadets for that matter, not only flying but gunnery, armament, bombing and some celestial navigation. The bombardiers and navigators keep teasing us and calling us taxi drivers all the time but when it comes right down to it we have to know as much as all the rest of the crew put together.

We used to get some of that commando drill in basic… Most of the men would more or less welcome some training like that though. The work that we have to do carries too much nervous and mental strain with it. Never ending alertness is the price of life for us. It tells on you and don't ever think it doesn't. You get to feeling as though you would just like to lay down and never move or do anything again for the rest of your life. Just about the time you get to thinking that someone yells at you though and you go on just the same as you have every other day…

Love

Ladd"

Ellington Field, Houston, Texas, June 24, 1943

Dear Ethel…

I never thought of Ichabod Crane in connection with my co-pilot but that is just who he looks like.

Love,

Ladd"

Ellington Field, Houston, Texas, June 20, 1943

"Dear Ethel…

It's so warm as I write that I have to rest my hand on an extra sheet of paper to keep the perspiration from spoiling the sheet on which I am writing. I have been the warmest for the longest period of time that I have ever been in my life since I arrived here at Ellington Field. It doesn't even cool off when it rains…

You asked if those uniforms I bought were "pinks." I only purchased one set of pinks because they are a uniform that you don't wear very often. They would be considered a class "B" uniform I think, that is sort of semi-formal. The official formal class "A" uniform is OD officers cap, khaki shirt and tie, forest-green blouse and pants to match for winter and the same for summer except it would all be khaki colored tropical worsted. Class "B" would be next and that could be pinks with a forest-green shirt and OD cap or forest-green pants and shirt to match. All outside of that has to be khaki except for the trench coat and that is pink. Khaki is considered class "E" and is what you wear most of the time during the summer except for very special occasions…

Love,

Ladd"

Ellington Field, Houston, Texas, June 27, 1943

"Dear Ethel…

We've been flying both day and night and you get awfully tired. That doesn't help to keep your spirits up.

A couple of nights ago I came in for a landing without lights. I kept letting down on my way into the field without the least idea of where the ground was at. Just a second too late I caught the reflection of my navigation lights on the ground and next thing I know I hit so hard that the old plane I was flying bounced a hundred feet back up in the air. We gave it full throttle and kept it flying somehow, climbed a ways circled the field and tried again. We put our landing gear down and couldn't believe the indicator that there still actually was any gear on the plane. We took a flashlight and looked out the window to try and see if there really were any wheels there. We couldn't tell for sure but we came in and they were there alright. When we got down the mechanics checked the plane over and the only thing wrong was a crack in the windshield from the jar. How we ever hit that hard without doing any more damage than that I don't know. It shook us up plenty and when the plane hit it sounded as if the whole thing fell apart. Every joint creaked and rattled. The only thing that saved us is that a plane seems to always strike a sort of glancing blow. It must be due to the air currents around the plane, something slightly similar to when you drop a book perfectly square onto another flat surface and it seems to hit as though it were cushioned. It's a lot different in a plane of course but the principle is the same...

Ethel, I'll have to tell you that the furlough situation looks entirely hopeless for us. I wrote to my folks and told them that if they wanted to see me about all that they could do would be to come down to Texas for my graduation. I told them that if they came they should bring you along if it was at all possible for you to come or if they could persuade you to come...

Love, Ladd"

Ellington Field, Houston, Texas, July 7, 1943

"Dear Ethel…

I have been buying some more of my officer's clothing and equipment off and on and I am beginning to wonder what I will ever do with it all. We will be issued our own parachutes and everything else before we leave here and everyplace we go all that stuff has to go with us. Before I get done moving around I suppose it will cost me a fortune in express charges.

I'm going to have to go to the flight line in about 15 minutes for night flying. I'm getting really tired. We have been flying every night and every day. I just happened to be lucky and didn't have to fly last night.

The old "dread" is coming around again. It's getting time for check rides and I hate to think of it. I would really hate to wash out just a couple of weeks before graduation. I don't think I have much reason to worry about that though. I'll have to close and get ready to fly in a few minutes.

Love, Ladd"

Ellington Field, Houston, Texas, July 8, 1943
"Dear Ethel...

Perhaps you know that Clayton Partridge is at a camp that is only a little ways from Ellington Field. We can see the camp from the air but don't dare fly anywhere near it because they will take a crack at us with anti-aircraft if we do. They shoot first and look afterwards to see who it was they shot. At night they keep spotting us with search lights just for practice I guess...

The reason I am able to write this letter is because we had a sand storm or dust storm this evening. It started clouding up with dark thick thunderclouds this afternoon and by 6 p.m. it got dark. We were expecting a real hard thunder storm. About 7:45 the storm struck, only instead of rain it was dark reddish brown dust coming down so thick that for a little while you could hardly see 50 ft. As the storm passed it didn't leave any dust behind but seemed to carry it all right along. We all felt pretty well pleased because it was enough to cause them to call off night flying...

Love, Ladd"

R E S T R I C T E D

nrb

HEADQUARTERS
ARMY AIR FORCES GULF COAST TRAINING CENTER
RANDOLPH FIELD, TEXAS

10 Jul 1943

PERSONNEL ORDERS)
                  :
NO.   15   )

E X T R A C T

   34. The following named Flight Officers, AC, and 2d Lts, AC, Class No.
43-G, having completed the required course of instruction at the AAFAFS,
Ellington Fld, Tex, are, under the provisions of AR 95-60, 20 Aug 42, and
AAF Regulations 50-7, 5 Feb 43, rated Pilot, eff 29 Jul 43:

NAME	SER. NO.	NAME	SER. NO.
		FLIGHT OFFICER, AC	
BOVITT, EDMUND J.	T122283	FOUTS, JOHN T.	T122287
CAHILL, EDWARD R., JR	T122284	McGLYNN, KEVIN P.	T122288
FISCHER, CHARLES A.	T122285	MARTEN, WILLIAM A., JR	T122289
FORD, HOMER L.	T122286	NESSLER, CHARLES A.	T122290
		2D LT, AC	
ABERNATHY, WILLIAM H.	0687520	CARTER, HARMON D.	0687544
ALDRIDGE, EUGENE F.	0687521	CHAFFEE, EDWARD F.	0687545
ALLENBRAND, J. B. (IO)	0687522	CHRISTENSEN, ALVIN M.	0687546
ALLMAN, JAMES L.	0687523	CLEVELAND, EDWARD D.	0687547
ANDRAS, ELLIS J.	0687524	COCHRAN, GEORGE W.	0687548
AVERY, HAROLD B.	0687525	COLEMAN, JAMES M.	0687549
BADLER, BERNARD	0687526	COLEMAN, STEPHEN D., JR	0687551
BARNETT, WILLIAM S.	0687527	COLLINS, GEORGE S., JR	0687550
BEACHNER, CARLTON G.	0687528	CORNELL, ARTHUR W., JR	0687552
BEAZLEY, MALCOLM K.	0687529	COVELL, NICHOLAS	0687553
BENNETT, CHESTER B.	0687530	CRANSTON, CHARLES E.	0687554
BLAYLOCK, JOHN A.	0687531	DADDARIO, FRANCIS E.	0687555
BOGEL, TOMPKINS N.	0687532	DANA, PHIL C.	0687556
BOLES, DOUGLAS L.	0687533	DAVIS, ARTHUR W.	0687557
BOSWELL, GWYNN A.	0687534	DESKIN, WILLIAM A., JR	0687558
BOWER, ROBERT R.	0687535	DESMOND, RODERT F.	0687559
BROUGHTON, NATHANIEL H., III	0687536	DIONNE, HENRY E.	0687560
BROWN, LEONARD	0687537	DOELL, HERMAN M.	0687561
BRUNDAGE, ROBERT S.	0687538	DONNELLY, EDWARD J.	0687562
BURDETTE, ROBERT T., JR	0687539	DUNSE, HAROLD F.	0687563
BURKE, CORNELL R.	0687540	DUTY, JERALD O.	0687564
BUSH, DONALD A.	0687541	EBERT, DALE	0687565
BUTTERFIELD, WILLIAM H.	0687542	EDWARDS, SCOTT M.	0687566
CAMPBELL, LAWSON D.	0687543	EIDEN, CHARLES T.	0687567

- 1 -

Page 1. *Orders that officially designated Dad as a pilot.*

(PO # 15, 10 Jul 43)

NAME	SER. NO.	NAME	SER. NO.
		2D LT, AC (CONTD)	
ERICKSON, ROGER W.	0687568	MALONEY, ROBERT F.	0687612
EVANS, HERBERT W.	0687569	MATTHEWS, PAUL M.	0687613
EVANS, ROBERT G.	0687571	MICKEY, HARRY F.	0687614
EVANS, WILLIAM J.	0687573	MILES, SAMUEL W.	0687615
FARMER, MATT	0687570	MILLER, RUEL H.	0687616
FELDT, ALBERT J.	0687572	MONTGOMERY, DAVID F.	0687617
FETTEROLF, CHARLES E., JR	0687574	MONSEN, ROY M.	0687618
FORT, WILLIAM G.	0687575	MORGAN, RALPH M.	0687619
FOUSHEE, WILLIAM C.	0687576	MORGAN, WESLEY E.	0687621
FOWLER, ROBERT L.	0687577	MORRISSEY, WILLIAM J.	0687620
FRANGENTE, WILLIAM H.	0687578	MULLETT, GEORGE S.	0687622
GARDNER, FRANCIS M.	0687579	MYLLMAKI, EDWARD E.	0687623
GHENT, JAMES R.	0687580	NEWTON, TYRE A.	0687624
GOODNOW, ARTHUR E.	0687581	O'BRIEN, THOMAS F.	0687625
GOODWIN, GEORGE T.	0687582	PAINTER, DONALD E.	0687626
GOPLEN, FRANCIS A.	0687583	PARKER, ROBERT L.	0687627
GRANGER, HAROLD D.	0687584	PARKS, RICHARD W.	0687628
GUSCOTT, GEORGE H., JR	0687585	PICKEL, KEITH M.	0687629
HALFEN, CHARLES N.	0687586	PONTBRIAND, CLIFFORD H.	0687630
HALL, KENNETH J.	0687587	PRINCE, CHARLES J.	0687631
HALSETH, ALLAN L.	0687588	PUCCIA, VINCENT J.	0687632
HARRIS, NORMAN	0687589	QUATER, GERALD L.	0687633
HEATON, JONAS	0687590	QUICK, HILLIS E.	0687634
HEINBAUGH, HAROLD H.	0687591	REGINA, JOHN D.	0687635
HELTON, EDWIN M.	0687592	ROBINSON, ALFORD L.	0687636
HERRING, CHARLES K.	0687593	RUSSELL, CHARLES C.	0687637
HICKS, CHARLES E.	0687594	SCHULER, PAUL J.	0687638
HILLYARD, HENRY H.	0687595	SCOTT, THOMAS H.	0687639
HORN, LADD L.	0687596	SEITZ, HAROLD M.	0687640
ITTEL, LLOYD D.	0687597	SPEARS, RALPH T.	0687641
JOHNSON, GEORGE L.	0687598	STATEN, HAROLD E.	0687642
KAUFMAN, MEYER	0687599	STEDMAN, HAROLD F.	0687643
KAYWORTH, EDWARD A.	0687600	STEWART, CLARENCE H., JR	0687644
LAJEUNESSE, LAWRENCE D.	0687601	TASSIN, LARRY L.	0687645
LOTHANER, JAMES K.	0687602	TEETER, JAMES I.	0687646
LOUDEN, JAMES L.	0687603	TOMPKINS, LOUIS W., JR	0687647
LOWSTETTER, ROBERT C.	0687604	TOURANGEAU, ARTHUR J., JR	0687648
McCLEARY, GEORGE C.	0687605	TRAVIS, JACK W.	0687649
McCLUNG, JOHN P.	0687606	URBAN, JOHN E.	0687650
McFARLAND, LAWRENCE U.	0687607	VANDERLEEST, GEORGE M.	0687651
McKINNEY, RALPH M.	0687608	VAUGHAN, HENRY C.	0687652
McLACHLAN, RICHARD	0687609	WEMPE, JOHN R.	0687653
McMINN, ROLAND A.	0687610	WESTLAKE, BROMBY S.	0687654
McQUAID, FRANK H.	0687611	YOUNG, HARRY S. B., JR	0687655

- 2 -

Page 2. *Orders that officially designated Dad as a pilot.*

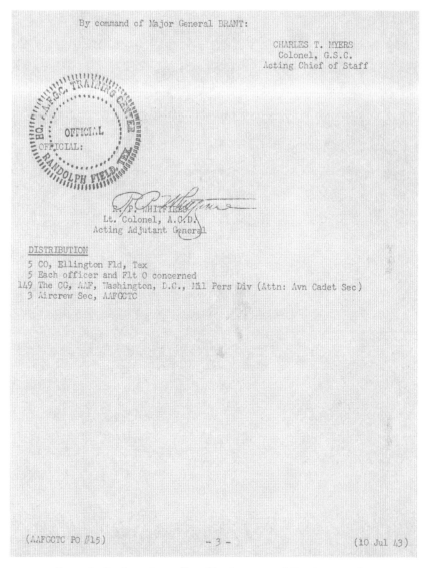

By command of Major General BRANT:

CHARLES T. MYERS
Colonel, G.S.C.
Acting Chief of Staff

OFFICIAL:

Lt. Colonel, A.G.D.
Acting Adjutant General

DISTRIBUTION

5 CO, Ellington Fld, Tex
5 Each officer and Flt O concerned
149 The CG, AAF, Washington, D.C., Mil Pers Div (Attn: Avn Cadet Sec)
3 Aircrew Sec, AAFCCTC

(AAFCCTC PO #15)   - 3 -   (10 Jul 43)

Page 3. Orders that officially designated Dad as a pilot.

Ellington Field, Houston, Texas, July 13, 1943

"Dear Ethel…

I'll tell you what I can about my "graduation." It won't be a fancy one like they used to have in peace time. There won't be any plane formations other than regular training flights by the underclass. There won't be any fancy uniforms either, just regular workday khaki with an officers cap and insignia. The graduation will be at 10 a.m. July 29 and if you are here, and I certainly hope you will be, you will be allowed to attend. There will probably be a couple of speeches by some of the higher officers and then the wings and commissions will be handed out. You and my mother will have to share the honor of pinning on those bars and wings…

I'm going to enclose a clipping from the paper that tells about all the trouble I helped to cause in Houston last night. I was flying the lead ship of the second element of planes that was identified as enemy…

Love

Ladd"

Entire Zone 4 Activated In Civilian Defense Drill

For the first time an entire zone, comprising one-ninth of the city, was activated in civilian defense drill Monday night. Zone 4, which includes the Montrose, Southampton and River Oaks sections, participated in the drill.

Ellington Field planes flew over that section and were identified as "enemy" planes at 9 p.m. Then some 500 air-raid wardens, the auxiliary firemen and emergency squads of Harris County, the Red Cross, A. W. V. S., and various aides, set to work to put out the fires, incendiary bombs, and effect rescues.

○ ○ ○

Two Scouts "Rescued."

At the Sidney Lanier Junior High School the wardens rescued two Boy Scouts from the top floor of the "burning" building. An imaginary bomb crater in front of the building complicated their work. The building was scaled with a rope ladder and then a rope and pulley system was set up by which the fire victims were lowered on stretchers.

The red flares representing the fire were so effective that uniformed neighbors were fooled and called the city fire department, which responded on a wild goose chase.

The rescuers found that the entire side of the South Main Baptist Church was so badly "bombed" that it was necessary to shoot a line from a marine gun all the way across it, before the rope ladder could be affixed.

○ ○ ○

Practice Advantageous.

Post Warden Robert W. Sell of Section 4 pointed out that widespread zone practices were advantageous because every worker must be present and participate in his special job. When sectors only are activated and all the workers are not present, help is called from other sectors. A surprise air-raid drill might be staged at any time.

Mr. Sell said he believes that the greatest need at present is for more wardens. Also needed is more practice in black-outs, which are called only by military officials. More wardens are needed to replace absentees.

The value of a city-wide practice is to be considered. Cities are bombed in sections rather than totally. A practice of that kind would be of special value to control center workers.

◆◆◆

Ellington Adds Two To 'Hall of Heroes'

The names of two Ellington Field-trained men have been added to the "Hall of Heroes" at the field, according to Col. W. H. Reid, commanding officer. They are

Clipping about the civilian defense drill that Dad mentioned in the letter.

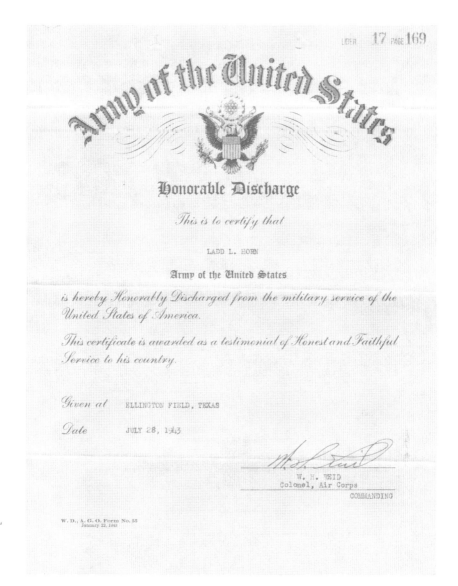

Honorable discharge at graduation from Ellington Field, Houston, TX.

Honorable discharge at graduation from Ellington Field, Houston, TX.

ID card issued on July 29, 1943 at Ellington Field, Houston, TX.

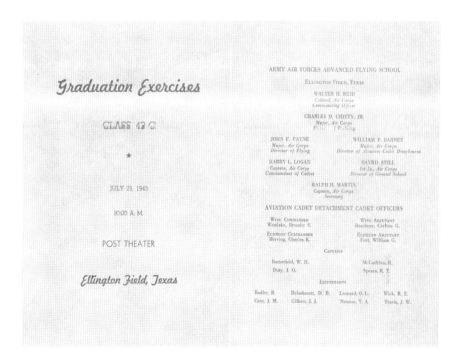

Graduation program from Ellington Field, Houston, TX, July 29, 1943.

HEADQUARTERS
ARMY AIR FORCES GULF COAST TRAINING CENTER 1FY-hwk
Office of the Commanding General

Randolph Field, Texas
In reply
July 29, 1943
refer to: 201 - Horn, Ladd Leonard

Subject: Temporary Appointment.

To   : Aviation Cadet Ladd Leonard Horn,
          U.S.A.,   A   0-687,596
          Ellington Field, Texas.

1. The Secretary of War has directed me to inform you that the President has appointed and commissioned you a temporary Second Lieutenant, Army of the United States, effective this date. Your serial number is shown after A above.

2. This commission will continue in force during the pleasure of the President of the United States for the time being, and for the duration of the war and six months thereafter unless sooner terminated.

3. There is inclosed herewith a form for oath of office which you are requested to execute and return. The execution and return of the required oath of office constitute an acceptance of your appointment. No other evidence of acceptance is required.

4. This letter should be retained by you as evidence of your appointment as no commissions will be issued during the war.

By Command of Major General BRANT:

J. E. McCord,   /s/
J. E. McCORD,   /t/
Lieut.Colonel, A.G.D.,
Asst.Adjutant General.

Inclosure:
Form for oath of office.

A CERTIFIED TRUE COPY:

VERL A. OBERLIN,
Major, Air Corps,
Executive Officer.

Official documentation for Dad's promotion to 2nd Lieutenant upon his graduation from Ellington Field, Houston, Texas.

BARS AND STRIPES

Ladd L. Horn, 54 Salisbury Avenue, Blasdell, has been graduated from Ellington Field. Houston, Tex., where he received the silver wings of an Army air pilot and a commission as second lieutenant.

Ellington Field is one of eleven advanced flying schools of the Gulf Coast Training Center of the Army Air Forces, which are producing thousands of pilots each 4½ weeks. News of the graduation came from the AAF Gulf Coast Training Center, Randolph Field, Texas.

Lieut. Horn

Buffalo area (Blasdell, NY?) newspaper announcement of Dad's graduation from Ellington Field, Houston, TX.

Ellington Field Class 43-G graduation book, July 29, 1943. Ladd L. Horn
top row, second from left.

Dad on graduation day, July 29, 1943, Ellington Field, Houston, TX. Picture taken at the hotel that Ethel O'Neil and his parents had stayed at.

Newton, Kansas, August 1, 1943 (On the way to Dodge City, Kansas)

"Dear Ethel

Well, so far so good. Here I am in Newton waiting to catch the 9:40 p.m. train for Dodge City.

Ladd"

Dodge City, Kansas, August 2, 1943

"Darling

I arrived at the field here Sunday 3 a.m. with another officer whom I met on the train. We couldn't find anyone around here at all except for the MPs at the gate so we just crawled into an empty barracks and went to sleep. We woke up at about 11 o'clock and went and reported in.

The field is fairly new but very dilapidated looking. Everything is dirt and dust and it is so hot that when you step out into the sun it is just like stepping into a blast furnace. The other day it was 113° in the shade and no shade. It hasn't rained for four months and the air is so dry that my lips and the inside of my nose have cracked until they bleed.

The way things stand here now it evidently won't be too bad except for the heat. My pay will be $291 a month and my board and room, laundry, cleaning, officers club dues and everything else put together will only come to $40 a month…

I'm in a room with another boy by the name of Cain, "Sugar" Cain, from southeast Alabama. He says those _____ Yankees hung that name on me as soon as they found out I was from Alabama and I never have been able to get away from it since….

According to present orders I may be here for 9 weeks or I may be here only until Sept. 4. If I stay for 9 weeks I will continue to fly B-26s but if I leave Sept. 4 I will be sent to a B-29 school. The B-29 is our largest bomber and carries a first, second and third pilot. I understand that all one of the pilots does is work the throttles and engine and propeller controls while the other two actually fly the plane…

We have more freedom on this post than any place else that I know of. Any time that you are off duty you may go to town and you may stay alright as long as you are back in time for duty in the morning. You also may bring your wife, parents, children or sweetheart on the post and they can even eat with you at the officers' mess…

Yours truly,

Ladd"

Dodge City, Kansas, August 8, 1943 *In this letter you will hear my dad very strongly expressing his desire for my mom to tell him that she wants to marry him some day. It was not a marriage proposal or demand to get married right away. He states that clearly in his next letter dated August 15th. Recognize that this letter was, in part, driven by the deaths of 5 men from his squadron in a single afternoon and his recognition that he might not live through training.*

"Dearest Ethel…

I suppose though that you think, "How could he love me as he says he does and still ask me to be his wife at a time like this? Doesn't he know how hard it would be for me not to be able to be with him? Doesn't he realize how hard it would be for me if he should fail to return and I should be left alone, perhaps even the mother of a coming child?" Ethel, certainly I have thought of those things and considered them and don't think that my heart didn't ache as I thought of them and thought too of the many young women who have had to withstand those same heartaches. Don't ever think that I could wish for you to have to go through anything like that and still, after all my reasoning and self judgement my heart cries out she must be mine, I just have to have her for my own and soon too.

I and the other young men with me, have lived very close to death in the past few months and even more so now. It has only been a miracle that more of us haven't been killed before now. That miracle more or less came to an end yesterday. We had 5 of the young men from our squadron killed yesterday in one afternoon. While we don't have any idea of who might be next still we know, that as long as we are flying these planes, according to the law of averages there will be five more of us gone by next Saturday. Flying these planes the losses are no greater in combat than they are in training and these men realize that. Knowing that they do you must understand that they have no fear of death itself, else they would long ago have fallen by the wayside. Many though, myself included, have another fear. That fear being that we may die without ever having known that most beloved of all girls as our wife. Each one says to himself, "My girl, even though she realizes what she might have to bear up under, even though she realizes the heartache she may have to suffer, loves me enough so that she will willingly and even longingly be mine." Each man hopes too that his girl will know and understand his desire that she should bear a child for him even though he might never see that child.

This, Ethel, is what I am afraid that you won't be able to understand and that is that that isn't just a selfish desire nor just a longing for self-satisfaction. It is something far deeper, something in reality unfathomable to human mind, something ordained of God to be and something that always will be as long as man lives upon this earth. Those desires do not exclude your feelings, your fear of heartache and loneliness, your fear of loss and unhappiness in the future; they recognize and make allowance for each feeling and fear that you have and each man who truly loves a girl thinks continuously in his heart of how he might be able to take away her fears and compensate for any feeling she might suffer. Because after all he is human he can't entirely succeed but nevertheless the intent is there.

Sweetheart, we have one whom we can trust who isn't human, one who can heal every heartache, one whom we can trust even that there should be no heartache for us unless it is his will. And if it's his will we will know that somewhere there is a good reason for it even though we might not know what that reason is. Why not trust him now for our strength and for our happiness…

Don't think that I don't respect your judgement or your wishes. After all, what you want means a lot to me and you must be able to understand that… I do respect your judgement and I understand that it is best to take time concerning such a matter. My only fear is that we don't have time to take. I want you today while I'm alive and can have you because tomorrow I may be gone. Perhaps that fear makes me unreasonable but please, Ethel, take what I have just said and put it with what has gone before and try to understand it as I mean it…

Yours, Ladd"

Dodge City, Kansas, August 15, 1943 *The New Testament that he received from Mom was carried on all his missions and through the end of the war.*
"Dear Ethel

I received the lovely Testament that you sent me yesterday and your letter this morning. You don't know how precious that testament will always be.

Ethel, I'm sorry that I made you feel so bad because of that letter I sent you. I didn't mean to do that to you and I'm sorry…

Honey I just tried to tell you what I wanted and how I felt inside… That was only what I want and lots of things I want aren't the same as what I can have…

Loving you, Ethel could I want you to have to ever suffer just those very things that I know you fear? Still, loving you, couldn't I wish that you would love me enough though to be willing to take the chance of suffering those things for me?…

I asked if you wouldn't be willing to suffer heartache or even heartbreak for me. You would be wouldn't you? That's what I wanted you to tell me. I didn't mean that letter as a proposal for marriage although the way I wrote it perhaps you took it that way…

Those two separate times at Houston when I asked you I thought you understood that I didn't mean for it to be right now. I just wanted you to promise me so that I would have a firm sure hope to build upon…

…. I want you to know that you want to be my wife whether it is possible or practical for us now or not. Understand, Ethel, that I said I want to know that you <u>want</u> to be my wife, not whether or not you will be…

Ethel, if this seems to conflict with what I wrote in my last letter and you can't quite understand remember that my feelings are all mixed up inside me and I don't quite know what to do or say or what is best or right… Please forgive me and try to love me just the same…

Love

Ladd"

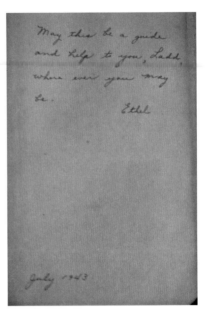

The New Testament and Psalms given to Dad by Ethel J. O'Neil in July of 1943. The note reading "May this be a guide and help to you where ever [sic] you may be. July 1943" is Ethel's note to Dad on the inside page. Dad carried this New Testament the whole time he was in North Africa, Sardinia, Corsica and France and was still reading it when he was in Atlantic City on May 20, 1945. These pictures were taken in 2022.

Dodge City, Kansas, August 20, 1943

"Dearest Ethel

They have just about killed me since I have been here. We have a schedule that runs from 6:45 a.m. to 8 o'clock at night but we have been working from 6:45 right through until 12:30 and 1 o'clock at night.

I was tired and kind of run down when I left Ellington and now with this I am about finished. If I last another week I will be doing good. If I can't make it they will probably ship me out to Brooks field at San Antonio for a while to the pilots' pool there… That is where they send all their "beat up" and "broken down" pilots to try and recondition them a little bit. Several of the boys I knew have already been shipped out of here. I guess we had already taken a little too much in the past year before we came here…

Love

Ladd"

Dodge City, Kansas, August 24, 1943

"Dear Ethel…

I don't know how much you know about the planes that I am flying so I will tell you a little. They are fast heavy planes with the worst reputation of any plane in the world in their class and size. They are also the heaviest plane of their size in the world and have the heaviest wing loading, also some of the heaviest armor and armament.

The ones that I am flying are just about brand new and are B-35s and B-41s. They are just a little larger than the old B-26 and have a power turret in the tail. The general appearance is identical except that the tail isn't pointed as it was in the older planes due to the new turret placed there.

The weight runs about 28,000 lb without crew, gas or any special equipment. With maximum load the weight may run up as high as 42,000 lb. Normal loaded weight is about 39,800 lb or just about 20 tons. The engines develop 4,000 horsepower and have four-bladed propellers that are 13 ½ ft in diameter. (Of course the engines are built by Henry Ford.) If you cut the power off the plane comes down at a 45° angle. You don't think that is steep until you fly one. The gliding ratio is about 1 to 1 or that is the plane will glide one foot forward for every foot it drops down. Most planes glide 6 or 7 ft forward for every foot down and some even make 12 ft.

900 gallons [sic] is about the minimum load of gas that we take off with and for long trips the plane can be equipped to carry about ½ a tank car of gas.

It takes 250 gallons of gas just to take off and climb up to 5,000 ft. After you are once up there of course it doesn't take nearly as much to keep going.

In 9 ½ hours I could fly coast to coast with one of these planes and I could fly home in from 5 to 6 h. I thought that I might get a chance to fly home but they limited us to 1,000 miles from the field and Buffalo is about 1,400 miles by air from here.

I saw one of these planes crash and burn last Sat. night. It got so hot that some of the slabs of armor plate burned like giant sparklers and lit the sky for several miles around…

I love you, honey

Ladd"

Dad's note on the back of this postcard: This is the plane that I am flying now. Aug. 1943 Dodge City, Kansas.

Dodge City, August 29, 1943

"Dear Ethel…

First of all the P.S. in my address stands for Pilot School. There is only one other at Del Rio, Texas. They have been set up mostly just to teach pilots of other planes how to fly B-26s. The 26s are a lot tougher than most planes to fly and the pilots need special schooling in them before they can take them up. If I get a card for a 26 that means that I am qualified to fly any plane there is. However if I am qualified to fly every other plane that there is it would not qualify me for a 26…

I'm still hanging on here somehow, but how I can make it I don't know. I've been so tired that I hardly knew what I was doing this past week. They were going to eliminate me from flying I got so bad. The Captain sent me up for a ride with the Operations Officer to prove to him that I couldn't fly anymore so that he could get rid of me. When I went up I was so tired that I didn't care about anything and I flew the plane just as though I didn't care. After we had been flying for a while he cut one engine out on me and I guess I was too tired to even show any surprise. I cut the switches and controls on the bad engine, feathered the prop and went right on flying just as though nothing at all had happened. When we got down and landed the operations officer moved me up to first pilot. The ceremony of which consisted of nothing more than that he stopped the plane on the runway climbed out of his seat and motioned me to take his place. All he said was "and don't ride the brakes." That's the one fault of almost every new pilot in one of these planes that's why he mentioned it.

When I got back to the flight room the Captain was waiting for me and he started talking all about how it was no disgrace to be eliminated from flying if you weren't able anymore and all such stuff. Also perhaps I would be able to fly some other type of plane sometime. I let him get pretty well talked out and then just casually remarked that I was flying first pilot now. He suddenly decided that he didn't care to talk to me anymore just then…

…Almost all the boys that I came through with are gone now. My roommate is in the hospital and several of the others have been sent to Brooks field. One of the fellows broke all of a sudden and is in the hospital. I was talking to him last night. The poor kid is actually dying from nothing more than just overwork, too much nervous strain and too much lonesomeness for his girl and his folks. He just seemed to all of a sudden lose all will to live. They put him in the hospital and gave him a private room with anything that he might want but nothing seems to arouse any interest in him. The doctors have all examined him and can't seem to find anything at all wrong with him and still he just grows weaker and thinner every day. He'll want a Coca Cola or something and they'll get it for him and after he has it he will just take a swallow or two and then set it down and forget about it. The same way with a book. He will read a page or two and then lay it down and forget about it. They have his girlfriend here and have allowed her to even lay with him and sleep with him in the hope of having her near him might bring some feeling or desire to drive him but he hardly seems to notice that she is there. Last night though when she was getting ready to go into town he seemed to realize she was going away for a while and he called her over to his bedside, reached up and drew her face down to his and kissed her but then afterwards he didn't seem to realize that she was still there or anything and didn't even say good bye to her when she left. After she had left I tried to get him to talk to me but he seemed just as though he was too weak to talk. Finally though he noticed my roommate who has had an operation on his spine and isn't able to bend his back enough to sit down yet or get around very well and he laughed at the hard time he was having and tried to tell me how funny it was to watch the other boy try to bend over.

Why they don't send him home and let him be with his folks I don't know. The Army just doesn't do some things I guess…

All my love

Ladd"

Dodge City, Kansas, September 5, 1943

Dear Ethel

…I've lost 10 more lbs of weight so I'm getting down to where there isn't too much left of me. As a matter of fact I weigh the same now as I did when I was 13 and 14 years old. I was supposed to be underweight then so I don't know what I am now.

For that matter your [*sic*] pretty lucky to even have a boyfriend who is alive right now after last Friday night. We came in to the field through a thunderstorm and did everything that it is supposed to be impossible to do in a plane without getting killed say nothing about doing it in a B-26. We came through a thunderstorm which is strictly taboo to start with. We came into the field from about 50 miles with so much turbulence that part of the time we were using the trim tabs to try to control the ship. It was raining so hard that you couldn't see anything and we came in at 900' off the ground when normally you never fly one of these ships under 2,000'. We couldn't make any radio contact and couldn't see enough to know which way the wind was from with the result we came in for a cross wind landing and making an approach at about 230 mph. We got down to about 15 ft off the ground before we realized the wind direction and made a 45° turn into the wind at about 10' off the ground and 200 mph. We set the plane down on a wet runway at 170 mph and then didn't know how we were going to stop it. Somehow or other we got traction enough to get stopped just about at the end of the runway. The poor enlisted men in the crew were so scared that they looked as though someone had taken a whitewash brush and daubed their faces with it. We were too busy to know enough to get scared I guess but they had to just sit there and sweat it out. The poor plane was shaking and vibrating so that the crew chief crawled through the bomb bays and clear into the tail section to see if the elevators were still holding on or half torn off. You don't have the least idea what we went through or never will have unless you can be in one of these planes for even just a normal landing sometime. Even men who have flown quite a bit get scared when they get in one of these planes and see the ground coming at them at a 45° angle and 160 mph. It's just like going down the first hill on the big roller coaster at Crystal Beach only twice as fast...

Love, Ladd"

Dodge City, Kansas, September 10, 1943

"Dear Ethel…

I was just figuring out the other day that on average I have been flying about 1,000 miles a day…Next week I start flying day and night both besides going to school. I will be flying about 15 to 1,800 miles a day then. The week after next I will be leaving here on a 5000 mile flight or perhaps even 9 or 10,000 miles. I don't know for sure or where I will be going either. I think that I will hit Detroit but don't expect to pass any closer than that to Buffalo.

Ladd"

Dodge City, Kansas, September 17, 1943

"Dear Ethel

I mailed you a small package today with a gift for you and also my two rings. If you wish you may keep the Air Corps ring as a souvenir or keepsake but take the other gold ring back to my parents… My fingers have grown too thin for me to keep the rings on so I figured I had better send them home rather than take a chance on losing them.

I've had about 8 hours sleep in the last three days so I guess you know just about how I am feeling…

…I passed my final check here yesterday…the rest will be just plain flying. I think that I will be able to complete my ground school work about the middle of next week and from then on for a while I will be free just to roam around the country for a while in a B-26…

A couple of afternoons ago I flew from Dodge City to Garden City, to the Rocky Mts. pretty well up north, then southeast to Denver, Colorado, around Colorado Springs, southwest to Pikes Peak, then back east to Great Bend, Kansas and circled there hunting for B-29s to race or dogfight with and then came back to Dodge City. The total time that I was away from the field was just about 4 hours. It would take just about a week to cover the same area in a car.

It took me 31 hours to come up here by train from Houston. I could go back with one of these planes in about 2 hours or just a little better. That's traveling only 15 times as fast…

Love, Ladd"

Dodge City, Kansas, September 17, 1943

"Dear Ethel

I am enclosing a picture of the planes that I fly here. It is from the October issue of "Air Trails."…

…As we say, "Roger Dodger, over, under and out."

Love, Ladd"

Picture enclosed in Dad's letter of September 17, 1943.

Dodge City, Kansas, September 26, 1943

"Dearest Ethel…

I'm pretty well finished up here and things won't be too hard for the next week or so…

Ladd"

Dodge City, Kansas, October 3, 1943

"Dear Ethel…

I have just about everything finished up here except for gathering up a few loose ends. I think that I will be leaving for MacDill Field, Florida or perhaps Barksdale, Louisiana about the middle of this week. There is also a slight chance that I might go to Klingsman, Arizona. I completed the course here with the highest average of any man on the field so I think that perhaps I will get my choice which is MacDill…

Love, Ladd"

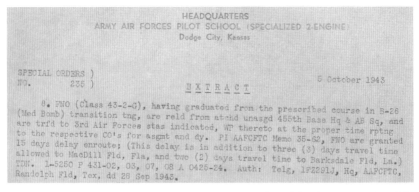

October 5, 1943 orders to transition to MacDill Field, Florida with a fifteen day leave and five days of travel.

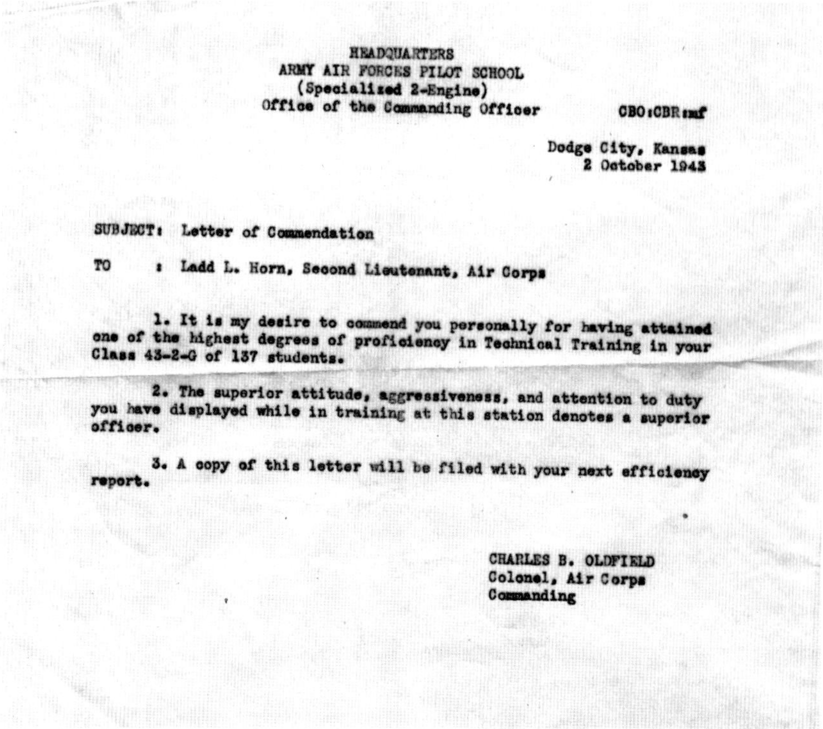

HEADQUARTERS
ARMY AIR FORCES PILOT SCHOOL
(Specialized 2-Engine)
Office of the Commanding Officer   CBO:CBR:mf

Dodge City, Kansas
2 October 1943

SUBJECT: Letter of Commendation

TO   : Ladd L. Horn, Second Lieutenant, Air Corps

1. It is my desire to commend you personally for having attained one of the highest degrees of proficiency in Technical Training in your Class 43-2-G of 137 students.

2. The superior attitude, aggressiveness, and attention to duty you have displayed while in training at this station denotes a superior officer.

3. A copy of this letter will be filed with your next efficiency report.

CHARLES B. OLDFIELD
Colonel, Air Corps
Commanding

Typewritten letter of commendation given to Dad by Colonel Charles B. Oldfield for having "...attained one of the highest degrees of proficiency in Technical Training in your class 43-2-G of 137 students." A handwritten copy was also given.

The following pictures were taken in Blasdell and Hamburg, NY in October 1943. Dad took advantage of his leave time ("delay") to visit his parents and Ethel O'Neil on his trip from Dodge City, Kansas to MacDill Field, Tampa Bay, Florida. MacDill Field, Florida was a short stop en route to Barksdale Field, Lake Charles, Louisiana.

October 1943 leave in Blasdell/Hamburg, NY. Upper picture: Dad and Ethel O'Neil with "Skook" on hunting trip. Lower picture: (left to right) Leonard August Horn (Dad's dad), "Skook", Dad, Ethel O'Neil and Frank Fuller (a friend; Batavia, NY) on a hunting trip.

Ethel O'Neil and "Skook."

Lower picture: Dad and "Skook" in front of his parents' house at 54 Salisbury Ave., Blasdell, NY. The house still stands today in 2022.

Ethel O'Neil with Dad in his parents' house on Salisbury Ave. Blasdell, NY.

Dad outside his parents' house at 54 Salisbury Ave., Blasdell, NY October 1943. Dad's writing on the envelope containing the picture: "Pre-combat pictures."

Picture of Ethel and Ladd in front of Ethel J. O'Neil's house on Bay View Road in Hamburg, NY. Date unknown, but based on a series of pictures that were marked, "Oct.-43 during delay from Dodge City to Lake Charles," *and comparing the uniform and Ethel's coat, it is almost certainly Dad's October 1943 leave between Dodge City, KS and MacDill Field, Tampa Bay, FL. Dad's writing on the envelope containing the picture:* "WWII pre-combat pictures."

MacDill Field, Tampa, Florida, October 25, 1943

"Dearest Ethel

Well, I arrived all right at MacDill yesterday evening. The weather, the field and Florida are all beautiful but some things stink pretty loudly including the salt water…

…I expect to leave this post pretty soon, perhaps as soon as 8 days… The whole bunch of us have been classed as limited co-pilots for the time being. Why? I don't know. To top that off they are issuing each one of us infantry uniforms and about a half a ton of infantry and jungle equipment… They are even issuing each one of us two small pup tents and waterproof sleeping bags. Whether we're going to turn out to be some kind of flying commandos or something remains to be seen. They have also dumped in a bunch of single engine pilots just graduated from advanced school who I think will become our co-pilots in time…

Love, Ladd"

Postcard of MacDill Field, Tampa Bay, FL that Dad saved.

Postcard of a "crash boat" from MacDill Field, Tampa Bay, Florida. So many B-26s crashed in Tampa Bay during training that the saying, "One a day in Tampa Bay" was known throughout the USAAF and beyond.

MacDill Field, Tampa, Florida, November 5, 1943

"Dearest Ethel...

...Its 10:45 p.m. and lights out at 11. I'm shipping out tomorrow on a troop train. We're going someplace near Lake Charles, Louisiana...

...We look like regular infantry troops... You should have a picture of me with a pistol belt, field pack, canteen, gas mask and steel helmet on. You'd get a kick out of it.

Last Saturday afternoon I was able to go over to St [*sic*] Cloud and stayed overnight to come back on Sunday. I went down purposely to see our place there because I figured it would probably be my last chance. I ate a tangerine off my own tangerine tree, an orange off my own orange tree, and a fig off my own fig tree, and then went and stood on the front steps of the house and cried. I just wanted the war to be over and to have you with me and to be there to stay with everything so quiet and calm and beautiful, with everything living and growing.

I wish that I had had you come as far as Washington with me... *(This is a reference, to a return trip from a furlough in Buffalo after his training in Dodge City, Kansas.)*

Yours truly

Ladd"

Train between MacDill Field, Tampa, Florida and Lake Charles, Louisiana, November 6, 1943

"Dear Ethel

I am writing to you from a Pullman Berth on a troop train somewhere between Mobile, Alabama and New Orleans. I'm really traveling in style this time if not very fast...

We left MacDill about 4:30 or 5:00 yesterday afternoon and have been traveling ever since to get this far. We pull into a siding for every other freight train on the line to go by. It took five trains to move us out. One train for each of the four squadrons in our group and a fifth train for baggage and equipment. I counted 59 jeeps alone for our outfit and we don't carry many jeeps in proportion to tugs, bomb carriers, bomb loaders, crash trucks and gas trucks. In addition to the trains all our planes are flying to our new base loaded with everything that they can carry. They don't mean much though because we only have 8 left. We had nine to leave for Lake Charles but one cracked up and burned right after takeoff. I don't know how we will ever do any flying if we don't soon get some more ships. Just since I have been in the outfit which is just two weeks Sunday we have lost about $2,000,000 worth of planes due to accident, inferior grades of gas and error. At that rate in three more weeks we'll be out of planes and be practically an infantry outfit.

We're beginning to call ourselves the 479th flying commandos. Most of us have been in the air only about once and a lot not at all in this outfit and all the rest has been infantry stuff.

Back to our train right now. It might interest you to know how it is made up. We have one car that is an orderly room and headquarters for the train then we have two cook cars to feed us, one car for a dispensary with a medical officer, one car for prisoners and the rest Pullman cars for the men. The enlisted men have to double up 2 to a berth but each officer gets a berth to himself. Each man is assigned to a car and must not leave that car from the time he enters it until he reaches the destination. Meals are served to each man at his seat in the car. It is brought down the aisles in large containers and dished out. Each man has his canteen, mess kit, and cup and wipes them clean after his meal with a paper napkin.

The meals on the train have been the best that I have had since I left home after my furlough. Meals at MacDill were poor and terribly expensive served by a civilian restaurant run on the field as a concession. The Army is feeding us on the train and the cost will be about 1/3, and for supper I had roast pork, mashed potatoes, salad, applesauce, peas, bread and butter, iced tea and "Cherryade." All cooked well and served good and hot and the iced drinks really ice cold.

Yours, Ladd"

Lake Charles Army Air Base (LCAAB), Lake Charles, Louisiana, November 10, 1943

"Dear Ethel…

This is quite a small camp and field. There are not really enough barracks for us and we are crowded together with barely 2 ft between our bunks. I've just got room enough to hang my clothes up and that's all.

We still don't have enough planes to do any flying to speak of. I have flown four hours one night since I came back from my furlough. Lots of the fellows haven't flown at all for six weeks… We overloaded their mess hall… The lunch room is mobbed all day and the PX is sold out… The Provost Marshall is complaining because of the odd mixture of G.I. uniforms and flying equipment and everything is going sour in general. Even the people in town are mad because our takeoffs are so low and fast that the civilians are scared of the planes coming over them and annoyed by all the noise. Even with lack of planes and equipment we are just a little bit too big for this field. We can't even get our planes into the hangars. The rudders stick up higher than the hanger eaves… They all look at these B-26s with sort of awe and then look at us as though we were crazy, shake their heads and walk off…

Lovingly

Ladd"

Lake Charles Army Air Base (LCAAB), Lake Charles, Louisiana, November 16, 1943

"Darling…

…I am just getting over a cold and had to take a yellow fever and typhus shot today. It seems as though my arm has been continuously sore from shots ever since I have been in the Army… The yellow fever makes me ache in all my joints though and to make it worse I have to get up and take physical training in the morning…

Ladd"

LCAAB Lake Charles, Louisiana, November 21, 1943

"Dear Ethel…

…It's two months all but a few days since I have flown a plane myself. I've put in just four hours co-pilot time in between…

They are getting things organized a little better now and I will have to expect to go across sometime late in February I guess. They've picked out about 12 of us to make a flight. I don't know what they will do with the rest of the fellows. There were more than 150 more pilots signed in this last bunch alone. The 12 of us I expect will start flying about 4 h a day beginning Monday. I hope we will get hold of some new ships and good tires pretty soon. These are pretty ricketty [*sic*] and well-worn that we have right now…

Sincerely and lovingly

Yours, Ladd"

LCAAB, Lake Charles, Louisiana, November 27, 1943

"Dear Ethel…

I have part of my crew now and probably will get the rest before long. I have a co-pilot, bombardier and Radio man [*sic*] so far. That means I only need an engineer and turret gunner to have a full crew. We will probably carry an extra gunner now though because it takes special training for a turret gunner and our planes all have ball turrets in the tails now. Also my bombardier is a combination bombardier and navigator and that means one less man to man a gun if you get in a fight.

The crew stands now—

1ˢᵗ pilot—Horn

Co-pilot—Roseman

Bomb & nav.—Larrabee

Radio man [*sic*]—Sparaco

Engineer—?

Gunner—?

Pilot, bombardier, radioman, and engineer are all gunners too of course. Our standard armament right now is 12 guns. Bombardier fires one, pilot fires five, radioman fires two, engineer fires two and turret gunner fires two. No matter how you figure it the pilot gets more work than anybody on this deal. The co-pilot does the least I believe. About all that he does is ride along as a spare part. Lots of times in the course of an entire flight the copilot won't do anything but move the landing gear handle up on takeoff and down again for the landing…

      Ladd"

LCAAB, Lake Charles, Louisiana, December 2, 1943

"Darling…

…I'm not certain right now whether I told you in my last letter or not that I was in the process of being checked out as a 1st pilot in the third air force [*sic*]. The check-out is complete now but it involved quite a bit of filling out of papers and etc. and also the wasting of most of two days trying to get the major to sign my certificate.

…the way things are going right now you can probably expect me to be in this country until about next April…

I'm learning right now to be a bombardier as well as a pilot. I don't know what good it will do me to know how to use a bomb sight but I'm learning nevertheless..

      Truly yours

      Ladd."

LCAAB, Lake Charles, Louisiana, December 5, 1943

"Dear Sweetheart…

I don't know whether you realize it or not Ethel but life is pretty hard for me in the army. It all goes against my nature terribly. Considering that you have the same feeling for me that I do for you, you are still lucky because after all you are at home and with your parents, sisters and friends. I have an army of men around me and not one man that I can chum with. I live day after day in nothing but a continual mess of drinking, smoking, swearing, dirty jokes and obscene stories. I never realized that people could be so wicked and that there could be so few decent ones in such a large group. I'm getting more and more disgusted each day with our young people in this country and I mean the young women too not just men…

Yours,

Ladd"

LCAAB, Lake Charles, Louisiana, December 12, 1943
"Darling…

You were right, I do have two new crew members but we're not taking flights together right now. My whole crew has been having all ground school work this past week and the pilots have been flying by themselves. Tomorrow morning though we are going on a skip-bombing mission. We have had three ships have close shaves with them lately. One had a bomb release late and just missed a Sulphur plant by about 100 ft. Another had the same thing happen and just missed a farmer's cow by about the same difference. The third plane had a really close one though. It dropped a skip bomb from about 25 ft. The bomb hit the ground and instead of skipping it did an upshot and hit the plane that had dropped it. The bomb went off just about the time it hit the plane but all it did was shake it up good. The crew was scared though for two days afterwards. I suppose it would make you feel scared for some time afterwards especially when you think of the ten bombs still left in the bomb bay any one of which might have exploded just from the jar even after the miracle of the bomb going off and not hurting the ship…

I'll have to say so long now and go fly but I'll be thinking of you continually.

Lovingly yours,

Ladd"

LCAAB, Lake Charles, Louisiana, December 14, 1943

"Dear Ethel…

My crew is complete now… I dropped five bombs yesterday on the skip bombing mission I told you about in my last letter…

Love,

Ladd"

LCAAB, Lake Charles, Louisiana, December 20, 1943

"Dear Ethel…

I'm not doing any long distance flying now as you asked and as far as a 1,000 mile radius is concerned we are confined to a 35 mile radius now which means we are just about never out of sight of our home field. The only time we go outside that 35 mile limit is on bombing missions and then we don't go over 100 miles to our targets…

It didn't snow in Lake Charles this past week but we almost froze to death just the same. Frost formed so thick on the plane wings that the men had to sweep it off with push brooms before we could take off. We had a couple of planes forced down by wing ice too which is rather unusual in this part of the country…

Love to my Sweetheart and every Christmas joy.

Ladd"

LCAAB, Lake Charles, Louisiana, December 26, 1943

"Darling

Here it is the day after Christmas…

I have been lucky and finally found one Christian young man that I can chum with. His name is Noble E. Brown and he is a Nazarene. He's married and he never was around at all until this last week. However his wife has gone home for a while to Nevada and now he is around the barracks as much as the rest of us…

Ladd"

LCAAB, Lake Charles, Louisiana,, December 31, 1943

"Dearest Ethel…

We had a little excitement here last night. The officers' club house burned down. There was supposed to be a grand opening tonight but it will have to be canceled indefinitely I guess…

All my love,
Ladd"

LCAAB, Lake Charles, Louisiana, January 2, 1944

"Darling…

I'm grounded right now because yesterday noon when I was just ready to take off a captain from the Medical Corps grabbed my wrist and took my pulse. My pulse was all screwy I guess so he grounds me and says if I'm not different in a few days I'll have to go down to the hospital and have a blood count taken. I don't know what he figures is wrong with me…

I feel proud to have you wear my regular pair *(Pilot's wings)* that they gave me when I graduated…

Love, Ladd"

LCAAB, Lake Charles, Louisiana, January 3, 1944

"Dear Ethel…

I was down to the dispensary this morning and saw a different doctor who says there is nothing wrong with me and ungrounded me again…

I can't help but keep wishing that this whole thing were over with. I haven't even seen any war yet and still I've had too much of it.

I guess I'm just a little bit too peaceful a man at heart...

Yours truly

Ladd"

LCAAB, Lake Charles, Louisiana, January 6, 1944

"Honey...

Do you know where I have just been? No less than St. Cloud, Florida. It just happened that I was sent over to Lakeland to bring a plane back and I was able to go to St. Cloud and see my folks for about 8 hours...

I have to close and go to sleep because I haven't slept at all in two days...

Love,

Ladd"

LCAAB, Lake Charles, Louisiana, January 9, 1944

"Dear Ethel...

From what they tell us now it is pretty definite that we will be over on the other side for the talked-of invasion of Europe. I didn't expect us to wind up in England but it appears as though we will now... *(Note that this is not what happened and shows the mixed and changing messages they received.)*

Love, Ladd"

LCAAB, Lake Charles, Louisiana, January 11, 1944

"Dearest Ethel...

Ladd"

Dad included this "Departure and Arrival Report" from January 10, 1944.

LCAAB, Lake Charles, Louisiana, January 13, 1944

"Darling…

My crew was changed some from what it was at the start. The way it stands now we have two Dutchmen, two Jews, and two Poles on it.

Co-pilot—Roseman—South Carolina Jew

Engineer—Fineman—Philadelphia Jew

Bombardier (combination bombardier and navigator)—Larrabe,—Massachusetts Dutchman or German

Radioman—Shultz—Chicago Pole

Gunner/Armorer—Olaska—Chicago Pole…

> All my love, Ladd"

LCAAB, Lake Charles, Louisiana, January 14-15, 1944

"Darling…

…I get so that I feel just all bitter and shriveled up inside. I hate the Army and the war and everything connected with it more and more every day. It just isn't good for you to live always with your heart full of bitterness and hate but I can't seem to make it go away…

> Ladd"

LCAAB, Lake Charles, Louisiana, January 16, 1944

"Honey…

> Love, Ladd"

1. A _____ _____ operating on any frequency between ____ and ____ K.C.'s has as its _____ _____ to "home" bomber aircraft to their station.

2. QDY indicates a _____ _____ is located on the magnetic course to steer to reach the airdrome.

3. Navigational aid consisting mainly of true bearings can be obtained from a _____ organization.

4. To relay a message to our home base we would use the facilities from a _____ and _____ station.

5. Type one FC/HF/DF station are equipped with the _____ approach and _____ approach.

6. Balloon barrage squeakers and the Darky distress system operates on a frequency of _____ and has a range of opproximately _____ miles.

7. The _____ operates a high powered transmitter usually on _____ K.C.'s to insure _____ transmission of all vital messages to aircraft in flight.

8. Upon leaving the coast of England the radio sets are tuned to ____ stations which operate on a frequency of ____ to ____ K.C.'s.

9. When using the SOS procedure the IFF should be placed in the _____ position.

10. True bearings and fixes can be obtained with the D/F loop by using the MF system operating between _____ and _____ K.C.'s.

11. Six high powered SBA transmitters located along the south and east coasts of England are known as: A. Splasher beacon. B. Main beacon. C. Jay beams.

12. The minimum altitude of a plane requesting a QDM is:
        A. 2000 ft.   B. 1000 ft.   C. 5000 ft.

13. When returning from a mission early with out a recall
        A. The IFF should be placed in the distress position.
        B. One should use C.W. identification.
        C. A strange part of the coast should be approached.

14. To obtain information on enemy beacons we can monitor
        A. 6710 K.C.'s   B. 3050 K.C.'s   C. 6240 K.C.'s.

15. All necessary information concerning the mission can be obtained from the :
        A. Bandit.   B. Flimsie.   C. Occult.

16-25.
    1. Scrw down key   ( ) Darky
    2. FC/HF   ( ) SOS
    3. MF/DF   ( ) QTE
    4. Ballon Barrage   ( ) QDM
    5. Distress stud   ( ) Ditching
    6. May day   ( ) SBA
    7. Beacon   ( ) fix
    8. Dinghy   ( ) squeaker
    9. True bearing   ( ) beacons
    10. Blind approach   ( ) Box Kite

Typical ground school "quiz" enclosed in the above letter.

LCAAB, Lake Charles, Louisiana, January 24, 1944

"Dear Ethel…

Saturday afternoon the field ran out of gas so that it was impossible to fly Saturday night. As a result I had a little spare time…

The end of February I go to POE, that is "port of embarkation." I can't say exactly where or when…

We lost a plane the other day out in the gulf with 7 men. That's kind of bad. Another one of the fellows I know was killed in an auto accident so the old bunch is thinning down pretty much. I hate to think what it will be when and if we come back from combat. It's getting to where none of the fellows are left that I started out with as it is. When I think of it doesn't hardly seem possible that many of them are dead…

Ladd"

LCAAB, Lake Charles, Louisiana, February 5, 1944
"Dear Ethel…

I've been getting just one meal a day quite often lately and that doesn't do any good. Candy bars and stuff in between might be alright but that doesn't take the place of a meal…

Lovingly

Ladd"

LCAAB, Lake Charles, Louisiana, February 7, 1944
"Dear Ethel…

I went skip bombing yesterday afternoon and out of 10 bombs I got 4 direct hits on a model of a medium tank and several others missed only from 5 to 10 ft. If I was in the tank I would hate to have one go off even 50 ft from me. They can do quite a bit of damage at 600 ft if you don't have any protection…

Love,

Ladd"

LCAAB, Lake Charles, Louisiana, February 19, 1944
"Dear Ethel…

This morning I had my physical exam and they hemmed and hawed about my knee a little bit but finally decided that it was O.K. That means I'm all set to go now. Everything else has been taken care of and I'm ready to pack and leave on a moment's notice. We haven't been alerted as yet but expect to be soon. We had a picture of our crew taken this afternoon. They claim that they'll have prints ready for us tomorrow… *(Dad was referring to the picture on the cover of this book and reproduced below.)*

All my love,

Ladd"

Flight Crew 12A. Left to right: Ladd L. Horn, Paul M. Roseman, William Webb, Warren E. Tupper, Harmon R. (Ralph) Summers, Bernard Fineman.

LCAAB, Lake Charles, Louisiana, February 21, 1944

"Dear Ethel…

Today I got the print of our crew picture from the photo lab. It isn't too bad, the only thing wrong with it that I can see is the subjects. The more that I see of myself the less I like me. Honestly, Honey, when I look at a picture of myself or when I look in a mirror I don't know how you could possibly ever care for me. I have the dopiest, silliest look of anyone I ever saw…

If you should hear that I'm missing in action or something don't give up hope either because some of the folks here just heard from their son and he had been reported killed in action nearly two years ago. He was in the Southwest Pacific when the war started and a couple of weeks after war broke out he was reported missing but was only separated from his own troops in jungle fighting and succeeded in getting back to his own lines about 3 or 4 weeks later. About a month after that he was reported missing again and nothing was heard of him for a couple of months at the end of which time word was again received that he had returned safely to his own lines. Very soon after however he was reported killed and as no further word reached home he was given up for lost. Just a couple of weeks ago though, nearly 22 months later, his parents received a nice long letter from him. He is alive, uninjured and in fair health but a prisoner in a Jap concentration camp. To the folks that knew him I guess it was just like having someone brought back from the grave…

Ladd"

LCAAB, Lake Charles, Louisiana, March 2, 1944

"Dearest Ethel…

We lost another plane in the Gulf yesterday. Both the Navy and one of our planes claimed yesterday that they had spotted 3 of the fellows in a life raft. Today they picked up the engineer floating around in his life vest but he was already dead and later they picked up the life raft with one of the other men still laying half in and half out of the raft but also dead. What became of the others they don't know. When you hear of these crews surviving in the South

Pacific for weeks it is really a miracle because our crews can't seem to survive even two days in the Gulf even in calm weather. I don't know whether the nervous strain and suspense makes them go crazy and leave the rafts or if they drink salt water and it kills them or what. Whatever the cause when they once down the plane in the Gulf none of them seem to live long enough for a boat to reach them.

My engineer was in pretty bad shape this morning. Every engineer that has slept across the aisle from him has either been killed or all crippled up. Three I think have been killed and a fourth or perhaps it is only the third (I'm not quite sure) is in the hospital with both legs broken in two places and one arm broken and numerous other bumps and bruises. He couldn't fly enough when he first came here but now he is pretty jittery about going up at all…

Sincerely and lovingly yours

Ladd"

See the story, "Into Africa" in "PART I The War as I Heard It" for the official orders for Flight Crew 12A to report to Hunter Field, GA.

COMBAT CREW PROGRESS AND QUALIFICATION CARD

FLYING TIME		TOTAL PREV.	PREV. BASIC	PHASE I	PHASE II	PHASE III	TOTAL	INST. CHECK	QUALIFIED DATE
PILOT:								FORMATION	2-1-44 / 2-2-44
2nd Lt. O-687596	DAY	124:00	223:04	49:10	47:40	0:00	443:54	FRONT GUNNERY	2-9-44
DUNN, L. L.	NIGHT	17:00	7:40	31:10	8:40	0:00		TORPEDO	None
	INST.	21:25	13:15	6:25	4:40	0:00	47:45	BOMBING	2-8-44
7 Months	LK.TR	20:00	23:10	15:00	1:00	0:00	59:10		

SERVICE YRS & MO

GROUND TRAINING COMPLETED
2-18-44 PHASE I 2-25-44 PHASE II PHASE III

FLYING TIME		TOTAL PREV.	PREV. BASIC	PHASE I	PHASE II	PHASE III	TOTAL	INST. CHECK	QUALIFIED DATE
CO-PILOT:								FORMATION	None
2nd Lt. O-758859	DAY	0:00	168:30	31:00	43:40	0:00	241:10	FRONT GUNNERY	None
ROSEMAN, P. H.	NIGHT	0:00	66:10	21:05	6:40	0:00	93:55	TORPEDO	None
	INST.	0:00	9:15	3:40	0:00	0:00	12:55	BOMBING	12-28-43
4 months	LK.TR	0:00	23:30	14:00	5:00	0:00	42:30		

SERVICE YRS & MO

GROUND TRAINING COMPLETED
2-18-44 PHASE I 2-25-44 PHASE II PHASE III

GROUND TRAINING					AIR TRAINING	
NAVIGATOR:	PHASE I	PHASE II	PHASE III	QUAL GUNNER	QUALIFIED	None
					NO. D.R. MISSIONS	11
					NO. C.L. MISSIONS	None
BOMBARDIER: 2d Lt. William G. Webb O750067	2-18-44	2-25-44		3-1-44	QUALIFIED	3-3-44
					NO. BOMBS DROPPED	104
ENG. GUNNER: Sgt. Bernard Pineman 33586506	2-18-44	2-25-44		1-25-44	QUALIFIED AS ENGINEER	12-24-43
RADIO GUNNER 3/Sgt Warren E. Tupper 31184224	2-18-44	2-25-44		1-25-44	QUALIFIED RADIO WORDS P/M	1-21-44 / 20
GUNNER: Sgt Harmon R Summers	2-18-44	2-25-44		1-28-44	ADD. QUALIF.	Armorer 8-29-43
					ADDITIONAL QUALIFICATIONS	

COMBAT CREW NO. 12
SHIPMENT NO. FM-420-CT

COMMANDING.
H. B. HANSON, JR.
Lt Col, Air Corps.

Crew 12A's "Progress and Qualification" card showing the combat readiness of each man in the crew.

On March 6, 1944 Dad mailed a postcard from New Orleans on his way through Florida to Hunter Field, GA. On March 7, 1944 he arrived at the Naval Air Station in Jacksonville, Florida. His crew was processed on March 10, 1944 at Hunter Field, GA.

The following letter written on March 13, 1944 was written from the cockpit of the new B-26 bomber that he picked up at Hunter Field, GA. His eventual POE (point of embarkation) for North Africa was Homestead Field, Florida. All return addresses on his letters from here on out are APO addresses and starting with his last US letter dated March 17, 1944, many letters were opened and censored. They have stamps or tape on the edges stating the examiner's review.

Uncertain location but highly likely Homestead Army Air Field, Homestead, FL** **March 13, 1944

"Dear Ethel…

I'm sitting in the cockpit of my plane writing this letter, it's really my plane this time and brand new too. I just about have to live in it now…

Love,

Ladd"

There is a break in letters from March 17, 1944 until the following letter written from Telergma, Algeria on April 1, 1944. The trip to Telergma, Algeria via the South Atlantic Air Ferry Route took place from March 18, 1944 to March 29, 1944.

Dad told me that before his crew and others arrived in Telergma, Algeria in the spring of 1944, the 17th Bombardment Group only had about six B-26s. There was a story told at the base that on the first mission that those six planes flew, they were unsuccessful. As Dad relayed it, one of the crews of those six planes was so frustrated about not using their bombs and not hitting the target, that they simply bombed/strafed the wreckage of a plane that had been shot down earlier and left in the desert. After the intelligence reports came back, they discovered that the Germans had been using the fuselage of that wreck as a high-ranking staff location. In their frustrated "bombing run" they had actually killed multiple high-ranking German officers.

Presumed location Telergma, Algeria though not stated in letter, April 1(?), 1944

"My Precious Sweetheart…

I had a little hard luck on the way over. I landed at a field in Liberia and had my wallet with about $65, my identification papers and everything stolen.

I just happened to have $30 stuck in another purse with my pilots rating and that has pulled me through. There isn't much to spend money on here though and I get all mixed up changing it anyway. In the last two weeks we've been using 6 or 8 different kinds.

I can tell you that I'm in North Africa but more than that I guess I better not say. Last week I visited Tunis while I had the chance…

Ladd"

Wallet carried all through flight training and USAAF WWII combat by Ladd Horn

Telergma, Algeria, April 2, 1944

"Darling…

I absolutely have to figure out some way of doing some laundry tomorrow. I haven't had any done or any way of doing any in three weeks…

Lovingly, Ladd"

Telergma, Algeria, April 3, 1944

"My Darling…

I'm writing once more by the light of a candle and keeping warm by the heat of a homemade gasoline stove. By the way I'm cooking bullion on the stove while I write this. When I finish I intend to whip up some hot chocolate too. Nice homey atmosphere don't you think?...it is nothing but loneliness and longing…

> I love you, Ladd"

When I was in my teens, Dad would sometimes describe the conditions in Telergma, Algeria. He said that you would sleep in your tent at night wearing, "every piece of clothing you had" including your sheepskin-lined flight jacket if you had one, and under as many blankets as you had because of how cold it got. The first man to wake up would turn on the gas (German gas fed through scavenged hydraulic lines from downed planes with a screw clamp to control the flow of gas) to the tent stove to heat up a little water for coffee or something warm. Then you would wear your heavy clothes and a flight jacket to the mess hall for breakfast. But, he said, by the time you got out of the mess hall, it was so hot that you had to strip down to just your T-shirt. He said that the temperature swings took their toll on you physically.

Telergma, Algeria, April 6, 1944

"Dearest Ethel…

…I used to think that 1,200 miles was a long way to be away from you but now it is 12,000. It just seems as though I can feel that extra distance. It feels just like a wall between us and I'm on the wrong side…

> Love, Ladd"

When I was in my teens, Dad told about an incident in Telergma, Algeria, in which, several of the other men came "screaming" out of one of the latrines. They were screaming about some kind of insect that was in the latrine sink and how awful it was. My dad thought that no insect could be bad enough to cause the "response" that these guys seemed to be displaying, so he went in. There in the sink was an insect that my dad said looked like a combination of a human and an insect with features from both with the head and facial features being human-like. He said that looking at it almost made him throw up. It must have been unusual because my dad was not afraid of much of anything and did not have a "weak stomach" for such things.

Telergma, Algeria, April 7, 1944

"Dear Ethel…

I visited Constantine today and did my monthly shopping. My rations for two weeks consist of 4 candy bars, 1 box of lemon drops, 4 packs of chewing gum, 2 bars of soap, 1 box of shoe polish and 1 jar of Vaseline. I also received 1 can of blended orange and grapefruit juice which is rather a treat. The pint can of juice has to last me for four weeks and the shoe polish for 8.

Constantine itself is a beautiful city to see from a distance. It is as modern as the World's Fair and as ancient as Rome, but inside it smells like the city dump on a hot day…

Ladd"

Dad was then moved from Telergma, Algeria to Villacidro, Sardinia. The official orders give a departure date of April 4, 1944; however I believe the transfer was delayed until April 9, 1944 as the previous letters are dated April 6 and 7, 1944 and are written from Telergma. Bernard Fineman's flight log says, "4/9/44 FC-47 Telergma to Villacidro Sardinia our crew #12 went as passengers. The new plane (42) 107730 was left in Telergma for the French government to use. When we arrived in Sardinia our crew was broken up. My co-pilot, radioman and myself stayed with the pilot. We were assigned to the 12 Air Force, then First Provisional Tactical Air Force 42nd Wing, 17th Bomb Group and 95th Bombardment Squadron."

U. S. RESTRICTED Equals BRITISH RESTRICTED

(SO #67, Hq, 42nd Wing (US), dtd 8 April 1944, continued)

6. The fol named O and EM, having been asgnd to this headquarters per competent authority, are further asgnd to orgns indicated and WP, without delay, rptg upon arrival to the CO thereat for dy. Perm chg of sta. TCNT TDN 91-66 P 431-02 1 A 0425-24.

17th Bomb Group (M)

2nd Lt.	DOMINIC V. FIACCO	0-687024	AC
2nd Lt.	RUSSELL C. KELLEY	0-815102	AC
Sgt.	Irwin W. Harder	17127154	
S/Sgt.	John S. Slirka	13128784	
2nd Lt.	JACOB MILLER	0-677751	AC
2nd Lt.	ROBERT T. PRATT	0-816154	AC
2nd Lt.	WILLIAM P. HINGLE	0-749920	AC
Sgt.	Rual E. Tubbs	19066380	
S/Sgt.	Irving L. Shapiro	32020277	
2nd Lt.	JOHN P. MARTINCON	0-686916	AC
S/Sgt.	William Solar	33477088	
Sgt.	Theodore C. Day	36575231	
2nd Lt.	JOHN C. BLAKE	0-686969	AC
2nd Lt.	ROY D. BISSETTE JR.	0-814630	AC
S/Sgt.	Thomas W. Powell	35532102	
Sgt.	Robert E. Irwin Jr.	33179138	
2nd Lt.	RAYMOND L. CONSTANT	0-751987	AC
2nd Lt.	RAYMOND P. BRITTON	0-815821	AC
F/O	SEYMOUR C. BASKOFF	T-1931	AC
S/Sgt.	Andrew J. Rutherford Jr.	53598600	
Sgt.	John S. Albright	33362842	
2nd Lt.	TOROLF H. EVLUND	0-808366	AC
2nd Lt.	GERALD B. LISZLK	0-810184	AC
S/Sgt.	Harold J. Shuck	35449031	
Sgt.	Alfred H. Bridge	11101024	
2nd Lt.	LADD L. HORN	0-687596	AC
2nd Lt.	PAUL M. POSEMAN	0-758859	AC
S/Sgt.	Warren B. Tipper	31183224	
Sgt.	Bernard (NMI) Fineman	33586506	
2nd Lt.	CHARLES J. OLSON	0-686589	AC
2nd Lt.	DONALD L. BREWER	0-746353	AC
2nd Lt.	GLENN E. MOORE	0-758835	AC
S/Sgt.	William F. Rhoads	19109607	
Sgt.	Nelson W. Crisler	32626225	

U. S. RESTRICTED Equals BRITISH RESTRICTED

- 2 -

April 8, 1944 orders assigning Dad and his crew to the 17th Bombardment Group.

Trunconi Air Base, Villacidro, Sardinia, April 13, 1944

"Darling…

Well, I moved again, hence no letter for a few days. To top it all off the last letter I wrote to you blew away in a dust storm the night before I left Africa.

I am now enjoying the warm sunshine and gentle breezes of Sardinia. I'm flying with the oldest outfit in the Air Corps…

I have about 3 h of combat time in now but no accredited mission as yet. I did have someone take one pot shot at me with a flak gun though.

I bought an accordion this evening so that I would have something to fill in my spare moments with. I'm going to fly over the target playing "Yankee Doodle Dandy" while my bombardier throws rotten eggs at Hitler. That is if I don't get the eggs for practicing around here…

Ladd"

This picture will give you some idea of the size of the cactus that everything was fenced with in Sardinia. The man in the picture is Capt. Radin, one of our navigators. *Note on back of duplicate picture:* Captain Radin, navigator. This will give you an idea of the size of the cactus everything was fenced with in Sardinia. Wheels down emergency one-engine landing, Sardinia 95th. Not on field, just out in farm country.

Some of the bombed out buildings in Sardinia. We had bombed them to get
the Germans out of Sardinia.

Italian guard at the gate to our tent area. He might have been either one of the local police or one of the POWs. We used the German and Italian POWs as guards. They weren't armed. They were happy to be with us and have a job. They knew that the Americans that were POWs were used as slave labor.

Paul Roseman(left) and Paul Martinson (right) of the 95th with my dog, Madam. That was while Martinson was still in fairly decent standing with us. They are sitting in front of our tent. It was warm weather and so most of the canvas is rolled up to let in the air. Normal flying personnel was 1,200 men and then in addition there were ground crews and support staff. Ground crews were generally assigned to a specific plane. But flying crews moved from plane to plane because you had to fly the planes that were "flyable." Planes that came in damaged were scheduled to go out the next day. The ground crews would work overnight to repair them. Usually the ground crews were around five men. The plane also had to be test flown before it was ready for the next mission. That is why flight crews were assigned to planes at the last minute.

Villacidro, Sardinia, April 18, 1944

"Darling…

I have quite a little combat time in now but still only one accredited mission and between times I have been doing some quite strenuous construction work. In the past few days I have built a chair complete with padded seat, back and padded arms. Today I built a cabinet to keep my clean laundry and toilet articles in. The hard thing is to get materials and nails to work with…

Within the next few days I expect to move into a house with three other fellows. We build our own here. Cement floors, tile walls and a G.I. tent to make the roof. That's 15' square so *(it)* makes plenty of room for four men…

Ladd"

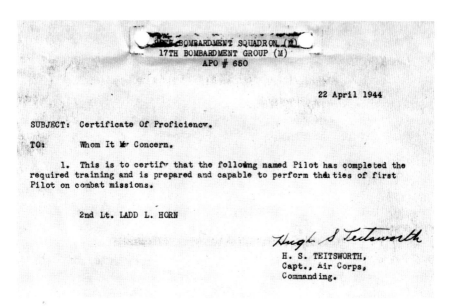

Dad's "Certificate of Proficiency" as a first pilot on combat missions.

Mud brick base for the tents to sit on in Sardinia. The mud for the bricks was dug up on site, screened, water added to make mud and then dried for a day or so and then assembled with mud mortar. The soldier in white, Donald (Chuckie) Barnett was our youngest pilot in the 95th. He had his 18th birthday about the time this picture was taken. His parents mailed him a birthday cake from the US and it arrived in one piece. It was the only time something like that had ever gotten through in one piece. He was supervising the construction of the tent set up for the officers of his tent crew. Donald became a career air force man and later fought in the Korean War. They built whole houses and municipal buildings with those mud blocks. *The note on back of the photo reads,* Barnett supervising construction of mud-brick tent base. He flew in Korea after WWII.

Dad was sent back to Telergma, Algeria as a B-26 pilot instructor in May of 1944. In the following letter he talks about instructing both French and American pilots. You can see his official papers designating him as "qualified as an instructor" in the story "An Italian Janitor, Two SM-55's and Italo Balbo" in "PART I The War as We Heard It."

Telergma, Algeria, May 5, 1944 (V-Mail)

"Dear Sweetheart…

(1)

I've had a stretch of combat and I'm back in N. Africa now. Of all things I am a French pilot instructor. I can't talk [*sic*] any French at all but I get by with a kind of sign language and object lesson combined. Drawing pictures helps some too. Afternoons sometimes I have to instruct American crews who have just arrived from the States. It keeps me pretty busy. (this letter will be in several sections)

(2)

Before I left Sardinia my name was put in along with several others with a recommendation to receive the air medal. Whether or not anything will ever come of it I don't know…

…The little girls that do our laundry for us will bring us some sometimes *(almonds)*. We give them a cake of soap and about 35 to 50 lira and they take our clothes down to the river and scrub them on the rocks. They do a

(3)

real good job for us, though.

I am trying to make up some things to take back to Sardinia with me. I have a light fixture made up from the formation bombing lights of a crashed plane and I am working on a desk lamp now. I am making it from parts of a worn out fighter plane. It will use four light bulbs from a plane which use 28 volts and are 30 watt bulbs. That makes it just right for the 110 volts that our generators put out. We have two generators driven by an old Model A Ford engine to make our lights over there.

Four of us have a nice house now. *(This was Dad's "Marauder Mansion" in Sardinia.)* I kind of hated to leave it and come here to live in a tent. I expect to go back to it before long though. It has a cement floor and is built of brick and tile. The tile wall comes up about 3 ft and then we have it screened off around from there up to the ceiling. We have a built in clothes

(4)

closet and it is plastered. We were able to get a regular porcelain sink and we have rigged up a system with running water by using hydraulic tubing from old planes. We were able to get a can of varnish so the place is pretty well fixed up. We have a sign out in front made by burning wood and then varnishing it. It has "Marauder Mansion" painted on it in blue and white letters and has a picture of a plane at one side.

Women washing clothes, Sardinia, Aug. 28, '44.

As soon as the weather gets a little warmer we figure to make awnings from the tent flaps. The weather is pretty nice up there though and we may not need them.

There has been a three day lapse of time since I started this page. I was suddenly called on to make a two day flight. I guess I can't tell you where I went or why.

(5) Telergma, May 8, 1944

Both engines on my plane quit running just as I landed at my home field… *(For the full story see "The Courier Trip" in "PART I The War as We Heard It.")*

(6-10) Telergma, May 10, 1944

Ladd"

Dad in front of the "Marauder Mansion" in Vilacidro, Sardinia with Mademoiselle on his lap.

"Marauder Mansion" sign on Dad's tent. 95th Squadron, Villacidro, Sardinia. Note: you can read P. M. Roseman and L. Horn on the sign. The building in the back is for another tent crew.

Paul Roseman at the "Marauder Mansion" sign, 95th Squadron, Villacidro, Sardinia.

ROBERT G. RINGO
605 S.W. JEFFERSON AVENUE
CORVALLIS, OREGON

COPY

May 27, 1994

Sent to
wrong man
the first time

Mr. William Baird
Editor
17th Bomb Group Newsletter
6776 N.E. - N.W. Highway
Dallas, Texas 75231

RE: 17th Bomb Squad Newsletter

Dear Bill:

Your last issue of the newsletter was worth my several
year's dues. I noticed the short note written by Ladd
Horn! I am enclosing an extra copy of this letter, and I
would appreciate it if you would forward it to Mr. Horn.

When I was dumped off at Ladd's tent in the Summer of
1944, Ladd Horn, Paul Roseman, and Johnny Martinson
took in one bewildered 19 year old flight officer. I
bunked with Ladd until he went home in late Winter or
early Spring of 1945.

What Ladd forgot to include in his note, was how
ingenious he was. We lived in luxury compared to the
rest of the men as a result of Ladd's ingenious. In our
tent we had a dark room, running water, and hot water.
Ladd was continuously building new bunks and whatever
else he could to make it comfortable.

Mr. William Baird
page 2
May 27, 1994

I have several fine pictures of Ladd and his dog, Madame.

It was a great pleasure to see Ladd's note, and I would appreciate it if you would forward a copy of this letter to Ladd.

Incidentally, I do have some pictures of Klein Beaumont who was a wonderful, warn person

Very truly yours,

Robert G. Ringo

RGR/mgr

Enclosure

pc: Mr. John Duensing
       Mr. George Moscovis
       Mr. Roy Jacobsen

Letter written by Robert Ringo to the editor of the 17th Bombardment Group newsletter about Dad and the ingenuity he displayed in adding "comfort" features in their tents in Sardinia, Corsica and Dijon, France.

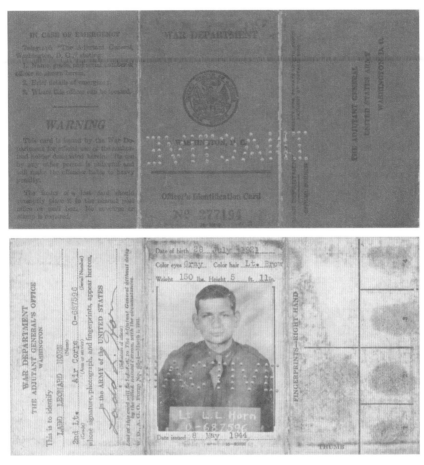

Dad's ID card issued May 8, 1944.

Telergma, Algeria, May 24, 1944

"Dearest Ethel

I can't seem to get the chance to write the way I should. They have kept me going all the time all day every day. I checked out my French students and now I have British and South Africans between times I flew American crews and every once in a while they would try to get me to slow time a plane with new engines besides.

The first mission flown by a French crew that the 95th Squadron had trained in Telergma. This was at takeoff in Sardinia. American plane with French markings. 1st Tactical Air Force Provisional.

The day before yesterday I pushed the button labeled spin crash and burn to top everything off. There'll be a souvenir in this letter. *(Dad is using the phrase, "pushed the button…" like we would use "punched my ticket." Dad is referring to being the instructor in the crash of the B-26B #47-17900 on May 22, 1944 which is described in the USAAF Accident Report #40522-504. Pictures and the accident report are included in Appendix 5.)*

Metal plate from B-26B #47-17900 the plane that Dad was in that crashed in Telergma, Algeria.

I'm going to enclose an engine plate from an Italian bomber too. You might keep it as a curiosity.

I think in my last letter I told you that I now own a dog. She is 7 ½ weeks old and just about as big as a pint of cider but full of vim and vigor. I now have a German army motorcycle of my own so my personal transportation problem is pretty well solved for the time being. *(See the story, "The Zundapp" in "PART I The War as I Heard It")* It is built rugged and will really get up and go. I have 7 tires that fit it so I figure that I can keep it rolling for some time. It really looked a wreck when I got it and still does for that matter but it really runs and rides nice [*sic*] and can pull away from almost anything on the road…

Ladd"

WAR DEPARTMENT
A.A.F Form No. 5
(Revised)

DIVIDUAL FLIGHT RECORD

NAME ....HORN, Ladd L. MONTH (S)....MAY 1944....19
RANK ....2nd Lieut., Air Corps. GROUP 17th Bombardment Group (M)
AERO. RATINGS....Pilot ORGANIZATION—Assigned 95th Bomb Sqdr
TRANSFERRED FROM ORG.—Attached for flying
TO DATE STATION APO # 650

Date	Duty	Mission Symbol	PILOT TIME BY AIRPLANE TYPE						Aircraft Model Symbol	No. Land ings	Other Than Pilot	REMARKS
			Attack	Bomb.	Obs.	Pursuit	Cargo	Training				
2	P	T		2:25					B-26C	1		BTC APO# 762
4	P	T		1:30					"	1		"
4	P	T		:55					"	1		"
5	P	T		2:30					" B	2		"
5	CP	T		2:35					"	1		"
6	P	T		2:30					"	2		"
6	P	T		2:45					" C	2		"
7	P	T		:30					" B	1		X-C
7	P	T		2:15					"	1		X-C
8	P	T		2:35					" C	4		BTC APO# 762
10	P	T		3:00					"	4		"
11	P	T		3:15					" B	4		"
12	P	T		3:20					"	2		"
13	P	T		:30					"	1		"
13	P	T		2:45					" C	2		"
15	P	T		2:10					" C	1		"
16	P	T		2:20					" B	4		"
17	P	T		2:10					"	3		"
18	P	T		2:25					" C	3		"
20	P	T		:50					" B	1		"
20	P	T		1:10					"	2		"
20	P	T		:30					" 1	1		"
23	P	T		2:30					"	6		"
23	P	T		1:40					"	1		"
26	P	T		1:15					"	1		"
27	P	T		1:50					"	1		"
29	P	T		1:15					"	1		"
30	P	T		1:00					"	1		"

	Total pilot time	Total other than pilot	Pilot time nonmilitary airplanes	
This report	54:25	54:25		
Previous reports this F. Y.	363:50	363:50	1:00	
Totals this fiscal year	418:15	418:15	1:00	
Totals previous years	230:45	230:45		
Totals to date	418:15 230:45	649:00	1:00	

* DUTY SYMBOLS
P—Pilot B—Bomber R—Radio operator
CP—Copilot OB—Observer PH—Photographer
N—Navigator E—Engineer O—Other crew
C—Command Pilot G—Gunner X—Passenger

NOTE.—When the airplane is assigned to an organization other than that to which the individual is assigned or attached for flying, show the airplane organization under Remarks, column 8.

Dad's individual flight record for May of 1944. Essentially all of May was spent training Allied pilots in Telergma, Algeria and doing courier flights to and from Sardinia. Most days show a short flight; some with up to six landings. The flights are all labelled as "T," i.e. transport flights.

Dad also told me the following in a general conversation. It was not a "recorded" story. During combat in North Africa and Sardinia, crews for each mission were made up of different people. This was necessitated by the fact that men were killed in action, crew members were sick, planes could not *be repaired in time for the next mission and a host of other reasons. At one of the bases we had a young guy (maybe twenty years old—Dad didn't remember his name) whose job it was to make up the crews for each day's mission. He would work all night checking on what planes could fly the next day, who was healthy and available for the mission, and who could work together. Dad says that he was good at the job and seemed to be able to put together competent crews with people who could work well together. Dad spent one night talking with him while he made up the crews for the next day. The guy told Dad something to the effect that, I'm just 20 years old and I am assigned to this job. But, I feel like I am signing the death warrant for these men who are going out on these missions. Dad said that he could understand the feeling because you knew that some of these men would not be coming back alive. Each morning as you went to the mess hall, there would be a set of sheets posted just outside the mess hall with the crew assignments. You would see several crews listed and then see names listed with KIA (killed in action) after their names. Dad said as the guys would read the crew assignments, sometimes they would learn for the first time who had been killed on the prior mission. Later in life, Dad could not look at a KIA automobile and not think about those lost in battle.*

Villacidro, Sardinia, June 3, 1944

"Dear Ethel…

…I'm back in Sardinia again…

You were mistaken about me ever being in Cuba. I meant to tell you that at the time I answered your letter thanking me for the Alligator purse. The leather in the purse came from Cuba, yes, but the purse was made and purchased in Puerto Rico.

It seems pretty good to be back here and in a nice house again after being down there in Africa. It is clean and cool and we have beautiful weather to top everything off. We even have a place to go swimming now but the water is so cold that you can hardly stand it...I have my motorcycle fixed up pretty good now so I don't have to worry about how to get places.

They are just harvesting oats here now and barley is just about ready. The best thing though is that the black sweet cherries are ripe. For just a small piece of candy or some little gadget or trinket the natives will give you a whole hatful of the cherries which are far better than the candy anyway...

All my love, Ladd"

Donkey pumping water to irrigate a garden. The picture was taken from the front door of our tent across the "camp road" we were on. This donkey woke me up nearly every morning. The picture was published in one of the other squadron books (I think it was Tannehill's book. The information is all correct.), but they got the location wrong. The donkey would pump water all day from *(starting at)* daybreak. He got water twice a day to water about 3 acres. I never figured it needed it because everything grew well without irrigation. I took the picture with my camera and I developed the pictures.

Scenery in front of our tent. This was typical transportation and the only traffic we had on our road other than US military vehicles.

Trying to repair a broken-down Italian tank in front of the "Marauder Mansion," 95th Squadron, Sardinia.

Villacidro, Sardinia, June 5, 1944

"Dear Ethel…

I have still been messing with that motorcycle the last few days. I've got it in pretty good shape now but still improving. I just about broke my neck with it a couple of nights ago. I hit a curve too fast to turn and went cross country [*sic*] through a lot of boulders.

The "puppy" that I got in Africa is doing pretty well. By the way her name is "Mademoiselle."…

Yours, Ladd"

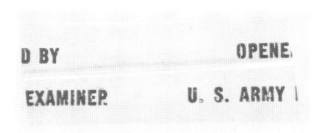

Typical US Army censor's tape marking the envelope as "opened and inspected."

Villacidro, Sardinia, June 11, 1944

"Dearest Ethel…

…Today my flight has the day off though. That means the day off from combat, we still have to slow time planes with new engines and test hop planes that have been repaired or overhauled…

…As far as the name of my plane is concerned I don't have a plane. They took my plane away from me and gave it to the Free French. In our outfit the planes are assigned to a crew chief who takes care of them and names them. The pilot and crew seldom fly the same plane two times in a row. The plane I flew on my last mission was "Pistol Packin' Mama" but most of the names are too dirty to mention…

Yours, Ladd"

Paul Roseman on the left. I can't identify the other man. The plane was
"Pistol Packin' Mama." The plane was on the beach in Corsica while our
outfit was still in Sardinia. We had four different damaged planes that bellied
in on the beach in Corsica when they came back from missions in northern
Italy and she was one of them. Roseman went up there just to see what the
plane looked like after it bellied in there. The ground crews had already been
up there and salvaged the engines off of them. If you had a badly crippled
plane, coming down on a beach was a pretty good option. You would come
in at water level and slide up on the beach. The planes were usually scrap,
but the crews got out alive.

Checking the map for mission route and target location.

Left to right - Paul Martinson, Guild and Stuttle. *(Date on back is in Dad's mom's handwriting. It is probably when she received it.)* It shows that one package gun was removed from the plane. They figured we weren't going to do enough strafing to make it worthwhile keeping the guns. They took them off to remove the weight, add bomb capacity and improve flight handling.

If the plane had set more than so many hours since the engine was run, the crew had to pull the props through so many revolutions before you could start the engine. The idea being that with the radial engine, the engine oil used to drain down into the lower cylinders. You didn't want one of the lower cylinders to compress on engine oil and blow a cylinder head or break a piston or arm. This is a picture of the crew following that manual procedure. Paul Martinson is the one with his arm up.

Martinson, Roseman, Duensing, *(and)* others sweating off mission. Sardinia, 95th.

Heading in from the line. 95th Sardinia.

One of our planes that came back with battle damage and had to "belly in" in
Sardinia

Villacidro, Sardinia, June 19, 1944

"Dearest Ethel…

Quite a few of the fellows are feeling kind of disgusted with their girls and folks at home. They are all receiving letters now saying how they know they would have liked to have been in on the invasion but they're glad they are safe in Sardinia instead. I wonder what kind of war they think we're fighting in Italy anyway. As yet this is still a bigger and tougher war than the invasion. It's over some of the roughest ground I ever saw in my life. This push that took Rome and moved on north was no holiday.

I'm going to enclose a souvenir of the plane that I was flying the other day. Just a couple splinters of the windshield where a jerry shell came too close for comfort…

…In three days I think it is it will be just 8 months since I last saw you…

Love,

Ladd"

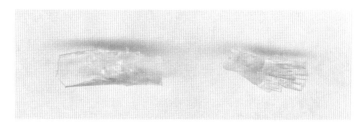

Two glass shards from a B-26 Windshield. See the story, "Flying Co-Pilot for Paul Roseman" in "PART I The War as I Heard It."

Villacidro, Sardinia, June 21, 1944 *(It is labeled June 20, 1944 but corrected in body of letter.)*

"Darling…

I'm pretty tired tonight, we had a rather long mission today. We took the puppy along, she has 2 missions and 1 air spare to her credit now. She really has the pep although she doesn't seem to eat hardly anything. She crawls under the pilot's seat and sleeps for most of the mission. The rest of us come back dog tired and the only dog in the outfit comes back full of vim, vigor and vitality.

I took that ride up into the mountains that I told you about in my last letter. It's really beautiful country, I wish you could see it with me. I brought back a slab of cork just the way it comes off the tree. They were cutting it on the mountain sides and hauling it out with oxen.

Oxen and motorcycles seem to be the chief means of transportation in this country. About 4 a.m. you hear the ox-carts start creaking down the road headed for town...

Love, Ladd"

Local scenery, Sardinia.

WAR DEPARTMENT A.A.F Form No. 5 (Revised)					INDIVIDUAL FLIGHT RECORD					

NAME HORN, Ladd L.
RANK 2nd Lieut., Air Corps.
AERO. RATINGS Pilot
TRANSFERRED FROM
TO DATE

MONTH (S) JUNE 1944 19
GROUP 17th Bombardment Group (M)
ORGANIZATION—Assigned 95th Bomb Sqdrn (M)
ORG.—Attached for flying
STATION APO # 650

1	2	3	4 Pilot Time by Airplane Type						5	6	7	8
Date	Day	Mission Symbol	Attack	Bomb.	Obs.	Pursuit	Cargo	Training	Aircraft Symbol Model	No. Landings	Other Than Pilot	Remarks
2	CP	C		4:15					B-26 C	1		Secret
3	CP	T		1:20					"	1		"
4	P	C		4:10					"	1		"
5	P	C		4:00					"	1		"
6	CP	C		4:15					" B	1		"
9	P	C		3:55					"	1		"
12	CP	C		4:15					"	1		"
13	P	C		3:45					" C	1		"
14	P	C		4:10					"	1		"
15	CP	C		4:15					"	1		"
16	P	C		2:40					" B	1		"
17	CP	C		3:50					"	1		"
21	P	C		4:40					" C	1		"

	9	10	11	12
TOTALS	Total pilot time	Total other than pilot	Pilot time nonmilitary airplanes	
This report	49:30	49:30		
Previous reports this F. Y.	418:15	418:15	1:00	
Totals this fiscal year	467:45	467:45	1:00	
Totals previous years	230:45	230:45		
Totals to date	467:45 230:45	698:30	1:00	

DUTY SYMBOLS
P—Pilot B—Bomber R—Radio operator
CP—Copilot OB—Observer PH—Photographer
N—Navigator E—Engineer O—Other crew
C—Command Pilot G—Gunner X—Passenger

NOTE.—When the airplane is assigned to an organization other than that to which the individual is assigned or attached for flying, show the airplane organization under Remarks, column 8.

Dad's individual flight record for June 1944 in Sardinia. Note that all flights were missions on which he was the command pilot except for a single transport flight. Note also that the missions were typically approximately 4 h duration.

The next few letters were written from the hospital in Cagliari, Sardinia. The following details are meant to help you understand the context. Dad was 5 feet 11 inches when he started his basic training at SAACC in San Antonio. As he served in Telergma and Sardinia, he was significantly affected by the *poor nutrition, the living conditions, and the stress of flying and sickness. While in Sardinia his weight dropped and his blood pressure was very low. He told me that mornings, he would wake up and lie there for a few minutes until he could sit up and rest on the top of his bed. He would "black out" for a few seconds, then come to and sit up with his legs over the side of the bed. He would brace himself with his arms on the bed and he would "black out" again. After he came to for the second time he would then stand up, holding onto the bed or anything else he could, taking care that he did not black out and fall. Slowly he would gain his strength and be able to make it to the mess hall and get moving for the mission that day. In June of 1944 while in Sardinia, Dad was scheduled for a mission. He tried to get out of bed, but instead, fell to the floor and threw up. His co-pilot, Paul Roseman, and his other tentmates decided that he needed to be in the field hospital. So, on June 26, 1944, Dad was taken to the field hospital at Cagliari, about 30 to 35 miles south of the other US air field at Decimomannu. He only weighed 132 pounds (at 5 feet 11 inches tall!) and had gastroenteritis (in one place Dad mentions hepatitis in a letter, but the hospital records show acute gastroenteritis, acute diarrhea and acute nasopharyngitis). According to his medical form dated March 10, 1945, he was hospitalized for five weeks. Once Dad was treated and had gained one pound, he was discharged for active duty and returned to the base at Villacidro. During his service, he was also grounded for one week for gastritis on 8/2/44 and for three days each on 6/8/44, 9/27/44 and 12/29/44 for upper respiratory infections.*

Cagliari, Sardinia, June 28, 1944

"Darling…

I'm in the 60th Station Hosp. but I don't guess I could say where. *(Based on other records and letters I know that the hospital was in Cagliari, Sardinia.)* Riding these G.I. trucks on the rough roads they have here has gotten the best of my stomach and kidneys for a little bit I guess. I was pretty sick for a few days but I'm not bad now…

I don't know what to write about unless I just tell you about the hospital. It evidently was a modern civilian hospital or sanitarium before the Army took it over. I'm in a ward with just one other fellow who is a bombardier… we have running water and a sink of our own in the ward. Each of us has a white enamel steel dressing table and a set of headphones. If we want to hear the latest BBC news we just plug the phones into the sockets at the heads of our beds. We get all the big chain programs from the states and England too from the American expeditionary station. Instead of having windows in our room we have a set of large double doors that open right outside and let the sun come in and the breeze blow through. We're on the second floor and looking out I look down on a blue lagoon and out to mountains four or five miles on the other side. There's the top of a pine tree that reaches just above our floor level and I can look through that over red tile roofs to evaporating pans for salt. They are just pools of sea water walled in, each one 2 or 3 acres in area and all arranged in neat rows and patterns. They are all different colors depending on the stage of evaporation. They start deep blue and work up through all the different shades until finally they turn a kind of red color, following the red they become tan, suntan and finally the finished product turns out a grayish white…

I don't know how to go about writing to my folks. If I tell them I'm in the hospital my mother will worry herself sick over me. She is probably all upset now because I haven't been able to write since last week. When you get this letter you had better tell her for me that I'm in the hospital, OK, not wounded and so on and so forth just in case she doesn't have a letter from me yet when you receive this.

At least I'm safe and they can't shoot at me while I'm here. That's a good angle to use to have a calming influence.

All my love

Ladd"

```
                    60th STATION HOSPITAL
                    OFFICE OF THE REGISTRAR
                    APO #763    U.S. ARMY


SUBJECT:  Report of Hospitalization.

TO      : The Commanding Officer, 95th Sq  17th Bomb Group

        1. Horn, Ladd  L. 2nd Lt. 0-687596        a member of your

command was admitted to this hospital on    26 June 1944

        2.His admission diagnosis was    Gastro-enteritis, acute


                                    For the Surgeon

                                    GEORGE C HICKMAN
                                    1st Lt., Med Adm C.,
                                    Registrar
```

Admission record for Dad's hospitalization on June 26, 1944 for gastroenteritis.

Cagliari, Sardinia, July 5, 1944

"Darling

I'm awfully sorry that I haven't written for a whole week but after that last letter I wrote to you (on the 28th I believe it was) I felt so sick that I didn't even write to my folks…I'm feeling much better now…

Yours,

Ladd"

Cagliari, Sardinia, July 6, 1944

"Dear Ethel…

Things are going along just about the same in the hospital...It is well ventilated and cool and every day is warm and sunny just like every other day. I hate to think about going back to the squadron and trying to get into the swing of things again. I don't want any more war. I never did want any for that matter. I'd just like to take my girl in my arms, hold her tight, cuddle her close and forget about everything else but her sweetness and the thrill of her lips. I think she's swell and just about the very, very best girl a fellow could ever have...I love her with all of my heart and I always will. I don't think there's another girl in the world that compares with her. Someday I'm coming home...

May God bless and keep for me the loveliest, sweetest girl I know of on this earth.

Yours,

Ladd."

Cagliari, Sardinia, July 10 (?), 1944

"Darling Sweetheart...

The day will come though when it is over when I can hear your voice again and feel you near me. I realize I'm a rather peculiar man and not at all handsome but I dearly love you, my sweetheart.

Ladd"

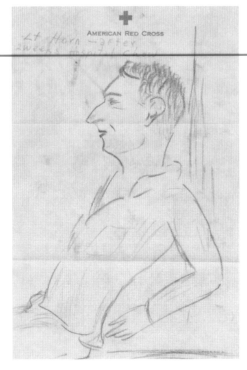

A sketch of Dad done by another patient in the hospital in Cagliari.

Cagliari, Sardinia, July 12, 1944

"Dear Ethel…

The European people to all appearances have become rotten to the core. While they have every modern convenience yet they are lazy, indolent and as dirty as the dirtiest you ever saw in the states. Their small towns stink until it just about turns my stomach. For the most part even Tunis which is a fairly modern city smells so bad that I can hardly stand it. To top it all off prostitution flourishes to an extent that would be unimaginable to you…

I heard a statement by a Russian major…"The people of the world seem to have no sense of social responsibility. I don't understand it. They live every man for himself. Even the common people of Russia wouldn't stand for it."…

…I can still take it, Eth, but it's awfully hard.

Love, Ladd"

Cagliari, Sardinia, July 19, 1944

"My Lovely Sweetheart…

Well, I've been in the hospital here for 3 weeks and 2 days and I still have no idea when I might get out. Some days I feel pretty good and others good for nothing. It's a sure thing I haven't gained any weight…

All my love,

Ladd"

Cagliari, Sardinia, July 20, 1944

"Dearest Ethel

I'm going to enclose a few clippings from our Army newspaper over here…

Yours,

Ladd"

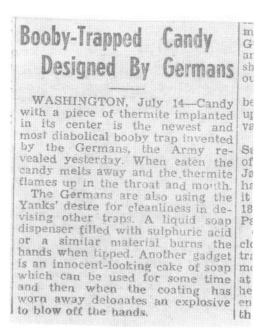

One of the enclosed clippings.

Cagliari, Sardinia, July 22, 1944

"Darling…

They have finally found out what is wrong with me. I have "hepatitis."…
It is a kind of jaundice except that you don't turn yellow from it. I have slight
intermittent fever and spells of nausea followed by diarrhea…

Ladd"

Cagliari, Sardinia, July 24, 1944

"Ethel dear…

That reminds me. What's the difference between a Rooster, Uncle Sam and
our Old Maid? The Rooster says cock-a-doodle-do

Uncle Sam says yankee-doodle-do

And the Old Maid says—any Dude 'll do…

Ladd"

Cagliari, Sardinia, July 27, 1944

"Darling…

…That reminds me, tomorrow I will be 23… *(Dad was born July 28, 1921)*

Love, Ladd"

Cagliari, Sardinia, July 30, 1944

"Darling…

I still don't know just when I'll get out of here…

I weigh 132 ½ lb right now. You'd better not tell my folks that though
because my mother would go wild. I used to weigh that much when I was 14
years old. When I went out with you just before I left for the army I weighed
162-165…

Ladd"

Villacidro, Sardinia, August 3, 1944

"Dearest Ethel…

…I was busy checking out of the hospital and getting settled back at my own squadron again…

All my love

Ladd"

Villacidro, Sardinia, August 4, 1944

"Darling…

This afternoon we were able to get some watermelon, muskmelon and peaches. I ate a whole small watermelon this afternoon by myself. We just now finished another one between four of us. We're saving the peaches for tomorrow morning and the muskmelons too. Yesterday I had 3 Coca-Colas, we're really getting the luxuries here now. We're having lots of fresh tomatoes…

All my love,

Ladd."

Villacidro, Sardinia, August 6, 1944

"Darling…

I have a snapshot of me, the pooch and the motorcycle taken on some of that film that you sent me. The pooch turned her head away from the camera just as the picture was taken but it isn't bad nevertheless. The tent in the background is just across the way from ours. I was sitting on the motorcycle in our front yard. Robert Ringo took the picture. He is a bombardier and the Italians call him the "Bambino Lt." He is 19 but is small and looks and acts about 14.

Ladd."

Me [*sic*] and Madam in Sardinia on my motorcycle during the one or two days I had after my hospitalization for hepatitis. *This picture was taken by Robert Ringo in Sardinia from the front yard of Dad's tent, the "Marauder Mansion" in early August 1944.*

Ringo sitting on two of our standard 1,000-lb bombs next to two 1,100-lb Navy armor-piercing bombs. We used a lot of Naval bombs because they were very destructive to reinforced concrete or if you want them to go into the foundation of a building. The Naval bombs are much more pointed. The mechanism in the background is the scaffolding that the ground crews used to work on the planes (to reach engines and wings...).

Note on the back of this picture: Robert Ringo on bombs Sardinia 9/44.

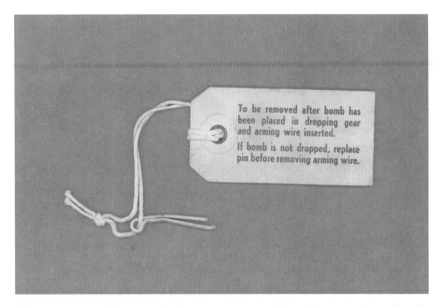

This is a tag and cotter pin that was removed in order to activate bombs when they were placed in the dropping gear after the arming wire had been inserted.

Villacidro, Sardinia, August 7, 1944

"Dearest Ethel…

I'm enclosing a snapshot of a German Ju 88 shot up on our field… They're quite a plane even with the substitution of materials that the Germans found necessary…

Love,

Ladd"

Remains of a German Ju 88 (a medium bomber that was the approximate size and capacity as our B-26s). It had a higher ceiling than our planes and stripped out they flew pretty fast—a lot faster than our P-39s could fly. They used some of them for observation planes. They stripped out the weight and flew high. For a while we had one fly over our field in Sardinia every other afternoon. They came over high enough that our anti-aircraft guns couldn't reach them. They were flying fast enough that the P-39 squadron we had stationed in Cagliari couldn't catch them. Their main reason for flying over was to count our planes to see what our losses had been. They would count what they thought were our operational planes. It was left by the Germans when the field in Sardinia was bombed because it had been damaged too severely.

This was the remains of a German Dornier (model 200 something) bomber left on our field in Sardinia. We always called the field "Villacidro" because the town was so closely linked to it. This is the type of bomber they used for bombing London and the rest of Great Britain.

This was a six-engine German glider shot down by B-26s over Sardinia in late 1943 or early 1944. They were built out of plumbing supplies— galvanized pipes all fitted together. They had six German Volkswagen engines. The idea being that if they couldn't make it by riding thermals over the Alps, they could give themselves a boost with those six engines and come out with enough altitude to reach North Africa as gliders. These gliders were manned with *(by a)* pilot and co-pilot. They were towed to a high altitude over southern Germany by fancy twin bombers (Twin bombers— Germans took one of their top level bombers, cut them off at mid-wing and joined them together so they flew as one plane.) The two planes had power enough to get one of these big gliders aloft. The gliders were huge with a heavy supply load and therefore no single bomber could tow them aloft. This glider was shot down before I got there. It was a last-ditch effort to get supplies to North Africa to support the German troops there in 1943/1944. Look at the picture with a magnifying glass. Some of the rubbish on the ground is oil and gas drums.

Villacidro, Sardinia, August 9, 1944

"Darling…

I'm enclosing a snapshot again. It shows just a little section of the main street of a town over here about the size of Hamburg. *(NY)* The street is just wide enough for two cars to pass. (I have heard of GI truck drivers getting stuck in some of these towns when the streets got so narrow that the trucks rubbed on the buildings on both sides at once.) The buildings are made of baked blocks of mud (that is sun baked) and have tile roofs. The door casings and window casings are cast out of cement and are the only solid parts that there are.

You have heard of running water enough times but these houses are equipped with walking water. If you don't believe me just look at the right hand edge of the picture. *(see the picture of Luigi in "Luigi's Mother's Laundry Service in Sardinia" in "PART I The War as I Heard It.")* That jug she is walking off with so nonchalantly with [*sic*], must weigh about 45 lbs too. The jug is heavy earthenware and holds 5 gals. Little donkey carts come around a little before meal times and everybody comes running out with those jugs on their heads to buy water to do their cooking.

By the way, 4 windows in one of those houses is just about maximum and very few of those have glass in them…

Shoes are practically unheard of as you'll be able to see by this picture and others that I'll probably send you…

All my love,

Ladd"

Villacidro, Sardinia, August 14, 1944

"Darling…

…I haven't written to you in the past 4 days because I was in Rome.

I've got a few things from Rome that I'm going to enclose and guess I had better explain about a little.

The pink slip is the stub from a ticket to "Aida" at the Royal Opera House of Rome. I attended the opening night there on the 12th. I had a box with another fellow that cost me $7.

That snack bar ticket is from the Red Cross in Rome. I got a kick out of it and kept a couple of them for souvenirs.

The white slip was my pass to get down in the catacombs. I wanted to sneak out a skull or some bones for souvenirs but they watch them too close [*sic*]. There are miles and miles of them of course but the guides only take you through a little ways…

By the way I had an audience with the Pope while I was over there not that I think much of him…

All my love,

Ladd."

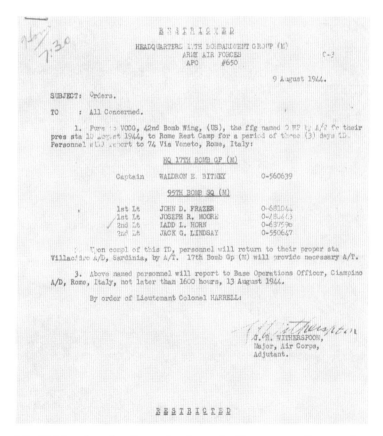

August 9, 1944 orders for three-day leave in Rome reporting on August 13, 1944 at the Ciampino Aerodrome.

Ticket to "Aida" at the Royal Opera House of Rome

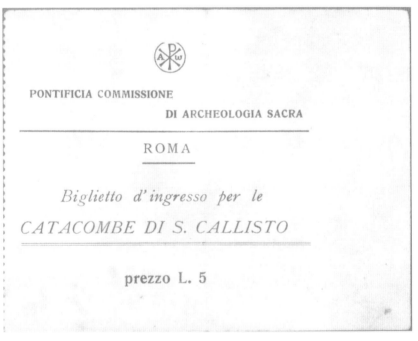

Ticket to the catacombs.

One lira note from Rome.

Rest leave in Rome after Rome was recaptured in June of 1944. "Zimmie" Zimmerman is on the left front (with cap). Zimmie fought on both sides of the war. He was going to college in Germany when the war started. They immediately inducted him into the German Airforce even though he was an American citizen. His parents were recent German immigrants. They trained him as one of their fighter pilots. This was prior to the US officially entering the war. His parents tried to get him extradited from Germany. They had about given up hope, but the last few days before the US declared war, the US government got him out. We don't know how they did it. He arrived back in the US to the news that he was now in the US Air Force. They retrained him as a bomber pilot. He was in the 95th Squadron with me. He had to go back and actually bomb the town where he had been living in Germany (and his grandparents still were). He did survive the war. He told us that those German pilots were the dirtiest people in some ways (sexual angle). All their jokes were relative to sex, nasty and dirty and so on. Even while he was in our outfit he got called up every once in a while to near the front to interrogate German POW air crews because his German was fluent and he could get leads because he had been flying with those same guys. He said that their main way of avoiding your interrogation was to deflect your question and give you extraneous information mixed with dirty stories.

Lace cloth souvenir from Rome.

Villacidro, Sardinia, August 15, 1944

"Dearest Ethel…

The other picture is one of Lt. Roseman my co-pilot on my motorcycle… One of the fellows took it and I borrowed the negative to get a print. I think I told you a while ago that he is a 1st lt now. I think I also explained some of the reasons why I will probably never be one. At least the chance is very remote. He is in for the Air Medal with 23 clusters too. It looks as though he'll get them all too and that means he'll have to wear three medals the same to get all the clusters on.

Roseman bracing Ringo. Roseman just made 1st lieutenant.

I'm going to enclose a picture from the inside of St. Peters Cathedral…

That reminds me of what the Italian guide said. In the cathedral there are a lot of statues by the great artists of early Rome and the middle ages. They are mostly of women, cherubs and angels, very few of whom have any great amount of clothes on. The guide said, 'We have a broad-minded pope now, the statues are all in their normal condition. When we have a narrow-minded pope we have to put lead skirts on the women and lead shorts on the cherubs, when we get a broad-minded pope we take them off again. The woman at the side of the alter has been dressed and undressed 7 times since the 16th century.'

I visited the house of Hermes where both Peter and Paul stayed just outside of Rome. The house is underground carved out of solid rock and is connected with the catacombs by passageways and stairways underground. The idea being to hide from the Romans when they got after them. In the catacombs nearly under the house are the tombs where Peter and Paul were buried. Peter was buried in the family tomb of Hermes and Paul in the tomb of another family right next to it. The tombs are like little chapels built in caverns hollowed out of the rock. They are built of marble stone and brick and very well preserved. The bodies, perhaps 10 or 15 were placed in niches in the stone walls and closed in by carved marble slabs. The slabs had names and dates on them in Latin much the same as we carve out tombstones now days [*sic*] only these were much more well done. Some have pictures of the good shepherd carrying a lamb or caring for his sheep and the work puts our modern artists to shame. In the catacombs there are some marble-base reliefs [*sic*] done less than 100 years after the death of Christ and they are beautiful. They tell the story of the New Testament in pictures. One that I looked at showed Jesus raising Lazarus from the dead, Mary washing his feet with her tears, Peter sinking when he tried to walk on the water and many others. The stories were told out in strips on the marble almost the way we tell stories in the comic strips now days [*sic*].

I've seen so much since I left the states that I can't begin to tell it in letters. Sometime, Honey, perhaps I can tell you in person. I'm hoping all the time for that day to come.

All my love

Ladd"

Vatican Obelisk in St. Peter's Square, August 13–15, 1944 when Dad was on leave in Rome.

Paper "postcard" Dad saved from Rome. Dad's words on the card are:
Buildings on the right are the Vatican. Center building is St. Peter's cathedral. Built in 400 A.D. largest church in the world. 490 ft floor to ceiling dome.

Temple to Apollo in Pompeii. View toward Mt. Vesuvius. Picture would have been taken between August 13–15, 1944 while Dad was on rest leave in Rome.

Described in letter written September 6, 1944: Two of the fellows walking down one of the streets of Pompeii.

Faraglioni Rocks off the Island of Capri. Picture taken August 13–15, 1944 while on rest leave in Rome.

This picture was taken from Monte Solaro on Capri Island, Italy looking toward Villa Jovis. The picture is printed backwards. The small island off the tip of Capri at Villa Jovis is just barely visible in the upper right of the picture. This picture was taken between August 13–15, 1944 when Dad was on rest leave in Rome.

Emperor Tiberius' palace ruins at Villa Jovis on Capris Island, Italy August 13–15, 1944 while Dad was on leave in Rome.

Emperor Tiberius' palace ruins at Villa Jovis on Capri Island, Italy August 13–15, 1944 when Dad was on rest leave in Rome.

Villacidro, Sardinia, August 18, 1944

"Dearest Ethel…

I'm going to enclose a snapshot of the "Bambino Lt." Robert Ringo who lives in the tent with us. Even in the picture he looks a little bit like a kid but not nearly so much so as he does in real life…

…We've got a big deal on today. We're going to build a dark room…

Love, Ladd."

Bob Ringo riding my German motorcycle. When we were moving out of Sardinia I sold it because I didn't want to have the job of moving it. I paid $40 for the motorcycle. I sold it to this guy *(not Bob Ringo)* for $80. I figured he should have the fun of moving it.

Note on back of picture: Roseman in front of our darkroom. Bomb crate darkroom where nearly all of these pictures were developed.

Original spy camera contact prints—done in Sardinia "Horn" photo lab shown in this photo. Canvas over a bomb crate with a GI mess kit to develop in. [*sic*] Makeshift chemicals, scraps of aerial surveillance film and Air Force paper [*sic*]. Camera was credit card size—about 3/8" thick with lens that imitated a brown shirt button. *(The)* Lens buttoned through *(the)* shirt buttonhole so *(that it)* was unnoticeable. Camera *(was)* inside *(the)* shirt.

The "bomb-crate darkroom" in Sardinia was a huge step up. In Telergma, Algeria, Dad had to use this "darkroom equipment." He would develop his film in his tent in his mess kit and helmet under an army blanket. When they moved to Corsica, Dad built another darkroom connected to their tent. However when they moved to Dijon, France, he once again resorted to using his helmet and mess kit under an army blanket in his tent. This picture of his canteen, mess kit and blanket was taken in 2022.

The left and right men are pilots. The one on the left was named Lindberg. The man in the middle was the head of S2. S2 was an intelligence agency. They interviewed you when you came back from a mission, checked all pictures that were taken by official photographers and kept up on intelligence issues. He wanted my "split-frame 27" from Sears and Roebuck. He wanted it because you could take a lot of pictures without much film and he had access to scrap film. He wanted the camera badly and tried to buy it from me or get it from me. When I left to come home I gave him the camera. His department issued the cameras that the official photographers received (They just picked men from the crews on a random basis and they gave the cameras back and S2 developed them.) Some of the larger pics I have are ones from S2. The man on the right was another pilot in the 95th.

Villacidro, Sardinia, August 21, 1944

"Dear Ethel…

Today the whole group has a day off. More or less a day of mourning. A group day off is something unheard of but this is one time it was just about necessary.

Don't worry too much about what I said in that one letter. As I said, a fellow can't come home just the same as he was when he left after this but I'm afraid you took a little wrong meaning of that. After all I will be a couple of years older and will probably look a little different. A fellow can't see the fellows he has been living with killed before his eyes without a chance and be just the same as before either. A lot of those things all added together change a person whether they want them to or not…

I'm enclosing a picture of myself in *Old Faithful*…

I sold my motorcycle last night. I made a profit of $75 on it besides having the use of it that I did….

After days like yesterday I wonder if I'll be around long enough to ever have the chance to spend any of what I have saved…

Yours truly

Ladd"

This plane is Old Faithful. *Dad is not the pilot in the picture. It looks like she had flown eighty-five missions at the time of the picture.*

Villacidro, Sardinia, August 22, 1944

"Darling...

I can't tell you which as yet but I have lost two members of my crew. Their folks must be notified by now but we're not allowed to write home their names until 90 days are up and that won't be for quite awhile [*sic*] yet. I didn't really know whether to tell you or not. I've been kind of pondering it for quite a while. A couple of days ago I thought it was the end for all of us.

You probably realize that this southern French invasion has thrown about twice the work onto us that we normally have had...I have to get up for a mission in the morning about 5:15. That dawn stuff kind of gets you. Things are pretty tough now though irregardless. The more whipped those Germans are the harder they fight. Their equipment and men are getting more concentrated all the time and that makes it bad for us even though we are winning.

Sweetheart, I do love you so,

Ladd."

Villacidro, Sardinia, August 25, 1944

"Dearest Ethel...

This combat is getting to be rough stuff. Now that the Germans are getting their backs to the wall it isn't a healthy business to fly over their lines any more.

I seem to be getting just about all the rough ones lately too...

Of the pictures that I am enclosing...the third shows how they let the little Italian kids run around here. The one in the picture is what we call a Sardo. They have light hair and skin and their features aren't the same as the persons we normally think of as being Italians. The little kids run naked or half naked until they're about old enough for school. It makes no difference whether they are girls or boys and no one notices or cares. It's just part of their way of living.

The standard with the kids is to wear a sort of short shirt that reaches to their waist and nothing else as you can see from the picture…There are two English words or perhaps I should say three that they all know, namely, "take it easy." They got them from that song, "Take it Easy" which has been very popular here and played over the Armed Forces radio a lot…

…When the missions get pretty rough though as they've been lately I begin to get worried for fear my plane might be one of those that doesn't come back. I hope not though.

All my love,

Ladd"

Note on back of picture written by Dad's mom, Freida May (Wenz) Horn:
Fall dress suit for Italian children. Sardinia. In letter of Aug 25–'44.

Villacidro, Sardinia, August 27, 1944

"Dearest Ethel…

I still only have 21 missions. I had a dry run today, that is my plane went out before we got to the target so I didn't get a mission…

Yours,

Ladd."

Villacidro, Sardinia, September 1, 1944

"Dear Sweetheart

I had a rather rough day yesterday and didn't get a chance to write to you. It's a rough life even if you don't weaken.

We had a long mission, 14 hours, incorporating a forced landing about 30 miles behind the front lines.

This afternoon I am having the Air Medal presented to me by General Webster. The Air Medal with one cluster. I have about 6 more clusters coming I think…

All my love,

Ladd"

Villacidro, Sardinia, September 3, 1944

"Dear Sweetheart…

Yesterday was a long hard day. We landed late in the evening with all of our gas gauges reading empty. One engine ran out of gas as we parked our plane.

This morning I have free until 1:30 and then I have to be ready for another mission. We'll probably come in late from it too…

The next picture shows a plane in flight with a shoreline in the background. I was flying on the wing of this ship when it took a direct hit from a German 5" naval gun. One of the fellows was on the ball and got a picture of it just as the shell burst. It showed the wreckage flying and one engine still running but with no more plane attached to it. *(See the pictures in* "Toulon: A Right-Wing Plane is Lost" *in "PART I The War as I Heard It")*

Another picture shows a bomb that Roseman addressed to Hitler from his little cousin *(nephew?)*…

Lovingly,

Ladd"

Villacidro, Sardinia, September 4, 1944
"Dear Ethel…

…I'm putting in a picture of *Old Faithful* too. It shows a couple of the crewmen working on the tail turret…

All my love,

Ladd"

Villacidro, Sardinia, September 9, 1944
"Dearest Ethel…

I'm beginning to pick up some of the lingo around here but I'm not as quick at it as some of the fellows. Some words are quite similar to English. If you can't think of the Italian or Sardo word for something you just try to think of an English word for it that isn't used much and you try first just the first one or two syllables of the word. If they don't understand try the whole word and add first "o" to the end of it, second "i" and if that still doesn't get them try an "e" on the end. 9 times out of ten the Sardos will understand one of the versions you render. For "very good" they use "multi grande." See how easy it works. I have to go "monjari" now. That is one that doesn't work. It means "eat."…

> All my love
>
> Ladd."

Villacidro, Sardinia, September 10, 1944

"Dear Sweetheart…

I'm going to have to leave the trimming of these prints up to you. I'm sending them in the rough. We developed 98 prints last evening and 70 the evening before, also 3 films. I guess you can see that we do need material to keep that up. I must have mailed about 40 prints to you so far and have about 30 new ones on hand that I will be enclosing…

> All my love,
>
> Ladd."

Somebody shipped a volleyball net and volleyball over to a son. When that came in, and he unpacked it, the fellows set it up and just went wild playing volleyball because they hadn't had a chance to do anything like that in years or months. The volleyball was in use continuously for 3–5 days maybe until it was so worn out it was no longer repairable. That was the end of volleyball as a sport over there.

A second shot of the volleyball game as in *(the previous picture)*. I don't think the volleyball ever stopped moving for the 3–5 days it took to wear it out. Note the guy in the background with the nice uniform on (left rear). It is quite likely that he was a POW. Often they had good German or Italian uniforms on. Compare that with the rag-tag get ups of the guys playing volleyball. Many of the Italian forces had surrendered at this time. We had a whole Italian tank crew that had surrendered. They wanted to fight with the Americans in France and moved their tanks up to the north end of Sardinia ready to ship for Toulon. Many of their tanks broke down along the way. The US refused to ship their equipment to Toulon because they said it was not good enough for the fighting in France. Ringo talked with those guys a lot. He knew a little Italian and they knew a little English. It was easy to make friends of them because they badly wanted to know what America and Americans were like and they desperately wanted the Americans to understand that they had not had a choice about fighting with the Axis armies. They didn't want us to think badly about them. They were amazed that as POWs we fed them and housed them as good or better than our troops. They had heard all kinds of stories about how badly POWs were treated by the US and Allied forces. Most of those stories came out of Germany where POWs were treated very badly. I think many were amazed that we used the POWs as guards and to do jobs that would help us out.

"Huckster" with horse and cart, Sardinia.

Villacidro, Sardinia, September 13, 1944

"Dearest Ethel…

…Don't feel too anxious, Honey, I'll be all right but I don't know how much longer it will be until we can come home. The Germans are whipped right now but they will make a desperate last ditch stand probably in the hope that they will be able to get better peace terms…

All my love,

Ladd"

Villacidro, Sardinia, September 14, 1944

"My Dear Sweetheart…

I didn't fly today because I had a blowout just before takeoff. It was a recapped tire and blew out while we were standing still waiting for our turn to take off. That tire never even lasted for its first takeoff say nothing about a landing …

There's a picture of my corner of the mansion. If you look close [*sic*] you can see your picture on the stand at the head of my bunk…

Yours,

Ladd"

Dad's corner of the "Marauder Mansion" 95th Squadron, Villacidro, Sardinia.

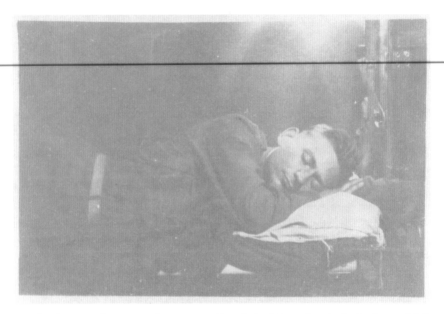

Dad asleep on his cot in his tent in Sardinia. Note the dark clothes which were wool. It was nearing fall and the weather was turning cold. The pole in the background is the pole to help swing the door shut. Canteen hanging on it 'cause there wasn't much room to put it elsewhere.

Villacidro, Sardinia, September 15, 1944

"Dearest Ethel…

We had a slight flood this afternoon. Some of the fellows had water a foot deep running in the back of their tents and pouring out the front door. We got a couple of puddles on the floor where water came in the ventilator at the peak but otherwise we kept dry…

Most of the pictures are self-explanatory I think. One shows General Webster presenting the air medals and one shows a couple of women sitting at the gate of their farm. One of them is spinning yarn, they're not even up to date enough to use a spinning wheel around here…

All my love,

Ladd."

The flood we had in Sardinia. This was a summer thunderstorm in Sardinia. Salvaging tent supplies and possessions out of the water. We were on the lower slopes of the mountain and so while it didn't happen too often, when it did rain like that, it flooded.

One of the fellows trying to salvage some stuff as it floats down the street.

This is a picture of our "Orderly Room" which was a converted German building. It was really the headquarters for the squadron. All orders came out of this building. They got just as much water as the rest of us did when the thunderstorms hit.

General Webster presenting medals. We were still temporarily attached to the 12th Air Force. Webster was a high level commander in the 12th Air Force. The tall man standing at the table is General Webster. That is about as close as I ever got to him. He felt that any man that was awarded a medal should have it handed to the man personally by a commander and "right then" (as near as possible). He would make a routine trip over to Villacidro and any man that had been awarded a medal would have it handed to him by the general. *Picture taken in Sardinia, mid-summer 1944.*

95th Squadron lined up at the medal presentation ceremony. The guy at the end standing out (shorter than everybody else) was the Squadron Commander. I think he is the same man as [*sic*] is doing the laundry in album Picture #81. If you look at the plane in the background, the guys are lined up along the wing. You can look at the leading edge of the wing and see the damage—some were patches and some were just from loose flak. This plane is well-used as you can see.

Sardinia. Flickinger receiving DFC 95th Squadron" *(There is another faint note on the back that reads something like the following;* One of the fellows receiving his DFC *Note: DFC stands for Distinguished Flying Cross.)*

Unknown women sitting at the gate to their farm. One is spinning wool. They don't even have spinning wheels. Sardinia, Summer 1944.

(Poretta) Corsica, France, October 1, 1944

"Dear Sweetheart...

I just had to write you a little note this evening. We've been in the midst of moving and flying both and I haven't had the chance to write before...

Boneyard when we arrived at Corsica. The remains are of Douglas A-20s. The group that was based there got hit by a group of German fighters while they were lined up for mission takeoff. The fighters bombed and strafed and put the whole operation out of business. So that is when we moved up there and took over on that field. Our fellows were curious about the A-20s and what they could salvage from the wreckage.

The mess hall for the officers. Basically it was a tent over picnic tables with no canvas on the side and there were holes in the tent. You can see all the different uniforms. The Germans were dressed meticulously with beautiful uniforms and nice wool. We as officers would be flying missions with a baseball cap, Natal boots instead of military boots and coveralls. Even the German POWs doing work for us had nice uniforms.

I have 30 missions now and one the other day was really rough but our ship got through ok.

We have a pretty good tent built up now and lined with blankets. We also have a gasoline stove for heating that we built. Gasoline is the only fuel obtainable here for heating purposes. I'll probably send you pictures of our home pretty soon. We have a chimney big enough for a boiler factory…

Ladd."

The tent in the left foreground is the tent that Ladd Horn, Robert Ringo, Paul Roseman, James Miller and Olsen lived in on Corsica for the 6 weeks or so that we were there. They had these huge trees in Corsica. I don't know the variety. They were very protective of them. There was one right at the end of the runway. We took off right over the top of the tree the whole time we were there. We were unable to get permission to remove it and neither was the Army Air Force. We figured if you got over that tree, you had it made for the mission. Look at the chimney on our tent (towers over the tent). That is the chimney for our little gasoline stove. When we packed up that tent to leave Corsica for France, that chimney barely protruded through the canvas of the tent because the balance had gradually melted off from the bottom— every so often the stove would get too hot and the zinc alloy would melt and drop a half inch or 3/4".

Dad washing his clothes in Corsica. We would boil our clothes. The trucks would bring water around to us that they didn't think was good enough to use for drinking water. They would fill drums and we would keep a German gasoline fire going under the drums until they would boil. It was probably a good practice because the conditions we lived under were not very sanitary. We didn't get any native laundry service in Corsica.

We had a row of commanding officers that insisted on flying in the lead plane. The Germans concentrated on shooting down those planes figuring they would get the high-ranking officers. We got down to this man who was a Captain. He was very nice. He became the commanding officer of the 95th. This is in Corsica, the first place we could do white laundry. White laundry was too easily seen by observation planes. *This picture was taken in October or November of 1944.*

Corsica, France, October 6, 1944

"Dear Sweetheart…

For once this morning I am just sitting by the fire and toasting my toes. It's been raining cats and dogs ever since late last evening…

I've started work on a darkroom in my spare moments and in a couple more days I think I will be doing some work in it. Due to the fact that winter is coming on I have built it as a part of the tent with an inside entrance. I think it will be warm enough even in the winter…

It will be just a year ago tomorrow that I came home from Dodge City and was able to see you for a little while. That seems so long ago now…

…I never seem to get tired of looking at pictures or making them either. Every snapshot is something new and interesting to me…

…Perhaps I told you in some of my letters about flying "Pistol Packing Mamma." I'm enclosing a picture of her after she laid her pistol down…*(See the picture with letter entitled, "Villacidro, Sardinia, June 11, 1944")*

Yours,

Ladd."

Corsica, France, October 9, 1944

"Darling…

Last evening I did the first work in my darkroom. I developed some 8-year-old [sic] film and printed it on 3-year-old [sic] paper. The results weren't entirely satisfactory but I did still get some pictures…

…The weather has been dark and dreary and muddy and my spirits have gotten into just about the same condition I guess. It seems sometimes as though I just can't wait to see you anymore and *(it seems)* as though time over here would [sic] never end. I hate to think of being here for the winter but it looks as though we will be…

Martinson is in France, Ringo is drunk, Roseman is well on his way to being drunk and trying to hold Ringo on his feet while he vomits. Roseman at least can take care of himself right up to the point where he passes out. The fellows get 2 ounces of rye whiskey after each mission and once every three months they get a quart per man. The liquor just came in a couple days ago and everything has been drunk out lately as the fellows say. These guys don't take it easy at all. They might go as much as several weeks without getting drunk and then they will drink until they pass out. Most of the liquor they get is native rot gut stuff and you never know what its effects are going to be.

Robert Ringo and his liquor ration. *This picture was taken at Longvic Field, Dijon, France.*

Roseman got some French cognac a few days ago that knocked him out completely. In 5 minutes he went from cold sober to unconscious. It took us 2 h and a half to bring him to. For a while we got scared we wouldn't be able to bring him out of it. We finally got him conscious enough so that we could force him to eat something. After that he vomited and then came around ok. We put him to bed and let him sleep it off. Roseman's worst fault when he gets drunk is that he wants to fight the Civil War over again. He says in the next civil war the south is going to win. To him everyone from north of Richmond is a "Nigger Lovin' Son of a _____ _____ ___." *Once again, please know that my Dad never approved of any racist or crude language but, unfortunately, it was part of what he heard daily during the war.* One of the last nights we were in Sardinia we got arguing over the Civil War and he went to shooting in the tent in the pitch dark with no one able to see what was going on.

We're going to make up some hot toast and chocolate right now. Ringo has gone to sleep and Roseman is still navigating pretty well…

Ladd."

The hardships, sickness, the awful reality of the war, the tragic loss of lives (and probably youthfulness) drove many of the men in the flight crews to drink to survive. Dad told me of one bombardier in the 95th Bomb Squadron who would go through extreme emotional cycles. As they were preparing for a mission, he would be talking about how they needed to stop Hitler in order to save the world and how they should bomb their whole army and all of their equipment. He would go on the mission, drop his bombs, and then later get the intelligence report. When he saw the damage his bombs had done, especially if he found that they had missed the bridges, industrial and military targets and hit some civilian areas instead, he couldn't take it. He would start drinking, acting depressed and talking about how the whole war was terrible and how he had murdered civilians. He might be down for a day or a few days. Then as he was assigned to the next mission, he would start talking again about how important it was that they get out there and destroy Hitler and his armies. This cycle was repeated mission after mission for the time he served.

Corsica, France, October 11, 1944

"Dear Sweetheart…

I don't know whether I'll have any more pictures to send to you or not. They made me stop developing our own and other facilities are just about impossible. I think maybe we'll get some kind of deal fixed up so that we can get pictures through…

Love,

Ladd"

Corsica, France, October 11, 1944

"Dear Ethel

Well, I'm back safe and sound from the mission but I'll have to admit I was a little worried about it this morning. I don't suppose I can say where it was to but it was to one of the "Hot" targets in Europe.

It has been long enough now so that I guess I can tell you Roseman, Fineman and I are the only ones left of my crew here. Fineman is flying as a bombardier now and is a staff sergeant. As far as he is concerned combat is more or less a picnic. All he worries about is promotions and medals. He has an air medal but he is one of these fellows who wants more and thinks he ought to get it. Sometimes of course he does but not often enough to suit him.

All my love,

Ladd"

Bernie Fineman just after his 60th mission pointing out where flak had hit his helmet. He had lacerations on his face and leg and a badly injured eye though you can't see them in the picture. I didn't take the picture, but I developed it.

December 17, 1944 *Longvic Air Base, Dijon, France. Bernard Fineman's helmet showing where shrapnel hit it.*

Corsica, France, October 17, 1944

"Dearest Ethel...

We didn't fly today so we went to work and dug a cesspool for our sink drain. It's harder to get rid of wash water in a sanitary manner than you imagine when you're used to just pouring it down a drain.

We've been doing quite a little cooking in the evenings. Lately we've been making macaroni and cheese. Our own recipe. It's my recipe for that matter I guess. I'll write it out for you and you can see what you think of it. It really tastes good to us. We take about 5 oz. of macaroni, boil it in about ½ gallon of salted water and drain it. Then we make a sauce out of 3 oz of cheese, 6 tablespoons of milk and a half tablespoon of sugar melted together on the stove with two tablespoons of butter. Pour that over the drained macaroni and kind of fold it in, put a lid over it and let it steam a little while on the stove with just a little fire under it. That makes a helping for about 3 of us and tastes better than anything we ever get in the mess hall. A helping of that, a slice of hot toast and cup of hot chocolate about 11p.m. on a cool evening is just about "it."

We soldered up a coffee pot for ourselves that holds about 16 cups and that is sitting on the stove now full of hot coffee. As long as there is no guard at the mess kitchen at night and as long as we get enough packages from home we won't be standing short...

I'm getting pretty tired of this army life but I guess I'll have to stick it out for a good long time yet...

All my love, Ladd"

Corsica, France, October 21, 1944

"Dearest Ethel...

We were presented with a Presidential Citation yesterday by General Cannon but I missed the ceremony. I was out on a weather mission and got back over the field just in time to see the end from the air.

I've always had an idea of what a person meant when they said something was "blown to smithereens" but I've got a better idea since yesterday. I saw a plane that had a 1,000 lb bomb accidentally explode in it. The plane was traveling about 130 mph when the explosion occurred and it was scattered in pieces from the size of a pinhead to about the size of a GI helmet over an area better than half a mile in diameter. The miracle of it is that after the explosion took place at that speed and with such terrific force two men stepped out of the very center of the explosion and one with only a little scratch under one eye; of three other men there wasn't even a grease spot left outside of a pair of shoes. A sixth man was just a headless, handless and footless corpse.

That is more or less of a horrible thing to describe but somehow we seem to look at things like that differently over here than we did at home. Rather than mourning over the men who were lost we rejoice over those who were left alive.

I have talked to two men who have survived similar accidents. One was an RAF man who was caught in the center of the same kind of explosion. He was the only man who survived and the only injury that he sustained was a partial loss of strength in his right arm due to a nerve being crushed by the explosion. The other man was an American pilot who was instructing in Africa at the same time that I was. He was flying co-pilot in a B-26 and they were taking off in formation with a bomb load. His ship collided with one of the other ships just after takeoff about 50' in the air. Both planes exploded and the wreckage fell to earth in small pieces. Several hours later they found this fellow wandering around in some farmer's fields adjacent to the landing field. He wasn't hurt whatsoever except that he couldn't remember what had happened between the time the ships came together and the time the other fellows found him. He was the only one to survive, in fact they never even found any bodies of the other men. Those are things almost impossible to understand but yet they happen every once in a while where explosions are concerned. Perhaps you remember once when we were kids and that little brick store on South Park up in Lackawanna blew up from gas. Two people in the store there walked right out through the solid brick wall and the wall just disintegrated before them. Neither of them were hurt much at all but there was nothing left of the building.

Speaking of explosions, we have built a hot water heater for our tent out of an empty oil drum and copper tubing from a wrecked plane. We're hoping that it won't explode. It heats from a copper coil that runs through our stove. Whenever the stove is lit just turn on the faucet and presto—hot water. I wish you could see our tent and see just how comfortable it is possible to live with nothing but makeshift equipment…

All my love

Ladd."

Corsica, France, October 25, 1944

"Dearest Ethel…

We've been having plenty of rain and we have had our hands full to quite an extent trying to keep our tent weatherproof. The other day it stood through a 65 to 75 mph gale with strong gusts so we were pretty well pleased with it but the wind didn't do it much good as far as being waterproof was concerned. I'm going to have to sleep tonight with a G.I. raincoat topping off my blankets. …They don't make them fly nearly as long or as many missions up there in England. Also if they fly a shuttle run they get double credit while we still only get single credit. Some of our missions we have taken off at first daylight and landed again at our own field as it was getting dusk. That is all water past the wheel now I hope…

All my love

Ladd"

Corsica, France, October 29, 1944

"My Darling…

I've a blank here to fill out right now in case I should be stranded overseas for 6 months after the war is over. The army is going to make our outfit into a sort of combined high school and university. As soon as the war is over we'll start in on 6 month "dehydrated" courses.

We're having quite a time around the tent here now. Roseman has a dog that moved in with us one day when it was cold and wet and we had a warm fire. He's been with us ever since and Ringo christened him "Stud" after our S-2 officer whose name is Stud Lawson. He and the dog do have some things in common at that. To top everything off "Madam" is in heat and half the dogs in camp are hanging around the tent. To make it worse yet she has the wrong idea about sex and wants to take the part of a male dog. We've been trying to get the right idea through her head but I don't know just what to do with a dog in such a case. It's something extremely unusual and none of the fellows around camp have ever seen or heard tell of such a thing before say nothing about knowing what to do about her.

I don't have to fly today and to all appearances I won't have to tomorrow either so I'm kind of planning on going "eel" fishing in the river near camp. Some of the fellows have been having pretty good luck. I'm going to rig up a line this afternoon and then try to get some worms for bait tonight.

The night before last I built myself a mousetrap. I set it and nothing came near it so last night I didn't bother to set it and this morning the bait was gone. Tonight I guess I'll set it again. Mice are an awful nuisance to us. We have to watch out for them getting into stuff all the time. Our next worst nuisance is Bees. They seem to be starved to death on the island here. The mess hall gets gallon cans of orange marmalade and if you open one of those cans and let it stand outside for a day the bees will come by the millions and the can will be just a living crawling mass. By the time the day is over there won't be anything left but dry pieces of orange peel in the can that are mixed in the marmalade. Every bit of the sweet will be gone and the tin will be shiny and slick as a whistle. They try to eat the marmalade right off your bread while you're putting it in your mouth. You can't brush them off long enough to take a bite. Ringo got stung on the inside of his lip a while ago that way…

Just so you'll know what ribbons I wear now I'm going to list them here for you… On my left breast at the extreme left I wear a European theatre ribbon with two bronze stars. One for the Italian campaign and one for the French. [*sic*] Next to that I wear a good conduct ribbon and to the right of that the air medal with one bronze cluster. If the orders go through that I have been recommended on I will have 2 silver clusters to add to the bronze one. On my right breast I wear a blue ribbon with a gold border for a presidential citation then I have the "Croix de Guerre avec Palme" from General De Gaulle for collaboration with the French, also if the orders go through on the second one I should be entitled to wear a gold cord around my left shoulder. The Croix de Guerre was given for quote, "Attacking and destroying many most important objectives in support of the French Army despite intense, heavy and accurate anti-aircraft fire."…

All my love,

Ladd"

Corsica, France, November 1, 1944

"Dearest Ethel…

We received some good news, that is that Tupper is a prisoner of war in Germany. *(Tupper was Dad's original radioman)* We had given him up for lost even though we didn't want to admit it so that news came as a happy surprise…

…It seems almost like something impossible, it has been so long since I have been able to do things on my own just as I pleased…

Ladd"

Corsica, France, November 2, 1944

"Darling…

Today we went eel fishing for a while but the river was too high and we didn't have any luck. It was a pleasant way to spend an afternoon though…

All my love, Ladd."

Shepherds in Corsica.

Corsica, France, November 9, 1944

"Darling…

I've been flying every day for a while and had a bad cold besides. The last two days I have been grounded but I felt too miserable to write before this. I have 39 missions now and chances for coming home don't look good for a long, long time…

You mentioned in your last letter that no one around home knew anything about Cannes. I thought everyone knew about it. Cannes is the center of the

French Riviera, the "hot spot" of Europe's greatest winter resort. The place where all the royalty of Europe congregates in peace time. [*sic*] It is there that Monte Carlo is located and you must certainly at some time or other at least heard about "The man that broke the bank at Monte Carlo." Also you should know by now that Cannes was where the troops went ashore for the invasion of Southern France. I haven't had a chance to get up there as yet but I haven't given up hopes. Anything is possible they say. In a place and at a time like this you don't know what might be coming next…

All my love, Ladd."

Corsica, France, November 11, 1944

"Dear Ethel…

Today I put in mission no. 40. It wasn't too bad but none are good. It was only 20 below up there and we had two fellows with frostbitten feet when we got back. Mine were numb and prickled a little bit but are ok. I had Roseman take a picture of me with a winter jacket on. If it turns out Ok I'll send you a print so that you can see what they are like. We have even an Eskimo just about beat…

All my love,

Ladd"

Dad dressed for cold weather in Corsica.

Corsica, France, November 15, 1944

"Dear Ethel…

That presidential citation that you mentioned is a unit citation. For quite some time we had the most accurate bombing record in the Air Force and that was the main reason for the presentation. You have to have two citations before you receive the badge that we wear. Just where we stand right now I don't know but it is mighty close to the top for accuracy.

I'm going to enclose some money that I think you might like to have as a souvenir. The 2 Franc bill is worth just a little better than 4¢. In actual use it corresponds about to a nickel in the States. It was printed since the so called "liberation" of France. The 20 Franc note is left from before the war. It is worth just about 43¢ and corresponds about to a half dollar. They don't have any metal money at all any more. Metal has been too scarce in these countries to waste it in making coins.

All my love, Ladd"

Corsica, France, November 17, 1944

"Dearest Ethel…

I flew a mission yesterday and was supposed to fly another today but I had a "dry run" as we call it. We had to turn back because we couldn't get enough power out of one of our engines. I'll probably have to go out in the morning again if the weather is good…

…I don't worry about when I'll get home—just whether or not I will get there.

As far as missions are concerned I have to figure on going between 65 and 70 and that number is more liable to be increased than decreased. The only way I can get home with less than that is on a medical disability.

The boys flying heavies here are supposed to fly 50 in order to go home but they are actually only flying about 35. They have a sort of line of demarcation set up and whenever they have a mission that goes beyond that line it counts 2 toward going home.

I have three snapshots for you that I am going to enclose…and another that shows 6 of those big birds that "Jerry" doesn't like to see darken his sky with their wings…

All my love,

Ladd"

Corsica, France, November 20, 1944

"Dearest Ethel…

I don't know what you will think of the other two pictures I am enclosing or what you will think of me for sending them to you. They are pictures that Roseman took and one shows the courtyard in the house of prostitution in Pompeii and the other shows a picture of the entrance. Roseman went through the place on a sight-seeing tour…

…I have 42 missions now but that is still a long way from 70. I don't know how long I'll have to wait.

Love, Ladd"

Courtyard of the house of prostitution in Pompei. Picture taken by Paul Roseman.

Longvic Air Base, Dijon, France, December 12, 1944

"Darling

I'm so sorry that you have had to wait so long for a letter from me.

We made a rather sudden and trying move from Corsica back in the middle of November and I have not had the chance to write. This morning I just arrived back at my outfit from a trip to Paris and I have had no sleep for 36 hours and very little then…

You asked what I had for my Thanksgiving dinner. Well, I had 6 "C" biscuits with preserved butter on them and a cup of cocoa made without milk. For breakfast that day I had a cake of dehydrated breakfast food and a cup of water and for supper a mess kit full of "C" ration stew and cup of coffee without cream. We are living in tents and the mud is up to our knees, the weather is cold and I'm telling you it's not very comfortable…

Ladd."

Longvic Air Base, Dijon, France, December 18, 1944

"Darling…

…This evening I just received a package from my folks that was mailed to me back when I was in the Hospital in Sardinia. The package was in very good shape, I don't know where it could have been all this time. It came in with a load of Christmas packages. Counting it as a Christmas package I have received 19 I believe so far for Christmas.

I have a little time this evening so I guess I had better explain this past month when you didn't receive any letters from me.

One day back about the middle of Nov. or a little after we went to briefing for a mission over Italy. Halfway through briefing the operations officer came in and said "The mission's canceled, pack your bags and load your planes, your [sic] leaving for France in an hour and a half" so an hour and a half later we took off for France. We found France to be a veritable mudhole and wading around in mud up to our knees we went to work pitching tents in sleet, rain, slush, mud and cold. Due to the short leave notice in Corsica we had nothing but our tents and personal equipment so it was pretty hard to set up any kind of housekeeping such as we were used to back there.

It drizzled and rained and sleeted and snowed for a week straight during which time we tried to fly, get our living quarters organized and keep clean. None of these things were successfully accomplished and we finally gave up. It's just impossible to keep the mud off, my clothes are caked about a quarter of an inch thick right now.

James Miller, Bob Ringo, Madam 95th Dijon.

Water supply truck in Dijon, France. [*sic*] This was a neighboring tent that he was delivering to. These guys were listed as being in combat, but this was their job. While the water was filtered, we still had to add Halazone and wait 20 minutes before we could drink it.

The road behind our tent and the neighborhood French kids playing around our tent. They were all curious about us and would hike down the road to watch what we were doing. Bob Ringo may have taken this picture.

Ole Olson giving Madam treats from the mess hall. Everyone used to bring treats by for Madam. That is what she lived on. Ole was a co-pilot at the time of this picture, but he moved up to pilot.

Last week just as we were beginning to get a little bit organized they called me in and said, "You're in charge of 6 men going to Paris you leave tomorrow morning at 8:30." So we left and went to Paris in G.I. trucks. I don't care if I never have another ride like that one.

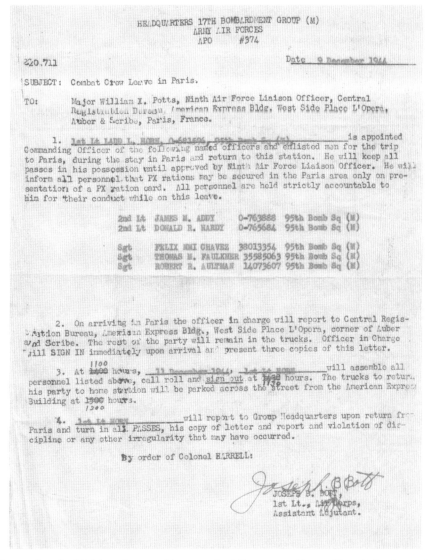

HEADQUARTERS 17TH BOMBARDMENT GROUP (M)
ARMY AIR FORCES
APO   #374

220.711   Date 9 December 1944

SUBJECT: Combat Crew Leave in Paris.

TO: Major William X. Potts, Ninth Air Force Liaison Officer, Central
          Registration Bureau, American Express Bldg, West Side Place L'Opera,
          Auber & Scribe, Paris, France.

        1. 1st Lt LADD L. HORN, O-551506, 95th Bomb Sq (M)   is appointed
Commanding Officer of the following named officers and enlisted men for the trip
to Paris, during the stay in Paris and return to this station. He will keep all
passes in his possession until approved by Ninth Air Force Liaison Officer. He will
inform all personnel that PX rations may be secured in the Paris area only on presentation of a PX ration card. All personnel are held strictly accountable to
him for their conduct while on this leave.

                2nd Lt JAMES M. ADDY   O-763888 95th Bomb Sq (M)
                2nd Lt DONALD R. HARDY   O-765684 95th Bomb Sq (M)

                Sgt   FELIX MMI CHAVEZ   38013354 95th Bomb Sq (M)
                Sgt   THOMAS M. FAULKNER 35585063 95th Bomb Sq (M)
                Sgt   ROBERT R. AULTMAN 14073607 95th Bomb Sq (M)

        2. On arriving in Paris the officer in charge will report to Central Regis-
tration Bureau, American Express Bldg., West Side Place L'Opera, corner of Auber
and Scribe. The rest of the party will remain in the trucks. Officer in Charge
will SIGN IN immediately upon arrival and present three copies of this letter.

        3. At 1100 hours, 11 December 1944, 1st Lt HORN   will assemble all
personnel listed above, call roll and sign out at 1730 hours. The trucks to return
his party to home station will be parked across the street from the American Express
Building at 1200 hours.

        4. 1st Lt HORN   will report to Group Headquarters upon return from
Paris and turn in all PASSES, his copy of letter and report and violation of discipline or any other irregularity that may have occurred.

                By order of Colonel BARRELL:

                                        JOSEPH B. BOTT,
                                        1st Lt., Air Corps,
                                        Assistant Adjutant.

*December 9, 1944 orders making my dad "commanding officer" for leave in
Paris. It was apparently a grueling trip from Longvic Airbase, Dijon to Paris
in the back of an Army truck.*

I had hoped to buy some things in Paris but as luck would have it all the
stores were closed while I was there. I stayed in the King Edward VII Hotel
on the Rue De L'Opera while I was there and had good meals served on tables
with tablecloths on them, ate with silverware for a change and had waiters with

white coats and black trousers. They even talked [*sic*] English in the hotel. It made me homesick, the most homesick that I've been since I came overseas.

I had "more fun than a barrel of monkeys" as the saying goes though [*sic*] riding the subway. It was the first time in my life that I ever had to ride on a subway and being in a foreign country made it even more interesting…I'm hoping to get a chance to go back again before too long and maybe I'll be able to buy more stuff then. I tried to buy a fancy pair of bedroom slippers for you but the price ran up to nearly $45.00 and I couldn't quite see that, besides I haven't been paid in two months.

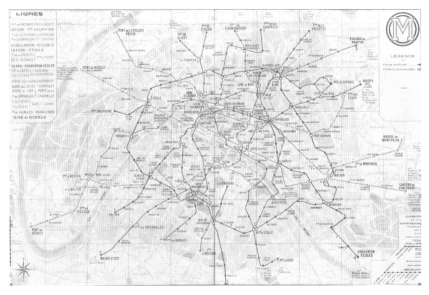

Subway map of Paris from Dad's leave December 9–11, 1944.

Since I've been back we have got our tent fixed up pretty well with stuff that we got from a German supply dump and we are living a little more comfortable [*sic*] but in pretty much of a mess just the same. At least we have a stove now so that we can keep warm.

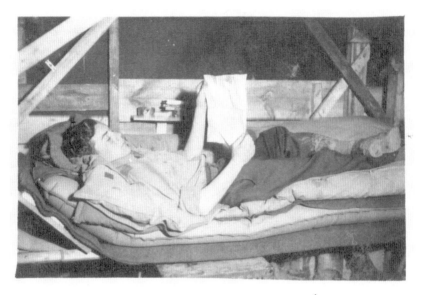

Bob Ringo Longvic Airbase, Dijon, France, 95th Squadron.

I'm entitled to three stars on my campaign ribbon now and I am in for thirteen (that is two silver and three bronze clusters) clusters on my air medal…

Sargt. [*sic*] Fineman, my engineer, has been wounded twice and has the Purple Heart with one cluster. He is in the hospital now. This last time he was hit in the eye with a piece of flak and I haven't heard as yet just how bad it was. Our Doc wasn't there to take care of him and a doctor from another squadron treated him and took him to the hospital.

So far I haven't even got [*sic*] scratched, I guess I'm pretty lucky after all.

On Nov. 24 a baby boy was born to Lt Roseman. He really thought he was somebody when he found out that it was a boy. We have been teasing him all along and telling him that he was going to have twin daughters instead of the boy that he wanted.

I'm going to enclose some pictures taken of me when I was in N. Africa. I think you'll get a kick out of them…

Picture of 2ⁿᵈ Lieutenant Ladd L. Horn, age 22 in Telergma, Algeria.

Eth, I'm so lonesome for you that I don't know how to tell you. I dreamed of you all last night. It was one of the most peculiar dreams that I ever had in my life. I fell asleep and started dreaming and then in the dream I fell asleep and dreamed about you. Still in the dream I woke up and there you were right beside me. I was so surprised that I said out loud, "Ethel can't be here, I'm in the Army and I'm overseas and she just can't be here." Right then you snuggled up close to me and pressed your cheek against mine and said "But I am here" so I reached out and put my arm around you only when I did you weren't there so I took my arm away and you were there so I tried to put both arms around you and you weren't there so I drew back a ways from you and looked and you were there. That went on for an indefinite period until I was completely dazed. Finally I sat up in bed and said to myself "Something is definitely wrong, I don't believe in the supernatural happening and a person can't vanish so the only thing I can see is that I must be sleeping. Maybe I had better wake up and find out, so I woke up and of course you weren't here. It was just getting daylight, it was drizzling out and as cold as could be without freezing and it was time to get up in a cold tent go to about a 4 hour briefing in an ice-cold auditorium with nothing but bomb fins to sit on and no breakfast to boot. It was the most disappointed feeling I've ever had in my life...

Darling, I love you,

Ladd"

Hotel des Invalides, Paris December 9–11, 1944 while Dad was on leave.

Napoleon's tomb in the Hotel des Invalides, Paris. Picture taken December 9–11, 1944 while Dad was on leave in Paris.

Cathédral Notre-Dame de Paris. Picture taken December 9–11, 1944 while Dad was on leave in Paris.

The Eiffel Tower and gardens. Picture taken December 9–11, 1944 while Dad was on leave in Paris.

Front and back views of an aluminum two-franc coin from Dad's Paris leave in December 1944.

Front and back views of a twenty-franc note from Dad's Paris leave in December 1944.

Paris, December 1944.

Arc de Triomphe du Carrousel Paris. Picture taken December 9–11, 1944 while Dad was on leave in Paris.

Palais Garnier, Paris. Picture taken December 9–11, 1944 while Dad was on leave in Paris.

" CHARMEUR D'OISEAUX "
DES TUILERIES, PARIS

Note on back of postcard: Here is an old man that I ran across in Paris. He has a daughter with five children living in California. If you give him ten or fifteen cents he will charm the sparrows and birds in the park for you. He just calls to the sparrows and they will come and sit in his hand and let him pet them and handle them. When he calls, birds come from all over and swarm about him.

Old man, "Bird Charmer," as in postcard. Photo taken December 9–11, 1944 while Dad was on leave in Paris.

Longvic Air Base, Dijon, France, December 21, 1944

"Dearest Ethel…

I'm going to enclose some pictures in this letter for you too. You say my mother would probably be shocked if she knew what was in some of my letters to you. What about yourself, I've been worried about how shocked you might be. My mother grew up with three brothers all of whom were rather rough customers and she isn't so easily shocked in some ways as you might think. You haven't had anything like that to harden you up so I have to worry the most about you…

Speaking of shocks and being hardened up to things I have had a few shocks and been hardened up some myself since I came overseas. The first shock that I got was when I arrived in Liberia in Africa and found the natives well-dressed and speaking English as their common language. The next shock that I got was when I arrived in N. Africa and found both men and women using the same rest rooms at the same time. A Frenchman in Tunis sent Roseman into a rest room along with a WAC and poor "Rosy" has never gotten over it since. The next shock coming along the line was upon arriving in Sardinia and finding the kids going naked to the waist from the bottom up. That was something I had expected of the natives in Liberia and not of the supposedly civilized Italians.

Then we came up to France and found the more "ritzy" French girls going naked to the waist from the top down. They seem to think nothing at all of an evening gown that reaches to the floor but leaves their breasts entirely bare. Just some of the dummy models in the store windows would make you blush if you had any sense of shame at all…

This deal of coming home doesn't look to me as though I have a chance before next spring and perhaps not before summer. We definitely can't come home unless there is someone to replace us and replacements just ain't [sic]. Then too if your squadron is under strength and crews are lost as they are lost they have to be replaced before you can be replaced…

Unless I should come home on a "medical" I'm afraid I'll have to go back to war though after a leave no matter how many missions I fly now…

Ladd"

Longvic Air Base, Dijon, France, December 25, 1944
"Merry Christmas Darling…

This has been more of a Merry Christmas for us over here than we expected although the two days before were rather rough. We were "stood down" today, (that is we didn't have to fly) also we had a fine Christmas dinner at 4:30. We had roast turkey, thousand island dressing, candied carrots, hot potato salad, giblet gravy, crushed pineapple and hot coffee. That was the only meal that we ate today but last night we stole a 12-lb, smoked ham and is it ever nice ham. I imagine it will suffer some before we go to bed tonight. We've got part of it already sliced and just waiting to be fried. We don't consider taking food as actually being stealing however I don't know just how wicked you would consider us for doing it.

Don't class our everyday food by the outline of that one meal however, when we stole the ham we had no anticipation of anything other than "C" rations for Christmas dinner. I'm so hungry for butter and milk right now that my mouth just waters to think about them. The last fresh milk that I had was at Hunter Field GA. Last March. That is better than 9 months ago now. You don't know how good milk is until you go for a long time without it.

Did I tell you before that we had our tent decorated for Christmas? We had a wreath and paper bell in our front window, an imitation Christmas tree and some red tinsel.

I received about 7 pakgs. [*sic*] In the past few days one of which contained my camera. Also Roseman and Ringo received packages and Ringo got to Paris while the stores were open and bought us a Radio, camera film and film clips and several other items to help make a Christmas out of today. It doesn't seem possible that it is Christmas though even at that…

…I have 47 missions in now and I won't be getting missions very fast this winter to all appearances. I'd like to get home by Easter but the middle of next summer looks more probable…

All my love

Ladd"

Longvic Air Base, Dijon, France, December 29, 1944

"Ethel dear…

…You can keep the cluster for me until I get home, that is if you can find it. They're not very big. This is a silver cluster and is equal to 5 bronze clusters.

I'm putting in a picture or two for you. The one of the planes in route formation I don't want you to lose no matter what. It would be next to impossible to get another and the picture has sentimental value as far as I am concerned...

I'm going to have to end this pretty shortly and go eat supper. It's just about time for them to start serving. The mess hall isn't heated and the weather is so cold that if you are late your "chow" isn't good for much. My dessert this noon had ice frozen in it by the time I got around to eat it.

I took some pictures to try to show what it was like here on Christmas day. All the trees were covered with white frost and it was really beautiful but I don't know whether the pictures will show it or not...

Darling yours,

Ladd."

Winter Comes to France

December 1944 view from our tent door. I got up that morning and all the ice crystals had formed on the trees. They were all fine white crystals that covered the tree limbs adding up to a few inches in diameter. We could get a picture like that because we were the last tent in the row. About halfway across the field would be where Ringo would throw up on mornings of missions. After he threw up he would come back to the tent and take a handful of aspirin.

Longvic Air Base, Dijon, France

"France 00:00 hr.

31 December ?

1 Jan. ?

1944 ?

1945 ?

    Happy

        New

            Year

            Love,

                Ladd"

Longvic Air Base, Dijon, France, January 2, 1945

"Dear Ethel…

…I guess you had a white Christmas this year by the sound of it.

Ours here was just barely white but very cold. The ground even now is frozen until it is as hard as concrete. It seems good not to have all that mud. I don't think I'll ever get my clothes clean again after all the mud we had. I never saw so much before in my life.

Roseman and I are now the two oldest men in our squadron. I don't mean by that that we are the oldest as far as our age is concerned but rather that we have been in the squadron longer than anyone else, no one excepted, not even the CO. That still doesn't bring us any closer to coming home though, in fact we're farther from coming home than ever.

I'm going to give you a little outline of the greatness of our outfit. In the last war this was Rickenbacker's squadron. At the start of this war it was Doolittle's. It is the oldest medium bomb squadron in existence and is part of the oldest group known as "The Daddy of 'Em All."

It was the first squadron to sink a sub in this war, the first to bomb Tokyo, the first to bomb all three Axis powers and the capitals of two, the first to receive a foreign citation and has maintained the most accurate bombing record of the entire Air Corps. It has been twice cited by the president for its fine work and once by General De Gaulle and just recently our group was commended as being the best bombardment group in the world. Since then I wouldn't blame them for changing their mind about it.

I don't know whether I have mentioned it to you before or not but I have visited Dijon, France a couple of times. It is a good-sized city and just about like an American town. They do have some crazy looking trolley cars though. I don't guess the looks matters as long as they run…

All my love,

Ladd"

Barge on the Canal de Bourgogne which passes through Dijon.

Another view of a barge on the Canal de Bourgogne which passes through
Dijon.

Picture of a woman working on the Canal de Bourgogne in Dijon, France.

Farmers loading hay wagons, Dijon, France.

Dijon. Seven horses in line on a sugar beet wagon. Across the road from our tent. [*sic*]

Second view: Dijon. Seven horses in line on a sugar beet wagon. Across the road from our tent. [*sic*]

French mail girl. She pedaled out from Dijon to the 95th regularly.

Longvic Air Base, Dijon, France, January 5, 6 1945

"Dearest Ethel…

Weather is ice cold here and we have been having quite a little snow. It's the first real stretch of cold weather and snow that I have seen in a long time.

In fact I believe it is 8 years since I went through a winter anyplace where it was cold…

They are sending Fineman home as I expected and that leaves Roseman and I as the only ones of the old school. We've seen quite a few changes take place in the past months. Roseman is rather anxious as he would like to see his son…

Yours truly,

Ladd"

Longvic Air Base, Dijon, France, January 11, 1945

"Dear Ethel…

It's been mighty cold here the past week. Our stove has been red hot just about steady. We melted the grate right out of it. We're pretty cozy though. We have hot and cold running water rigged up from crashed plane parts and gas drums. We've found that hot and cold water are two of the greatest comforts in life. We never appreciated them much at home…

Yours,

Ladd"

Longvic Air Base, Dijon, France, January 16, 1954

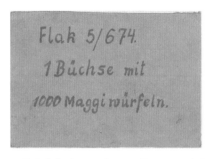

German flak label sent home January 16, 1945.

Longvic Air Base, Dijon, France, January 18, 1945

"Dear Ethel

I'm writing before mission time this morning. Truck time was moved back an hour so I have that much extra time…

Things are still cold and snowy here. This is the longest stretch of cold without any change or thaw that I have ever seen…

I don't know as I ever told you before but you might be interested. Roseman's wife was All American Girl of 1942…

We're getting so that the four of us drink two gallons of coffee per evening. I don't know what we will do when we get home. We brew it up really strong and call it "Black Death." I doubt that any normal person could drink it…

I hate to think of another 6 or 8 months over here and then perhaps only a short while at home before I have to leave again.

Maybe those Russians will be getting on the ball again though and help things out a little. I certainly hope so.

All my love,
Ladd"

Longvic Air Base, Dijon, France, January 23, 1945

"Darling…

I've been flying pretty regular [*sic*] lately and have 50 missions now. It's pretty cold hard flying now though. I'm hoping to get home by next summer but the way things look right now I don't know what to expect.

It has been snowing out off and on all day but we haven't had any of those big snows like you have had. What we've had has been headache enough though.

Truly yours

Ladd."

Longvic Air Base, Dijon, France, January 25, 1945

"Darling...

We didn't go on the mission today because it started snowing too hard. It was just about noon anyway though by the time we got back from briefing.

In case you would be interested in how we spend a day I'll outline this one which is typical of a good many when the weather is bad. We got up at 7:30 and had breakfast which is from 7:30 to 8:30. After breakfast I wrote that short letter to you and then got into my flying clothes and caught the 9:45 truck to Group Headquarters for briefing, after about an hour and a half of briefing word came on the teletype that the target time had been delayed 24 h so then it was trucks back home again. By the time we got home it was time for dinner. After eating we had to fill the gas tank for our stove and get 10 gallons of gas extra. You pump the gas from drums and carry it about ¼ of a mile so that is more of a job than it sounds like. Then we heated 5 gallons of water on the stove and used that to thaw out a 50 gallon drum of water so that we could pump it into the tent for use. That again is more of a job than it sounds like. When all your life you have been able to go to a faucet and turn it on for water you don't realize what a necessity water is for living either.

After that I spent a couple of hours checking out a new man on operating procedures to some extent. By then it was time to get cleaned up for supper and go to the mess hall to eat.

After supper we went up to sqd. [*sic*] headquarters to check on the mission schedule for tomorrow and to see if we had any mail which we didn't. We came back to the tent and I wrote a letter to my folks and then started on the letter to you. Now it is almost bedtime...

Ladd."

Longvic Air Base, Dijon, France, January 25, 1945

"Dearest Ethel…

…Miller went to town before chow, Roseman is in London and Ringo had gone to visit some fellows that he knows. That left our tent abnormally quiet…

Truly yours,

Ladd"

Longvic Air Base, Dijon, France, January 27, 1945

"Darling…

We've been getting reports today that the Russians are only 90 miles from Berlin and that they have isolated East Prussia from Germany proper. That sounds mighty good to me. I just hope that they keep on going for a while. We didn't fly again today because of snow and weather. You can't get many missions in during this time of year.

Yours,

Ladd"

Longvic Air Base, Dijon, France, February 1, 1945

"Dear Ethel…

It's now more than 15 months since I last saw you and in another month and a half I'll have one year of overseas service in. I'm afraid it's going to be nearly two years between meetings for us this time…

All my love,

Ladd."

Longvic Air Base, Dijon, France February 4, 1945

"Dear Sweetheart...

I don't guess I ever told you but I went to town with Miller a while back to get a haircut. Miller can talk [*sic*] quite a little more of this French than I can with the result that I wound up with a Clark Gable haircut and a wave in my hair. Miller thought it was just it but I couldn't help but feel like a sissy...

love,

Ladd."

Longvic Air Base, Dijon, France, February 5, 1945

"Dear Ethel

Guess what! Last evening I received the Christmas package that you sent me.

It said not to open until Dec 25 on the label but I couldn't see waiting for 11 months so I opened it right away...

All my love, Ladd"

Longvic Air Base, Dijon, France, February 11, 1945

"Dear Sweetheart...

It appears that in the near future it may be possible for me to take up some job other than flying in the Air Force. I've been trying to make up my mind about it but have come to no conclusion as yet. The main consideration being that if I should go into the other work it would mean remaining overseas for quite some time longer than if I should continue flying. However, when I did come home I would be coming home to stay whereas if I continue flying I will come home only to leave soon afterward for further duty probably in another theatre of war...

I am going to enclose two pictures for you. One is of Fineman just before he went home. He is pointing to a hole in his helmet but it didn't show up very good in the picture…

All my love,
Ladd"

9:00AM [*sic*] Longvic Air Base, Dijon, France, February 14, 1945

"To my Valentine

Dear Ethel…

---

1 mission

9:00 P.M.

…They are sending Roseman home and I'm hoping to be next but don't think because I say that that it will be right away. I would say that there are hopes in about 4 months.

I have 53 missions now. I don't know what 53 sounds like to you but it sounds like an awfully lot to us guys over here…

That card printed in German that you asked about was one that I got from a German mess hall. It was a label on a stock shelf. I've got a whole batch of them…

Ladd"

Longvic Air Base, Dijon, France, February 17, 1945

"Darling…

If you want to know about Roseman and the "All American Girl" I'll tell you. She worked in Washington as secretary for the Senator from Georgia. Roseman was a Soda Jerk in the corner drugstore near the Senator's Washington office. She would come in in spare time and buy a Coke or a soda every once in a while. They were both from the south and both had a southern accent…

Sincerely and lovingly yours,

Ladd."

Longvic Air Base, Dijon, France, February 20, 1945

"Dear Sweetheart…

…I have 55 missions now and I'm getting them in at a pretty good clip lately. Replacements have been pretty good too…

All my love, Ladd"

Longvic Air Base, Dijon, France, February 22, 1945

"Dear Sweetheart…

I have 57 missions now and expect to get another one tomorrow…

Ladd."

Longvic Air Base, Dijon, France, February 24, 1945

"My dear Sweetheart…

I have 58 missions now and almost got my 59th one today but didn't quite make it. Perhaps I'll get it tomorrow.

Yours,

Ladd."

Longvic Air Base, Dijon, France, February 26, 1945

"Dearest Ethel…

I have 59 missions now and if I go out today I'll have 60. That's beginning to get pretty well up there…

…I believe that I told you that I'm in the 1st TAF, that is 1st Tactical Air Force. When you see anything in the papers about the 1st TAF or 1st TAC why that's about us…

> All my love,
>
> Ladd"

Longvic Air Base, Dijon, France, February 27, 1945

"Dear Ethel…

Well two days have passed since I wrote you telling you that I expect to put in that mission 60 and I still haven't got it in but perhaps tomorrow I will or by the next day at least…

> Love, Ladd"

Longvic Air Base, Dijon, France, March 2, 1945

"Darling…

I have 60 missions now. I put my 60th one in yesterday and today I just laid around. It's the first time in I don't know how long that I have spent a whole day without doing anything…

> Ladd"

Longvic Air Base, Dijon, France, March 3, 1945

"My Darling…

Today I almost got my 61st mission but the weather prevented me. Tomorrow for once I am not on any schedule that I know of so I will be able to do as I please which will probably be lying in bed. I think perhaps I will take a walk around the countryside though and take some pictures. I know of one special one that I want to take. It is a skeleton hanging from a tree. Gruesome…

> Sincerely yours,
>
> Ladd"

Dad's last mission, his sixty-fourth, was flown in the plane, Old Faithful, *between March 4ᵗʰ and March 11ᵗʰ 1945. (see, "My Sixty-Fourth and Final Bombing Mission" in "PART I The War as I Heard It.")*

Longvic Air Base, Dijon, France, March 5, 1945

"Dear Sweetheart…

I have some news that I hope will sound good to you. It is this, I hope to be coming home sometime about the 10ᵗʰ of April. That is if everything goes right but don't pin too great hopes on it.

I was offered a job as flying aid to General Webster or General Devers. I refused. I don't know whether you will think I did right or not but it meant staying overseas and sweating out the end of the war without coming home. I couldn't quite see it. They offered the same jobs to four of the fellows that I know and they all refused too so I guess mine was a normal reaction…

All my love, Ladd"

Longvic Air Base, Dijon, France, March 8, 1945

"Dearest Ethel…

My orders are in for me to come home but as yet they haven't been passed by higher headquarters. It's quite certain that they will be though.

I suppose I should be very happy as this is what I have been looking forward to for the past year but I have been feeling rather downhearted instead. I can't help but think of the fellows I knew that will never be coming home again. When I think back its surprising how many there actually are. Sometimes I can hardly believe that I have come this far and am still alive.

I'm frightened too, Eth, for fear you won't care for me any more when I come home. I don't know whether I'll seem any different to you than when I last saw you or not. I've tried not to let myself change, at least not in any way that mattered, but whether I'm really different or not I don't know. I know this much that since I have been away I have done nothing that I couldn't tell you about without blushing or being ashamed. Above all else, Honey, I love you, if such a thing is possible, more dearly than when I last held you close and felt your lips pressed tenderly to mine…

Love, Ladd"

95th B. Sqd. 17th B. Grp. (M) AFF
APO-374 c/o PM N.Y.C.
France, 9, March, 1945

"Dear Ethel

I am AO today, that is Airdrome [*sic*] Officer, and seeing that there is a typewriter handy I thought that I might as well use it to write to you. It is the first time that I have used one in about 6 years and I really surprised myself when I started writing. I didn't think that I would even remember where the letters were but I can write right along with it except for when I come to special characters once in a while.

I have some extra special news to put in this letter, you have probably already guessed what it is though, You're right, my orders are here for me to come home.

The next few days I will be quite busy turning equipment in, packing, and straightening out my affairs so I don't suppose you had better expect any more letters after this one…

Pray for me now as always, my loved one.

Yours,

Ladd"

HEADQUARTERS 42ND BOMB WING (US)   G-8
APO   374

8 March 1945.

SPECIAL ORDERS)
              :   E X T R A C T
NUMBER   51)

    1. The fol named O & EM, orgns indicated, are reld from
asgmt thereto, are asgnd to the Casual Pool, 70th Reinforcement
Depot (AAF), AAF Station 591, APO 658, and WP, to the 134th
Reinforcement Battalion (AAF), APO 633, for transportation to
the UK to await transportation to the Zone of the Interior.
Letter, Hq, United States Strategic Air Forces in Europe, file
370.5, subject: "Procedure for Return of Individuals", and
inclosures thereto, 15 November 1944 and ETOUSA Circulars 110,
as amended, and 124, 1944, will be complied with. Correspondents
and publishers will be notified to discontinue mailing letters
and publications until they receive notification of new address.
V-Mail notice to correspondents and publishers, WD AGO Form 971-1,
may be used for this purpose. Information concerning WD, Army or
personal activities of a military nature within this theater will
not be discussed in private or public and will not be disclosed
by means of newspapers, magazines, books, lectures, or radio, or
any other method, without prior approval through WD Bureau of
Public Relations or the appropriate PRO of army installations.
Travel via mil, navel, or commercial acft, belligerent vessel,
rail, or GMT is authorized. TCNT TDN Perm chg of sta. 60-114 P
431-02 A 212/60425. (Auth: Section III, War Department Circular
372, 13 September 1944, letter, Hq, United States Strategic Air
Forces in Europe, subject: "Combat Crew Rehabilitation Policy",
3 December 1944, and paragraph 16, Memorandum 35-6, Hq, First
Tactical Air Force (Prov), 22 Jan 45.)

                    Hq, 42nd Bomb Wing (US)

Major   RALPH I. BURGE   0399653   AC

               320th Bomb Gp (M)

Captain   FRED J. MUELLER   0683751   AC
Captain   LAFAYETTE R. WELCH   0808916   AC
1st Lt.   WESLEY E. OTTERMAN   0690146   AC
1st Lt.   DOMENIC J. GRAMANO   0750136   AC
T/Sgt.   Terry E. Metcalf   20934972
S/Sgt.   Lincoln A. Soldati   11033098
T/Sgt.   Julius C. Blum   33596615
T/Sgt.   Alvin L. Christenson   37560218
T/Sgt.   Carter H. Harrington   38426814
S/Sgt.   LeRoy W. Lindquist   36368790

               17th Bomb Gp (M)

1st Lt.   LADD L. HORN   0687596   AC
1st Lt.   LEROY C. WATSON   0815437   AC
1st Lt.   JOHN A. ZIMMERMANN   0697467   AC
1st Lt.   LAWRENCE D. MUELLER   01683416   AC
1st Lt.   GEORGE R. DOTT   0820728   AC
T/Sgt.   Blaine C. McElfresh   33430755
T/Sgt.   Paul O. Herron   15106007
T/Sgt.   Theodore C. Dey   36575231
T/Sgt.   Jurek J. Kozlowski   33601390

March 8, 1945 orders for release from the 42nd Wing and travel to the UK
for eventual transport to the USA.

Dad's "release from service" orders were signed on March 8, 1945. He proceeded to London to wait for transport to the US. In London, he and the other men with him knew little about the city. By chance they met Jacqueline Cochran (the famous woman pioneer pilot who held many aviation records, played a large role in getting women into pilot training and founded and directed the effort that became the Women Air Force Service Pilots, WASP, program) and a friend of hers on the street. She asked about them because she saw they had 12th Air Force patches. They told her that they were from the 17th Bomb Group. She was very interested in their experiences flying B-26s and after some conversation offered to host them for the next few days. She hosted them at several dinners, probing them for information about the bombers and their performance on missions. Dad saved a stamp that was made in her honor.

Air Force patches. 12th Air Force patches were issued for travel from France to England.

Dad traveled to the USA by ship (see the story, "My Return Home" in "PART I The War as I Heard It") arriving in Boston on April 22, 1945. Dad moved to the Fort Dix "Receiving Station" in Atlantic City, NJ for processing. His first meeting was held in the Ritz-Carlton Hotel, Room 428. On April 25, 1945, he was granted twenty-one days leave plus two days of travel with a return date of May 17, 1945. When he returned to Fort Dix, he stayed in the Ritz-Carlton Hotel (Room 1010) for eight nights. He was then granted thirteen days leave and one day of travel starting on June 10, 1945 to return to his family in Blasdell, NY and then was required to be back on base by June 24, 1945. He was honorably discharged at Fort Dix on July 11, 1945. Interestingly, this was exactly three years to the day from when he entered the service based on his draft notice.

The following are excerpts from a few letters Dad wrote to Mom from the Ritz-Carlton Hotel in Atlantic City.

Atlantic City, NJ, May 19, 1945

"Dearest Ethel…

I arrived here ok. Yesterday afternoon…Today they kept me pretty busy with lectures and one thing and another. We had an orientation lecture first, then talks by the Chaplain and a Red Cross officer on morale, morals and special service activities. We also had a sex lecture and movie which I guess you know are standard procedure every time we report in to a new base or new outfit. A rather long session on the G.I. Bill of Rights wound up the day.

I have no idea what they are going to do with me as yet. There is a very slight possibility that I might get a discharge…

All my love,

Ladd.

P.S. I guess you can see that the Air Corps has some class. I'm staying at the ritziest hotel in Atlantic City…"

Dad's final individual flight record showing he had no flying time in April and May of 1944. His cumulative flying time was just shy of 900 hours including 230 of "student pilot time."

Atlantic City, NJ, May 20, 1945

"Dear Sweetheart…

I wasn't scheduled for anything today so I slept late, until 10:30 to be exact…about 11:15 or so I went downstairs to the lobby, read the news bulletin and then ate lunch (breakfast for me).

After lunch I went for a walk down the "Board Walk." I walked from our Hotel all the way to the north end of the walk and back again. What with window shopping and all it took me 4 hours…

…(my meal by the way, even though it's an Army mess cost me $1.00.) Yesterday evening it cost me $1.25…read my testament (the one you gave me 2 years ago) for about two hours. I read a couple of chapters in Romans, the whole book of Revelation and several chapters of Psalms.

There were three verses in Psalms that sort of took my fancy and sounded awfully good to me. They were Psalms 4:8 and Psalms 27:13, and 14.

When I had finished reading I prayed for a while and I want to ask right here, Eth, that you pray too, often and earnestly concerning our coming marriage. If the day comes that we are married I want it to be just the most perfect marriage that could possibly be and I know that you do too but how could we expect it to be perfect if we shun God's help in the matter? I know that you won't and I want you to know that I won't either…

Yours, Ladd"

Atlantic City, NJ, May 21, 1945

"Darling…

Today I drew some travel pay, filled out my income tax report and took exhaustive psychological tests. My brain is still traveling in circles with an endless procession of questions spinning around in it. All stuff such as: Do you bite your fingernails? If not why not? Did you ever bite them? Do people annoy you? Do you want to bite them? Well, why don't you? Were you more scared on your last mission than your first? Would you like to have more peace and quiet? Do the hours of darkness seem long to you? Do you worry? Do you dream about combat? Would you rather play baseball or be an artist? Are you noisy? Do you wish you could make yourself talk more? Do you like to think things through? Is the army an easy solution to your problems? Are you widowed, divorced, separated or single? Do you like women? If your [*sic*] married, why? Would you like to live alone?

That stuff went on endlessly for nearly 5 hours…

Tenderly and lovingly yours,

Ladd."

Atlantic City, NJ, May 22, 1945

"Darling

I'm just too happy about it to keep it a secret. I'm being discharged from the army. I just found out about 10:30 this morning. I didn't know whether to laugh, cry or jump up and down and yell. It's just about a positive certainty but I won't have my papers for about a week or 10 days yet.

In line with this I want you to do something for me, that is not to tell anyone as yet through whom my mother might find out. I'm afraid that if I told her I was being discharged and then something went wrong so that I wasn't she wouldn't be able to take it very well…

All my love

Ladd"

Atlantic City, NJ, May 25, 1945

"Dear Sweetheart

This morning I received your letter dated May 22 with the clippings enclosed. If I said that I was very pleased it wouldn't begin to express how happy I was to get it. After all those clippings are a thrill that comes once in a lifetime, aren't they? I hope that in later years we can look at them and be just as happy about them as we are now.

Honey, you ought to know how happy I am about your wearing my ring. For the past three years there has been nothing that I wanted more unless it was to actually have you as my own…

…I thought I would be spending another year in the Army at least…

I've just been watching something different than I have ever seen before. There are about 10 men down on the beach doing mining, *(and)* although it is for silver and gold I don't know whether mining is the proper term to call it. They are going along the beach in front of the big hotels here and shoveling the top layer of about 10" of sand into piles about a truckload each. They have tables about like the picnic tables at Chestnut Ridge only with window screen tops and they set these beside the piles of sand that they have shoveled up. You can probably guess the rest. They just sift the pile of sand through the screen and pick out the nickels, dimes, quarters and jewelry that have been lost on the beach the past year by the thousands of people who came here…

Yours,

Ladd."

Horn-O'Neil

Mr. and Mrs. Matthew M. O'Neil of Bay View Rd., Hamburg, announce the engagement of their daughter, Ethel Jane, to Lieut. Ladd L. Horn, USAAF, son of Mr. and Mrs. Leonard A. Horn, 54 Salisbury Ave., Blasdell. Lieut. Horn is home on leave after completing a tour on duty with the Twelfth Air Force in the European theater. He has been awarded the ETO ribbon with three campaign stars, the air medal with nine oak clusters, the Croix de Guerre Avec Palm and the presidential citation.

Engagement notice in a Hamburg/Buffalo paper May 18, 1945. The date was determined by a letter from Ethel J. Horn to Ladd L. Horn dated May 22, 1945 saying that the announcement was in the past Friday's paper.

NJ, June 5, 1945

"When I got to Dix they told me to go back home for 4 more days as they are too busy to take care of us fellows right now…The morning of the 9th they will be ready to start processing me as they call it…

…As I've told you before I won't stand for a weekend marriage or a weekend honeymoon. We have no right to expect more than one marriage and honeymoon in our lives so the first ones have to be right. I want our marriage to be just about the most joyous time of our lives and I want us to have time enough to enjoy ourselves as we please and to the fullest extent possible…

Yours in Him and through His graciousness, Ladd"

NJ, June 7, 1945

"Dear Ethel…

Honey, know above all else though know that I do love you with all my heart and my every thought is of you…you're so very precious to me.

All my love,

Ladd"

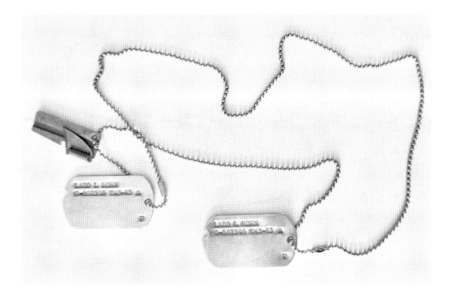

At this point, the stories and letters from Dad are ended. I trust that through my dad's words you have experienced WWII in a fresh and "human" way. Some may call Dad a hero—and these stories show that he is—but I will always love him not because of his time fighting for our freedom, but rather for his love and care for Mom and our family and for his love for his Savior, Jesus Christ.

Thank you, Dad!

Appendices

Appendix 1

Brief Life History of 1ˢᵗ Lieutenant Ladd Leonard Horn

Born July 28, 1921 to Freida M. (Wenz) Horn and Leonard A. Horn

Attended Blasdell High School, NY

Enlisted in the USAAF on June 20, 1942

Drafted and then entered the US Army on July 11, 1942

Completed twin-engine flight training on July 28, 1943

Commissioned as 2ⁿᵈ Lieutenant July 29, 1943

Left the US for Telergma, Algeria March 18, 1944

Promoted to 1ˢᵗ Lieutenant September 3, 1944

Completed his sixty-fourth bombing mission on March 1, 1945

Arrived back in the US in Boston on April 22, 1945

"Processed" at Fort Dix, Atlantic City, NJ

Honorably discharged on July 11, 1945

Married Ethel J. O'Neil of Hamburg, NY on September 15, 1945

Graduated from the University of Buffalo as an electrical engineer in 1951

Father of two children: Keith A. Horn (October 15, 1953) and Judy L. Horn (December 19, 1958)

Worked at Fedders Air Conditioning, Andco, Dustex and API

Died 10/16/2016

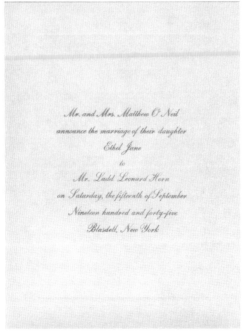

1ˢᵗ Lieutenant Ladd L. Horn and Ethel J. O'Neil Wedding on September 15, 1945.

1ˢᵗ Lieutenant Ladd L. Horn funeral, October 22, 2016. Buried in Hillcrest Cemetery, Hamburg, NY.

Appendix 2

Information Regarding the USAAF (US Army Air Force)
(versus the Army Air Services, Army Air Corps and the Air Force)

Dad always made it clear that he was in the US Army Air Force, the USAAF. At his funeral, he had an Air Force color guard. Some of his papers, including discharge and separation papers, are titled US Army Air Corps. Dad was, in fact, correct. He was in the Army and he was part of the USAAF not the Army Air Services, Army Air Corps or the Air Force. The following information explains the assignment and the potential "confusion."

As air combat increased in importance to the Army and as they moved into WWII, the division evolved and changed significantly during 1941 and 1942. Here is the historical sequence:

- *Division of Military Aeronautics—May 20, 1918 to May 24, 1918*
- *Air Services, US Army—May 24, 1918 to July 2, 1926*
- *US Army Air Corps—July 2, 1926 to June 20, 1941; The Air Corps was abolished as an administrative organization on March 9, 1942.*
- *US Army Air Force—June 20, 1941 to September 17, 1947*
- *On September 26, 1947, the USAAF with all personnel was transferred to the Air Force, the USAF. The final transfer order was dated June 22, 1949.*

Dad entered the Army in July of 1942 and was discharged in July of 1945. All of his service was therefore under the Army title of US Army Air Force (USAAF). The reason he had an Air Force color guard at his funeral, was because the USAAF had been transferred with all personnel to the US Air Force after his military service. Some of his official paperwork is titled, "US Army Air Corps," because the US Army Air Corps was in existence until June of 1941 and some of the forms used by staff for his records in 1942 still had the old title.

Appendix 3

Dad's Training Bases with Dates of Assignment

1. *Fort Niagara, Niagara, NY: July 11, 1942 to approximately August 5, 1942.*

2. *Mitchell Field, Long Island: approximately August 7, 1942 to August 14, 1942.*

3. *Blytheville Army Air Field, Blytheville, Arkansas: August 17, 1942 to approximately September 7, 1942.*

4. *Nashville, Tennessee: September 9 to September 19, 1942.*

5. *Lackland Air Force Base, Kelly Field, San Antonio, Texas (The San Antonio Aviation Cadet Center or SAACC): Group I, Squadron II, Flight A, Arrived approximately September 22, 1942 (first letter written is September 25, 1942), left for Harmon Flying School, Bruce Field, Ballinger, Texas, on January 15, 1943.*

6. *Bruce Field, Ballinger, Texas: January 15, 1943 (January 18, 1943 is the first training flight recorded in his pilot's log book) Class 43-G, graduated on March 17, 1943, left for San Angelo, Texas on March 21, 1943.*

7. *Goodfellow Field, San Angelo, Texas: March 21, 1943 (March 26, 1943 is the first training flight recorded in his pilot's log book) Class 43-G, completed training on May 22, 1943 and he left for Ellington Field on May 24, 1943.*

8. *Ellington Field, Houston, Texas: approximately May 25, 1943; Class 43-G graduation was on July 29, 1943. The following day, July 30, he left for Dodge City, Kansas.*

9. *Dodge City, Kansas: August 1, 1943 to October 5, 1943. Orders granted fifteen days leave and three days travel time to MacDill Field, Florida.*

10. *MacDill Field, Tampa Bay, Florida: October 24, 1943 (Picture 585—note on back—says October 1943—delay en route from Dodge City to Tampa Bay, Florida) to November 5, 1943.*

11. *Lake Charles Air Field, Lake Charles, Louisiana: November 9–10, 1943 336th Bombardment Group to approximately March 4, 1944.*

12. *Hunter Field, Savannah, Georgia: March 8, 1944 to March 16, 1944.*

13. *Homestead Army Air Field, Homestead, Florida: March 16, 1944 to March 18, 1944.*

Crew 12A left Homestead, Florida for Puerto Rico on March 18, 1944. (Their orders to leave for Casablanca, Morocco are dated March 15, 1944.)

Appendix 4

*Dad's Crew When He Left the USA for Casablanca, Morocco
(Crew12A assigned in Lake Charles, LA)*

Dad trained for combat duty at Lake Charles, LA. It was there that his six-man crew (Crew 12A) was formed. (Note that in combat they often would have a seven- or eight-man crew due to including a photographer and others.) Leaving the USA from Homestead, FL, Dad's crew included:

- *Ladd L. Horn, Pilot (Serial No. 0687596)*
- *Paul M. Roseman, Co-Pilot (Serial No. 0758859)*
- *William (Bill) C. Webb, Bombardier (Serial No. 0750057)*
- *Warren E. Tupper, Radioman (Serial No. 31181224)*
- *Harmon R. Summers (the crew never called him by his first name, so Dad couldn't remember it. I later found it listed on the orders to move to Hunter Field, Georgia.), Tail Gunner (Serial No. 39288084)*
- *Bernard Fineman, Flight Engineer (Serial No. 33586506)*

Dad gave me the following information about his original Crew 12A in a general conversation that was not part of our recorded sessions:

In Natal, Brazil on their way to North Africa, they were told that they were overloaded for the trip to the Ascension Islands (they were carrying extra machine guns, parts and even cases of rations) and so they had to leave two of their crew behind. Bill Webb (bombardier) and Harmon R. Summers (tail gunner) were taken out of the crew and later shipped over with other crews. When Webb and Summers arrived later they were not placed with Dad in the 17th Bomb Group, 95th Squadron. Instead they were assigned to the 320th because it was short on personnel.

Dad's flight engineer, Bernie Fineman, was Jewish. His copilot, Paul

Roseman, was not. Paul Roseman always carried a card signed by his pastor that showed that he was from a German, Lutheran church. He wanted to be sure that if he were shot down and captured, the Germans would know he was not Jewish. On the flip side, Bernie Fineman, who was Jewish, simply didn't care. He felt he was doing what he needed to do and was going to do it no matter what the outcome.

The following are Dad's words regarding the fate of his crew:

At the time I left Dijon, there were three survivors from my original crew, we thought—Bernie Fineman, Paul Roseman, who had been transferred to ATC after sixty-five missions, and myself [*sic*]. I found out later that Warren Tupper had survived after spending time as a POW.

Tupper had volunteered for a special radio mission to try and get his missions in faster to get home sooner. The plane he was on was shot down. He bailed out OK. We got word, apparently through the Red Cross, that he had survived and was headed for one of the Stalag Lufts. But no further word was ever received so we eventually gave him up. The last I heard he was still alive and living in Florida. He is getting old though (like the rest of us). He was thirty-seven when we went overseas, and probably the oldest man in the 17th Bomb Group except perhaps Doc. Brown.

The following information was found at
https://www.fold3.com/page/84136316-robert-e-shank/stories

Lt Robert E Shank was a B-26 Pilot during WWII with the 17th Bomb Group, 95th Bomb Squadron and was shot down over Bergamo, Italy on the way to the Target of Villacidro Airdrome, Italy.... It appears that Lt Robert Shank, Lt Robt. Burch, S/Sgt Nelson Clairmont, S/Sgt Warren Tupper and Sgt

Samuel Tracy were all MIA and eventually "Returned to Duty". . . . . . . while Lt Vernon Morris and S/Sgt Robt. O'Donnell were KIA.

Obituary for Bernard Fineman, Dad's flight engineer

FINEMAN
BERNARD, May 30, 2012 of Philadelphia, Pa., Husband of the late Marian (nee Wilson), Father of Dr. Steven Fineman (Juanita Elefante) and Amy (Stewart) Kupperman. Also survived by 4 grandchildren and 2 great-grandchildren. He was a proud WWII veteran who flew 60 missions and was shot down twice. Relatives and friends are invited to graveside services Friday, June 1, 12:30 P.M. at Haym Salomon Memorial Park (Frazer). Contributions in his memory may be made to a charity of the donor's choice. www.levinefuneral.com

Dad's words continued:

Paul Roseman corresponded with me for a while after he was in the ATC but then I received no more letters. Trying to check up on him, the only word I could get was that he was known to be deceased. Fine thing after surviving sixty-five combat missions. I still miss "Rosy" after all these years. He was probably my closest friend and associate the whole time I was in service. Bernie Fineman, Warren Tupper and Bob Ringo, who was a tentmate the whole time I was in the 95th, were right in there close too.

Harmon R. Summers was lost in a crash on Sardinia. His plane *(flying with a different crew)* flew into the mountain on Sardinia during a night flight *(presumably Punta La Marmora, elevation 6017 feet, which is to the East of Villacidro).*

Appendix 5

*War Department USAAF Accident Report #40522-504 of the 12th AFT
(The 17th Bomb Group, 95th Squadron was attached to the 12th Air Force
Tactical)*

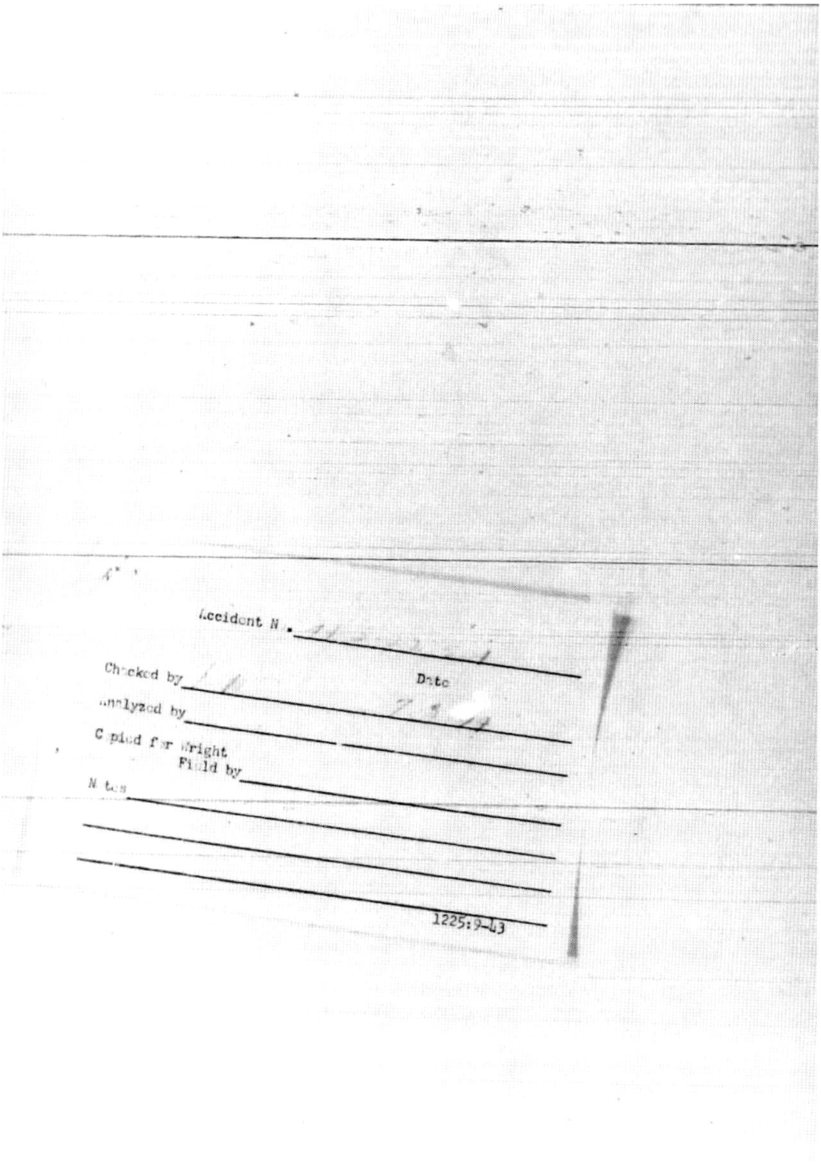

Accident N.

Checked by

Date

analyzed by

Copied for Wright
Field by

Notes

1225: 9-43

WAR DEPARTMENT
AAF FORM NO. 14
(Revised May 15, 1942)

ACCIDENT NO. 490

BTC AFO 762

WAR DEPARTMENT
U. S. ARMY AIR FORCES
REPORT OF AIRCRAFT ACCIDENTS

(1) PLACE B.T.C., AFO 762.   (2) DATE 22 May 1944   (3) TIME 1030

AIRCRAFT: (4) TYPE & MODEL B-26B   (5) AF NO. 41-17900 (6) STATION BTC AFO 762

ORGANIZATION: (7) 12 AFTTBC 12AF   (8) BTC   (9) 1st Bomb Tng Sq
                    (Command & Air Force)   (Group)   (Squadron)

PERSONNEL

DUTY	NAME (Last name first)	RATING	ASN	RANK	PERSONNEL CLASS	BRANCH	IP or Comd	RESULT to PERSONNEL	USE OF PARACHUTE
P	Horn, Ladd L.	P	0687596	2nd Lt		AC	12AF	None	
D	Overed, Martin	P	328310V	1st Lt		RAF	RAF	None	
CP	Rowland, Eric N	P	1158782	Sgt	(26)	RAF	RAF	None	
E	Working, Frederick L.	E	15085021	S/Sgt		AC	12AF	None	

RECEIVED JUN 19 1944

PILOT

(20) Overed, Martin (21) 328310V (22) 1st Lt (23) 06   (24) RAF
L.name F.name M.I.   ASN   Rank   Personnel class   Branch

Assigned (25) RAF   (26)   (27) 14th   (28) B.N.A.F.   Station
          Command & Air Force   Group   Squadron   Station

Attached for flying (29) 12AFTTBC 12AF (30) BTC (31) 1st Bomb Tng Sq (32) BTC AFO 762
                    Command & Air Force   Group   Squadron   Station

Original rating (33) Pilot (34) 4/17/43 Present (36) Pilot (36) 4/17/43 Last (37)
              Rating   Date rating   Rating   Date rating   Date

First Pilot Hours:
(at the time of this accident)
38) This type . . . . _____   (42) Instrument time last 6 mos. _____
39) This model . . . . _____   (43) Instrument time last 30 days _____
40) Last 90 days . . . . 17/150   (44) Night time last 6 months _____
41) Total . . . . 217/150   (45) Night time last 30 days _____

AIRCRAFT DAMAGE

DAMAGE				(49) List of damaged parts
Aircraft	X			Right wing and aileron damaged beyond repair
Engine(s)	X			Right engine - sudden stoppage
Propeller(s)	X			Right prop damaged beyond repair

Weather at the time of accident _____ CAVU

Was the pilot flying on instruments at the time of accident? No
Was flight from BTC AFO 762 (53) To Local (54) Kind of clearance Contact

Specific mission Training
Nature of accident Landing accident - right main landing gear collapsed on landing
Cause of accident Pilot Error
Report form been submitted? Yes

RESTRICTED

DESCRIPTION OF ACCIDENT

(Brief narrative of accident. Include statement of responsibility and recommendations for action to prevent repetition)

On 22 May 1944, B-26B, Serial Number 41-17900, while in the process of landing to the east on the Twlergns black-top runway, stalled in from approximately twenty (20) feet, breaking the right axle completely off the right main strut, tearing the right main strut out of its mount, causing the aircraft to veer to the right off the runway, with the right wing on the ground. A fire started under the right engine nacelle but was extinguished by the fire trucks. There was no injury to personnel.

The cause of the accident is attributed to a hard landing, the impact causing the axle on the right wheel to break completely off. The wheel and tire were found about 2000 feet ahead of the accident, the tire still inflated. This was the second accident of this type, the first occuring during take-off.

Responsibility for the accident is believed to be 100% pilot error on the part of the instructor pilot, Lt Horn, since the student pilot actually at the controls was believed by this committee to have been inexperienced in this type aircraft. The student was in the process of making his fourth left seat landing. It is felt that had the instructor pilot displayed the required mental alertness, the accident would have been avoided.

There are no recommendations to be made.

Signature _David J. Jones, Lt. Col. A.C._
(Investigating Officer)

Raymond H. Lipscomb, Maj. A.C.
(Committee Member)

_____
(Committee Member)

AIRCRAFT ACCIDENT

(20) Horn, Ladd L. (21) O-687596 (22) 2nd Lt. (23) 18 (24) AC
     L.name F.name M.I.   ASN   Rank   Personnel class   Branch

Assigned(25) 12 AF (26) 17th (27) 95th (28) APO 650
              Command & Air Force   Group   Squadron   Station

Attached for flying(29) 12 AFTBC 12 AF (30) B.T.C. (31)Tr Sqdn #1 (32) BTC APO 762
                        Command & Air Force   Group   Squadron   Station

Original rating(33) Pilot (34) 7/29/43 Present(35) Pilot (36) 7/29/43 Inst.(37) --
                    Rating   Date rating   Rating   Date rating   Date

First Pilot Hours: Time estimated
(at the time of this accident)Forms 5 not available
(38) This type . . . . 296:35 (42)Instrument time last 6 mos. --
(39) This model. . . . . 309:25 (43)Instrument time last 30 days --
(40) last 30 days. . . . . 130:25 (44)Night time last 6 months   --
(41) Total . . . . 339:25 (45)Night time last 30 days   --

1st Bombardment Training Squadron
Bombardment Training Center
APO 762, U. S. Army
24 May 1944

S T A T E M E N T

TO WHOM IT MAY CONCERN:

In the crash landing of B-26 type aircraft #41-17900 on the date of May 22, 1944, I was acting as instructor pilot and flying in the right seat of the aircraft. The student, Lieutenant Owered, RAF, was receiving transition training in the B-26 and was in the process of shooting what would have been his fourth left seat landing in that type aircraft.

We turned on to the approach for a landing from west to east on "This Year" strip. His air speed was 150 MPH as he rolled out level on the approach and dropped his flaps. About 1/3 of the way down the approach his airspeed dropped to a little below 145 MPH. I cautioned him about the low air speed and as we were definitely not undershooting he dropped the nose of the aircraft to regain the airspeed rather than adding any more throttle. This resulted in a rather steep but not abnormal descent. At about 45 to 50 feet in the air, just short of the end of the runway, he started his flare out. The air speed at this time was just under 150 MPH, probably about 148 MPH.

About 1/3 of the way through the flare out I started to reach over to put my hands on the prop pitch and cowl flaps to be ready to adjust them when we touched down. Just as I leaned slightly to the left to reach them more easily, I felt the plane sort of settle or start to mush. I made a wild grab for the controls and glanced toward the air speed. Just as I touched the controls of the plane, the aircraft stalled completely and we fell the rest of the way to the runway. The airspeed at the time I first glanced at it was reading about 137 or 138 MPH. As the plane stalled onto the runway the air speed was still reading slightly over 130 MPH. I judged the altitude when I first felt the plane mush to be about 20 to 25 feet and the completely stalled condition developed between 10 and 15 feet in the air. As the main gear of the aircraft struck the runway there was a sharp report and it felt as though the right tire had blown out. I veered immediately out the switches and I cut the mixture controls. Just as I cut the mixture the right gear collapsed completely and the plane veered to the right off the runway. As the plane came to a stop I unlatched the hatches and climbed out. I jumped down off the right side of the nose and saw that a small fire had already started in the right engine nacelle apparently around the fuel strainer or the fuel line coming into it.

LADD L. HAR
2nd Lt., AC,
Pilot.

Ladd L. Har

Royal Air Force
Bombardment Training Center
APO 762, U. S. Army
25 May 1944

S T A T E M E N T

TO WHOM IT MAY CONCERN:

The accident occurred while flattening out prior to landing. During the final approach I let the air speed drop to about 142 m.p.h. indicated air speed, so I dropped the nose to increase speed, approaching at a fairly steep angle. I flattened out rather quickly, and the aircraft responded sluggishly to the controls, dropping in from about ten feet. The aircraft landed heavily on the main gear and the right leg apparently collapsed. The aircraft swung to the right and I switched off the ignition and master switches. When the aircraft stopped the right engine was seen to be afire. Nobody was hurt, and the fire was extinguished.

M Owened.
MARTIN OWENED,
1st Lt., RAF,
Pilot.

EIGHTEENTH AIRWAYS COMMUNICATIONS SQUADRON, AAF.,
U S ARMY., APO 762

22 MAY 1944

SUBJECT: AIRCRAFT ACCIDENT.

TO   :   WHOM IT MAY CONCERN.

      1.   AIRCRAFT NO. 900, PILOT 2ND LT. E.L. HORN, WAS
CLEARED BY "THIS YEAR" TOWER FOR LANDING BEST TO EAST, WHILE
ON FINAL APPROACH. UPON REACHING THE END OF THE RUNWAY THE
PLANE SEEMED TO SUDDENLY DROP DOWN FROM ABOUT 25 OR THIRTY
FEET. THE IMPACT WAS SO GREAT THAT IT CAUSED THE RIGHT
LANDING GEAR TO COLLAPSE THUS CAUSING HIM TO GROUND LOOP TO
THE RIGHT OF THE RUNWAY.

      2.   ALL NECESSARY PERSONS WERE NOTIFIED OF THE CRASH
AND FIREFIGHTERS WERE ON THE SCENE IMMEDIATELY.

      3.   DAMAGE TO AIRCRAFT AND PERSONNEL UNKNOWN BY OPERATORS
IN TOWER.

                              CECIL W. ABLES
                              T/SGT. AIR CORPS.,
                              CHIEF OPERATOR.

FIRST BOMBARDMENT TRAINING SQUADRON
OFFICE OF THE ENGINEERING OFFICER

22 May 1944

SUBJECT : ACCIDENT REPORT ON B-26B2 # 41-17900.
TO   : BASE ENGINEERING OFFICER,. APO # 762 U.S.ARMY.

     1. On or about 10:30 22 May 1944,. Pilot 2nd. Lt. L.L. Horn was flying aircraft # 41-17900. After a normal approach a very hard landing broke the axle on the right strut, and collapsed the right strut. Aircraft caught fire.

     2. Extent of damage noted.

        a. Right wing damaged beyond repair.
        b. Right Engine and Nacelle damaged by fire.
        c. Right Engine had sudden Stoppage. (T.O. 02-1-15)
        d. Right Prop damaged beyond repair.
        e. Right aileron damaged beyond repair
        f. Right strut torn from mounting, damaged beyond repair.

     3. Disposition: Aircraft turned to the 20th ADG. for salvage.

     4. Recommendations: Unsatisfactory Report being submitted on defective part.

     5. Remarks: None

                          Joseph O. Whitsett
                          Capt. Air Corps
                          Engineering Officer.

                   1st Ind.   RNL/crd

BASE ENGINEERING OFFICE, Bombardment Training Center, A.P.O. 762, U.S. Army, 24 May 1944.

TO: Base Operations Officer, Bombardment Training Center, A.P.O. 762, U.S. Army.

     1. Noted and forwarded for your information.

                        RAYMOND N. LIPSCOMB,
                        Major, Air Corps,
                        Base Engineering Officer.

ADDED: 3 Incls.
       Incl #1 - U.R. #44-71
       Incl #2 - Photo of Defective Part.
       Incl #3 - "   "   "   "

A. A. F. [illegible]
[illegible]
([illegible])

[illegible] REPORT
(A.A.F. [illegible] 1-54)

Station [illegible] No. _____ 44-71 _____   [illegible] 5-22-44 _____

[illegible] APO 762 C/O U.S.Army _____   [illegible] 1st Bomb Wing 3d, Bn.

[illegible] S.L.Martin B-26B-4 A/C#41-17900 _____

[illegible] Strut,hydraulic,Cleveland Pneumatic
Part #257090

[illegible]:

1. Right main landing gear wheel came off as aircraft was landing. Investigation revealed that the axle had broken at the union of the axle and the hydraulic strut.

2. Historical data:
   (a) Strut,hydraulic,Cleveland Pneumatic Part #257090
   (b) G.L.Martin B-26B-4 A/C#41-17900
   (c) Original Installation
   (d) Total Time: 654:25
   (e) Acceptance date: Unknown.

3. Corrective action taken: None (Aircraft crashed).

4. Previous reports submitted: One (1).

5. Disposition: Turned in to the 20th A.D.Group,APO 528 C/O U.S.Army,for salvage.

6. Recommendations: None.

7. Enclosures: Two(2) photographs. Ten(10) of each.

For the Commanding Officer

Joseph G. Whitsett
Captain, Air Corps
Engineering Officer

HEADQUARTERS FOURTH TRAINING CENTER
OFFICE OF THE AIRCRAFT ACCIDENT INVESTIGATING OFFICER
APO 762, U. S. Army

2 June 1944

SUBJECT: Report of Aircraft Accident Investigation Committee.

TO : Commanding Officer, B.T.C., APO 762, U. S. Army.

1. The Aircraft Accident Investigation Committee met at 1530 hours, 26 May 1944 in the investigation of the accident of B-24, 941-17900, which occurred 22 May 1944 at B.T.C., APO 762.

2. The findings of the Committee are herewith submitted for the information of all concerned.

3. This report was delayed in excess of ten days due to the fact that a member of the Aircraft Accident Investigation Committee was on detached service to another station at the time of completion of this report, and therefore was unable to sign the Form 14.

David S. Jones
DAVID S. JONES,
Lt. Col., Air Corps,
President.

INCLOSURES:
Incl #1 - Report of A/C Accident
Exhibit A - Pilot's Statement
Exhibit B - Student Pilot's Statement
Exhibit C - Tower Operator's Statement
Exhibit D - Report of Engineering Officer
Exhibit E - Unsatisfactory Report
Exhibits F, G, and H - Photographs

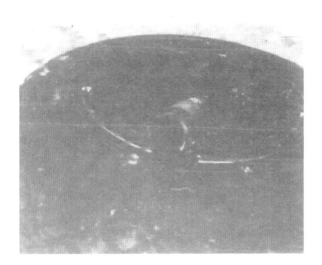

Appendix 6

Fred Harms

The following is independent information on the Harms family that was originally posted on the South Dakota Department of Veterans Affairs. (It has since been moved/removed.) Note that in the following submission there is a mix-up between Fred and Herbert Harms (identified by my notes in italics). Herbert was the infantryman and Fred was the B-26 pilot. The location of Fred Harms' death, France, may also be a mistake based on information from the website, honorstates.com.

"Fred, Donald, Herbert and Joyce Harms

Mr. and Mrs. Harms have three sons and a daughter in the army, and all are graduates of Tripp High School. Cpl. Fred H. Harms *(Note: This is a mistake. This was Herbert Harms who was in the infantry.)* entered the army in January 1942, and left the United States in September 1943, for Ireland. He went from England to France and was in the invasion on D-Day. Sgt. Herbert Harms *(Note: This is Fred Harms who trained with my dad in the USAAF in 1942 and 1943 in the US)* entered the army in August 1942, and has been located in all parts of the United States. Lt. Donald Harms entered the army in October 1942, and left the United States in January 1944, for Hawaii, and is now in New Guinea. Miss Joyce Harms is a cadet nurse and entered in June 1944. Mr. and Mrs. Harms received word from the war department March 10 of the death of their oldest son, Sgt. Fred Harms, 30. *(This was Herbert.)* The notice stated he was killed in action February 27. He was a member of a reconnaissance group. He had just been awarded the Purple Heart for wounds on his hands when a booby trap exploded while he was on patrol duty in Germany. Apparently, he recovered sufficiently to return to action on the German front and then lost his life. Mr. and Mrs. Henry Harms received word their son Lt. Donald had been killed in action in Luzon. A few months ago, they received a similar message telling of the death of another son Fred in France *(Note: Germany based on information from the honorstates website)*. This is a double blow for this family and one can well imagine their grief. Another son is expected home this week. His outfit is about ready for overseas service. *(Note: These last two statements about another son cannot be correct. According to the previous parts of the article, all three sons, Herbert Donald and Fred were dead.)* Donald received the Purple Heart for wounds received in action east of Olongapo. He recovered from his wounds and was back in action when he was killed. Lt. Harms was a platoon leader of Company F, 152nd Infantry, and saw action in his regiment's 16-day battle for strategic and heavily fortified Zig Zag Pass, east of Olongapo, which opened another route to Manila. He was with the 38th (cyclone) Division on Luzon. He also received the Asia-Pacific ribbon with three Bronze Stars and a Bronze Arrowhead and the Philippine ribbon with two bronze stars. These ribbons were awarded to him prior to March 21. While stationed at Luzon, Don contracted Dengue fever and was hospitalized. He recovered after two weeks, and was sent back into active duty until his death.

Submitted 8/19/01"

Appendix 7

The Death of 1ˢᵗ Lieutenant Joseph T. Schoeps

The following information is from the ETVMA website
https://etvma.org/veterans/arlyn-l-lones-8320/

Arlyn L. Lones was a crew member on Pilot Joseph T. Schoeps' plane, New York Central II, *when it went down.*

Aircraft B-26 B41 with serial number 42-43308 departed from Dijon Airbase in France on a bombing mission to Kaiserslautern in Germany. Statement from 2ⁿᵈ Lt. Joseph H. Herbert, Air Corps, 37th Bomb Squadron:

> I first observed plane no. 68 when fire broke out on the left side of the ship, while the plane was still in the formation. It broke away to the left of the formation in a gradual glide. I saw two men leave the rear of the plane in rapid succession while the plane was at 10,000 feet just after it broke formation. Then seconds later a third man left the rear of the ship at an altitude of about 10,000 feet. Five seconds later a 4ᵗʰ man left the ship. I observed flame in front of this man when he bailed out but I cannot say if his chute was afire or not, or just what was burning. The flame lasted for 3 or 4 seconds and went out, after which time I lost sight of the ship and the 4 men who bailed out. I only observed the chutes of the first two men who bailed out to open. The last two I did not observe.
>
> The plane stayed in a dive until it reached an altitude of about 3000 feet. At this altitude the plane went into a steep dive and spiraled to the ground. At 13:00 hours the plane crashed at Fischbach near Pirmasens. A German interrogator mentioned to a crewmember that Sgt. Lones was found in the crashed plane but his body was recovered

near Alsenborn. After the liberation he received information from Squadron personnel in England that Sgt Lones was machine-gunned after arriving on the ground by the Germans. Only SSgt Draper and SSgt Reesha survived.

Crewmembers

Pilot, Joseph T. Schoeps

Co-Pilot, Major Hugh S. Teitsworth, Jr.

Bombardier, 1st Lt Camillo W. Tensi

Navigator,. 2nd Lt Edward J. Purdy

Radio Gunner, SSgt Jimmie A. Reesha

Engineer Gunner, SSgt Arlyn L. Lones

Armorer Gunner, Pvt Gerald R. Draper

Also, at https://www.asisbiz.com/il2/B-26-Marauder/1942043308.html

USAAF 42-43308 Martin B-26B-40-MA Marauder

USAAF serial number S/N: 42-43308 Martin B-26B-40-MA Marauder

*1942043308, 42-43308 Martin B-26B-40-MA Marauder Fate: Shot Down Unit: 17BG95BS **Remarks:** 17BG95BS Code:68 named: The New York Central II shot down by AAA over Germany Jan 1, 1945. MACR-11110, Disposal: 01-Jan-45*

Appendix 8

Information We Have on Sixteen of Dad's Sixty-four Missions.
(The information comes from Dad's handwritten notes, the flight log of
Bernard Fineman, flight engineer on some of Dad's sixty-four missions, and
from miscellaneous documents Dad had in his files.)

The following missions were recorded in Bernard Fineman's flight log:

- Date 4/12/44 #54 B-26—Villacidro to Imperia Railroad bridge. Pilot Borden; Co-Pilot Horn; Engineer Fineman

- 4/14/44 #66 B-26—Villacidro to Aresso Railroad bridge. Pilot Dacus; Co-Pilot Horn; Engineer Fineman

- 4/24/44 #67 B-26—Villacidro to Aresso Railroad bridge. Pilot Horn; Co-Pilot Dorothy

- 6/2/44 #66 B-26—Villacidro to Pisaniono. Pilot Dorothy; Co-Pilot Horn; Engineer Fineman

- 6/4/44 #62 B-26—Villacidro to Civita Castellana Bridge. Pilot Horn; Co-Pilot Roseman; Engineer Fineman

- 6/10/44 #56 B-26—Villacidro to Ficulle Highway Bridge. Pilot Horn; Co-Pilot Roseman; Engineer Fineman

- 6/21/44 #60 B-26—Villacidro to Pontecoroni Railroad bridge. Pilot Horn; Co-Pilot Hildebrandt; Engineer Fineman

- 8/17/44 #58 B-26—Villacidro to St. Julienne Railroad viaduct. Pilot Roseman; Co-Pilot Horn; Engineer Fineman

- 8/26/44 #62 B-26—Gun position at Marseille, France. Pilot Horn ; Co-Pilot Burnett ; Engineer Fineman

- 8/28/44 #65 B-26—Villacidro to Villa Franco Airfield. Pilot Horn; Co-Pilot Solomski; Engineer Fineman

The following trips or missions were described by Ladd L. Horn:

- 8/31/44—Bridge East of Terraro, Italy. Mission to railroad bridge at Poleslla was a failure. Didn't drop bombs. Had a little flak and was accurate. Ship 52 was badly damaged. Landed in Italy. Ships stayed overnight. Couldn't get gas. Crew was Lts Horn, Carter, E.M. Grippo, Drapper. Bombs were 1,000#. Landed at Cecina for gas. Tactical Sergeant Debbert F. Kretschman (sixty combat missions).
- 9(8)/12/44 - Ship #60 Firenzula buildings and troops. Lts Loard, Horn and Gunnels and Hughes. "Milk run." Frags dropped at 10,800 feet. Dad's note says 8/12/44, but the official citation says 9/12/44.

The following missions were recorded in typed, proposed citations

- 9/17/44—Piacenza railroad bridge.
- 9/23/44—Palazzola Railroad Bridge. "Milk run" from Corsica. Lts. Duensing, Horn, Ringo, Hardy, E.M. Aultman
- 12/1/1944—Bridge on Rhine River. No drop because of overcast. Lts. Padgett, Horn, Burroughs, Gardelli, EM Vlack, Kostant. Col. Perwin flew with us.
- 2/25/45 Seigelsbach ammunition dump, Germany.

Appendix 9

Ladd Leonard Horn
WWII Military Awards

First Lieutenant

B-26 Martin Marauder pilot WWII (medium-range bomber)in the 42nd Wing, 17th Bomb Group, 95th Squadron, Crew #12A of the US Army Air Force (USAAF). Served in North Africa (Telergma, Algeria), Sardinia, Italy and Corsica and Dijon, France. Completed sixty-four missions.

Awards

- *Letter of Commendation from Charles Barnard (Barney) Oldfield, Dodge City, Kansas for "…one of the highest degrees of proficiency in Technical Training in your class…"*
- *Air medal (August 23, 1944) with thirteen oak leaf clusters (Two silver and three bronze based on information in letter to Ethel J. Horn.)*
- *Mediterranean Theater of Operations Ribbon with two bronze battle stars (same as first two stars below)*
- *European Theater of Operations Ribbon with two bronze battle stars (same as second two stars below)*
- *Rome-Arno Campaign bronze battle star (Jan. 22, 1944–Sept. 9, 1944)*
- *North Apennines Campaign bronze battle star (Sept. 10, 1944–Nov. 21, 1944)*
- *South France Campaign bronze battle star (Aug. 15, 1944–Sept 14, 1944)*
- *Rhineland Campaign bronze battle star (Sept. 15, 1944–March 21, 1944)*

- *Croix de Guerre avec Palmes from Charles DeGaulle (Granted August 8, 1944 for the support of the Allied offensive in Italy that began on May 11, 1944.)*
- *The 17th Bomb Group received two presidential unit citations (DUC's): 1. Rome Ciampino north and south aerodromes on January 22, 1944 for gallantry and proficiency, and 2. Schweinfurt, Germany on April 10, 1945.*
- *Posthumously awarded the NYS Conspicuous Service Cross 9642 with four silver devices and one gold device, the NYS Medal of Merit with one silver shield and one gold shield and the NYS Conspicuous Service Star with two silver shields*

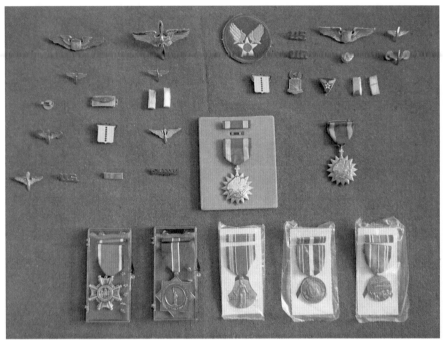

*Insignia and medals/honors awarded to Ladd L. Horn. Identification, left to right, top to bottom: **Row 1**, pilot's wings, prop and wings for crush cap, USAAF shoulder patch, two US lapel pins, pilot's wings, honorable discharge pin (under pilot's wings), two prop and wings lapel pins; **Row 2** two prop and wings lapel pins, 17th bombardment group insignia (Toujour au Danger) Distinctive Unit insignia pin Southeast Flying Training Command, 12th Air Force star and wings pin (Dad was not part of the 12th, but was issued 12th Air Force pins and patches when on leave to hide the identity of the 95th Squadron personnel), lieutenant rank bars; **Row 3** (left side only) Air Medal bar, identification insignia, lieutenant's bars; **Row 4** prop and wings lapel pin, 17th Bombardment Group insignia, prop and wings lapel pin, Air Medal and bars (issued with posthumous application for NYS awards), original Air Medal; **Row 5** prop and wings lapel pin, US lapel pin, lieutenant rank bar, Croix de Guerre avec Palmes ribbon; **Row 6** NYS Conspicuous Service Cross with four silver and one gold devices, NYS Conspicuous Service Star with two silver shields, WWII Victory Medal, NYS Medal for Merit with one silver and one gold shield, European-African-Middle Eastern Campaign Medal and ribbon. The oak leaf clusters and battle stars are not shown.*

Winter uniform with US and prop and wings lapel pins, honorable discharge patch, DUC ribbon, pilot's wings, Air Medal ribbon with oak leaf clusters, European-African-Middle Eastern Campaign ribbon with battle stars and Croix de Guerre avec Palmes ribbon. This picture was taken in 2022.

R E S T R I C T E D

HEADQUARTERS TWELFTH AIR FORCE
APO 650

SPECIAL ORDERS)
     :   3 September 1944
NUMBER 226)

E X T R A C T

  2. By direction of the President and pursuant to authority
contained in letter Headquarters NATOUSA, 16 May 1944, and letter
Headquarters AAF/MTO, 24 May 1944, subject: Authority to Make
Combat Promotions in the AUS, file AG 210.1/402-P, the following
officers having clearly demonstrated their fitness for promotion
by outstanding performance in actual combat, are temporarily
promoted in the Army of the United States to grades indicated,
effective this date. Date of rank is date of this order, unless
otherwise indicated after name. These promotions, unless sooner
terminated, terminate automatically at the expiration of the
emergency and six months thereafter, at which time the officers
will revert to their permanent grade. No oath of office or
acceptance is required. In accordance with provisions of Public
Law 746, 77th Congress, promotion is deemed to have been accepted
as of date of this order, and under the provisions of the same law,
officers are entitled to receive pay and allowances of the higher
grade from such date.

2ND LT TO 1ST LT

GEORGE F ALLEN 01683350 AC	LADD L HORN 0687596 AC
ROBERT J BURNS 0761555 AC	JACK G LINDSAY 0550647 AC
DAN B CORDELL 01683341 AC	WILLIAM PETTINGILL JR 01683346 AC
JOSEPH G COTTON 01683333 AC	LESTER W ROBINSON 0765085 AC
EARL W HALL 0815322 AC	GEORGE J WILLIAMS JR 0761284 AC
WILLIAM A HENDERSON 01683353 AC	RICHARD L WILLIS 0755485 AC
	JOHN A ZIMMERMANN 0697467 AC

   *   *   *   *

By command of Major General CANNON:

            JOHN W MONAHAN,
            Colonel, AC
            Chief of Staff

OFFICIAL:

WILLIAM W. DICK,
Colonel, A.G.D.,
Adjutant General

Official documentation of Dad's promotion to 1st Lieutenant September 3, 1944.

In June of 1947 the Secretary of War directed the issuance of a commission in the highest rank obtained to each honorably discharged officer in the Army. This is Dad's 1st Lieutenant commission from that directive.

B-26 Pilot Promoted

First pilot of a B-26 Marauder with the 12th Air Force in Sardinia, Ladd L. Horn, son of Mr. and Mrs. Leonard A. Horn, 54 Salisbury Ave., Blasdell, has been advanced from second to first lieutenant. Overseas since last March, he recently received the Air Medal with one Oak Leaf Cluster.

Newspaper announcement of Dad's promotion from 2nd Lieutenant to 1st Lieutenant.

PROPOSED CITATION

LADD L. HORN, O-687596, First Lieutenant, Air Corps, 37th Bombardment Squadron, 17th Bombardment Group. For meritorious achievement while participating in aerial flight as pilot of a B-26 type aircraft. While attacking enemy positions at Firenzuola, Italy, on 12 September 1944, Lieutenant Horn flew his plane with superior skill, keeping in perfect formation enabling his bombardier to release all his bombs in the target area, thereby aiding his flight to bomb with accuracy and devastating effect. Lieutenant Horn's courage and flying skill have reflected great credit upon himself and the United States Army Air Forces.
Blasdell, New York.

PROPOSED CITATION

LADD L. HORN, O-687596, Second Lieutenant, Air Corps, 37th Bombardment Squadron, 17th Bombardment Group. For meritorious achievement while participating in aerial flight as pilot of a B-26 type aircraft. While flying in an attack on the Piacenza railroad bridge in Italy, on 17 September 1944, Lieutenant Horn piloted his plane in perfect formation enabling his bombardier to release all his bombs in the target area, thereby aiding his flight to severely damage the bridge and block the west approach. Lieutenant Horn's skill in combat has reflected great credit upon himself and the United States Army Air Forces. Blasdell, New York.

Two examples of award citation proposals. The first is for a bombing mission at Firenzuola, Italy on September 12, 1944 and the second is for a mission to destroy the Piacenza, Italy railroad bridge on September 17, 1944.

95TH BOMBARDMENT SQUADRON (M) AAF
17TH BOMBARDMENT GROUP (M) AAF
APO   374

DATE   10 July 1945

SUBJECT : Battle Participation Award.

TO   : Whom It May Concern.

This is to certify that   1st Lt. Ladd L. Horn

ASN   O-687596   is entitled to wear a Bronze Battle Star for participat-

ing in the   Rome-Arno   Campaign, from Jan. 22,1944

to   Sept. 9, 1944   .

Authority: Ltr., MTOUSA, File AG 200.6/040 P-n, dated 30 December 1944

VERIFIED BY :

JAMES P. BRADFORD,
Captain, Air Corps,
Adjutant.

Official paperwork for Dad's Bronze Star award for the Rome-Arnot Campaign.

95TH BOMBARDMENT SQUADRON (M) AAF
17TH BOMBARDMENT GROUP (M) AAF
APO   374

DATE 22 July 1945

SUBJECT : Battle Participation Award.

TO   : Whom It May Concern.

This is to certify that   1st Lt Ladd L. Horn

ASN 0-687596   is entitled to wear a Bronze Battle Star for participat-

ing in the   North Appenines   Campaign, from   10 Sept. 1944

to   21 Nov. 1944   .

Authority: Letter MTOUSA Jd 6 July 1945 AG 200.6/040 F-0

VERIFIED BY :

JAMES F. BRADFORD,
Captain, Air Corps,
Adjutant.

*Official paperwork for Dad's Bronze Star award for the North Appenines
Campaign.*

95TH BOMBARDMENT SQUADRON (M) AAF
17TH BOMBARDMENT GROUP (M) AAF
APO   374

DATE   22 July 1945

SUBJECT :   Battle Participation Award.

TO   :   Whom It May Concern.

This is to certify that   1st Lt. Ladd L. Horn

ASN O-687 596   is entitled to wear a Bronze Battle Star for participating

in the   Rhineland   Campaign, from   15 Sept. 1944

to   21 March 1945   .

Authority: Leter ETOUSA Dd. 14 April 1945 AG 200.6 Op Ga.

VERIFIED BY:

JAMES P. BRADFORD,
Captain, Air Corps,
Adjutant.

*Official paperwork for Dad's Bronze Star award for the Rhineland
Campaign.*

95TH BOMBARDMENT SQUADRON (M) AAF
17TH BOMBARDMENT GROUP (M) AAF
APO   374

DATE 10 July 1945

SUBJECT :   Battle Participation Award.

TO   '   : Whom It May Concern.

This is to certify that 1st Lt. Ladd L. Horn

ASN 0-687596 is entitled to wear a Bronze Battle Star for participat-

ing in the   South France   Campaign, from Aug. 15, 1944

to   Sept. 14, 1944   .

Authority: Ltr., MTOUSA, File, AG 200.6/040 P-0, dated 30 December 1944

VERIFIED BY :

JAMES P. BRADFORD,
Captain, Air Corps,
Adjutant.

Official paperwork for Dad's Bronze Star award for the South France Campaign.

HEADQUARTERS

TWELFTH  AIR FORCE

The Air Medal

is awarded

Ladd L. Horn, Second Lieutenant, Air Corps

17th Bombardment Group (M)

by direction of the President, under the provisions of Army Regulation 600-45 as amended, and pursuant to authority vested in me by the Commanding General, Mediterranean Theater of Operations.

Citation

For meritorious achievement while participating in aerial flight as pilot of a B-26 type aircraft during an attack upon a rail road viaduct at Incisa-in-Valdarno, Italy on 23 April 1944. Lieutenant Horn's proficiency in combat reflects great credit upon himself and the Military Service of the United States.

JOHN K. CANNON
Major General, USA
Commanding

G. O. No. ___139, 23 August 1944___

Official award paperwork for the Air Medal for Dad's mission on April 23, 1944 to bomb a railroad viaduct at Incisa in Val d'Arno, Italy

HEADQUARTERS
FIRST TACTICAL AIR FORCE (PROV)
APO   374

C I T A T I O N

9th OLC
Air Medal

LADDL. HORN, O-687596, First Lieutenant, Air Corps, 95th Bombardment Squadron, 17th Bombardment Group. For meritorious achievement while participating in aerial flight as pilot of a B-26 type aircraft. On 25 February 1945, Lieutenant Horn was a member of a formation which attacked the huge enemy ammunition dump at Seigelsbach, Germany. Piloting his plane with extraordinary skill, Lieutenant Horn kept his plane in perfect formation enabling his bombardier to drop all his bombs in the target area, thereby aiding the formation to cover the area with an excellent concentration of bombs causing widespread destruction and terrific explosions. Lt. Horn's outstanding flying skill has reflected great credit upon himself and the United States Army Air Forces. Entered military service from: Blasdell, New York.

Awarded by Par._____, Sec._____, General Order _76____.

Hq., First TACAF (Prov), dated _3 April 1945_____.

Citation paperwork for the 9th Oak Leaf Cluster for the Air Medal for Dad's mission on April 23, 1944 to bomb a railroad viaduct at Incisa-in-Valdarno, Italy

HEADQUARTERS 42ND BOMBARDMENT WING (US)
APO   650

19 September 1944

This is to Certify

That on 8 August 1944, 2nd. Lt. Ladd L. Horn, O-687596
95th Bombardment Squadron (M)
was a member of the 17th Bombardment Group (M) which as a part of the

42nd Bombardment Wing (M), was cited by General de Gaulle,

President of the Provisional Government of the French Republic

and Chief of the Armies, by Order Number 44 of the French Air

Force with the

Croix de Guerre avec Palme

for its outstanding part in the preparation and support of the

Allied offensive in Italy which began on 11 May 1944, by atta-

cking and destroying many most important objectives in support

of the French Army, despite intense, heavy and accurate anti-

aircraft fire.

JOHN F. DOYLE
Colonel, Air Corps,
Commanding.

Authenticated:

R.G. HARRELL, JR.,
Colonel, Air Corps,
Commanding
17th Bomb Group (M)

Official award paperwork for the Croix de Guerre avec Palme (Award August 8, 1944; paperwork September 19, 1944).

(Duplicate of Air Medal Credential)

Headquarters

Twelfth Air Force.

The Air Medal
is awarded

Ladd L. Harn, 2nd Lieutant, Air Corps
17th Bombardment Group (M)

By direction of the President, under the provisions of Army Regulation 600-45 as amended, and pursuant to authority vested in me by the Commanding General, Mediterranean Theater of Operations.

Citation

For meritorious achievement while participating in aerial flight as pilot of a B-26 type aircraft during an attack upon a railroad viaduct at Incisa-in-Valdarno, Italy on 23 April 1944. Lieutenant Harn's proficiency in combat reflects great credit upon himself and the Military Service of the United States.

John K. Cannon
John K. Cannon
Major General, U.S.A.

G.O. No. 139, 23 August 1944. Commanding.

Official

This document, and the following two, show the interesting, handwritten, duplicate copies that were always made of awards. This document is for Dad's Air Medal. Compare these with the official paperwork on p. 669.

(Duplicate of Citation for Croix de Guerre, avec Palme)

Headquarters 42nd Bombardment Wing (M.S)
APO 650   19 September 1944.

This is to Certify.

That on 8 August 1944 2nd Lt. Louis L. Horn 0-687596 was a member of the 95th Bombardment Squadron (M) 17th Bombardment Group (M) which as a part of the 42nd Bombardment Wing (M), was cited by General de Gaulle, President of the Provisional Government of the French Republic and Chief of the Armies, by Order Number 44 of the French Air Force

Croix de Guerre avec Palme

for its outstanding part in the preparation and support of the Allied offensive in Italy which began on 11 May 1944, by attacking and destroying many most important objectives in support of the French Army, despite intense, heavy and accurate anti-aircraft fire.

Authenticated:
R. O. Harrell, Jr.,
Colonel, Air Corps,
Comanding
17th Bomb Group (M)

John P. Doyle
Colonel, Air Corps,
Commanding.

Handwritten duplicate of the official award of the Croix de Guerre avc Palme.

(Duplicate copy)

Reck from War Dept.,
U.S. Postal Service
APO-802 MAY 13-45

Headquarters
First Tactical Air Force (PROV)
APO-   374

- - - - - - - Citation - - - - - - - -
9th Oak Leaf Cluster
Air Medal

Ladd L. Horn, O-687596 First Lieutenant,
Air Corps, 95th Bombardment Squadron,
17th Bombardment Group,
For meritorious achievement while participating in aerial flight as pilot of
a B-26 type aircraft. On February 25, 1945,
Lieutenant Horn was a member of a
formation which attacked the huge
enemy ammunition dumps at
Seigelsbach, Germany. Piloting his plane
with extraordinary skill.
Lieutenant Horn kept his plane in
perfect formation enabling his bombardier
to drop all his bombs in the target area
thereby aiding the formation to cover the
area with an excellent concentrations of
bombs causing widespread destruction
and terrific explosions. Lt. Horn's outstanding flying skill has reflected great
credit upon himself and the United States
army Air Forces. Entered Military Service
from Blasdell, N.Y. Awarded by Par-. Sec. General Order
76. Hd., First T.A.C.A.F. (Prov). Dated 3-April-1945.

Handwritten, duplicate copy of the award of a 9th oak leaf cluster for the Air Medal.

Military and Naval Affairs

ANDREW M. CUOMO
Governor
Commander-in-Chief

ANTHONY P. GERMAN
Major General
The Adjutant General

APR 1 6 2018

Mr. Keith A. Horn
133 North Avenue
Rochester, NY 14626

Dear Mr. Horn:

This is in response to your request for the award of the New York State Medal for Merit and New York State Conspicuous Service Cross on behalf of your late father, Mr. Ladd L. Horn.

A review of the documentation provided has been made in accordance with the criteria outlined in the Division of Military and Naval Affairs Regulation 672-1 (Decorations, Awards, and Honors – State Military Awards). I am pleased to inform you it has been determined that your father was eligible to receive a New York State Medal for Merit with one silver shield and one gold shield, New York State Conspicuous Service Cross 9642 with four silver devices and one gold device, New York State Conspicuous Service Star with two silver shields and companion certificates.

May these medals serve as a memento of your father's honorable service in the Armed Forces of the United States and to the state of New York.

Sincerely,

JAMES M. HUELLE, Director
Government Affairs

Enclosures

New York State award documentation for the Medal of Merit with one silver and one gold shield.

FOR

CONSPICUOUS SERVICE

STATE OF NEW YORK

UNITED STATES OF AMERICA

To all who shall see these presents, Greeting:

THE GOVERNOR

on behalf of our Representatives in the Legislature of the State has this day conferred upon

LADD L. HORN

First Lieutenant, Air Corps/Army of the United States

the Cross ordered to be awarded to those who have rendered Conspicuous Services to our people.

Medal No: 9642

In Testimony Whereof we have caused our Military and Naval Seal to be hereunto affixed.

Witness   ANDREW M. CUOMO

Governor of our said State, Commander in Chief of our Military and Naval Forces at our City of Albany this _____ 26th _____ day of _____ FEBRUARY _____ in the year of our Lord two thousand and _____ EIGHTEEN _____ and in the two hundred and _____ FORTY-FIRST _____ year of the Independence of the United States.

New York State award documentation for the Conspicuous Service Cross with four silver devices and one gold device.

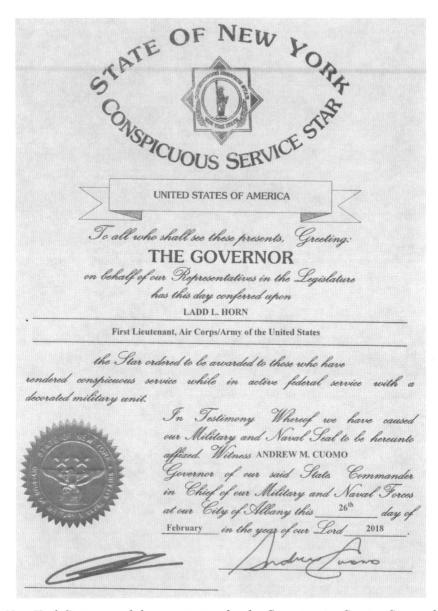

New York State award documentation for the Conspicuous Service Star with two silver shields. These awards were granted posthumously.

Appendix 10

Presidential DUCs Awarded to the 17th Bombardment Group (Note: All non-applicable sections have been redacted)

Ciampino, Italy

GENERA L ORDERS, No. 83

WAR DEPARTMENT, WASHINGTON 25, D. C., 27 October 1944

Section MEDAL OF HONOR-Award ---
--------------- I

AIR MEDAL-Awards ---
-- II BATTLE HONORS-Citations of units --
------ III

III-BATTLE HONORS.-1. An authorized by Executive Order No. 9396 (sec. I, Bull. 22, WD,

1943), superseding Executive Order No. 9075 (sec. III, Bull. 11, WD, 1942), citation of the following unit in General Orders, No. 179, Headquarters Twelfth Air Force, 28 September 1944, as

approved by the Commanding General, United States Army forces in the North African Theater of Operations, is confirmed under the provisions of section IV, Circular No. 333, War Department. 1943, in the name of the President of the United States as public evidence of deserved honor and

distinction. The citation reads as follows:

The *17th Bombardment Group (M)* is cited for outstanding performance of duty in action against the enemy in the Mediterranean Theater of Operations on 13 January 1944. In preparation for the Allied landings at Nettuno, Italy, which were effected on 22 January 1944, 341 medium bombers of the Twelfth Air Force attacked five German fighter bases in the Rome area on 13 January 1944. As a result of the outstanding success of these operations, in which the 42d Wing alone amounted for the destruction of 50 percent of the German fighter aircraft in central Italy, the enemy was forced to withdraw his remaining fighter strength to airdromes further north, drastically reducing his ability to offer effective resistance to the beachhead assault. With its own commanding officer charged with the planning and execution of the 42d Wing's part in this effort, the *17th Bombardment Group (M)*, leading the 320th Group over Rome Ciampino north and south airdromes, exhibited such gallantry and combat proficiency as to set it above and apart from other units participating in the same engagement. Taking off from its Sardinian base at 1130 hours, the group made landfall on the Italian coast immediately north of Anzio. Distinguished themselves through extraordinary heroism and unswerving resolution in the face of accurate heavy antiaircraft fire which continuously tracked the formation from Anzio to the target, and until it had recrossed the coast, the bomber combat teams coordinated flawlessly in completing their mission. Maintaining the compact formation required for maximum accuracy, despite the unceasing barrage which damaged 12 aircraft and wounded a number of crew members, each pilot held his airplane on the long deliberate bomb run which enabled the thirty-five B-26's to drop each one of their 4,116 fragmentation bombs precisely in the assigned dispersal area, destroying or severely damaging 13 of the 16 German fighters present. The consistently superior performance of the *17th Bombardment group (M)*, of which this outstanding mission is but one example of many in which all bombs were dropped within 200 yards of the target, and one of the

215 flown between 1 January and 31 July 1944, which compiled the unparalleled over-all accuracy average of 63.07 percent, upholds the highest traditions of the Army Air Forces and reflects great credit on the personnel of the *17th Bombardment Group (M)* and the military service of the United States.

BY ORDER OF THE SECRETARY OF WAS: G. C. MARSHALL, *Chief of Staff*

OFFICIAL: ROBERT H. DUNLOP, *Brigadier General, Acting The Adjutant General*

RECEIVES UNIT

CITATION

A 12th AAF B-26 Marauder base:

First Lt. Ladd L. Horn of 54 Salisbury Avenue, has served overseas 7 months as a pilot with the AAF's oldest B-26 Marauder group, which has been cited by the President for "outstanding performance of duty in armed conflict with the enemy," during a January 13, 1944 mission over Rome Ciampino North and South airdromes, in preparation for the Allied landings at Nettuno, Italy on January 22nd, 1944.

He is entitled to wear the blue and gold framed Distinguished Unit Badge, the only army award worn above the right hand blouse pocket. His Bombardment Wing was recently cited by General de Gaulle, Chief of the French Armies, for outstanding bombing support of Allied ground forces in Central Italy.

His was the first B-26 group in Major General John K. Cannon's 12th AAF to complete 400 missions and, as the Presidential citation mentions, flew 215 missions between 1 January, 1944 and 31 July 1944, during which period it reflected great credit on the military service of the United States.

— V —

RECENTLY RE-ASSIGNED

Herald Advance Nov. 9-1944

The "Harold Advance" announcement (November 9, 1944) of the unit citation for the north and south aerodromes, Ciampino, Italy.

Schweinfurt, Germany

GENERAL ORDERS No. 58

WAR DEPARTMENT WASHINGTON 25, D. C., 19 July 1945

Section MEDAL OF HONOR-Posthumous awards -------------------------------
------------- I

MEDAL OF HONOR-Award ----------- ---------------------------------------
--- II DISTINGUISHED-SERVICE MEDAL-Awards --------------------------
----------- III LEGION OF MERIT-Awards ---------------------------------------
-------------------- IV SOLDIER'S MEDAL-Awards -------------------------------
------------------------- V BRONZE STAR MEDAL-Awards --------------------
--------------------------------- VI BATTLE HONORS-Citation of units --------
-- VII BATTLE HONORS-Changes in
section I, WD General Orders 33, 1945 ------------- VIII

8. The *17th Bombardment Group* is cited for outstanding performance of
duty in action against the enemy in the European Theater of Operations on
10 April 1945. Following the Rhine River crossings made on a large scalp by
Allied armies, the 42d United States Infantry Division arrived at the outskirts
of the fortress city of Schweinfurt, Germany, an important communications
center. With its advance toward Nuremberg and Munich impeded by
numerous strong points in this city, which constituted one of the principal
German-held defense bastions, it was necessary to neutralize Schweinfurt by
air bombardment. The magnificent air cooperation provided the 42d Division
by the 42d Bombardment Wing on this noteworthy occasion is an eloquent
tribute to the effectiveness of air-ground coordination and teamwork. The
preeminent part played by the *17th Bombardment Group* set it above and
apart from other units participating in the same engagement and insured the

effectiveness of these operations as a whole. After taking off from their base at Dijon, France, at 0915 hours on 10 April 1945, sixty-eight B-26 aircraft from the group commenced their bombing run near the objective amid a barrage of heavy and accurate antiaircraft fire which damaged 15 of the attacking Marauders. The twelve flights of bombers resolutely persevered on their course over the target in perfect formation and accomplished the bombing with incredible precision. Photo reconnaissance revealed that the 133 tons of bombs released on the objective by the *17th Bombardment Group* achieved unparalleled destruction. Such extensive damage was inflicted upon the city by blast and fire that military effectiveness of the enemy troops defending the city was paralyzed. The success of this mission, so typical of the superior bombing of the *17th Bombardment Group,* was so catastrophic for the enemy that the 42d Division was able to seize Schweinfurt with virtually no opposition, thereby accelerating the advance of the Seventh Army toward Nuremberg and Munich, thus bringing to a more rapid conclusion the ultimate victory of the Allies. The thoroughness of mission planning and the precision of execution attest to the efficiency, elan, and determination of the combat crews. The superior results achieved are attributable to the extensive cooperation and devotion to duty displayed by the ground crews, and administrative staffs who made possible such an exceptional achievement. The enormous damage inflicted upon enemy installations by the *17th Bombardment Group* in the Mediterranean and European Theaters of Operations, during a period of 29 consecutive months of air warfare, was accomplished by a consistently high bombing accuracy which is believed to be without precedent. Through its unique and highly successful performance against the enemy in 606 bombing missions, the *17th Bombardment Group* has won for itself an enviable position in the Army Air Forces which has reflected the greatest credit on the group conforming to the most illustrious traditions of the United States military service. (General

Orders 128, Headquarters First Tactical Air Force (Provisional), 19 May 1945, as approved by Commanding General, European Theater of Operations.)

[AG 370.24 (12 Jul 45)]

BY ORDER OF THE SECRETARY OF WAR G. C. MARSHALL *Chief of Staff*

OFFICIAL: EDWARD F. WITSELL *Major General Acting The Adjutant General*

Appendix 11

Poems to Her Son, 1st Lt. Ladd L. Horn,
by Mrs. Leonard A. Horn
[Freida May (Wenz) Horn]

"A Soldier's Post War Welcome"

And when you come back

This dear little shack

With all its crooks and angles

Will be waiting here

Filled with good cheer,

And Love and Hope and Gladness!

The palms with their fronds,

The pines with their cones,

The turks with their caps of red

And the cedars white, in their sheer delight

Will sway and bow

As they only know how,

For a Soldier is home tonight!

The trees with their fruit

The owl with his hoot

The flame vine all aglow

With the century plant

Will stand guard tonight

With row on row

Of swords held low

For a soldier is home from the fight!

And when you come back

To this dear little shack,

Every window will be bright,

And the radiant light

Throughout the night

Will tell of a joy that is ours by right,

For the boy that has grown

Into manhood's own,

Is Our Soldier that is home tonight!

Dedicated to our only & well-beloved Son
Composed by his mother, Mrs. L. A. Horn
Lt. Ladd L. Horn—0-687596
While at Lake Charles, LA 2/11/44

"To My Pilot Son"

Whether near or far

On land—In air

Oh, how my best thoughts dart,

Straight from the heart o' me,

For you're a part o' me,

My valiant Ladd!

Whether soon or late,

Unsung or great,

Oh, how thankful I will be,

For the good fight fought

As a Christian ought—

Fought by my son and me!

When the battle's done,

And the trophies won,

Oh, how happy I shall be;

For like a Great Bird singing,

My dear son shall come winging—

HOME to this heart o' me!

Composed at midnight Dec. 4, 1943
Dedicated to our only son, Ladd
Blasdell, NY. Mrs. L. Horn

"Red Roses"

1.

He's off to the war

Like men of yore,

But his heart is home with you—

And his promise to you

Will soon come true,

In deep red rose time!

Cho:

Deep red roses,

Deep red roses,

And his love for you

He is sending through

Deep red roses!

2.

And on his return

His heart will yearn

For the one he loved so well—

And the ring that he wore

Will be his no more

In deep red rose time!

Words and music composed by
Mrs. Leonard A. Horn and lovingly and affectionately,
Dedicated to Ethel
Mar. 18, 1944
St. Cloud, Florida

"Since You're Away"

The sunshine is as bright
Yet it never seems quite
As it should, since you're away.

The flowers are as pretty,
Yet this little city
Isn't the same, since you're away.

The fruit is as sweet
Yet it isn't the treat
It was, before you went away.

The nights are moonlight
Yet it isn't the sight
It was before you went away.

The trees are so great
And still stand as straight,
But there's a difference, since you went away.

And life's so disconcerting
"As we keep on yearning
While you're away."

I wish you'd come back
For there's something I lack
And I can't seem to find it

Since you went away!

Blasdell, NY
Mother 3/30/44
Just returned from Florida

"My Prayer" (A Mother's Prayer)

God, I commit to your care and keeping
The son thou gavest me;
Thou who knowest a mother's weeping,
Who alone her heart's depths see—
God, care for that one who's so precious to me!

Keep him today where 'ere he may be,
On the land, in the air, or out at sea;
And at night, be thou nigh
High in the sky,
And fly in his ship;
If it pleaseth thee
God, keep my son, so precious to me!

And God, all that I plead for
Myself and my son,
I ask for each mother, aye, everyone
With this prayer in her heart,
Or these words on her tongue,
God bless and keep my only son!

Blasdell, NY 3/30/44
Mother

"What Makes Me Proud"
"Silver Wings"

What makes me proud?

Well it's not the gold buttons

That my soldier son wears

That are able to make me proud,

Nor the bar on his coat,

Nor that on his hat,

Which most folks acclaim so loud.

There are other things more deep,

And I love to think

As the night hours creep,

Not of his "Silver Wings"—

But the man underneath!

And it's not his uniform

That I am looking at,

Nor that crease in his trousers,

Nor his "hot" pilot's hat;

But that which stands sure,

When the world turns flat;

Not his "Silver Wings"—

But his heart, under that.

And it's not his ship

That he flies so well,

Nor the stories of battle

He yet may tell;

But his faith in God

Tried and true,

And his love for the other "five of his crew"

And six pairs of wings!

(of course, I'm proud too.)

For he's a Christian soldier

Through and Through!

Composed and dedicated to the "Father" of my pilot son,
Lt. Ladd L. Horn- 0-687596
Blasdell, NY April 5, 1944
Mother

"My Gift" (Extravaganza)

I'd gather the moonbeams

Out of the night.

And a shaft of light, dazzling white,

And pluck the stars from their field of blue—

And scatter them all in your path for you

As a gift supreme

On your natal day!

I'd combine the soft twitter

Of the mocking bird

That oft through the night

'Till the morning is heard—

With dawn's first ray

At the break of day,

When I lift my heart to God to pray

For you my son—

Far away, on your natal day!

I'd glean all the color

From the Florida sky

As the sun sets, deep in the west,

And the rainbow hue of a promise true

With the pot of gold and the only clue—

To the natal gift I am sending you!

Then with the flash of the Cardinal

The blue of the Jay—

The gold of the Lark,

As he flies away—

And the glint of the fins

Of the great black bass

That lie in the pools

We so often pass…-

I'd weave them all

Into tapestry fine,

A "Joseph's coat" of "Love," a sign,

And cast it round your shoulders straight

As a shield from the world

And all of its hate.

Then with nothing left but pleasures pure

And love and peace forever secure,

I'd commit you to God

And His Own way—

All this, - And more—

For your natal day!

Ladd celebrated his 23rd birthday
In the hospital at Sardinia
(cause—Hepatitis)
Composed, Blasdell, NY Apr. 29, 1944
With deepest love & affection I dedicate this to you, son,
On your 23rd birthday, Mother

"Just A'wearying"

I get so lonesome and weary

A'waiting and longing for you,

A'hoping and watching and praying

This great war soon be thru.

May God give me strength

To be faithful

And yielding to Him

May I know

All the joy or the sorrow I feel,

Comes just from whatever I sow.

He that has promised is faithful,

He alone is able to keep,

He looketh upon the inside—

He will forgive if I weep.

May hatred and greed
Soon vanish away,
And God restore peace to all the earth
May all of our boys be back at last,
For a world of glorious worth!

Blasdell, NY Mrs. Leonard A. Horn
Aged 54 today, 5/14/44
"May His be all the glory"

"Toast to Marauder Mansion"

Here's to the Marauder Mansion,
Here on Sardinia Isle,
Here's to the men that built it,
Here's to their GI style!

Here's to the concrete foundation,
Here's to the tile in the wall,
Here's to the brick in the corners,
But God is the "Chief Stone" of all!

Here's to the men's willing labor,
Here's to their constant smile,
Here's to their courage in combat,
Making a world worth while [*sic*]!

Here's to the place they call "home",

Here's to their strength they renew,

Here's to "Marauder Mansion"

God grant wars soon may be thru!

Dedicated with love & deep appreciation
Of his capabilities
To my son, Lt. Ladd L. Horn
Mother
Blasdell, NY 7/4/44

"Air Way Castles"

I ride in a mist

From dawn till night

For I fly in a Ship

And I hold on tight!

With my head in the clouds,

And my feet on the land,

I search for my son,

But God holds my hand.

I watch at the Flight Line,

I "sweat out my ship",

My parachute's ready

For a hazardous trip.

When the ships "take off",

I follow each one,

For somewhere there,

Flies my Pilot Son!

Where your treasure is

There your heart will be;

So sometimes I slip

Straight out to the sea!

In my phantom ship

I fly light and free---

For I've passengers now!

God, My Son, My Husband

And --- Me!

*Composed July 6. 1944 while anxiously awaiting word from my
son, Lt. Ladd based somewhere in Sardinia, Italy.
Received letter written by him the "same day" (7/6/44)
saying he was in the hospital there.*

Mrs. L. A. Horn

"Reminiscence"

I stand at the marimba alone, to play,

But tho'ts keep wandering far away

To a boy, who once stood right at my side,

As one and another of the hymns we tried.

The vibraharp next I try,

But you can't read notes

With a tear in your eye,

And a haunting melody
Sweet and clear
Wafting itself on your sensitive ear
When the boy who played it isn't here.

By the accordion there
Stands the musical saw,
Silent and straight with the bow,
And the resonant chimes and the bells
And the bowls and all he held so dear,
Seem strangely dumb and incomplete,
When the boy who played them isn't here.

But some day soon
When the war is won,
And our "Boy" is home again,
We'll shout and sing a great AMEN
For the men of the world will be free!
And we'll play again
As we used to then---
The glory, hallelujah jubilee!

August 1944
Composed by Mrs. Leonard A. Horn
Blasdell, 19, NY

Appendix 12

Allan Cooper Sketch

Sketch of *(a)* WWII pilot by Allan Cooper. Allan Cooper was a noted artist and movie actor at the time he enlisted in the AAF. This could have significant value. He made *(this)* sketch specifically for me in my presence. LLH 12-5-15 *(Note that the picture being held up in the sketch is of the girl in the ad on the back side of the sketch shown in the right hand picture. I have not found any information on Allan Cooper other than this picture and my dad's notes.)*